Proclaiming
Jesus

Essays on the
Centrality of Christ in
the Church in Honor of
Joseph M. Stowell

Proclaiming
Jesus

Thomas H. L. Cornman
GENERAL EDITOR

MOODY PUBLISHERS
CHICAGO

Cover Design: Paetzold Associates
Interior Design: Ragont Design
Editors: Allan Sholes, Jim Vincent

ISBN: 0-8024-6511-0
ISBN-13: 978-0-8024-6511-5

We hope you enjoy this book from Moody Publishers. Our goal is to provide high-quality, thought-provoking books and products that connect truth to your real needs and challenges. For more information on other books and products written and produced from a biblical perspective, go to www.moodypublishers.com or write to:

Moody Publishers
820 N. LaSalle Boulevard
Chicago, IL 60610

1 3 5 7 9 10 8 6 4 2

Printed in the United States of America

CONTENTS

INTRODUCTION

by Thomas H. L. Cornman

Jesus—that name above all names. Jesus—Lord, Savior, King of Kings. The pages you are about to read seek to focus on the proclamation of the central figure of both human and divine history. Jesus divides and unifies. He causes fights and binds up those who are wounded. He has been the subject of countless books, the focus of passionate debates, and the catalyst for lives of sacrifice and martyrdom. Some have attempted to dismiss Him while others have sought to prove His existence and importance. He has been called a good moral teacher, a deceiver, a figment of men's imaginations, and God Himself. His name is spoken both in reverence and cursing. Regardless of what people might think of Him, nearly everyone has an opinion. And, in the modern world there is a growing unrest about Him.

In 1987, Joseph M. Stowell III became the seventh president of the Moody Bible Institute in Chicago. Over the course of his eighteen years at the helm, he fell more in love with Jesus. That passion welling up inside him prompted him to write a number of books focusing on Jesus Christ. Students heard about his love for Jesus in their chapel services. Those who worked closely with him saw how serious he was about the primacy of Jesus in his thoughts and actions. As society viewed Jesus more as a polarizer, and even when some Christian leaders began to grow silent about His name, Joe Stowell remained firm in his commitment. He would proclaim Jesus.

In *The Trouble with Jesus*, his Gold Medallion winning book, Dr. Stowell wrote about an incident while serving as president of Moody Bible Institute in the days following the 9/11 terrorist attacks on America. Joe Stowell was among a large audience of religious and political leaders at the Chicago Prayer Breakfast, who heard the main speaker suggest rather strongly that the belief that Jesus is the only way to the Father divided people. The "Jesus only" tradition should be replaced by a new tradition in which all beliefs are equal The men and women present gave the speaker a thunderous standing ovation.

Thoughts raced through Joe Stowell's mind. "For the first time in my life I was being asked to deny Jesus. By joining in the standing ovation I would affirm the speaker's premise that it was best to give up the tradition that divided us. It was clear. The only way I could stand was to turn my back on Jesus. . . . At that breakfast I made a decision to stick up for Jesus whenever and wherever . . . regardless. Though I knew that this decision might come at a cost, I was ready to take it on."[1] He remained seated, at the risk of being looked upon as part of the problem.

Coupled with his deep love for Jesus was Joe Stowell's absolute commitment to the centrality of the universal church to accomplish Christ's plan on earth. It only made sense that his love for Christ, the head of the church, should lead to his love for the body of Christ, the church. A few years back, when the faculty were working through a curriculum change, Joe asked us to show him where the church figured in the new curriculum. It's not that the church wasn't there. It was in the spiritual life course and the systematic theology offerings. It appeared here and there. His point was that having the church spread throughout the curriculum without a place of focus could result in its losing its centrality. He wouldn't accept excuses. The church had to be prominent in the curriculum. After we refashioned the program to position the church in its proper place, Dr. Stowell was ready to pronounce his blessing on our new course of study.

After all—Jesus, truly God and truly man—is the head of the church. He came to call out His beloved to Himself and to place her at the center of His program *to redeem a lost and dying world.* It is through the church that Christ has determined to accomplish His purpose in the world today.

In days past we could expect those who lived around us to understand who Jesus was and to acknowledge the basic message of Christianity. They might not embrace Jesus themselves, but the concepts of the Bible and its basic story line were not foreign to them. For a growing part of our world today, those ideas are now a mystery. Gone is the tacit respect for the man from Galilee. Strange are the ideas of the cross and resurrection. Narrow-minded and bigoted are those who would dare to say that Jesus Christ is the only way to God. Sadly, a depth of awareness of Jesus, the purpose of His church, and the message of the Bible are dimming even within the evangelical church.

It seemed fitting to the MBI undergraduate faculty that a compilation of essays in honor of our former president should focus on his twin passions for Christ and His church. To that end we have attempted to address the core aspects of the life of the church through the lens of Christology. Each faculty author has chosen an area of expertise and has examined the proclamation of Jesus Christ within that context. Their assignment: offer scholarship, theological reflection, up-to-date commentary, and practical ministry responses concerning their chosen topics. The first three chapters focus on preaching about Jesus within the bounds of Scripture. Chapters 4 and 5 seek to establish the place of Jesus within the context of the historic tradition of Christianity through an examination of ante-Nicene Christianity and the Reformation. These chapters bring us back to critical periods in the history of the church when it was confronted with the reality of taking unpopular stands for Jesus Christ. (In chapter 4 we are reminded that the Christians of the first three centuries were hated for being exclusive in their faith and for their undying loyalty to the Son of God. The fifth chapter calls us to remember the struggles of those who sought to re-establish the primacy of Christ through a call to understand the Lord's Supper and baptism afresh.)

Chapters 6 and 7 challenge us to remain committed to an intelligent faith. This faith of the heart is also a faith of the head. We do not abandon those God-given mental faculties in order to believe.

The final chapters, 8 through 13, address key issues that the church must examine anew if it is to remain faithful in its proclamation of Jesus. They reflect the changing dynamics of a post-Christian world and areas of ministry concern where the church must remain intentional in the days ahead. What does the example of Jesus' temptation have to offer leaders in the church when they face their own temptations? How do Christians continue to communicate the reality of all that Jesus is to a world, both near and far, which is quite different from the world of the previous generation?

Since 1886, the Moody Bible Institute has been training and educating men and women to serve the cause of Christ throughout the world. The mission of the education division of MBI has been to provide education in biblical and theological studies, combined with practical training and experience, for preparing workers capable of going into the fields, which are white for the harvest. In this effort we now join forces with our colleagues at Moody Publishers to move outside the Chicago classroom to engage both the heads and hearts of pastors and Christian workers in calling them to love Jesus and take up the challenge of His cause in an ever-changing world.

The Moody faculty and administration value the legacy of former president Joseph M. Stowell III. This collection of essays is meant to honor his contribution to the cause of Christ at Moody and around the globe.

> *But we preach Christ crucified, to Jews a stumbling block and to Gentiles foolishness, but to those who are called, both Jews and Greeks, Christ the power of God and the wisdom of God.*
>
> —1 Corinthians 1:23–24

Thomas H. L. Cornman is dean of the undergraduate school at the Moody Bible Institute. He holds the Ph.D. degree in United States history from the University of Illinois, Chicago, as well as degrees from Philadelphia Biblical University, Talbot School of Theology, La Mirada, California, and Temple University, Philadelphia.

NOTE

1. Joseph M. Stowell, *The Trouble with Jesus* (Chicago: Moody, 2003), 22–23.

Chapter 1

PROCLAIMING JESUS FROM THE HEBREW BIBLE

The Virgin Birth as Predicted in the Hebrew Scriptures

by Michael Rydelnik

How important is the virgin birth of the Messiah Jesus to authentic biblical faith? When "modernism" in biblical and theological studies began to erode the rudiments of orthodox Christianity, some of the leading American Protestant thinkers articulated "the five fundamentals of the faith" in the early 1900s.[1] In so doing, they established the five essentials of doctrine, namely, the inerrancy of the Scriptures, the virgin birth and deity of Jesus Christ, the substitutionary death of Christ and salvation by God's grace through faith, the physical resurrection of Jesus, and the personal and visible return of Christ.[2] At that time, the virgin birth was included among the absolutes that Christians must believe.

THE VIRGIN BIRTH IN QUESTION

It appears that postmodern Christianity has evolved to such an extent that affirming absolutes of faith is disconcerting. In his book

Velvet Elvis, Rob Bell compares doctrine to springs on a trampoline. Doctrines are not God, merely a means of "fuller, deeper, richer understanding of the mysterious being who is God."[3] While Bell sees the value of these "springs," he does not view them as essential. According to him, when we view certain doctrines as essential we are treating them like bricks and not springs. Here's how he illustrates this point:

> Somebody recently gave me a videotape of a lecture given by a man who travels around speaking about the creation of the world. At one point in his lecture he said if you deny that God created the world in six literal twenty-four-hour days, then you are denying that Jesus ever died on the cross. It's a bizarre leap of logic to make, I would say.
>
> But he was serious.
>
> It hit me while I was watching that, for him, faith isn't a trampoline; it's a wall of bricks. Each of the core doctrines for him is like an individual brick that stacks on top on the others. If you pull one out, the whole wall starts to crumble. It appears quite strong and rigid, but if you begin to rethink or discuss even one brick, the whole thing is in danger. Like he said, no six-day creation equals no cross. Remove one, and the whole wall wobbles.
>
> What if tomorrow someone digs up definitive proof that Jesus had a real, earthly, biological father named Larry, and archaeologists find Larry's tomb and DNA samples and prove beyond a shadow of a doubt that the virgin birth was really just a bit of mythologizing the Gospel writers threw in to appeal to the followers of the Mithra and Dionysian religious cults that were hugely popular the time of Jesus, whose gods had virgin births? But what if, as you study the origin of the word *virgin*, you discover that the word *virgin* in the gospel of Matthew actually comes from the book of Isaiah, and then you find out that in the Hebrew language at that time, the word *virgin* could mean several things. And what if you discover that in the first century being "born of a virgin"

also referred to a child whose mother became pregnant the first time she had intercourse?

What if that spring was seriously questioned?

Could a person keep jumping? Could a person still love God? Could you still be a Christian?

Is the way of Jesus still the best possible way to live?

Or does the whole thing fall apart?[4]

After this discussion, Bell does affirm the historic Christian faith, including the virgin birth. But then he asks, "But if the whole faith falls apart when we reexamine and rethink one spring, then it wasn't that strong in the first place, was it?"[5]

While Bell rightly distinguishes between God Himself and the doctrines that teach us about Him, his illustration falls flat. The reason is that the two doctrines he uses in his illustration are really not comparable. While six-day creationism has its merits, most evangelicals would not consider it an essential of the faith. On the other hand, most would deem the virgin birth an absolute.

Bell's conjecture regarding "Larry, the human father of Jesus" is troublesome, not because he believes it, but rather because evangelicals have accepted some of the presuppositions involved in spinning it. For centuries Christians understood Isaiah 7 to be a prediction of the virgin birth. Now it is not uncommon for evangelicals to assert that the Hebrew word Isaiah used merely means "young woman" and does not contain the nuance of "virgin." Moreover, some view the passage not as a prediction of Messiah's birth but rather of a child born in Isaiah's day. These positions are taken not to deny a biblical essential but to affirm biblical scholarship. Furthermore, evangelicals are not only failing to see Isaiah 7 as a messianic prediction but also minimizing the significance of other traditional messianic prophecies.

Such positions can potentially lead to a spiritual disaster because so much of the identification of Jesus of Nazareth as Messiah relies on His being the fulfillment of messianic prophecy. For example, when the doubting John the Baptist sent his disciples from prison to ask Jesus, "Are You the Expected One, or shall we look for someone else?" (Matthew 11:3), Jesus replied by quoting from Isaiah 35 and 61 to show that He was the Messiah because He had fulfilled messianic prophecy.

Plainly, Jesus considered the messianic hope to be the central message of the Old Testament. Jesus revealed His view of Old Testament messianic prophecy in two post-resurrection encounters recorded in Luke 24:25–27 (teaching the two disciples on the Emmaus Road) and Luke 24:33, 44–46 (teaching in the gathering of the eleven). On those two occasions, Luke intended to demonstrate that Jesus understood the Old Testament to point to the Messiah.

That Jesus believed the whole of the Old Testament predicted the Messiah is evident in His emphasis on the word "all" in both encounters. Jesus rebuked the men on the road to Emmaus for being slow to believe in *all* that the prophets spoke (Luke 24:25); He explained the Scriptures about the Messiah beginning with Moses and *all* the prophets (Luke 24:27); He interpreted the message about the Messiah in *all* the Scriptures (Luke 24:27); to the eleven remaining disciples He affirmed that He had to fulfill *all* that was written about Him in the Law, the Prophets, and the Writings (cf. Luke 24:44). This emphasis on "all" shows that Jesus saw the Messiah not merely in occasional isolated texts, but in all the Scriptures.[6] Ellison has correctly observed, based on this passage, "The whole Old Testament, and not merely an anthology of proof passages, was looked on as referring to Christ Jesus."[7]

In reviewing these two encounters, it becomes evident that Jesus believed that the messianic prophecies were sufficiently clear that the two disciples on the Emmaus Road should have understood their meaning. He chided them for being "foolish men and slow of heart to believe in all that the prophets have spoken!" (Luke 24:25). The implication was that the disciples should have recognized the events of the crucifixion and the reports of the resurrection as fulfillments of Old Testament prophecy. The prophecies were not so unclear that the disciples could be excused for their failure to understand. (He did not say, "O poor men of faith, you could not understand what the prophets had spoken of Me because they had not yet been given their full sense of meaning [their *sensus plenior*] until this very moment as I am explaining them to you!") As A. T. Robertson remarked, "Jesus found himself in the Old Testament, a thing that some modern scholars do not seem to be able to do."[8]

The book of Acts also demonstrates the evidential value of messianic prophecy. In that book, the central message of the apostles was that Jesus was both Lord and Messiah (Acts 2:36). According to F. F. Bruce, the apostles substantiated their claim with two arguments, one from prophecy and the other from miracles. They proclaimed that "the prophetic Scriptures which foretold Messiah's coming have been fulfilled by the ministry, suffering and triumph of Jesus, and the mighty works which He performed were so many 'signs' that in Him the messianic age had arrived."[9] Both of these arguments were brought together in their proclamation of the resurrection of Jesus, which was both a mighty work of God and a direct fulfillment of messianic prophecy.

Peter's second sermon is a prime example of the apostolic message as it relates to messianic prophecy. At Solomon's Colonnade, after the healing of the lame man (Acts 3:11–26), Peter proclaimed: "But the things which God announced beforehand by the mouth of all the prophets that His Christ would suffer, He has thus fulfilled" (Acts 3:18). Having called on the crowd to believe in Jesus as the eschatological Prophet like Moses foretold by Moses himself, Peter further claimed, "all the prophets who have spoken, from Samuel and his successors onward, also announced these days" (Acts 3:24).

For now, postmodern evangelicals can maintain their faith in Jesus even if they, in Rob Bell's words, question a spring or two. But ultimately, without this primary foundation of faith, the bricks will indeed collapse. Before too long, without messianic prophecy, how can we even affirm that Jesus is truly the promised Messiah? And when we can no longer maintain that, our faith will cease to be recognizably Christian.

Just as Rob Bell cited Isaiah 7 in his example, it seems that if we are to proclaim Jesus from the Old Testament, it will be necessary to address this seemingly troublesome passage. Is it possible to view Isaiah's prophecy as a direct messianic prediction while still practicing sound exegesis? In this next section, that is precisely what I propose to do.

THE VIRGIN BIRTH IN PROPHECY

In my experience, Isaiah 7:14 is the most controversial of messianic prophecies. Disputes revolve around a variety of issues, chiefly, the meaning of the word *almah*, the relationship of Isaiah's "sign" to the context, the way the original readers of the prophecy would have understood it, and Matthew's citation of this verse in support of the virgin birth.

As a result, interpreters have divided into three primary views of the passage, and even among these views, expositors present their own unique perspectives. The first view, held by many traditional Christian interpreters, is to see the prophecy as a *direct prediction* of the virgin birth of the Messiah. Taking different approaches as to how the prophecy relates to the original context, they each conclude that the word *almah* means "virgin" and refers to the mother of Jesus. Another position, frequently held by critics and Jewish interpreters, is that of a purely *historical interpretation*. It takes the fulfillment of Isaiah's promise to be that a young woman in the eighth century BC would have sexual relations and then give birth to a child, and this event would serve as a sort of hourglass for Judah: Before that child reached a certain age, the two kings threatening Judah would be removed.

Third, a common approach by contemporary Christian scholars is to view the prophecy as having some sort of *dual or multiple fulfillments.* It would see Isaiah referring to the natural birth of a child in his own day to function as a sign to Judah. Nevertheless, these interpreters would contend that this does not exhaust the meaning. Rather, by double fulfillment (*sensus plenior* type), a later rereading, progressive fulfillment, or even by the use of first-century Jewish hermeneutics, the prophecy also refers to the virgin birth of Jesus.

I believe that by placing the prophecy in context, through a careful reading of the text of Isaiah 7 and by relating it to inner biblical interpretations of the passage, a view that supports a direct prediction of the virgin birth makes the most sense. That would explain Matthew's reason for citing Isaiah 7:14 as a prediction of the virgin birth.

The Context of the Prophecy

The historical setting of the prophecy was a threat against Judah around the year 734 BC. At that time, Rezin, king of Syria (Aram) and Pekah, king of the northern kingdom of Israel, formed an anti-Assyrian alliance. They, in turn, wanted Ahaz, king of Judah, to join their alliance. When he refused, they decided to make war against Ahaz to force the issue (7:1). The northern alliance against Ahaz caused great fear (7:2) in the royal family of David because the goal was not just to conquer Judah but also to "set up the son of Tabeel as king" in the place of Ahaz (7:6). Their plan would place a more pliable king on the throne and also put an end to the Davidic house. This threat provides a significant detail in understanding the passage. While some have contended that there would be no reason to foretell the coming of the Messiah, the danger to the house of David explains the messianic concerns of the passage. It was the Davidic covenant (2 Sam. 7:12–16; 1 Chron. 17:11–14) that led to the expectation of a future Messiah who would be a descendant of David. Therefore, if Ahaz and the entire royal house were to be destroyed, it would bring an end to the messianic hope. A long-term prophecy of the birth of Messiah would assure the Davidic house and the readers of the scroll of Isaiah that the messianic hope was indeed secure.

With this threat looming, the Lord sent Isaiah to give assurance to Ahaz, telling the prophet to meet Ahaz at "the end of the conduit of the upper pool, on the highway to the fuller's field" and specifically to bring his son, Shear-jashub (7:3). Frequently, commentators overlook this command to bring the boy as if it were an unnecessary detail. Nevertheless, it seems strange to think that Isaiah would include this precise requirement without it having any significance. As we will see, this seemingly minor detail plays a significant role in understanding the passage.

At the conduit of the upper pool, Isaiah gave Ahaz his God-directed message: "It shall not stand nor shall it come to pass" (7:7). The Lord, through Isaiah, promised that the attack would not succeed and the alliance would be broken. In fact, Isaiah predicted that within sixty-five years, the northern kingdom of Israel would no longer be recognized as a people (7:8). This prediction came true in three phases: First, when Tiglath-pileser, king of Assyria, conquered Israel in 732 BC, sending many captives back to Assyria (2 Kings 15:29). Second, when Assyria destroyed the northern kingdom in 721, deporting much of the Israelite population to Assyria and settling the land of Israel with other peoples (2 Kings 17:24ff). It was completely fulfilled in 669 when Ashurbanapal enacted the final population transfers between Israel and Assyria (Ezra 4:2, 10). Thus in 669, sixty-five years from the date of the events described in Isaiah's prophecy, the northern kingdom was indeed shattered so that it was "no longer a people" (7:8), and the land was inhabited by Samaritans, a people of mixed ethnicity.[10]

To confirm the promise that the attack on Judah would not succeed, the Lord offered a sign of to Ahaz of his own choosing.[11] The king was told to make the sign as "deep as Sheol or high as heaven" (7:11). This is an obvious merism,[12] calling Ahaz to ask God to provide a sign that would be stupendous enough to provide faith. Although the Hebrew word for "sign" does not necessarily require a miracle, it does include the supernatural within its range of meaning (cf. Deut. 6:22). In light of the nature of the offer, it appears that Ahaz was to ask for a miraculous sign.

Nevertheless, Ahaz, with false piety, refused to test God. The disingenuous nature of his response is plain in that this is a king who had so little regard for the Lord that he practiced idolatry, even offering his own son as a child sacrifice to Molech (2 Kings 16:3; 2 Chron. 28:3). While he might claim biblical justification (Deut. 6:16) for his refusal to ask or to test the Lord (7:12), this seems ridiculous because the Lord Himself had just called upon him to do so. So, when Ahaz was under his greatest threat, he refused the Lord's comfort and rejected the offer to ask for a sign. In response, Isaiah declared that nonetheless, the Lord would give a sign—one that would become a source of controversy for generations.

The Contents of the Prophecy

The most significant difficulty in interpreting the prophecy is that on a cursory reading, it appears that the sign would be fulfilled within just a couple of years of Isaiah's meeting with the king and not more than seven hundred years later with the birth of Jesus. The reason for this difficulty is the failure to read the prophecy carefully and pick up the clues the author has left. A close reading of the text will disclose that there is not one prophecy but two different prophecies—a long-term prediction addressed to the house of David (7:13–15) and a short-term prediction addressed to Ahaz (7:16ff).

The Long-Term Prophecy to the House of David—
The Birth of Messiah (Isaiah 7:13–15)

Since the northern alliance was threatening to replace Ahaz with the son of Tabeel, the entire house of David was endangered. Were Syria

21

and Israel to succeed, the messianic promise of a future son of David who would have an eternal house, kingdom, and throne (2 Sam. 7:16) would be demolished. This prospect provided the need for a long term sign of hope, that despite the menace to the Davidic line, the Messiah would be born, with the sign of His coming being His virgin birth. The details of this prophecy are as follows:

"Listen now, O house of David." Isaiah's declaration of the Lord's sign shifts the direction of the prophecy away from Ahaz to the whole house of David. This is evident not only from the vocative "O house of David" but also from the change of the pronoun "you." In 7:10–11, when addressing Ahaz alone, the second person *singular* pronoun was used. However, in 7:13–14, Isaiah used the second person *plural*. This is not an obvious change in the English Bible which translates both the singular and plural as "you," but it is plainly so in the Hebrew text.[13] The reason for the shift is that God was clearly fed up with this wicked and sanctimonious king, so Isaiah addressed the royal house he represented. Moreover, it was not only Ahaz that was being threatened but also the entire house of David.

"Therefore the Lord Himself will give you a sign." Although Ahaz, as the head of the house of David, has tried God's patience, Isaiah promised that the Lord Himself would still grant a sign—but one which would now be of God's own choosing. As mentioned above, the Hebrew word for *sign* can refer to the miraculous or the non-miraculous. However, in light of the previous offer of a sign "as deep as Sheol or high as heaven" it would appear that the sign to follow would be of a miraculous nature. Moreover, this is how Isaiah uses the same word in the parallel situation with Hezekiah (Isa. 38:1–8). There, as a "sign" that Hezekiah's life would be extended, the shadow on the stairway would miraculously retreat ten steps (38:7–8).[14]

"Behold, a virgin will be with child and bear a son." The Lord called special attention to the ensuing sign with the word "behold." When used in similar constructions in the Hebrew Bible (Gen. 16:11; 17:20;

Judg. 13:5–7), the word "behold" serves to bring attention to a birth of special importance.[15] The sign that the Lord promised the house of David is that of a pregnant *almah* who would bear a son. The use of the article (frequently untranslated in modern English versions) with the word *almah* indicates that the Lord has a specific woman in mind. It is not some generic woman in the court of Ahaz but one whom the prophet sees in particular.

Controversy has surrounded the word *almah* since the second century, when Aquila substituted "young woman" (Greek, *neanis*) in his Greek translation of the Hebrew Bible for the LXX translation of "virgin" (*parthenos*). Was Isaiah speaking of a virgin or merely a young woman?[16] Various arguments have been put forward to make the case for translating the word as virgin.

Etymologically, *almah* is derived from a word that means "to be sexually strong, sexually mature, sexually ripe or ready."[17] This would seem to emphasize the age of the woman (pubescent) rather than indicating whether she was sexually active. Cyrus Gordon has argued that ancient (pre-Mosaic) Ugaritic, which is a cognate of Hebrew, used the parallel word for *almah* of a virgin goddess. Since the Ugaritic annunciation formula used a very similar construction to Isaiah 7:14, Gordon concluded that *almah* should rightly be translated "virgin."[18] Furthermore, many have maintained that the Septuagint translation of *almah* with the Greek word *parthenos* (virgin) is evidence that in the pre-Christian era, the word was understood as referring to virginity.[19]

The best way to determine the meaning of the *almah* is by examining its usage throughout the Hebrew Bible. If there were one place in Scripture where *almah* were to refer to a non-virgin, it would dismiss the translation of the word as "virgin." However, in every situation, the word is used either of a virgin or in an indeterminate, neutral sense.

- **Genesis 24:43.** Here Rebekah, the soon-to-be wife of Isaac, is called an *almah*. This chapter of Genesis describes Rebekah, as a "girl" (24:14—*na'arah*), a virgin (24:16—*bethulah*), and a maiden (24:43—*almah*). These three synonyms are used to describe a virginal young woman.

- **Exodus 2:8.** In this passage, Miriam, the sister of Moses, is called an *almah*. As a young girl, still in the home of her parents, we may imply that it includes the idea that she was a virgin.

- **Psalm 46:1.** In this verse, the superscription uses the word as a musical direction. So it is indeterminate, not supporting or contradicting the meaning virgin.

- **Psalm 68:25.** This verse refers to a musical worship procession in which *alamot* (plural of *almah*) play the timbrels. Perhaps this verse is indeterminate, not speaking to the virginity of the maidens. But possibly it hints at virginity because it calls to mind Jephthah's daughter who lamented her being offered as a sacrifice to the Lord (Judg. 11:34–40). While some commentators believe that Jephthah's daughter was an actual human sacrifice, others maintain that Jephthah gave her to lifelong service in the tabernacle. Thus, she was never to marry, and she went with her friends to mourn her virginity. If this is the case, then perhaps it indicates that serving in the temple was restricted to virgins. Therefore, the damsels in the temple worship procession, spoken of in Psalm 68:25, would be virgins.

- **1 Chronicles 15:20.** Once again, the word is used as a musical direction. So it is neutral, not supporting or contradicting the meaning virgin.

- **Song of Solomon 1:3.** This verse refers to the love of the *alamot* for Solomon. These are not married women but maidens who wanted husbands but have not yet been married. Therefore, the word would imply the concept of virginity.

- **Song of Solomon 6:8.** This description of the king's harem includes three categories: sixty queens, eighty concubines, and *alamot* without number. The queens are those whom the king has married, the concubines are those with whom he has had sexual relations, and the *alamot* are the virgins who will one day be elevated to either concubine or queenly status. If these *alamot* were not virgins, they would be in the concubine category. Hence the use of the word here is of virgins.

A final verse, in Proverbs, is the most controversial of the usages, since it describes "the way of a man with a maid [*almah*]" (30:19). The entire proverb is found in 30:18–19 and refers to four wonderful and incomprehensible things: an eagle in the sky, a serpent on a rock, a ship in the sea, and a man with an *almah*. Some have maintained that what unites these four is in each one something disappears. A soaring eagle is easily lost from sight. A serpent quickly slithers off the rock, disappearing from sight. A ship can be lost in a fraction of time. And a virgin can lose her virginity to a young man very quickly. Even if this were the true interpretation of the proverb, the word *almah* would indeed be virgin. But since there is no moral evil in the first three examples, it seems unlikely that the fourth would call extramarital sex "wonderful." Moreover, the contrast with the adulterous woman in 30:20 would imply that the *almah* in the previous verse was not engaged in illicit sex.

Probably the best way to understand this proverb is as referring to the mysterious and wonderful qualities of youthful attraction.[20] Thus, it once again would refer to a virgin.

In every use in the Hebrew Bible, the word *almah* either refers to a virgin or has a neutral sense.[21] Based on this study, it appears that Isaiah chose his words with precision. While the Hebrew *bethulah* could refer to a virgin of any age, *almah* would refer to a virgin who has just arrived at puberty. She is a maiden in the truest and purest sense. So, there does not seem to be cause to abandon the traditional interpretation of *almah* as a "virgin" except for an anti-supernatural or anti-messianic bias.[22]

This virgin, according to the translation, will be with child. However, the Hebrew in the verse is even more emphatic. It uses the feminine singular adjective *harah* ("pregnant"), which would more accurately be translated "the virgin is pregnant," or "the pregnant virgin." Were it not for the context calling for a sign as deep as sheol or high as heaven, such a translation would seem impossible. However, the prophet, by vision, sees a specific pregnant virgin before him,[23] who would be the sign of hope for the house of David. This indeed would meet the qualification of being "deep as Sheol or high as heaven."

"And she will call His name Immanuel." The virgin mother of the child will recognize his special nature. Therefore, she will give Him the title "Immanuel" which means "God with us."[24] The message to Judah was that God would be with them in a special way through this child. The title hints at the divine nature of the boy. Even clearer is Isaiah 8:8, in which the prophet, describing the Assyrian conquest of Judah, says that the Assyrians will sweep over Judah "and the spread of its wings will fill the breadth of your land, O Immanuel." Were the child Immanuel not divine, Isaiah would not identify the land as belonging to Him. Moreover, in the next great vision of the coming Davidic king (Isa. 9:6), the child receives other divine throne titles including Mighty God and Father of Eternity ("Eternal Father").[25] Isaiah was not merely promising a future Davidic king who would secure the line of David; he was not only promising that He would have a supernatural birth. Ultimately, the prophet has revealed that the Messiah would be God in the flesh, Immanuel.[26]

"He will eat curds and honey" (v. 15). The Lord continues His description of the virgin-born Davidic Messiah, giving a clue to the situation into which He would be born. Many mistake the curds and honey He would eat as the food of royalty, ignoring the context in Isaiah 7 itself. Later in the chapter it speaks of the coming Assyrian oppression, when Assyria would shave the land (7:20). At that time, fields would not be cultivated and would become pastures for oxen and

sheep (7:23–25). The effect of this will be an overabundance of dairy (or curds) because of the pasturing of livestock and an excess of honey, because bees will be able to pollinate the wild flowers. Therefore, because of the "abundance of the milk produced" a man "will eat curds, for everyone that is left within the land will eat curds and honey" (7:21–22). So, in this passage, curds and honey does not represent the food of royalty, but rather the food of oppression.

The point, then, of 7:15 describing the future virgin-born Davidic king eating curds and honey is to emphasize that He would be born during a time of political oppression. In other words, the prophecy of Messiah concludes with a hint that He will be born and grow up ("know[ing] enough to refuse evil and choose good") at a time when Judah is oppressed by a foreign power.[27]

With this Isaiah has completed his first prophetic message. With the northern confederation of Syria and Israel threatening to remove Ahaz with a substitute king, the entire house of David was imperiled, and with it, the messianic hope. Isaiah has come with a message of hope—the future Son of David would indeed be born someday. The supernatural sign that would reveal His identity is that He would be born of a young virgin and have a miraculous divine nature. Moreover, He would grow up during a time of oppression over the Jewish people and their land. With the assurance that the house of David and the messianic hope are both secure, the prophet turned his attention to the immediate threat and gave a near prophecy to wicked King Ahaz.

The Short-Term Prophecy to Ahaz—
The Sign of Shear-jashub (Isaiah 7:16ff)

While many have considered verse 16 to be a continuation of the prophecy in 7:13–15, they miss the point as revealed in the grammar of the passage. The opening phrase in Hebrew reflects a strong adversative, showing an obvious disjunction between the child described in 7:13–15 and the one described in verse 16. *The New International*

Version and the *New Living Translation* are two recent English versions that have caught this nuance, beginning 7:16 with the words "*but before*" to indicate the contrast. There is a different child in view in this verse.[28]

So who is the child in 7:16? In light of Isaiah being directed to bring his own son to the confrontation with the king at the conduit of the upper pool (cf. 7:3), it makes more sense to identify the lad as Shear-jashub. Otherwise there would be no purpose for God directing Isaiah to bring the boy. Thus having promised the virgin birth of the Messiah (7:13–15), the prophet then points to the very small boy whom he has brought along and says, "But before *this* lad [using the article with a demonstrative force] knows enough to refuse evil and choose good, the land whose two kings you dread will be forsaken" (author translation).[29] In this way, Shear-jashub functioned as a sign to the king. Appropriately, Isaiah could tell Judah in the very next chapter, "Behold, I and the children whom the Lord has given me are for signs and wonders in Israel from the Lord of hosts, who dwells on Mount Zion" (8:18).

To whom does Isaiah make this prediction? What is not evident in the English text is plain in the Hebrew. The prophet returns to using the second person singular pronoun in 7:16 ("the land whose two kings *you* dread"). In 7:10–11 he used the singular to address King Ahaz. Then, when addressing the house of David with the prophecy of Messiah, he shifted to the plural. But in 7:16, he addressed King Ahaz, using the singular pronoun once again and giving him a near prophecy: before Shear–jashub would be able to discern good from evil, the northern confederacy attacking Judah would fail. Within two years, Tiglath–pileser defeated both Israel and Syria, just as the prophet had predicted.

Having completed his long-term prophecy, Isaiah gave a short-term prophecy. In doing so he followed a frequent pattern in his book. He consistently did this so his readership could have confidence in the distant prediction by observing the fulfillment of the near one.[30]

The Confirmation of the Prophecy

The messianic interpretation of Isaiah 7:13–15 does not only stand strongly through a careful reading of the text itself, but it is also confirmed by inner-biblical allusions to the prophecy. While some have argued that only Matthew 1:23 reads Isaiah 7:14 as a messianic prophecy, that is really not the case. Isaiah himself substantiates the messianic reading with two passages that follow, as does Isaiah's contemporary Micah.

Isaiah 9:6–7

After giving hope to the house of David that the promise of the Davidic covenant was secure—as would be seen in the birth of Immanuel (7:13–15)—Isaiah proceeded to identify when the Son of David would come. He described the time of judgment to fall on Judah (Isaiah 8) when Judah would be "hard-pressed and famished" and in "distress and darkness" (8:21–22). At that time "the people who walk in darkness will see a great light; those who live in a dark land, the light will shine on them" (9:2). This light was the Son of David described in Isaiah 7:13–15. He was the child who would be born and given four glorious, twofold titles, "Wonderful Counselor, Mighty God, Eternal Father, Prince of Peace" (9:6). He would sit "on the throne of David and over his kingdom, to establish it and uphold it with justice and righteousness from then on and forevermore" (9:7). Just as this future king would be called Immanuel, indicating His deity, so also would the other throne titles reflect His divine nature.[31] The point of Isaiah 9:1–7 was to alert the house of David that the virgin-born king for whom they were to look would come only after a long period of darkness. Nevertheless, He would indeed come, possessing a divine nature, to establish a righteous and eternal kingdom.

Isaiah 11:1–10

Although Isaiah 9 clarified that the Son of David would come after a time of darkness, Isaiah 11 elucidated even further that Immanuel, the virgin-born Child, on whose hopes the entire house of David rests, would come in the distant future. Only after the mighty tree of David had been cut down with "a terrible crash" (10:33) and the Davidic dynasty had become a mere stump, then a shoot would "spring from the stem of Jesse" (11:1). This king from David's line would be empowered by the Spirit of God and establish a righteous reign (11:2–5). His kingdom would be so peaceful that it would even alter the nature of predatory animals (11:6–9). He would not just be the king of Israel, but when He comes all "the nations will resort to the root of Jesse" (11:10). This description is an inner-textual clarification of the king as described in Isaiah 9, giving further details of His peaceful and righteous reign.

Robert Culver has conceded that perhaps Isaiah 7:13–15 is a difficult passage and hard to identify as messianic without careful reading. However, it becomes clearly messianic "when one continues to the final verses of the prophecy,"[32] referring to Isaiah 9 and 11. He adds that reading Isaiah 7:13–15 within the context of these other passages would cause a reader to "understand that a virgin was someday to bear a very human baby whose very character would be divine."[33]

Certainly, the prophet has included these passages in the book of Immanuel, as Isaiah 7–12 is frequently called, to clarify in whom it is that the house of David should pin their hopes. It was the child written about in Isaiah 7:13–15, namely the future, Davidic Messiah who would be "God with us."[34]

Micah 5:3

The prophet Micah, a contemporary of Isaiah, provides an intertextual confirmation of the messianic reading of Isaiah 7:13–15. Located in the well-known prophecy of the Messiah's birth in Bethlehem (Micah 5:2–5), this prophecy is clearly related to Messiah's birth. It identified His human origin ("But as for you, Bethlehem Ephrathah, . . . from you One will go forth for Me to be ruler in Israel"), His eternal nature ("from long ago, from the days of eternity"), and the time of His coming ("when she who is in labor has borne a child"). This last phrase has long been recognized as an inter-textual reference to the virgin birth in Isaiah 7:13–15.[35]

The passage indicates that Israel will be abandoned (referring to the captivity and exile) until she who is in labor has given birth to the Son of David. Only after this birth will the remnant of Messiah's brethren reunite as a nation (they will "return to the sons of Israel."). The reason they will be able to return is the glorious reign of the Messiah of whom it says, "This One will be our peace" (5:5).

Micah 5:2–5 has multiple allusions and references to the book of Immanuel. Both Micah 5 and Isaiah 7 refer to the Messiah's birth. Both refer to the pregnant woman giving birth. Both allude to His divine nature (Micah saying He comes from long ago and the days of eternity and Isaiah calling Him Immanuel, Mighty God, and Father of Eternity). Both Micah ("He will arise and shepherd His flock in the strength of the Lord" 5:4) and Isaiah (9:7; 11:1–10) refer to the glorious reign of the Messiah. Both point out that Messiah will be the source of peace for Israel. (Micah: "This One will be our peace." Isaiah: "His name shall be called . . . the Prince of Peace.")

These many intertextual references are significant. If a plainly messianic passage like Micah 5:2–5[36] cites Isaiah 7:13–15, it shows that the earliest interpretation of Isaiah 7:14, and no less an inspired interpretation, recognizes the messianic prophecy of the virgin birth.

Matthew 1:23

Matthew's use of Isaiah 7:14 in his narrative of the virgin birth has been regarded in a variety of ways. Some have taken it as a double fulfillment, or *sensus plenior*, while others view it as an example of typical fulfillment. Yet others consider it as nothing more than a midrash pesher interpretation, i.e., creative exegesis under the inspiration of the Holy Spirit. Some see it as a misuse of Isaiah who, they allege, was not referring to the virgin birth in any way at all. However, it appears to me that Matthew was following a careful and close reading of Isaiah[37] and recognized that the prediction given to the house of David had found its fulfillment in the virgin birth of Jesus of Nazareth. Immanuel had come just as prophesied eight centuries earlier. God was with Israel.

THE VIRGIN BIRTH IN PROCLAMATION

We end where we began. What if Jesus did indeed have a human father named Larry? What if the Gospel writers were merely mythologizing to make their message more palatable to pagans? What if Isaiah's prediction referred to a young woman giving birth to a child via natural means in eighth-century-BC Judah? According to postmodern Christianity, these are insignificant questions. This approach says that faith in Jesus is still the truth and works even if the virgin birth is questioned or even rejected. But truth is foundational to faith. We must believe in Jesus not because "it works" but because it is true. In fact, He is the truth.

It appears that, according to prophecy, the Messiah's virgin birth was an essential to be believed for two reasons. One, the virgin birth was to be a major sign to confirm Messiah Jesus' position as the messianic Son of David. If Jesus of Nazareth had a human father named Larry or Joseph, it would prove that He really was not the Messiah. No matter how good a life one could lead by believing in Jesus, such a life would be a sham, because that belief would not save anyone. Following Jesus changes our lives because He truly *is* the Messiah.

Two, the virgin birth is in some way related to Jesus' deity. The prediction foretells that the Messiah would be Immanuel or "God with us." Luke, when recording the virgin birth, records the angel's message to Mary: "The Holy Spirit will come upon you, and the power of the Most High will overshadow you; and for that reason the holy

Child shall be called the Son of God" (Luke 1:35). Just as Isaiah related the virgin birth to Messiah being God with us, so Luke associates the virgin birth as the basis for Jesus being the Son of God, or deity. Foundational to our faith is that God became a man in order to redeem us. Without the virgin birth we deny the doctrine of Messiah's deity and lose the truth of His atonement.

To go back to Rob Bell's analogy, he would say that the doctrine of the virgin birth should not be viewed as a brick but as a spring, important but nonessential. In a world where truth has become relative and absolutes unacceptable, it is still necessary to proclaim the virgin birth as not a brick or a spring, but as a foundation. Without it our confidence that Jesus is Messiah and God would indeed crumble.

Michael Rydelnik is professor of Jewish studies at the Moody Bible Institute. An alumnus of MBI, he has earned the D. Miss. degree from Trinity Evangelical Divinity School, Deerfield, Illinois, along with degrees from Dallas Theological Seminary and Azusa Pacific University in Azusa, California.

NOTES

1. Initially, "fundamentalism" was a theological movement, affirming certain fundamentals of the faith. By the middle of the twentieth century, it became associated with forms of sociological separatism that were, in reality, trivial and not fundamental. In 1979, when Islamic students captured the United States embassy in Teheran, news media began to call the Iranian captors Islamic "fundamentalists." As a result, the term "fundamentalist" has now developed a pejorative meaning, associated with extremism and radicalism.

2. William W. Sweet, *The Story of Religion in America* (Grand Rapids: Baker, 1979), 407–09.

3. Rob Bell, *Velvet Elvis* (Grand Rapids: Zondervan, 2005), 22.

4. Ibid., 26–27.

5. Ibid., 27.

6. I. Howard Marshall, *Commentary on Luke: A Commentary on the Greek Text, The New International Greek Testament Commentary,* ed. I. Howard Marshall and W. Ward Gasque (Grand Rapids: Eerdmans, 1979), 897.

7. H. L. Ellison, *The Centrality of the Messianic Idea in the Old Testament* (London: Tyndale, 1957), 6.

8. A. T. Robertson, *Word Pictures in the New Testament,* vol. 2. (Nashville: Broadman, 1930), 294.

9. F. F. Bruce, *The Defense of the Gospel in the New Testament* (Grand Rapids: Eerdmans, 1959), 13–14.

10. Cf. John J. Davis and John C. Whitcomb, *A History of Israel* (Grand Rapids: Baker, 1980), 429–34.

11. John H. Walton has speculated that Isaiah 7:10 ("Then the Lord spoke again to Ahaz . . .") begins a new setting for the prophecy at a later time and that Isaiah and his son Shear-jashub were no longer present at the conduit of the upper pool. He also cites a number of sources both supporting and rejecting this conjecture in "Isaiah 7:14: What's In a Name?" *Journal of the Evangelical Theological Society* 30, no. 3 (September 1987): 289. John Oswalt correctly affirms that 7:10 is a continuation of Isaiah's meeting at the upper pool. He writes that the word "*again* may merely indicate a second part of a single conversation, vv. 3–9 being the promise and vv. 10, 11 the challenge (cf. Gen. 18:29, etc.). There being no evidence of a change in time or location, it seems best to see the paragraph as a direct continuation of vv. 1–9" in *The Book of Isaiah: Chapters 1–39, The New International Commentary on the Old Testament,* ed. R. K. Harrison (Grand Rapids: Eerdmans, 1986), 204.

12. A merism is a figure of speech in which "the totality or whole is substituted by two contrasting or opposite parts"; cf. Roy B. Zuck, *Basic Bible Interpretation* (Wheaton, Ill.: Victor, 1991), 151.

13. English cries out with the need for a distinct second person plural. Hence the southern colloquialism "y'all" or the Brooklynese "youse."

14. See the discussion of the word *sign* [Heb. *'ot*] in David L. Cooper, *Messiah: His Nature and Person* (Los Angeles: Biblical Research Society, 1933), 136–37.

15. Note that E. J. Young not only cites these verses but also shows that the Ras Shamra literature does the same in *Studies in Isaiah.* (Grand Rapids: Eerdmans, 1954), 159–60.

16. Evangelical John H. Walton has made the case for translating *almah* as "young woman" in the *New International Dictionary of Old Testament Theology and Exegesis.* His strongest argument is that when used as an abstract noun in Isaiah 54:4, *'alumim* is used with "a metaphorical attribution of this term to Israel, she is also described as having a husband (v. 5) and being barren (v. 1). In parallel phrases the 'shame' of her *'alumim* is paired with the shame of her widowhood." He maintains that this "would suggest a close connection with childbearing," thus concluding that the word does not indicate virginity. However, a closer look at Isa. 54:4 will demonstrate that while Israel is indeed being spoken of figuratively as a woman, the promise the Lord is making is that "you will forget the shame of your *youth ('alumim)* and the reproach of your widowhood you will remember no more." The contrast is between Israel's youth (before she married, hence a virgin) and when she was a widow (again with no husband, after she married). Isaiah's use of the abstract noun *'alumim* would seem to indicate virginity.

17. Francis Brown, S. Driver and C. Briggs, *Hebrew and English Lexicon* (1952; repr., Peabody, Mass.: Hendrickson, 1996), 761.

18. Cyrus H. Gordon, "Almah in Isaiah 7:14," *Journal of the Bible and Religion* 21, no. 2 (April 1953): 106.

19. For example, cf. Edward E. Hindson, *Isaiah's Immanuel* (Phillipsburg, N.J.: Presbyterian and Reformed. 1978), 67–68. *Theological Dictionary of the New Testament,* Gerhard Kittel, Gerhard Friedrich, eds., Geoffrey W. Bromiley, trans., has maintained that the word *parthenos* did not yet mean "virgin" when the LXX was translated. While this is questionable, it is certainly incorrect about the Isaiah translator's understanding of the term. The translator understood *almah* as virgin and so rendered the feminine singular adjective *harah* ("pregnant") as a feminine singular verb ("will conceive"). Surprisingly, most interpreters miss what has long been seen as an attempt by the translator to come to terms with the "difficulty" of a "pregnant virgin" in Isaiah 7:14.

20. This is the view of Hindson, *Israel's Immanuel,* 38–39, and David Hubbard, who translates it "the way of a man with a virgin and describes it as "the positive picture of romance" in contrast "with the warnings against illicit relations" in *Mastering the Old Testament: Proverbs* (Waco, Tex.: Word, 1989), 465–66. William McKane, while denying that *'almah* means "virgin," interprets the proverb as referring to the "irresistible and inexplicable attraction which draws together the man and the woman." Cf. McKane, *Proverbs: A New Approach* (Philadelphia: Westminster, 1970), 658.

21. For a more thorough discussion of the meaning of *almah* see Richard Niessen, "The Virginity of the *'almah* in Isaiah 7:14," *Bibliotheca Sacra* 546 (April–June, 1980): 133–50.

22. The anti-messianic bias is readily apparent in the great Jewish biblical commentator Rashi, who interprets *almah* as "virgin" in Song of Solomon 1:3 and 6:8 but argues for "young woman" in Isaiah 7:14. This same bias motivated Aquila in his second century Greek translation of the Hebrew Bible, changing the LXX *parthenos* to *neanis* (young girl).

23. This explains why he speaks of a future event in the present tense.

24. Some have objected to Matthew's use of this passage in the birth narrative (Matt. 1:23) because Mary did not name the child "Immanuel." However, "Immanuel" is not the given name of the Messiah. Rather, it was to be seen as a symbolic, descriptive throne title. Similarly, David's son was given the name Solomon but his descriptive royal title was "Jedidiah" or "Beloved of the Lord" (2 Sam. 12:24–25).

25. Translating *'avi* as "Father of Eternity" is preferable because it is the more literal rendering. Moreover, it avoids the Christological problem of calling the Son the Father. Thus, in Isa. 9:6 this Son is the Author of Time or Creator.

26. Cf. Robert L. Reymond, *Jesus: Divine Messiah: The Old Testament Witness* (Fearn, Ross-shire, U.K.: Christian Focus, 2003), 31–34.

27. The "curds and honey" serve as figures for an oppressed land: natural rather than cultivated products; cf. vv. 22–23. "Fulfillment: the moral growth of Jesus, learning to distinguish between good and evil (cf. Luke 2:40, 52), yet in a land that was afflicted —as it worked out historically, by the Romans—and no longer ruled by the dynasty of David." J. Barton Payne, *The Encyclopedia of Biblical Prophecy* (Grand Rapids: Baker, 1973), 293.

28. John Calvin and more recently Robert Vasholz ("Isaiah and Ahaz: A Brief History of Crisis in Isaiah 7 and 8," *Presbyterion: Covenant Seminary Review* XIII:2 (Fall 1987): 82–83.) recognized the adversative phrase *ki b'terem* as signaling a new and different

boy under discussion. Although Oswalt writes, "It is not necessary to separate v. 16 from v. 15; in fact, the opening *ki* of verse 16 can be taken as causal, indicating why the child will eat curds and honey: Judah will be delivered from her neighbors' threat" (213). This neglects the strong adversative nuance of the first two Hebrew words when used together. Moreover, the causal nuance makes no sense if the curds and honey represent the food of oppression as they plainly do in the next paragraph.

29. Calvin and Vasholz ("Isaiah and Ahaz," 83) maintain that 7:16 begins a second prophecy but that it is not a particular boy, rather a generic child, leading to the idea "but before for the boy will know enough to refuse evil and choose good." To come to this view, they must claim a generic use of the article, which is not supported by the context. Cooper, *Messiah: His Nature and Person*, 150–51, and Arnold Fruchtenbaum, *Messianic Christology* (Tustin, Calif.: Ariel Press, 1998), 37, have recognized that the boy is Shear-jashub but mistakenly and without syntactical warrant begin his description in 7:15, seeing only 7:13–14 as referring to the Messiah. To my knowledge, only William Kelly in *An Exposition of the Book of Isaiah* (London: Paternoster, 1897), 144–45, has written that 7:16 begins a second distinct near prophecy and identified the lad as Shear-jashub. (He states that others hold this view, but he does not give attribution to anyone.)

30. Vasholz, "Isaiah and Ahaz," 82.

31. While some have objected to finding the deity of the Messiah in the Hebrew Bible, it appears that this is purely circular reasoning. It begins with the presumption that the Hebrew Scriptures do not reveal a divine Messiah. Then every passage that appears to indicate the deity of the future Messiah is dismissed because "the Hebrew Scriptures do not reveal a divine Messiah." The classic defense of taking Isaiah 9:6 as referring to Messiah as God is John D. Davis's, "The Child Whose Name Is Wonderful," *Biblical and Theological Studies* (New York: Scribners, 1912). For another authoritative defense of Messiah's deity in the Hebrew Scriptures see Benjamin Breckinridge Warfield, "The Divine Messiah in the Old Testament," *Christology and Criticism* (New York: Oxford, 1921).

32. Robert D. Culver, "Were the Old Testament Prophecies Really Prophetic?" *Can I Trust My Bible?* ed. Howard Vos (Chicago: Moody, 1963), 104.

33. Ibid.

34. Moreover, the author also provides an inner-textual reference between the Messiah of Isaiah 11 and the Suffering Servant of Isaiah 52:13–53:12. Just as the Messiah would spring from the "root of Jesse," He would also be compared to a "root out of parched ground" (Isa. 53:2). When all the inner-biblical dots are connected in Isaiah, it serves to inform the reader that: (a) the future son of David would be the virgin-born Immanuel (Isa. 7:13–15); (b) He would be God in the flesh (Isa. 9:6); (c) He would reign over a righteous and peaceful, eternal kingdom (Isa. 9:7; 11:1–10); and (d) He would accomplish this only after His substitutionary death and resurrection (Isa. 52:13–53:12).

35. Norman Snaith, while denying the messianic interpretation of both Isaiah 7:13–15 and Micah 5:2–5, has recognized that Micah is indeed referring to the Isaiah passage in *Amos, Hosea, and Micah* (London: Epworth Press, 1960), 95. Snaith admits that Micah 5 is referring to the birth of a great king, who, as heir to the Davidic throne, would be endowed with remarkable qualities.

36. Certainly some have disputed that Micah 5:2–5 is messianic and have regarded it as

nothing more than hope for the restoration of a Davidic king. Nevertheless, the messianic interpretation is ancient and well established. It is only those interpreters with a presumption that the Old Testament has no messianic hope at all who seem to reject the messianic interpretation of Micah 5:2–5.

37. Some might object that the careful reading available to Matthew was not understandable to Ahaz, who might be considered "the original audience" of this prophecy. This objection fails to understand the nature of the Bible as a text. While Ahaz did receive this prophecy in a particular time and place, all we have of it is a textual record of that event in the composition known as the book of Isaiah. Thus, Ahaz is not the original audience of the book of Isaiah but a character in the inspired narrative written in the book. The audience of the book is eighth-century-BC Judah, to whom a careful reading of the visible compositional strategies was available. They could read it in context with Isaiah 9 and 11 just as any reader of the book of Isaiah can after them. In other words, what was available and understandable to Matthew was also available and understandable to the original readers.

Chapter 2

PROCLAIMING JESUS IN THE GOSPELS

Entering the Kingdom of Heaven in Matthew

by Michael Vanlaningham

Very little of the gospel is in the Gospels—so argue a few Bible teachers. Further, parts, if not the whole, of the Gospels are pure law, they say.[1]

For years in my own pastoral work I was not comfortable with such statements, yet functioned as if it were true whenever I presented the gospel in my preaching, which I did nearly every time I preached. In my personal and public evangelizing I used the familiar texts in Romans and Ephesians. Pitifully little ever came from Matthew, Mark, and Luke, though John fared a bit better. That is no longer the case. There is plenty of the gospel in the Gospels.

This chapter will examine the means of salvation in Matthew's gospel to provide a launching pad for using it and the other Gospels when preaching the centrality of Christ for salvation. We'll narrow our focus to Matthew's remarks about entering the kingdom of heaven, which occur six times in his gospel (5:20; 7:21; 18:3; 19:23, 24; 23:13) and examine them to determine the entrance requirements for the kingdom.

THE IDENTITY OF THE KINGDOM OF GOD— THE KINGDOM OF HEAVEN[2]

As one might anticipate, New Testament scholars outside of evangelicalism have proposed a bewildering number of explanations as to the identity of the kingdom of God or heaven.[3] It is well beyond the scope of this chapter to consider these options in any detail.

Within the evangelical camp, virtually all believe in some form of the kingdom of God. For example, while there are significant differences between them, historic premillennialists and dispensational premillennialists believe in a future, literal reign of Christ upon the earth in which He eliminates His adversaries. He will then rule with absolute control over a literal geopolitical entity, establish true peace, and suspend the curse upon creation.[4] Amillennialists maintain that the church is the fulfillment of the Old Testament promises about a restored rule of God over the world with Israel at the pinnacle of the kingdom. The church is that kingdom. Christ currently rules and reigns in that promised kingdom. During this present age of "the-church-is-the-kingdom," Satan is bound and the gospel will spread throughout and have a profoundly positive impact upon the world. After this reign of Christ through the church, Satan will deceive the nations, resulting in widespread apostasy, Christ will return physically to earth to destroy His enemies and institute the eternal state.[5]

Finally, postmillennialists believe that the kingdom is being broadened in the world through the evangelizing and educating work of the church, and—according to a more recent development of postmillennialism through the theonomist and Christian reconstructionist movement—through seeking to bring the world under the gracious and powerful law of God.[6] Leading postmillennialist Kenneth Gentry writes,

Postmillennialism expects the proclaiming of the Spirit-blessed gospel of Jesus Christ to win the vast majority of human beings to salvation in the present age. Increasing gospel success will gradually produce a time in history prior to Christ's return in which faith, righteousness, peace, and prosperity will prevail in the affairs of people and of nations. After an extensive era of such conditions the Lord will return visibly, bodily, and in great glory, ending history with the general resurrection and the great judgment of all humankind.[7]

To make clear my position in this chapter, I offer the following brief summary of a dispensational view of the kingdom, the primary focus being on the teaching of the Gospels. In them the initial announcements of the kingdom are made to Mary regarding her Son, of whom the angel Gabriel says, "God will give Him the throne of His father David; and He will reign over the house of Jacob forever, and His kingdom will have no end" (Luke 1:32–33). Gabriel appears to reiterate the Davidic Covenant found in 2 Samuel 7, in which God promised David a son who would rule and reign over His kingdom Israel forever. The verbal parallels[8] with Luke 1 are instructive: Both passages use the words "house" (*oikos*; Luke 1:33; 2 Sam. 7:13, 16), "throne" (*thronos*; Luke 1:32; 2 Sam. 7:13, 16), "son" (*hyios*, Luke 1:32; 2 Sam. 7:14) "kingdom" (*basileia*, Luke 1:33; 2 Sam. 7:16), and "forever" (*eis tous aiōnas*, Luke 1:33; *eis ton aiōna*, 2 Sam. 7:16).[9] These suggest that Jesus has come, among other things, to fulfill the role as the quintessential Son of David.[10] They also suggest that the Gospel writers had an apologetic purpose, to argue for Jesus fulfilling the promises regarding David's seed ruling over David's kingdom.

Both in the horizons of Mary's experience and that of Luke's readers, it makes the best sense to see this kingdom as the same one promised in the Hebrew Scriptures. It is a literal kingdom with a ruling king, exercising authority over a literal people and a literal land. The amillennial and postmillennial understanding of the kingdom, and even to an extent the understanding of historic premillennialism, requires a significant shift in thinking away from the Old Testament (OT) concept of this kingdom. These approaches subordinate the role of Israel in the kingdom and unduly exalt the role of the church. It is exceedingly unlikely that this is the sense of the kingdom offered in the advent of the Messiah.

With the arrival of John the Baptist and his preaching, and later of Jesus and the disciples, the message was simply, "Repent, for the kingdom of God [or heaven] is at hand" (Matt. 3:2; 4:17; 10:7; Mark 1:15). It appears from the Baptist's citation of Isaiah 40:3 in John 1:23 that he anticipated a literal return of God to Israel. (See also the evangelists' reference to Isaiah 40 in Matt. 3:3; Mark 1:3; and in Luke 1:76 his reference to Mal. 3:1, in which a similar "preparing the way of the Lord", theme is found.) Since the evangelist offered no explanation of this kingdom for which he was sent to prepare the people, it seems best to ascribe to his message the usual OT understanding about a restored kingdom. The initial preaching of Jesus is similar. Only later in His ministry does He appear to add the more "spiritual" aspects of the kingdom in His teaching. These, however, should not be seen as "replacing" or "superseding" those promises so that the kingdom becomes altogether different from that seen in the OT.[11] Instead these are spiritual dimensions of the kingdom, complementary forms related to the OT ones, called "mysteries" of the kingdom (Matt. 13:11)—i.e., truths about the kingdom not seen, or at least not seen clearly, in the OT.[12] But even when Jesus embarks on teaching about these spiritual aspects, *He nowhere corrects John's idea of the literal kingdom*, which seems odd if Jesus were presenting new teaching at loggerheads with the Baptist.

Darrell Bock argues that there is a considerable amount of overlap between the teachings of Jesus and the OT teaching on the earth-shattering coming of the kingdom of God, whose kingdom would be mediated through the seed of David. There will be a calamitous coming of the kingdom as the OT predicts, but it will be preceded by the more secret, spiritual aspects of it in the world not foreseen in the OT, without any contradiction.[13] In addition, the original message was limited to Israel (Matt. 10:5–7; 15:24), but this makes the best sense if one understands that Christ came to *Israel* to sit upon *David's throne*.

An important question remains: Is the church in the present era the kingdom of God?[14] Dispensational writers respond with "No." When examining the concept of the kingdom in the New Testament epistles, the vast majority of references to the kingdom picture it as something future for the members of the church, as something that will be inherited.[15] Nevertheless, those members are equally said to be "citizens of the kingdom" right now, though its full establishment is future.[16] The kingdom is not to be equated with the church, but the church is the community through which the kingdom currently operates in the world. The body of Christ functions as an ambassador of the King and His kingdom,[17] is an heir with Christ to the future kingdom, and will reign with Christ in that future kingdom.[18] Nevertheless, the church is not the kingdom.

In terms of entering the kingdom, amillennialists maintain that when one enters the body of Christ, the church, by means of grace through faith (salvation), he is then in the kingdom. Dispensationalists and some historical premillennialists maintain that while the full-blown coming of the kingdom is future, the mystery form of it seen presently in the church must be entered now to assure inclusion in it with its climatic arrival. Postmillennialists say that one must be a part of the church, which will be instrumental in ushering in the kingdom in the future. All agree that no one is *automatically* in the kingdom. It must be entered, and there are entrance requirements to be met. Matthew explains what those are.

Exposition of "Entering the Kingdom" Passages

Once again, six passages in Matthew's gospel contain the phrase "enter the kingdom of heaven."[19] Those passages are 5:20; 7:21; 18:3; 19:23 (verse 24 uses the related "kingdom of God") and 23:13. What follows will seek to provide a brief exposition of each passage to clarify the fact that Jesus taught salvation by grace through faith—to borrow a phrase anachronistically from Paul.

Matthew 5:20

"For I say to you that unless your righteousness surpasses that of the scribes and Pharisees, you will not enter the kingdom of heaven."

At first glance, it appears that Jesus is teaching that the means for entering the kingdom relate to the practice of righteousness, and this is frequently how the verse is viewed.

A number of factors weigh against this understanding, three of which will be explored here. First, neither the verse nor the immediate context establishes how this righteousness is gained.[20] It is possible that it is established through the fulfillment of the "deeper teaching" of Jesus laid out in the antithetical statements of Matt. 5:21–48, but this understanding tends to wrest 5:20 from its contextual moorings, to be considered in the next point.

Second, the word "righteousness" (*dikaiosynē*) occurs in Matthew's gospel seven times, in 3:15 ("Permit it at this time; for in this way it is fitting for us to fulfill all righteousness."); 5:6 ("Blessed are those who hunger and thirst for righteousness"); 5:10 ("Blessed are those who have been persecuted for the sake of righteousness"); the passage under consideration (5:20); 6:1 ("Beware of practicing your righteousness before men"); 6:33 ("But seek first His kingdom and His righteousness"); and 21:32 ("For John came to you in the way of righteousness"). The word appears to have two connotations in Matthew: ethical behavior in keeping with the teachings of Jesus (Matt. 6:1; 5:10, perhaps 20), and God's delivering or vindicating action on behalf of His people (Matt. 5:6; 6:33), which can have a present and future (eschatological) component.

The uses most relevant for this discussion are 5:6 and 6:33, inasmuch as they appear to put the responsibility for gaining righteousness upon the hearer or reader, while the other passages (3:15; 5:10; 6:1; and 21:32) speak of John and Jesus' fulfillment of righteousness, or righteousness in the individual is presupposed.[21] "Poor in spirit" in 5:3 emphasizes not only the likelihood of economic poverty but also the spiritual bankruptcy of the one who is promised the kingdom.[22] In keeping with 5:6, these people who are blessed do not possess righteousness; they hunger and thirst for it, and the promise is extended to them that "they will be satisfied"—a divine passive, so that *God* is the one who fills them. Much the same could be said of Matt. 6:33, where both the kingdom and righteousness are sought along with the mundane necessities of life. The verb "shall be added" is another divine passive, but should not be restricted to the provision of food, water, and clothing alone. The Gentiles eagerly seek (*epizēteō*) these things, but the disciple is to seek (*zēteō*) the kingdom and His righteousness, and the implication is that both can be obtained, with the staples provided in the process. Since it is God who provides His people with righteousness, it is unlikely that the context allows for 5:20 to be understood as a proof text for bald works-righteousness. This puts God's gift of righteousness (in 5:6) at odds with the ethical demands of righteousness suggested by 5:20, something that would cause an intolerable tension.[23] Because of God's work emphasized in 5:6, it seems preferable to see a synthesis between the two aspects of righteousness at work in 5:20, not unlike Paul's connection between grace and works in Eph 2:8–10. Donald A. Hagner writes:

> The larger context of the verse (e.g., the grace of the beatitudes) forbids
> us to conclude that entrance into the kingdom depends, in a cause-effect

relationship, upon personal moral attainments. The verse is addressed, it must be remembered, to those who are the recipients of the kingdom. Entrance into the kingdom is God's gift; but to belong to the kingdom means to follow Jesus' teaching. Hence, the kingdom and the righteousness of the kingdom go together; they cannot be separated. And it follows that without this righteousness there can be no entrance into the kingdom (cf. 6:33).[24]

Third, the deficiency of the scribes and Pharisees is worth exploring. It is possible that through their scrupulous observance of the oral tradition they had domesticated the law and thereby neglected the weightier aspects of it (Matt. 23:23).[25] But it is unlikely that "doing more of the law" or "doing better at it" would have solved their problem. Instead, as Guelich suggests in light of the first and third beatitudes and the "But I say to you" statements in the last part of Matthew 5, their fundamental problem was that they failed to possess and exhibit a righteousness *that had Jesus as its focus instead of Moses or their own oral traditions.* The righteousness that His disciples would possess would be fraught with persecution as stated in 5:10 ("for the sake of righteousness," *heneken dikaiosynês*), which, in the context of 5:11, is persecution "because of Me" (*heneken emou*). In principle, it is hard to see how the scribes and Pharisees would have objected to the righteousness Jesus lays out in 5:21–48, except for the fact that He claims to be its authoritative source and that His new teaching supersedes the content of OT law.[26] The main problem of "the righteousness of the scribes and Pharisees" was that their system of righteousness bypassed Jesus. Guelich writes:

Contrary to the opinion of some, 5:20 does not demand a more rigorous keeping of the Law or a keeping of a more rigorous Law or interpretation of the Law. Rather, Jesus, according to Matthew, demands a *righteousness* congruent with his coming. *Righteousness* necessary for

46

entrance into the Kingdom connotes the conduct in keeping with the will of the Father, conduct that stems from the new relationships and possibilities inherent in the presence of the age of salvation and implicit in the demands of 5:21–7:12. The *righteousness of the scribes and Pharisees* was inadequate because it did not stem from the eschatological moment of God's redemptive activity in Jesus' Messianic ministry, restoring the broken relationships between himself and his people as well as among his people, enabling them to live in keeping with his will. . . . . Whereas Paul distinguished qualitatively between a "righteousness of my own, based on the Law" and "that which is through faith in Christ" (Phil. 3:9), Matthew used a quantitative comparison to express the ultimate inadequacy of "Pharisaic righteousness" for entrance into the Kingdom in view of Jesus' coming and ministry (5:17, 18, 21–48; 6:1–18).[27]

In concluding the discussion of this passage, if the righteousness needed to surpass that of the scribes and Pharisees comes as a gift from God, and focuses upon Christ and His teachings as the authoritative prophet and Messiah from God, then we cannot be very far from the teachings of the apostle Paul.

Matthew 7:21

"Not everyone who says to Me, 'Lord, Lord,' will enter the kingdom of heaven, but he who does the will of My Father who is in heaven will enter."

Once again, a cursory reading of the passage might suggest that "doing the will of My Father" requires some work that would merit entrance into the kingdom. While this is possible, it is not a necessary understanding of the verse in its context.

It is not completely clear what the connection of 7:21 is with the section before (7:15–20), in which warnings about false prophets predominate. It is likely that the discussion of false prophets continues into 7:21ff (note 7:22, "Many will say to Me on that day, 'Lord, Lord, did we not prophesy in Your name . . . ?'"), but the emphasis appears to shift from their deeds to their words or claims, and from recognition by others to Christ's refusal to recognize them in the future.[28] They do exhibit good deeds, one of them being their confession of Christ. They speak to Jesus the words "Lord, Lord." It is difficult to be dogmatic about the content of the knowledge or belief of these people regarding Christ's deity simply by the use of the word "Lord."[29] Whether or not these people barred from the kingdom were fully orthodox in their view of Christ, their problem remains.

Equally unclear is what Jesus means by "doing the will of My Father." More than likely it refers to doing what is commanded in the Sermon on the Mount.[30] These false prophets are not guilty of being passive. So precisely what is their problem?

This can be answered several ways. First, these false prophets assume that the good deeds of prophesying, exorcism, and effecting miracles are the prerequisites for entering the kingdom of heaven. Their claims of having ministered in Christ's name may not be false, but their outcome indicates that their feats are insufficient.[31] Here doing the will of God in order to enter the kingdom is *apparently quite different from what these miracle workers are doing.* Hagner observes:

> The persons are thus not criticized for their charismatic activities but for their dependence upon them as a substitute for the righteousness taught by Jesus. We may conclude that charismatic activities, done apart from this righteousness, have no self-contained importance and are in themselves insufficient for entry into the kingdom of heaven.[32]

It seems reasonable that if *these* amazing good works are insufficient for fitting one for the kingdom, then *any* good works would be equally futile.

Second, these false ministers are wolves in sheep's clothing; they are not sheep, even though they look like it.[33] Jesus also calls them bad trees, not good (7:17–18); they produce thorns and thistles, not grapes and figs (7:16); and they are destined for the fires of judgment, not the kingdom of heaven (7:19). Hence the false prophets are of a nature totally different from the sheep. On that basis their evil deeds—only bad trees produce bad fruit—and even their supposedly good deeds and miracles are rejected. These false prophets, then, have a nature different from those who possess the kingdom.

Finally, if doing "the will of My Father who is in heaven" is found essentially in the teachings of Jesus in the Sermon on the Mount, then part of that "doing" in the Sermon involves meeting the implicit conditions of the "grace" beatitudes in Matt. 5:3–6, i.e., being spiritually bankrupt and hungering and thirsting for righteousness. As we have seen, this should be understood as a righteousness given by God along with the kingdom itself as a gift (6:33), and which is riveted upon the new authority and the person of Jesus Christ (5:10–11). It would be an interpretive mistake to omit these elements from "doing the will of My Father" in 7:21.

Matthew 18:3

"Truly I say to you, unless you are converted and become like children, you will not enter the kingdom of heaven."

In this passage, we are on more familiar turf than some of the other "entering the kingdom" passages, as the childlikeness required for entrance is much easier to harmonize with the doctrine of grace found elsewhere in the New Testament.

In Matthew 18:2, Jesus calls a child and enacts a lesson with him or her, carried out in verse 3 ff. Though there are tragic exceptions, children tend to be highly valued in the West, but that was not always the case in first-century Judaism. The rabbis several generations later would classify children as on par with the deaf, dumb, and simpleminded.[34] To use a child as the protagonist of such an object lesson would have been graphic for the disciples. He warns the disciples, first, "[U]nless you are converted . . . you will not enter the kingdom of heaven." The word "converted," which in English is often understood as a change from one religion to another, is an unfortunate translation of *straphēte* (from the verb *strephō*), which usually carries the sense in religious contexts of "to experience an inward change, turn, change,"[35] or "to change one's manner of life, with the implication of turning toward God—to change one's ways, to turn to God, to repent."[36]

Second, Jesus says, "Unless you . . . become like children, you will not enter the kingdom of heaven." A host of proposals exists about the precise point of the analogy. Davies and Allison give a sampling of the views, which include openness, trust in God, spontaneity, receiving the kingdom as a child would receive a gift, being humble, learning to embrace God as Father, and their own proposal that becoming like a child means beginning afresh in one's religious life.[37] Determining the more likely option is not easy, but Jesus immediately follows this statement with the one enjoining humility in 18:4, and this throws considerable light on the sense of becoming like a child in verse 3. It is likely, then, that becoming like a child, in context, means having a lack of pretension or concern about status, which, as 18:1 suggests, is the problem the disciples exhibited that evoked Jesus' warning.[38]

Third, this humility can be identified more precisely from the context, and should not be viewed strictly as being humble in status in a social sense, as children of that day were. Two factors suggest it is humble dependence on God that constitutes the childlike humility that readies one for the kingdom. First, to be precise, the humility of the child is not mentioned in 18:3, and when Jesus broaches it in 18:4, it is in connection with being great in the kingdom of heaven, not getting into it. It is possible that the childlikeness necessary for entrance into the kingdom is of a nature different from the childlike humility for greatness in the kingdom.

Second, even allowing for the key element in 18:3 being humility, this is a certain kind of humility. Walter Grundmann writes, "Jesus is speaking to adults. He is conscious of their lost childlikeness before God. He thus gives humility a special nuance. It is to become a child again before God, i.e., to trust Him utterly, to expect everything from Him and nothing from self."[39] The context supports Grundmann's contention. In 18:6, Jesus warns, "[W]hoever causes one of these little ones who believe in Me to stumble, it would be better for him to have a heavy millstone hung around his neck, and to be drowned in the depth of the sea." Here a prime characteristic of childlikeness is believing in Jesus.[40] Furthermore, in 18:10, 12–13, Jesus presents the extreme care of the Father toward "these little ones," His seeking them, switching the analogy to sheep that have strayed, and His joy at finding one who was lost. This acute concern of the Father implies that to become like children to enter the kingdom of heaven in this context requires a humility that entrusts itself to God and His provision.

Matthew 19:23–24

> And Jesus said to His disciples, "Truly I say to you, it is hard for a rich man to enter the kingdom of heaven. Again I say to you, it is easier for a camel to go through the eye of a needle, than for a rich man to enter the kingdom of God."

When read in its context, this passage is one of the more difficult ones for those who study Paul's biblical writings. The main problem stems from Jesus' strong words in Matt. 19:16–21:

> And someone came to Him and said, "Teacher, what good thing shall I do that I may obtain eternal life?" And He said to him, "Why are you asking Me about what is good? There is only One who is good; but if you wish to enter into life, keep the commandments." Then he said to Him, "Which ones?" And Jesus said, "You shall not commit murder; You shall

not commit adultery; You shall not steal; You shall not bear false witness; Honor your father and mother; and You shall love your neighbor as yourself." The young man said to Him, "All these things I have kept; what am I still lacking?" Jesus said to him, "If you wish to be complete, go and sell your possessions and give to the poor, and you will have treasure in heaven; and come, follow Me."

It is puzzling as to why Jesus gives such a strong exhortation related to keeping the law in order to "obtain eternal life" (19:16), to "enter into life" (19:17), and to "enter the kingdom of heaven" (19:23, 24).[41] There is less of a contradiction here than there might seem with the rest of the New Testament. Several points in the passage will be considered.

First, the question as posed by the Rich Young Ruler underscores the idea that he sees obtaining life as contingent upon something good he must do. The word "good thing" is *agathon*, an adjective used in this sentence as a noun (a common construction with Greek adjectives).[42] This is clear enough. But what is not so clear is Jesus' response, where the interpretive waters are seriously muddied by most English translations.[43] It is common to translate the sentence in 19:17, "Why are you asking Me about what is good?" It would be preferable to translate it, "Why are you asking Me *about a good thing* [a work]?"[44] Jesus' response in Greek more obviously addresses the man's question about doing a good thing to obtain eternal life than most English versions suggest.

Jesus immediately follows with, "There is only One who is good" (19:17b) (*agathos*, the same adjective, used again as a noun). With this statement He presents the theme He will make explicit in 19:26, that one's entrance into the kingdom of heaven ultimately results from God's work on behalf of the individual, and not from good deeds. At this point, "One who is good" (again, *agathos*) refers not to something one does to obtain eternal life, but to *God Himself.* This suggests that the key to obtaining eternal life in this text is not found in doing something good, but in the good person of God.

I would be more comfortable if Jesus (and Matthew) had omitted 19:17b–25, and cut right to the "grace" part of the pericope in v. 26. But it is in this section that He plays the "works" card with the Rich Young Ruler, confounding more than a few of us, I suspect. In light of Jesus' emphasis in the passage on obtaining eternal life residing in God and not man's deeds, it is probably best to see Jesus' exhortation to keep the law as a move on His part to challenge the man's assumption that he, by his deeds, could obtain eternal life. If one could keep the commandments, then he probably could obtain it. But Jesus is showing by His interaction with the man, beginning especially in verse 18, that this is not possible.

Some popular writers emphasize that Jesus refers to the second table of the law, those commandments dealing with one's relationship to other people. From there, they maintain that Jesus then challenges the man on his view of money, that he had actually made it his god, thus violating the first table of the law (man's relationship to God).[45] But I doubt that this is the case. It seems instead that Jesus is challenging the Rich Young Ruler on his insistence that he has fully kept even the second table of the Law (Matt. 19:20), i.e., that he had not committed murder, adultery, and the other sins. There is no clear indication in the text that the Rich Young Ruler's main problem was that his wealth became his idol. His main problem lies precisely in the very things Jesus delineates in vv. 18–19, including loving one's neighbor as himself (Lev. 19:18). This last command is emphasized in Matthew's gospel in contrast to Mark and Luke (cf. besides here, Matt. 5:43; 22:39; Mark 12:31, 33; and Luke 10:27 refer to it only once each). The mention of loving one's neighbor is important in light of what happens in 19:21.

Jesus actually challenges him on his insistence that he had kept these laws, those that relate to one's relationships with others. In verse 21, when Jesus commands him to sell everything and give it to the poor, Jesus is simply reiterating Lev. 19:18. The Rich Young Ruler maintained that he had done all these things, including Lev. 19:18. Jesus calls his bluff, and tells him to sell his possessions and give to the poor, by which he would then be loving his neighbor as himself. Because of the Rich Young Ruler's sense of deficiency (v. 20), he probably never really had kept the second table of the law very well.[46] When Jesus goes on in verse 26 to say that "with people this [being saved, v. 25] is impossible," He further demonstrates that the Rich Young Ruler *had not* and *would not* keep the second table of the law adequately to obtain eternal life, and that he *could not* do so as well. In the same way that the Rich Young Ruler had a wrong view of doing "good deeds" to obtain eternal life, inasmuch as it is God who gives it, so also here Jesus says that gaining eternal life, aka getting into the kingdom, depends on God.

The astonishment of the disciples in verse 25 comes from the fact that early Judaism regarded wealth as an indication of God's favor and positive esteem of a person. They thought He would not give wealth to one who was a sinner. Hence, it if was hard for a rich man (upon whom the favor of God appeared to rest) to get into the kingdom, how could anyone else hope to do so? Again, Jesus responds by saying it is ultimately God's work. It seems, then, that in this passage we have Paul's doctrines of total depravity (Rom. 3:9–20), total inability (Rom. 2:1–11; 8:7–8), and salvation as God's gracious work apart from meritorious deeds by the individual (Eph. 2:8–9).

Matthew 23:13

"But woe to you, scribes and Pharisees, hypocrites, because you shut off the kingdom of heaven from people; for you do not enter in yourselves, nor do you allow those who are entering to go in."

Neither Matthew nor Jesus tells the reader how the scribes and Pharisees hinder their own or others' entrance into the kingdom.[47] There are clues, however. Looking at the broader context preceding Matthew 23, when both John the Baptist and Jesus came on the scene, they preached the nearness of the kingdom of heaven. As Jesus called them to repentance and to Himself, He was calling them equally to the kingdom. The Pharisees and others largely rejected Him, shutting themselves off from the kingdom He proclaimed. In this sense they "do not enter" into the kingdom themselves. And when they warned the people to avoid Him, they were hindering them as well (e.g., Matt. 9:33–34; 11:19; 12:23–24; 15:14; 16:12; 21:15–17).[48]

The more immediate context gives other clues as well. In Matt. 22:41–46, the failure of the religious leaders was that they did not recognize who Jesus really was, and so rejected Him.[49] Matthew 23:37–39 contains the climax of Jesus' denunciation of the religious leaders. The fundamental failure in those verses is their refusal to come to Jesus for spiritual deliverance and shelter.

If all this is on target, then entering the kingdom of heaven in Matt. 23:13 involves a sympathetic embracing of Jesus Christ, something that the religious leaders did not do, and that they discouraged others from doing as well. Once again, entering the kingdom does not appear to be a consequence of good works, but involves instead a positive connection with Jesus Christ.

HOW TO ENTER THE KINGDOM OF GOD

It is time to pull together the threads of this discussion. Entering the kingdom of heaven in Matthew's gospel seems to be tied to meritorious works that one must do, given a superficial reading of the texts. But Jesus makes it clear that the righteousness one must possess to enter the kingdom has to exceed that of the scribes and Pharisees (Matt. 5:20). The context of that statement indicates that God will satisfy those who crave this righteousness (5:6), suggesting that the righteousness is not exactly in their possession, and that the kingdom belongs to those who are spiritually destitute (5:3).

Spectacular deeds are also insufficient to gain entrance into the kingdom (7:21–23), and depending upon them for admission into the kingdom is misguided. Instead, a change of nature is required (from wolves to sheep, bad trees to good), and comes as a gift through the righteousness that God gives (5:3, 6). *One enters the kingdom of heaven only as he or she exercises complete dependence, in full humility and faith, upon God as the heavenly Father* (18:3–4, 6). In fact, it is impossible for an individual to enter the kingdom of heaven on his own, because he cannot and will not keep the law well enough to warrant a right standing before God, whereby such entrance is obtained (19:16–24). *One's way into the kingdom comes in one's allegiance to Jesus Christ,* and being excluded from the kingdom comes from a refusal to embrace Him.

The parallels with Paul are obvious. We have, in Matthew's gospel, the doctrines of total depravity and total inability so that people cannot improve their standing before God on their own, the futility of good works to obtain righteousness and merit eternal life, righteousness as a gift from God that rescues one from the eternal consequences of his or her sins, and righteousness obtained only by faith in Jesus Christ.

There is plenty of grace in the Gospels, or, put another way, there is plenty of the gospel in the Gospels. They can, and should, be used in our proclamation of the centrality of Christ as the sole mediator of God's grace to the lost world.

Michael Vanlaningham is professor of Bible at the Moody Bible Institute. He earned his Ph.D. from Trinity Evangelical Divinity School, Deerfield, Illinois, and also has academic degrees from Nebraska Wesleyan University, Lincoln, Nebraska, and Talbot Theological Seminary, La Mirada, California. He has served as a pastor for more than fifteen years.

NOTES

1. For example, Hans Windisch, *The Meaning of the Sermon on the Mount: A Contribution to the Historical Understanding of the Gospels and to the Problem of Their True Exegesis,* trans. S. MacLean Gilmour (Philadelphia: Westminster, 1951), 27–29, 71–73; Lewis Sperry Chafer, *Systematic Theology,* vol. 4 (Dallas: Dallas Seminary, 1948), 214–25; vol. 5, 105–14, both in connection with the Sermon on the Mount.

2. Matthew mostly uses the phrase "kingdom of heaven" vis-à-vis "kingdom of God" in the other gospels. Probably the simplest and best explanation of this is that he was apparently writing to a messianic Jewish audience, i.e., one that was Jewish in background and had embraced Christ as Savior and Messiah. Because a cavalier use of "God" would have been offensive to such an audience, "heaven" is used by metonomy for "God." Soree Ulrich Luz, *Matthew 1–7,* trans. Wilhelm C. Linss (Minneapolis: Fortress, 1989), 167.

3. For an older but admirable discussion of many of the options, see George E. Ladd, "Kingdom of God—Reign or Realm?" *Journal of Biblical Literature* 81 (1962): 230–38; more recently, see Mark Saucy, *The Kingdom of God in the Teaching of Jesus in 20th Century Theology* (Dallas: Word, 1997). Joel Marcus reduces the meaning of *basileia,* "kingdom," to the sovereign power of God breaking into the world through Christ, and indicates that it refers to God's "dominion" but not God's "domain." I will argue that, based on evidence in the Gospels and drawn from the OT, this is both overly reductionistic and a false distinction. The concept of "kingdom" on the lips of John the Baptist and Jesus surely includes elements of both, depending on the context.

4. A summary of the overlap between historic and dispensational premillennialism on the nature of the kingdom of God is found in Millard Erickson, *Contemporary Options in Eschatology* (Grand Rapids: Baker, 1977), 101–3; Idem., *Christian Theology* (Grand Rapids: Baker, 1985, one-volume edition 1987), 1209–12; and Stanley J. Grenz, *The Millennial Maze* (Downers Grove, Ill.: InterVarsity, 1992), 128–29. For a summary of the differences between historic and dispensational premillennialism, see Grenz, *Millennial Maze,* 129–31.

5. This is the summary of Kim Riddlebarger, *A Case for Amillennialism: Understanding the End Times* (Grand Rapids: Baker, 2003), 31–32.

6. The classic presentation of postmillennialism remains Loraine Boettner, *The Millennium* (Philadelphia: Presbyterian and Reformed, 1957), 3–105. See also J. Marcellus Kik, *An Eschatology of Victory* (Phillipsburg, N.J.: Presbyterian and Reformed, 1971) (for Kik's view of the millennium, cf. especially 4–14, 204–13). The notable theonomists include Greg Bahnsen, *Theonomy in Christian Ethics* (Phillipsburg, N.J.: Presbyterian and Reformed, 1977); Rousas John Rushdoony, *The Institutes of Biblical Law* (Phillipsburg, N.J.: Presbyterian and Reformed, 1984).

7. Kenneth L. Gentry Jr., "Postmillennialism," *Three Views on the Millennium and Beyond,* ed. Darrell L. Bock (Grand Rapids: Zondervan, 1999), 13–14. For a more detailed discussion, see Gentry's *He Shall Have Dominion: A Postmillennial Eschatology* (Tyler, Tex.: Institute for Christian Economics, 1997), 65–93, especially 65–73.

8. The verbal parallels are drawn between the LXX (the ancient Greek translation of the Hebrew Scriptures) and the New Testament texts.

9. Raymond E. Brown notes these similarities and their significance in *The Birth of the Messiah*, 2nd ed. (New York: Doubleday, 1993), 310–11. In the chronicler's parallel passage to 2 Samuel 7, the parallels with Luke also exist. For "house," see 1 Chron. 17:12, 14; for "throne," 1 Chron. 17:12, 14; "son," 1 Chron. 17:13; "kingdom," 1 Chron. 17:11, 14; and finally "forever," 1 Chron. 17:12, 14. See also Ps. 89:29, 36–37.

10. It is clear that early Judaism (aka Second Temple Judaism or the "Intertestamental Period") had not quenched the Jewish hope for *the* Son of David. For this, see Markus Bockmuehl, *This Jesus: Martyr, Lord Messiah* (Downers Grove, Ill.: InterVarsity, 1994), 42–51. This is probably one of the main themes of Matthew's gospel, which begins, "The record of the genealogy of Jesus the Messiah, the son of David . . . ." Only after establishing that *Jesus* is *the* prophesied Son of David does Matthew then begin the genealogy proper with Abraham, though David is still clearly emphasized, serving as the fulcrum for the entire list (Matt. 1:17).

11. Contrast with O. T. Allis, *Prophecy and the Church* (Philadelphia: Presbyterian and Reformed, 1945), 70–75; and Clarence Bass, *Backgrounds to Dispensationalism* (Grand Rapids: Eerdmans, 1960), 29–30.

12. Perhaps most noteworthy are the parables found in Matthew 13, in which the kingdom is seen growing in a gradual, permeating way which could be secretly discovered by those who enter it, vis-à-vis the earth-shattering, cataclysmic coming of the kingdom to the earth as seen in Daniel 2 and 7. But note that the "spiritual aspect" or "mysteries of the kingdom" in Matthew 13 follow only after what S. Lewis Johnson calls the national rejection of Jesus in Matthew 12. Starting in Matthew 13, Jesus teaches the crowds almost exclusively in parables as an act of judgment, and never again speaks of the nearness of the kingdom, yet speaks extensively of the kingdom during the present age (especially in the parables of Matthew 13). If the King is rejected, what happens to the kingdom He offered? It is in abeyance, with the "mysteries of the kingdom" in play (S. Lewis Johnson, "The Argument of Matthew," *Bibliotheca Sacra* 112 (1955): 149–51). Alva J. McClain says that the full-blown kingdom is then postponed and the mysteries of the kingdom become applicable, a theme Jesus introduces in Matthew 13. But none of this should be understood to preclude a full and future coming of the kingdom as anticipated by the OT prophets. Alva J. McClain, *The Greatness of the Kingdom* (Grand Rapids: Zondervan, 1959), 321–25.

13. Darrell L. Bock, *Jesus According to Scripture* (Grand Rapids: Baker, 2002), 570–79.

14. For a detailed discussion of this issue, see Darrell L. Bock and Craig A. Blaising, *Progressive Dispensationalism* (Wheaton, Ill.: Victor, 1993), 255–70; Robert L. Saucy, *The Case for Progressive Dispensationalism* (Grand Rapids: Zondervan, 1993), 102–10.

15. See 1 Cor. 6:9; Gal. 5:21; Eph. 5:5; Rom. 8:17; 2 Thess. 1:5; 2 Tim. 4:18.

16. See Col. 1:13; 1 Thess. 2:12; Rom. 14:17; 1 Cor. 4:20; Phil. 3:20.

17. 2 Cor. 5:20.

18. Rev. 3:21; 1 Cor. 4:8; 2 Tim. 2:12; Rev. 5:10; 1 Cor. 6:1–3. See Eric Sauer, *From Eternity to Eternity* (Grand Rapids: Eerdmans, 1952), 92–93.

19. There are other sayings in which "entering" is prominent. Those include *entering life* (18:8–9; 19:17), *the joy of your master* (25:21, 23), and the *narrow way* (7:13–14). Only entering the kingdom will be considered here.

20. This is the observation of D. A. Carson, "Matthew," *The Expositor's Bible Commentary*, vol. 8, ed. Frank E. Gaebelein (Grand Rapids: Zondervan, 1984), 147. Carson cites Isaiah 61:3 in support of the concept that *the Messiah* would establish a people typified by righteousness.

21. An enormous debate exists regarding the precise meaning of "righteousness" in the OT, early Judaism, the Gospels, and especially in Paul's epistles. For the issues and bibliography, see Mark A. Seifrid, "Righteousness Language in the Hebrew Scriptures and Early Judaism," in *Justification and Variegated Nomism: Volume One: The Complexities of Second Temple Judaism,* ed. D. A. Carson et al. (Grand Rapids: Baker, 2001), 414–42; Peter Stuhlmacher, *Revisiting Paul's Doctrine of Justification* (Downers Grove, Ill.: InterVarsity, 2001), 13–31. Summarizing the main points in the discussion would lead down a rabbit trail from which there would be no hope of return.

22. Craig L. Blomberg, *Matthew* in *The New American Commentary*, vol. 22 (Nashville: Broadman, 1992), 98–100.

23. Robert Guelich, *The Sermon on the Mount* (Dallas: Word, 1982), 85–88, 157–61, 346–48.

24. Donald A. Hagner, "Matthew 1–13" in *Word Biblical Commentary*, vol. 33a (Dallas: Word, 1993), 109. The "grace of the beatitudes," to use Hagner's expression, is further supported by the parallels between the first three beatitudes of Matt. 5:3–5, and Isa. 61:1–11, where God establishes righteousness (the deliverance of His people and justice) in the world.

25. Leon Morris, *The Gospel According to Matthew* (Grand Rapids: Eerdmans, 1992), 111; Carson, "Matthew," 147.

26. For an excellent discussion of what Jesus is doing in the Sermon on the Mount, cf. Douglas J. Moo, "Jesus and the Authority of the Mosaic Law," *Journal for the Study of the New Testament* 20, no. 1 (February 1984): 17–23. Moo argues that the key to the antithetical statements in Matthew 5 is not found in some supposed correction of Pharisaical teaching, or explication of the "deeper teaching of the Law"—though surely His instruction does not contradict the law. But the OT nowhere hints at the equation that anger is tantamount to murder, or lust to adultery. What Jesus is doing is giving *new revelation* ("But *I* say to you [as over-against the law]" 5:22, 28, 32, 34, 39, 44), to establish His prophetic authority in keeping with the promise of a prophet like Moses who would come (Deut. 18:15, 18; 34:10–12; see Acts 3:19–23 for its fulfillment in Jesus). If His followers embrace Him as this authoritative one who presents His own system of righteousness, then the persecution becomes understandable and inevitable.

27. Guelich, *Sermon on the Mount*, 159, italics his.

28. Morris, *Matthew*, 179, believes that those in view in 7:21–22 are no longer the false prophets, but instead "false followers."

29. Carson, "Matthew," 192–93.

30. In Luke 6:46, the Lucan parallel to this verse, Jesus says, "Why do you call Me, 'Lord, Lord,' and do not do what I say?" This suggests that doing the will of the Father is doing what Jesus taught in Matthew, especially in the Sermon on the Mount.

31. Carson, "Matthew," 193.

32. Hagner, "Matthew 1–13," 186.

33. Petri Luomanen, *Entering the Kingdom* (Tübingen, Germany: Mohr, 1998), 99–100, observes, " . . . [I]s not the address [*kyrie*, 'Lord'] the very sheep's clothing the prophets have put on? They look as if they were Christians, but in reality they are entirely something else. Furthermore . . . they are coming from *outside* . . . Matthew's own community" (99).

34. Joachim Jeremias, *New Testament Theology, Part One: The Proclamation of Jesus* (London: SCM, 1971), 227, n. 2.

35. Walter Bauer, et al., *A Greek-English Lexicon of the New Testament and other Early Christian Literature*, 3rd ed. (Chicago: University of Chicago, 2000), 948–49.

36. Johannes P. Louw and Eugene A. Nida, *Greek-English Lexicon of the New Testament Based on Semantic Domains*, 2nd ed., vol. 1 (New York: United Bible Societies, 1989), 510. Louw and Nida also offer the possibility that the verb might mean "to change one's belief, with focus upon that to which one turns—'to turn to, to come to believe, to come to accept'" (ibid., 373). It is tempting to make something of the passive form of the verb "are converted" and hanging the converting work upon God alone and thus claim grace. But *strephō* can have a passive form with an active or reflexive sense "to turn" or "to turn *oneself*," as it is used in John 20:14; Acts 7:39, 42; 13:46 (Abbott-Smith, *A Manual Greek Lexicon of the New Testament* [Edinburgh: T.&T. Clark, 1973], 420).

37. W. C. Davies and Dale C. Allison, *A Critical and Exegetical Commentary on the Gospel According to Saint Matthew*, vol. 2, (Edinburgh: T.&T. Clark, 1988), 757–58.

38. Robert H. Mounce, Matthew, in *New International Bible Commentary* (Peabody, Mass.: Hendrickson, 1991), 173-74. See also R. T. France, "Matthew," in *Tyndale New Testament Commentary* (Grand Rapids: Eerdmans, 1985), 270; and Hagner, *Matthew 14–28*, 517-18. France and Hagner maintain that the key here is not some characteristic exhibited typically by children, but their lack of status in Jewish culture of the first century. But on this they probably go too far.

39. Walter Grundmann, [*tapeinov, ktl*] *Theological Dictionary of the New Testament*, vol. 8, ed. Gerhard Friedrich, trans. and ed. Geoffrey W. Bromiley (Grand Rapids: Eerdmans, 1972), 17. See also Donald Guthrie, *New Testament Theology* (Downers Grove, Ill.: InterVarsity, 1981), 577.

40. R. T. France points out that Matt. 18:6 is the only place in Matthew, Mark, and Luke where the phrase "believe in Me [Jesus]" is presented as the basis for one's proper relationship with God and as the right response not only to Jesus' wonder-working power but to the message of the gospel as well. In Matt. 8:10–13, it is the exemplary faith of the centurion that will qualify him, and others like him, to participate in the great messianic banquet which is the kingdom. Finally, in Matt. 21:31–32, it is the reputed sinners who will get into the kingdom instead of the religious leaders because those sinners *believed* the Baptist's message regarding "the way of righteousness." France writes, "Faith is not just the key to Jesus' miraculous work, it is also the way into the kingdom of God" ("Faith," *A Dictionary of Jesus and the Gospels*, eds. Joel B. Green and Scot McKnight [Downers Grove, Ill.: InterVarsity, 1992], 223-24; citation from 224).

41. Each of these should be understood as essentially synonymous. Robert L. Thomas notes that the discussion of this episode moves to the theme of obtaining salvation, suggesting that receiving eternal life (19:16), entering the kingdom (19:23), and being saved (19:25) are synonymous; see Robert L. Thomas, "The Rich Young Man in Matthew," *Grace Theological Journal* 3, no. 2, (Fall 1982): 258.

42. *Agathon* here is a neuter singular accusative adjective, used as a substantive (like a noun). We do the same thing in English. In the *Black Stallion* movies, Alec calls his horse "the Black," in effect using the adjective "black"—as a proper name, as a noun.

43. The New American Standard Bible, English Standard Version, New International Version, Today's New International Version, Revised Standard Version, New Revised Standard Version, and New English Translation all, translate the phrase essentially, "Why are you asking Me about what is good?" The King James and New King James adopt an inferior reading based on the Textus Receptus.

44. In v. 17, the word is spelled slightly differently because it is used differently in the sentence. In v. 16 it is *agathon*, but in v. 17 it is *agathou*, a genitive singular neuter adjective. Note also the different emphasis in Mark and Luke. Mark 10:17-18 and Luke 18:18-19 apparently draw attention to the implications for the man's Christology in the wake of his calling Jesus "Good Teacher." But our concern is with Matthew's account, which gives a unique emphasis of the episode as it transpired.

45. Representatives of this view include Herschel H. Hobbs, *An Exposition of the Four Gospels*, vol. 1 (Grand Rapids: Baker, 1996), 265; and Warren Wiersbe, *The Bible Exposition Commentary*, vol. 1 (Wheaton, Ill.: Victor, 1989), 73.

46. See Robert H. Mounce, *Matthew, in New International Biblical Commentary* (Peabody, Mass.: Hendrickson, 1991), 184.

47. Davies and Allison (*Saint Matthew*, vol. 3, 286) propose that the hindrance comes from the heavy burdens placed upon people as mentioned in 23:4, or the persecution of Christian missionaries who are seeking to include others in the kingdom. The second proposal is unlikely because of the anachronism it involves (when Jesus spoke, there were no Christian missionaries), and the first is unlikely because, as Carson notes, "This [the act of hindering] does not refer to their casuistry that obscured fundamental questions of conduct and made it difficult for people to obey God's law fully. . . . Conduct is not mentioned here, only entrance into the kingdom. Though proper conduct is essential, it admits no one into the kingdom" ("Matthew," 477).

48. Morris, *Matthew*, 579, suggests this approach.

49. Carson, "Matthew," 477–78.

Chapter 3

PROCLAIMING JESUS TO NONBELIEVERS

The Gospel According to the Preaching in Acts

by Gerald W. Peterman

Pastor, you're not preaching the gospel!" I heard this comment one Sunday from a member of a small church I was serving in the Midwest. I wondered if he thought I was preaching heresy, so I asked him to explain. As it turns out, he meant that I was not rehearsing the essential elements of the plan of salvation in every Sunday sermon. My interaction with this believer, and with many since then, sent me back to Scripture, asking about the nature of preaching and the content of the gospel. In particular, I have been reading and rereading the sermons in Acts, seeking to define the gospel and to craft a model for evangelistic preaching.

Why take time to define the gospel? There are many reasons, but I will mention four. First, even many of those who have been believers for many years sometimes have trouble articulating the gospel message.[1] You and I need clarity for the sake of our own personal evangelism.

Second, the gospel is often truncated. As Will Metzger points out in his book *Tell the Truth*, since about 1900 a new method of evangelism has led to the preaching of an oversimplified gospel, a gospel that is not wholly faithful to the New Testament.[2] This simplification leads us to ask, What are the essential elements of the gospel?

Third, changes in society, especially in the West, constrain us to clarify how to communicate the gospel to people saturated in postmodern ways of thinking.[3] Since these individuals have very little of the biblical worldview that used to characterize average people, we need to ask, How should we present the message about Jesus to the people of our time?

Definitions of the Gospel

Fourth, in English, as in ancient Greek, the word *gospel* can have several meanings: (1) It could be a written narrative about Jesus' life, teaching, and work; so we can refer to *The Gospel According to Matthew*.[4] With such a usage, we do not mean all that can be known about Jesus and His work, but rather that which Matthew has chosen to tell.[5] (2) The gospel could be "the whole counsel of God" (Acts 20:27 ESV) that is, all that Christianity teaches about God, humans, sin, salvation, and Christian life. As an example of this use of the word, the book *This We Believe* says rightly, "the Gospel requires of all believers worship . . . and calls us to live as obedient servants of Christ and as his emissaries in the world."[6] Instead of the word *gospel* here, we could just as well insert the word *Scripture*. For further uses of *gospel* with the sense of all that Christianity teaches see Romans 11:28; 1 Corinthians 9:14; Philippians 1:27; 2 Thessalonians 1:8. (3) The word *gospel* could refer narrowly to the information a non-Christian needs to hear in order to believe and be saved (e.g., Romans 1:16; 1 Corinthians 4:15; 15:1; Ephesians 6:15; Galatians 1:6). This is the meaning the member of my congregation was using.

Because we can use the word *gospel* these three ways, then the phrases "preach the gospel" and "do evangelism" can also take on broad meanings.[7] This broad usage can sometimes lead to confusing statements. For example, in his book *Evangelistic Preaching That Connects*, Craig Loscalzo says, "An evangelistic sermon may urge a congregation to supply hungry people with food. It may challenge people to roll up their sleeves and get their hands dirty building a house for a homeless family."[8] Here Loscalzo is using *evangelism* according to definition 2 above. Certainly he does not mean that "supply hungry people with food" is an appropriate response to the question, "What must I do to be saved?"

For the purpose of this essay, I will focus on the third definition of *gospel*: the information a non-Christian needs to hear in order to believe and be saved. We will look at the words and acts of the apostles in the book of Acts to define the content of the gospel.

WHY THE GOSPEL ACCORDING TO ACTS?

Why go to the book of Acts to define the gospel? Here are three reasons. First, we go to Acts because it is superior to the epistles for quickly grasping the gospel. In the New Testament letters we find the gospel as it is explained to Christians, or what I would call the gospel for the church. According to Paul's thesis statement in Romans 1:16–17, he will unpack the righteousness of God seen in the gospel. But we have sixteen chapters, not Four Spiritual Laws![9] Nevertheless, the length of Romans is not surprising; there is much that Christians need to know about their faith (or the gospel, definition 2).

Second, the Acts of the Apostles provides us with a firsthand report of the gospel being preached. I am not looking for a secondhand report about the preaching of the gospel, as we have in Philippians 1:12–18 or 1 Corinthians 15:1–5, for example. Those passages are helpful for a full theological definition of the gospel but will not be used in this chapter because, again, they are reports or explanations directed to Christians. They are not actual examples of evangelism.

The most important reason to define the gospel through the book of Acts is that *only here in the New Testament do we have examples of actual evangelistic sermons preached to non-Christians*. It seems that as a method, this is the first place to go to answer the question, When we preach the gospel to non-Christians, what are the essential elements?

What passages of Acts will we investigate? Several could be included, but I have chosen the following: Peter's Pentecost message (Acts 2:14–40); Peter's message after healing the lame man (Acts 3:12–26); Peter's message to Cornelius and his family (Acts 10:34–43); Paul's message at the synagogue in Pisidian Antioch (Acts 13:16–41); and Paul's message to the Stoic and Epicurean philosophers in Athens (Acts 17:22–31).[10] With each of these we will summarize the essentials of the message. Then we will compare the five messages in order to answer that key question: When we preach the gospel to non-Christians, what are the essential elements?

GOSPEL PREACHING IN ACTS

Before looking at the individual messages, there remain two more issues to settle. First, I take it that Luke, the writer, does not give us transcripts of the messages. They are too short for that. One can read Peter's Pentecost sermon aloud in only three to four minutes, and it is unreasonable to conclude he actually spoke for such a short period. The rest of the evangelistic messages are similarly short. Rather than giving a transcript, Luke has given us summaries of the messages.

Further, these summaries are not summaries of the way Luke himself would present the gospel. So, for instance, whereas in the gospel named after him Luke goes back to the infancy of Jesus, the preachers in Acts never do. They begin with John the Baptist.[11] It is true that the speeches have a "remarkable coherence."[12] This unity of message, however, does not prove that Luke composed the speeches, as some scholars contend.[13] The evangelistic tracts "The Bridge to Eternal Life," "Steps to Peace with God," "Do You Know?" and "Have You Heard the Four Spiritual Laws?"[14] also display remarkable coherence. But it would be false to conclude that the same author wrote them.

I could give more evidence that Luke has not freely composed the messages, but instead I will proceed with the working assumption that he has presented what the apostles themselves preached. These summaries, though abbreviated from the original spoken words, are faithful to the original content and situation.[15]

Second, each message has similarities and differences. For the sake of the clarity of my presentation here I will ask four questions of each message:

1. **Context:** What in the context draws out this message?
2. **Jesus:** What does the speaker say about Jesus?
3. **Sin:** What is said about the listeners' sin or need for salvation?
4. **Offer/Command:** What is offered to the listeners, and what are the listeners encouraged or commanded to do?

Let's begin asking those questions with the account of Pentecost recorded in Acts 2:14–40.

Acts 2:14–40

Context: The coming of the Holy Spirit on the day of Pentecost brings speaking in tongues, which draws the attention of a crowd that is in Jerusalem for the festival (vv. 5–11). The ruckus leads some to suppose that the 120 followers are drunk (v. 13). This gives Peter his starting point. He claims that the apostles aren't drunk; rather the unusual commotion they hear is the fulfillment of a prophecy from Joel: God will pour out His Spirit in the last days (vv. 14–21, citing Joel 2:28–32).[16]

Jesus: From the miracle of tongues, Peter moves quickly to proclaiming Jesus, saying He was approved by God, that He performed miracles (v. 22), that the people of Jerusalem killed Him,[17] nailing Him to the cross (v. 23).[18] But God raised Him from the dead (v. 24). Peter finds scriptural prediction of the resurrection in Psalm 16:8–11, especially verse 10: "For You will not abandon my soul to Sheol; nor will You allow Your Holy One to undergo decay." Since David, the Psalm writer, did see corruption in the grave, Peter concludes that the reference must be to David's great Son, the Messiah Jesus, who has been raised from the dead (Acts 2:29–31).

Peter reiterates the resurrection of Jesus,[19] adding that He has been exalted to the right hand of God and that He has poured out what Peter's listeners see here: the Old Testament promise of the Spirit (vv. 32–34). This is a point that Luke will come back to repeatedly: "The establishment of the church and its mission is the object of prophecy."[20] So Peter returns to the original question: "What does this mean?" (v. 12). It is that the promise of the Holy Spirit has been fulfilled through Jesus. Even though the citation of Joel is contextually motivated, it is integral to the message.

Sin: Peter repeats, first, the accusation that those of Jerusalem killed God's Christ and, second, Christ's current position: This Jesus whom you killed is Lord and Christ (v. 36). Scriptural proof plus eyewitness testimony (v. 32) bring certain knowledge that God made Jesus the Lord.[21] In this message the sin of Peter's audience is the sin of misunderstanding Messiah Jesus during His earthly ministry, of rejecting Him, and indeed of participating in Jesus' death.

Offer/Command: Then the crowd asks Peter and the rest of the apostles, "What shall we do?" Peter responds: "Repent, and each of you be baptized in the name of Jesus Christ for the forgiveness of your sins; and you will receive the gift of the Holy Spirit" (v. 38). First, they must turn from their earlier sinful assessment of who Jesus is and consequent rejection of Him. Repentance from this rejection implies acceptance. Second, they must demonstrate their acceptance in the standard way: baptism.[22] The results will be forgiveness of sins and reception of the Holy Spirit.

Before leaving this first message, let me return to the subjects Jesus, sin, and offer/command. It is true that "salvation is linked with calling on the name of 'Lord Jesus the Messiah'—that is, with the recognition and acknowledgement of Jesus' messianic dignity . . . " But in Peter's Pentecost sermon there is no indication that Jesus' "death on the cross achieved the atonement for sin."[23] We might think that the shocking message of a *crucified* Messiah would lead Peter to explain *why*, in God's plan, Jesus had to die. But he gives no explanation. I will come back to this point in the conclusion.

Acts 3:12–26

Context: Similar to Peter's Pentecost message, in Acts 3 a miracle draws a crowd, which becomes the apostle's audience. Upon going to the temple at the hour of prayer, John and Peter encounter a lame man, whom Peter heals. The astonishment of the crowd provides the opening Peter takes.

Jesus: Peter says that God glorified Jesus, the one whom Peter's listeners denied before Pilate (v. 13). This Jesus is God's servant, probably referring to the servant of Isaiah (v. 13), and is also the author of life (v. 15). Moule comments: "In Acts 3, the intention is to explain how it is that glorious and daring claims are now being made for a recently crucified criminal; and the method is to identify him with the Suffering Servant who was indeed, according to Isa. 53, treated like a criminal, and whose vindication also has the authority of Scripture."[24] Though He was killed, God raised Him from the dead, of which Peter and others are witness.[25] This Jesus is alive and active in His witnesses, for a lame man's healing has come through the name of Jesus and by faith in His name (v. 16).

Sin: As with his earlier message, Peter charges his listeners with the sin of rejecting Messiah. Peter says that his audience's betrayal of Jesus came though ignorance and has in fact fulfilled the Old Testament prediction that the Christ had to suffer (vv. 17–18; cf. Luke 24:46–49).

Offer/Command: But now what they must do is repent (v. 19a), and if they do so they will receive forgiveness of sins and refreshing from the Lord (vv. 19b–20). Refreshing is probably a reference to the Holy Spirit, as He was promised to those who repent in 2:38. Here Peter digresses into how Jesus fulfills all that Moses and the prophets have said. In this fulfillment God sent Jesus "for you first . . . to bless you by turning every one of you from your wickedness"[26] (v. 26).

Acts 10:34–43

Context: Acts 10 brings us to a very different situation: the first Gentiles come to Christ. This event is very important to Luke, as seen by his reporting the story three times (10:1–48; 11:4–15; and 15:7–9), giving nearly two full chapters to these events.[27] The conversion of Cornelius and his family brings another level of fulfillment of Jesus' prediction in Acts 1:8. God goes to work in "two simultaneous theatres of action," namely, the Jewish world and the Gentile world.[28] Through a series of events orchestrated by the Holy Spirit (e.g., angelic appearances, a vision, God's voice from heaven), Peter and Cornelius are brought together in the Gentile's home.

Jesus: In this message to Gentiles Peter does not stress the fulfillment of Old Testament Scripture as in his Pentecost speech, nor does he accuse his audience of guilt in Jesus' death. He assumes his listeners are familiar with the basic events surrounding Jesus' life and ministry (v. 37), saying that God sent His Word, preaching peace through Jesus (v. 36). This Jesus was anointed by God, performed miracles (v. 38), and is Lord of all (v. 36). Further, as with both of his earlier messages, this Jesus was crucified, raised, and witnessed to (vv. 39–41). This Jesus is designated Judge of the living and the dead (v. 42).

Sin: Unlike the messages in Acts 2 and 3, this passage makes no explicit reference to the sin of the hearers. Peter makes implicit reference to their sin, however, when he says that every believer receives forgiveness of sins (v. 43). Luke has already shown in 10:1–8 how close Cornelius was to Judaism.[29] Consequently, as a worshiper of the God of the Old Testament, he would have had a good idea what this sin was.

Offer/Command: In 10:43 Peter makes passing reference to Old Testament fulfillment, saying, "Of Him all the prophets bear witness that through His name everyone who believes in Him receives forgiveness of sins." Two comments here: First, this is an implicit command and offer, not an explicit one.[30] We do not find Peter commanding his hearers to repent as in 2:38 and 3:19. But this is as far as the message goes, for Luke tells us next that while Peter was still speaking the Holy Spirit fell on the listeners. Second, it is uncertain just exactly which prophets bear witness that everyone who believes in Him receives forgiveness of sins through His name. C. K. Barrett refers to Isaiah (33:24; 55:7) and Jeremiah (31:34) as possibilities.[31] Rather than referring to a particular passage of the Old Testament, Peter's comment is probably best taken as a summarizing statement. It would be similar to saying, "God loves sinners, both men and women." Even though this exact sentence is not found anywhere in the Bible, it is a true summary of its teaching.

Acts 13:16–41

Context: Here we have the longest evangelistic message Luke reports.[32] On the first missionary journey, Paul and Barnabas enter the synagogue of Pisidian Antioch. After the reading of the Law, they are invited to speak a word of encouragement to the people (v. 15). Paul launches into a rehearsal of Israel's history from the Exodus to the arrival of David (vv. 16–22). This is characteristic of messages we have seen thus far that are directed to Jews; they hold the "conviction that God's promises in Scripture were fulfilled in Jesus' mission."[33]

Jesus: From this David, God has raised up for Israel a Savior, Jesus (v. 23). Jesus was announced beforehand by John the Baptist (v. 24). Even though this word of salvation was for the children of Abraham, those in Jerusalem, because they were ignorant of who Jesus was, asked Pilate to execute Him (vv. 27–29). But God raised Him from the dead and gave Him to be seen after His resurrection by those who would be witnesses to the resurrection (vv. 30–31). This resurrection (mentioned four times in vv. 30, 33, 34, and 37) was in accordance with the predictions of Scripture found in Psalm 2:7 and 16:10, demonstrating that in Jesus God is fulfilling promises made to the fathers (vv. 32–37).

Sin: As with Peter's message to Cornelius, so also here, no explicit reference is made to the sin of Paul's audience. Though Jews, they are not guilty of rejecting Jesus as Peter's hearers were. Nevertheless, the reference to forgiveness of sins through Jesus (v. 39) assumes the need for forgiveness and would be quite comprehensible to Jews and proselytes familiar with the Old Testament.

Offer/Command: From the mention of promises, Paul moves directly to forgiveness, saying, "Let it be known to you, brethren, that through Him forgiveness of sins is proclaimed to you" (v. 38).[34] Again, as with Peter's message to Cornelius, there is no call to repentance. Those in the synagogue of Pisidian have not previously heard of, and have not formed erroneous views about, Messiah Jesus. So Paul, in language reminiscent of Romans, says that in this One (Jesus) everyone who believes is justified (v. 39).[35] Here we have an implicit offer of forgiveness as well as an implicit command to receive it through faith. Paul's explicit words, however, are a warning about disbelief—disbelief of a kind warned about in Habakkuk 1:5: "I am doing something in your days—you would not believe if you were told." This warning serves as a call to receive Messiah and so avoid judgment.

Acts 17:22–31[36]

Context: Unlike any other message we have seen thus far, the gospel is preached to Gentiles who have no prior knowledge of the God of the Old Testament. Acts 17 puts Paul in Athens, where he is grieved by the many idols he sees, even one dedicated to an unknown god (v. 23). So he reasoned with Jews and Gentile worshipers in the synagogue and with all those who happened to be in the marketplace (v. 17). Some Stoic and Epicurean philosophers[37] heard him speaking about Jesus and the resurrection. These philosophers had the authority to judge what Paul was teaching, so they took him to the Areopagus, inviting him to explain it.[38]

Jesus: Unlike other messages, Acts 17 is quite sparse in details about Jesus. Indeed, it is the only one of our messages that does not refer to Him by name.[39] Yet Stanley Porter, in his book *The Paul of Acts*, errs in saying that the balance of Paul's message is all wrong.[40] Paul cannot present the Savior until he provides the context that is necessary for him to be understood. Thus, Paul's primary concern, as with his message at Lystra (Acts 14:15–17), is to correct polytheistic ways of thinking and explain what God is really like. Since He is creator, polytheism and pantheism are precluded. The Lord's sovereign care is seen in that He gives "all people life and breath and everything" (17:25). Yet while being sovereign over human needs and human boundaries (v. 26), He is also immanent; He is not far from each one of us (vv. 27–28). Understandably, Paul does not quote the Old Testament. Instead he contextualizes his message, proving this last point with a citation from Aratus, a pagan poet from the third century BC (v. 28).[41]

The bottom line is this: idolatry is foolish and reprehensible. God's tolerance for the ignorance of idolatry has come to an end with the work of Jesus.[42] Now He commands all people everywhere to repent. Paul's argument is brief, but probably his full message contained an expanded critique of idolatry along the lines of Isaiah 44–45 and Romans 1:18–32.[43]

Sin: Every other message we have looked at mentioned the forgiveness or cleansing of sins (2:38; 3:19; 10:43; 13:38). It is understandable that this phrase would be absent here, since it has such a Jewish flavor. Yet the sin of the hearers is not absent: they are guilty of ignorance about God (vv. 23, 29–30). This ignorance God has overlooked in the past but will no longer; He has fixed a day when it will be judged (v. 31). The clear indication is that such ignorance, if not corrected, will result in condemnation.

Offer/Command: Paul's listeners must repent from their previous wrong thoughts about God (v. 30). Although this command has a very Jewish ring to it, Guy D. Nave has studied the concept of repentance in the ancient world and has shown that pagans such as Stoic and Epicurean philosophers would understand such a call to repentance. They further would understand the implication that repentance is a means to escape punishment.[44]

IN CONCLUSION:
ESSENTIAL ELEMENTS OF THE GOSPEL

Several obvious features of the gospel preaching by the apostles Peter and Paul emerge in Acts. These common features point to the essential elements of the gospel. To aid us further in definition, we will look at elements commonly included in modern evangelism that are *not* included in the preaching of Acts.[45] Consequently, we have two sections: (1) what the preachers in Acts never say, and (2) what the preachers in Acts always say.

What the Preachers in Acts Never Say

"God Loves You."

We might be shocked to learn that these evangelists do not say, "God loves you and has a wonderful plan for your life." It is certainly true that God exercises sovereign care over all that He has made. Before the Areopagus, Paul refers to this care saying that God "gives to all people life and breath and all things" (17:25). The term *love*, however, is not used.[46]

As for the love of God and modern evangelism, Metzger says, "Let us open up the love of God to sinners in a striking and winsome way."[47] Rick Warren, in his best-selling book *The Purpose Driven Life*, says that real life only starts after one has received Jesus and believed in Jesus. Regarding what to believe, he urges his readers: "*Believe God loves you and made you for his purposes. Believe you were made to last forever. Believe God has chosen you to have a relationship with Jesus, who died on the cross for you.*"[48] Similarly, references to the love of God are commonplace in evangelistic tracts.

We could ask why the love of God is not mentioned in the evangelism of Acts and why, in contrast, such references are ubiquitous in modern evangelism. Putting this question to my students, I have often received the answer that people in the twenty-first century question God's love. A lengthy response could be made, but I will restrict myself to three comments.

First, references to the love of God flood American society. From television programs as diverse as *Oprah* and *Law & Order SVU*, to interstate billboards, to such non-Christian books as *Friendship with God: An Uncommon Dialogue*,[49] the belief is everywhere. Whether society as a whole *understands* the love of God is another question. But it is beyond doubt that God is believed to be loving.

Second, in Scripture the love of God is not democratic or two-dimensional. There is a unique, filial love of God for His Son (John 5:20), a love of God for a sinful world system (John 3:16), a love of God that makes us His children (1 John 3:1), and a love of God that is conditional (John 10:17).[50] This multifaceted and robust love could easily be emptied of its meaning and impact if indiscriminately broadcast to a society that inherently defines the love of God as flat and sentimental.

Third, we may be tempted to include reference to the love of God in evangelism in order to make our message more palpable. Certainly believers in Jesus have no desire to make the gospel offensive just for the sake of being offensive. On the other hand, it might be worth pondering whether the love of God is part of the gospel according to the preaching in Acts or whether we as believers add a reference to the love of God because we desire to please our non-Christian listeners.

As in the twenty-first century, so also in the first century, talk about the love of God was not uncommon among polytheistic Gentiles.[51] In both cases, however, this love is misunderstood as bringing comfort where none ought to be found—that is, they believe in the love of God while they are in rebellion against Him. Thus evangelism that emphasizes the love of God without being faithful to evangelistic themes of Acts can easily perpetuate a dangerous misunderstanding of the meaning and expression of God's love. It is therefore imperative our listeners know the unique position of Christ, the danger that faces their own souls, and the forgiveness that is offered them.

"Jesus Died for Your Sins."

The preachers in Acts do not say, "Jesus died for our (or your) sins." As noted earlier (cf. especially our discussion in Acts 2:14–40), the apostolic preaching in Acts does not offer audiences a theological explanation for the death of Jesus. Yet in our century, this theological explanation is a standard element in many presentations of the gospel. We should ask why Luke doesn't report this as a standard element in Acts.

There are two possible answers to this question: (1) It could be that the preachers of Acts used statements such as "Jesus died for our sins," but Luke, because he is offering an abbreviated report of the messages, has chosen to leave that statement out. If so, it would seem that his motivation was he did not consider it to be a crucial part of the gospel.[52] In my view, this first option is not the best. (2) Perhaps the preachers of Acts did not use statements such as "Jesus died for our sins." Marshall excludes this option, saying that "there is no doubt that teaching that

'Jesus died for our sins' formed part of the primitive gospel of the church (1 Cor. 15:3)."[53] Right away we see Marshall using the epistles only to define the gospel, without due consideration to the actual preaching of the gospel in Acts. Rather than wondering if Luke has misrepresented the preachers of Acts, as Marshall does,[54] it seems better to consider it a serious possibility that the preachers of Acts did not did say, "Jesus died for our sins." Of course, if such statements were not used, Luke would not report them.

Regardless of which possibility actually occurred, we are left with a stark contrast, for in much of contemporary evangelism "Jesus died for our (or your) sins" is encouraged, indeed nearly mandated. For example, Hybels and Mittelberg, when telling Christians how to present the gospel to non-believers, state that "The central truth of the gospel is that Christ died in our place."[55] Davy, defining the gospel using only 1 Corinthians 15:1–6 and Luke 24:46–48, says the death of Jesus for sins is an essential element that must be communicated.[56] "Steps to Peace with God," "The Bridge to Eternal Life," and "Have You Heard the Four Spiritual Laws?" include similar statements.

Many authors point out that Luke does not stress the salvific function of Jesus' death.[57] It is certainly not the case that Luke is ignorant of substitutionary atonement; in his reporting of the Last Supper, he alone among the synoptic writers adds that Christ's blood is given "for you."[58] Likewise in Acts 20:28, during Paul's farewell speech to the Ephesian elders, Luke tells us that Paul refers to the death of Jesus as atonement, saying that God "obtained [the church] with his own blood."[59] But while Luke is not ignorant of the salvific function of Jesus' death, it is true that he does not stress atonement. The reference to giving one's life as a ransom for many (Mark 10:45, Matthew 20:28) is not recorded by Luke. Rather than stressing atonement, "salvation is offered by Jesus the Saviour on the basis of His resurrection."[60] For example, in Acts 13 Luke says that Paul goes quickly from resurrection (v. 37) to forgiveness of sins (v. 38).

Of course, Luke isn't the only one who uses such language. Paul connects salvation and resurrection, telling the church at Rome that Jesus "was delivered up for our trespasses and raised for our justification" (Rom. 4:25 ESV). Jesus died for our sins, or a similar statement, is commonly made when, for example, Paul writes to Christians (e.g., Romans 5:8; 1 Corinthians 15:3; Galatians 1:4; Titus 2:14; compare 1 John 2:2). Similarly with Acts 20:28, we have *the only sermon in Acts* where a theological explanation for the death of Christ is offered. Paul refers to the blood of Christ, but he "is not evangelizing but recalling an already evangelized community to its deepest insights."[61]

Thus, if the evangelistic sermons in Acts enlighten us at all, we should at least rethink the common practice of preaching to non-believers, "Jesus died for our (or your) sins."[62] According to the preaching in Acts, the apostles didn't.

Noting a lack of mention of God's love and Christ's death for sins in Acts is not to say that these themes never have a place when sharing the gospel. Indeed, the New Testament is replete with references to both (John 3:16; Romans 5:8; 1 Corinthians 15:3; Galatians 1:4). But it challenges us to note that the preachers of Acts, orthodox to the core, chose to underscore different themes for their audiences. It is these themes—and the lessons they teach—to which we now turn.

What the Preachers in Acts Always Say

Jesus and Resurrection

Here I am in hearty agreement with Affirmation Ten of *This We Believe*: "We affirm that the bodily resurrection of Christ from the dead is essential to the biblical Gospel (1 Cor. 15:14)."[63] Indeed, the preachers in Acts always mention the resurrection. Even though Luke has given abbreviated reports of the messages, in some of them resurrection is mentioned three or four times.

In contrast to the preaching of Acts, resurrection is an element that is sometimes left out of modern evangelism. In my view, this is a sad omission. For example, Hybels and Mittelberg, when telling Christians how to present the gospel to non-believers, make no mention of resurrection. The tract of Evangelism Explosion, *Do You Know?* says, "Transfer your trust from what *you* have been doing to what *Christ* has done for you on His cross." However, no mention is made to resurrection.[64] We affirm that the bodily resurrection of Christ from the dead is essential to the biblical gospel.

One can easily see why resurrection is stressed in Acts. Jews and Greeks could conclude that a *crucified* Messiah is a contradiction, an absurdity. That is, since Jesus suffered and died, indeed was crucified, He must have been rejected by God. But the opposite is the case; the Resurrected One was not rejected by God. On the contrary, the preachers always give information about Jesus' approval by God: Acts 2 says He is Lord and Christ (v. 36); Acts 3 calls Him the Author of Life (v. 15 NIV); Acts 10 says God was with Him (v. 38); Acts 13 calls Him Savior (v. 23; compare 5:31);[65] Acts 17 says God appointed Him judge (v. 31). God was and is at work powerfully in Jesus, especially by raising Him from the dead. By repeatedly stressing the resurrection, Acts broadcasts a glorified Savior, a mighty Savior, and a victorious Savior. We should do no less.

Sin and the Offer

Because Luke's thought is steeped in the Old Testament, the message of forgiveness of sins is common to Jews as well as to Gentiles. Further, Paul says forgiveness is part of his commission to preach (Acts 26:17–18). Because of their nature as summaries, the speeches of Acts can be quite cursory in pointing out specific sins. Jerusalemites are guilty of rejecting Jesus; Athenians of false views about God. No specific sins are mentioned, however, in Acts 10 and 13. Nevertheless, in the book of Acts "sins are deemed a universal human problem."[66] The solution to this problem is Jesus; those who believe are promised forgiveness (2:38; 3:19; 5:31; 10:43; 13:38; 26:18). The exception is the

Areopagus speech, where Paul implies that through repentance one can escape judgment (17:30–31).

We live in a world filled with those alienated from God and each other. They easily understand forgiveness, knowing that along with forgiveness for wrongs against God comes a changed relationship with Him. It is an honor to offer this forgiveness to all who will listen.

Repentance/Faith

It comes as no surprise that either repentance or faith is always included in these Acts passages. Repentance is demanded in Acts 2, 3, and 17, whereas faith is the appeal in Acts 10 and 13. It is unwise to drive a wedge between repentance and faith.[67] The reason for the variation is not hard to find. The preachers of Acts 2, 3, and 17 find fault with the listeners' view of Jesus or God. In the former two chapters, Peter blames the death of Jesus on his hearers, the people of Jerusalem. In the latter, Paul faults the people of Athens with polytheistic views of God. The logical corollary of abandoning these false views is accepting the true teaching presented by the apostles.

The faith called for in the sermons of Acts has as its object the person of Jesus Christ. In our age it is common to speak of trusting "the finished work of Christ as Savior."[68] It would be unwise to draw a sharp distinction between the person of Christ and His work. Nevertheless, the language of trusting in the finished work of Christ is foreign to early church evangelism. The apostles call listeners to trust a person, not His work.

In the twenty-first-century Western world, millions have heard information about Jesus and reached false conclusions about Him. Some say He never existed, others that He was merely a good man or perhaps a prophet. We encourage, even when appropriate demand, that they repent from these false views.

The Core Message

Having looked at the preaching of Acts, I do not wish to imply that when communicating the gospel we need to slavishly imitate Peter's and Paul's sermons. The preachers of Acts themselves, even though they had a core message, were flexible.[69] And as noted earlier, the New Testament offers rich insights on other themes that can be drawn upon when required by the occasion and audience. We would be wise, however, to ponder their core message and ask what implications there are for evangelism and indeed for our own devotional lives.

In this core, first, they present Jesus as the One in whom God is working. To those who know the Old Testament, they announce that through Christ God is fulfilling the promises He made in the prophets (Acts 3:18; 10:43). To those with no Old Testament knowledge, Paul speaks of a man whom God has appointed (Jesus), through whom He will judge the world (Acts 17:31). This presentation of Jesus is especially crucial today, when many religions and cults claim that God is at work through their leader or prophet. Gospel preachers in Acts clearly refute that by presenting Christ as the *only* one through whom God works.

Second, because Jesus has God's approval, He did not remain in the grave after His execution, but was raised from the dead. The preaching of Acts is replete with references to resurrection. In keeping with His resurrection, Jesus has an exalted position: Lord, Christ, Servant, Savior, Author of Life, and Judge of all.

Again in a world with multiplicity of religions, it is crucial for people to understand that Jesus Christ holds a position in the universe that no one else holds. He is, therefore, the final Arbiter and Judge before whom we all must give an account.

Finally, without reference to the death of Christ as sacrifice, the preachers of Acts offer forgiveness of sins to anyone and everyone who will abandon false views of Christ and trust in this exalted, resurrected Lord. It is the treasure of the church to teach on such great truths as the atonement, the incarnation, the deity of Christ and the Trinity. Those who have come into the family of God learn these truths in all their richness and blessing (e.g., Romans 3:21–26; Philippians 2:5–11). But such rich doctrines, comforting as they can be when understood in the proper context, can be incomprehensible to the non-Christian. On the other hand, forgiveness and trust are readily grasped and applied. Forgiveness presupposes wrong-doing and a broken relationship. But the Author of Life and Judge of all is willing to mend the relationship by offering forgiveness to all who will come to Him.

Gerald W. Peterman is interim chairperson and professor of Bible at the Moody Bible Institute. He holds the Ph.D. degree from King's College, London, and academic degrees from Trinity Evangelical Divinity School, Deerfield, Illinois, and the University of Florida.

NOTES

1. Bill Hybels and Mark Mittelberg, *Becoming a Contagious Christian* (Grand Rapids: Zondervan, 1994). Thanks to Matthew Franke and Glenn Gresham (chaplains, U.S. Air Force) who commented on a draft of this chapter.

2. Will Metzger, *Tell the Truth*, 3rd ed. (Downers Grove, Ill.: InterVarsity, 2002), 34.

3. See *Telling the Truth: Evangelizing Postmoderns*, ed. D. A. Carson (Grand Rapids: Zondervan, 2000).

4. In the New Testament itself, we do not see the word *gospel* being used to refer to a narrative. The books written by Matthew, Mark, Luke, and John came to be called the Gospels in the early church (e.g., *Didache* 8:2, 2 Clement 8:5, Diognetus 11:6, *Origen against Celsus* 1:9).

5. That the Gospel writers have selected certain parts of Jesus' life and work to relate is clear from John's statement in 20:30, ESV "Jesus did many other signs in the presence of the disciples, which are not written in this book."

6. *This We Believe*, ed. John N. Akers, John H. Armstrong, and John D. Woodbridge, (Grand Rapids: Zondervan, 2000), 240–43. See also Paul's desire to preach the gospel to the Christians in Rome (Rom. 1:15).

7. Köstenberger and O'Brien note "Paul employs the *euangelion* word-group to cover the whole range of evangelistic and teaching ministry—from the initial proclamation of the gospel to the building up of believers and grounding them firmly in the faith." Andreas J. Köstenberger and Peter T. O'Brien, *Salvation to the Ends of the Earth* (Downers Grove, Ill.: InterVarsity, 2001), 183.

8. *Evangelistic Preaching That Connects* (Downers Grove, Ill.: InterVarsity, 1995), 121. Similarly, using definition 2, Loscalzo writes, "The gospel is for unbelievers and believers too" (159).

9. I refer to the evangelistic tract *Have You Heard of the Four Spiritual Laws?* © 1995–2002, Campus Crusade for Christ.

10. The truncated message of Paul to the people of Lystra (Acts 14:15–17) will not be treated separately, since no reference is made to Jesus. Elements from it are referred to in my treatment of Paul's Areopagus speech (Acts 17:22–31). I have omitted Paul's apologetic speeches (Acts 22:1–21; 24:10–21; 26:2–23; and 28:17–20) since they are more a defense of his ministry than an explanation of his message.

11. See Richard Bauckham, "Kerymatic Summaries in the Speeches of Acts," *History, Literature and Society in the Book of Acts*, ed. Ben Witherington III (Cambridge, England: Cambridge Univ. Press, 1996), 185–217.

12. Marion L. Soards, *The Speeches in Acts: Their Content, Context, and Concerns* (Louisville: Westminster/John Knox, 1994), 14.

13. Luke composed the speeches according to, for example, Eduard Schweizer, "Concerning the Speeches of Acts," *Studies in Luke–Acts*, ed. Leander Keck and J. Louis Martyn (Philadelphia: Fortress Press, 1980), 208–16.

14. I will refer to these four tools regularly. They have the following copyrights and publishers: *The Bridge to Eternal Life,* © 1998 Detroit Baptist Theological Seminary; *Steps to Peace with God* © 1998 Billy Graham Evangelistic Association; *Have You Heard of the Four Spiritual Laws?*, © 1995–2002 Campus Crusade for Christ; *Do You Know?* © 2003 Evangelism Explosion International.

15. For a readable summary in defense of the view that Acts gives faithful summaries see Eckhart Schnabel, *Early Christian Mission, Volume 1: Jesus and the Twelve*, (Downers Grove, Ill.: InterVarsity, 2004), 398–400. For a fuller explanation of the issues see Conrad Gempf, "Public Speaking and Published Accounts," *The Book of Acts in Its First-Century Setting*, ed. Bruce W. Winter and Andrew D. Clarke (Grand Rapids: Eerdmans, 1993), 259–303.

16. Concerning the promise of the Spirit one could as easily go to Ezekiel 36:27, but Joel is the prophet who connects the promised Spirit with miraculous signs, which are the presenting issue at the beginning of Peter's message.

17. On the guilt for Jesus' death being ascribed to Jerusalem, see Jon A. Weatherly's sound conclusion that Luke holds directly responsible for the death of Jesus only Jerusalemites and their leaders. There is no intention on Luke's part to condemn or denigrate Jews generally (*Jewish Responsibility for the Death of Jesus in Luke–Acts, Journal for the Study of the New Testament Supplement Series*, 106 [Sheffield, UK: Sheffield Academic Press, 1994]: 97, 175, 271).

18. The NIV and NASB add the word 'cross' here, although the Greek text does not have the word, in order to help provide comprehensible English. Literally it is: this one having nailed they killed. Acts does not use the word for the cross (*stauros*), although he uses *crucify* twice (Acts 2:36 and 4:10).

19. Peter mentions the resurrection of Jesus three times (vv. 24, 31, 32) in his message.

20. I. Howard Marshall, *New Testament Theology: Many Witnesses, One Gospel* (Downers Grove, Ill.: InterVarsity, 2004), 172.

21. Ernst Haenchen, *The Acts of the Apostles* (Philadelphia: Westminster Press, 1971), 183.

22. It is debated whether Acts 2:38 teaches that water baptism is required for salvation. In my view, during the New Testament age conversion to Christ was so closely associated with baptism, that one could simply use baptism as shorthand label for conversion (as Paul uses it in Romans 6:3 and Galatians 3:27). But that is not the same as saying water baptism causes forgiveness; it does not. See the discussion in *History, Literature and Society*, ed. Witherington, 154–155; Schnabel, *Early Christian Mission*, vol. 2, 1442; and Wayne Grudem, *Systematic Theology* (Grand Rapids: Zondervan, 1994), 966–87.

23. *Contra* Schnabel, *Early Christian Mission*, vol. 1, 404.

24. C. F. D. Moule, "The Christology of Acts," in *Studies in Luke–Acts*, edited by Leander E. Keck, and J. Louis Martyn (Philadelphia: Fortress Press, 1980), 169–170. See also Peter Stuhlmacher, "Isaiah 53 in the Gospels and Acts," in *The Suffering Servant: Isaiah 53 in Jewish and Christian Sources*, ed. Bernd Janowski, and Peter Stuhlmacher, trans. Daniel P. Bailey (Grand Rapids: Eerdmans, 2004), 147–62.

25. Note the pattern with *killed, raised,* and *witnesses* in close connection (3:15), also seen in 2:31–32 and 10:39–42.

26. With "first" here we have a hint of the gospel's later expansion to the Gentiles (Schnabel, *Mission*, vol. 1, 704).

27. As is pointed out by many others. See, for example, C. K. Barrett, *Acts* (Edinburgh: T & T Clark, 1994), 491; and Ben Witherington III, *The Acts of the Apostles* (Grand Rapids: Eerdmans, 1998), 340. On such repetition see R. D. Witherup, "Cornelius Over and Over Again: 'Functional Redundancy' in the Acts of the Apostles," *Journal for the Study of the New Testament* 49, (1993): 45–66.

28. Loveday Alexander, "'This Is That': The Authority of Scripture in the Acts of the Apostles," *The Princeton Seminary Bulletin* 25, (2004): 198.

29. Barrett, *Acts*, 493.

30. One wonders, therefore, if in modern evangelism an explicit command and offer is required.

31. Barrett, *Acts*, 528. Luke 24:27 also refers to "all the prophets" speaking of Jesus.

32. Acts 13:16–41 has 426 words compared to 326 in Acts 2:14–40 and 182 in Acts 10:34–43.

33. Schnabel, *Early Christian Mission,* vol. 2, 1549.

34. Again, this move from ancient promise to present forgiveness is probably based on OT texts such as Jeremiah 31:31–34 (cf. Acts 10:43).

35. Justification is a primary theme in Romans (e.g., 2:13; 3:24, 26; 5:1) but only here in Acts, in a sermon of Paul, is the word *justify* used. Here we have evidence that Luke has been faithful in presenting the apostle's own preaching. Yet Witherington wisely adds, "It is dangerous to assume that the way Paul addresses Christians in his letters would be exactly identical to the way he would address non-Christians in his missionary preaching" (*Acts*, 414, note 230).

36. For a summary of Paul's message with reflections on applying his method to mod-

ern evangelism see D. A. Carson's chapter "On Heralding the Gospel in a Pluralistic Culture," in his *The Gagging of God: When Christianity Confronts Pluralism* (Grand Rapids: Zondervan, 1996), 491–514, and his "Athens Revisited," in *Telling the Truth*, 384–398. My discussion is indebted to Carson. See also Schnabel, *Mission*, 1392–1404. For reflections on the use of natural theology in Paul's evangelism and our own, see Lynn Allan Losie, "Paul's Speech on Areopagus: A Model of Cross-cultural Evangelism," *Mission in Acts: Ancient Narratives in Contemporary Context*, ed. Robert L. Gallagher, and Paul Hertig (New York: Orbis Books, 2004), 221–238.

37. For a brief description of these philosophic systems, see Schnabel, *Early Christian Mission*, vol. 2, 1396–98.

38. See Bruce W. Winter, "On Introducing Gods to Athens: An Alternative Reading of Acts 17:18–20," *Tyndale Bulletin* 47, (1996), 71–90.

39. Jesus is named in 2:32; 3:13; 10:38; and 13:23.

40. Stanley Porter, *The Paul of Acts: Essays in Literary Criticism, Rhetoric and Theology* (Tübingen, Germany: Mohr-Siebeck, 1999), 124.

41. Schnabel, *Mission*, vol. 2, 1552–53.

42. Soards, *Speeches*, 192.

43. Carson, "Athens Revisited," 394.

44. Guy D. Nave, *The Role and Function of Repentance in Luke–Acts* (Atlanta: Society of Biblical Literature, 2002), 66–68.

45. I understand that by referring to what the preachers in Acts never say I am constructing an argument from silence and that such arguments are inherently weak. Nevertheless, I refer to what the preachers in Acts never say in order to fully illustrate one of my primary points: the common elements of modern evangelism often diverge from those of biblical evangelism.

46. We should be careful about drawing firm conclusions from mere lexical statistics, but I note in passing that the common Greek words for *love*, both verb and noun *agapō*, *agapē*, and *filew*, are absent from Acts.

47. Metzger, *Tell the Truth*, 69.

48. Rick Warren, *The Purpose Driven Life* (Grand Rapids: Zondervan, 2002), 58; emphasis added.

49. Neale Donald Walsch, *Friendship with God* (New York: Berkeley Books, 1999). *Friendship with God* is another installment in Walsch's best-selling series *Conversations with God*.

50. See further D. A. Carson, *The Difficult Doctrine of the Love of God* (Wheaton, Ill.: Crossway, 2000).

51. Among Jews, see Josephus, *Antiquities* 8.314, *On Sobriety*, XIII.64 and *The Worse Attacks the Better*; among Gentiles, see Diochrysostom, Discourses 1:17 and 30.26.

52. As a reminder, here I mean the *gospel* by definition 3 above (the plan of salvation). Luke doubtless would consider "Jesus died for our sins" to be a crucial element of the gospel by definition 2 (all that Christianity teaches).

53. I. Howard Marshall, *Luke: Historian and Theologian* (Downers Grove, Ill.: Inter-Varsity, 1998), 174.

54. Ibid.

55. Hybels, *Contagious*, 152. Similarly see Warren, *Purpose Driven Life*, 58; Richard Wagner, *Christianity for Dummies* (Hoboken, N.J.: Wiley Publishing, 2004), 52; Lee Strobel, *The Case for Christ* (Grand Rapids: Zondervan, 1998), 268.

56. Davy, "The Gospel for a New Generation," in *Telling the Truth*, 355.

57. "The cross is not viewed as a salvific act [in the book of Acts]," G. Walter Hanson, "The Preaching and Defense of Paul," ed. I. Howard Marshall and David Peterson, *Witness to the Gospel: The Theology of Acts* (Grand Rapids: Eerdmans, 1998), 301.

58. Darrell Bock, *Luke* (Grand Rapids: Baker, 1996), 1728.

59. So the ESV. Alternatively, this verse could be translated "the church of God which He acquired through the blood of His own one" (that is, through Jesus). This view is supported by Murray J. Harris, *Jesus as God: The New Testament Use of Theos in Reference to Jesus* (Grand Rapids: Baker, 1992), 141. Marshall calls this translation possible but unusual (*Theology*, 167).

60. Hanson, "The Preaching and Defense of Paul," 301.

61. Moule, "Christology of Acts," 171.

62. Conversely, we ought not to assume that, as a standard practice, we should preach to Christians in the same way the apostles preached to non-believers (*contra* Peter Lim, "The Preaching of the Word: A Theology of Preaching Based on the Book of Acts," Th.M. Thesis, Calvin Theological Seminary, 1998).

63. Akers, Armstrong, and Woodbridge, *This We Believe*, 244.

64. "Do You Know?" (emphasis original), in Hybels and Mittelberg, *Contagious Christian*, 149–64. In contrast, reference to resurrection is included in "The Bridge to Eternal Life" and in "Steps to Peace with God."

65. As Navone points out, referring to Jesus as Savior (5:31, 13:23) and Lord (2:36; see also 9:1; 16:31) was politically inflammatory, since in the first-century world Caesar was considered Lord and Savior (John Navone, "Luke–Acts and the Roman Empire," *The Bible Today* 42 [2004]: 233). Yet the apostles refused to back down from this potentially offensive message.

66. Christoph Stenschke, "The Need for Salvation," in *Witness to the Gospel*, 134.

67. As is done, for example, by Zane Hodges, *Absolutely Free! A Biblical Reply to Lordship Salvation* (Grand Rapids: Zondervan, 1989).

68. Michael P. Andrus, "Turning to God: Conversion Beyond Mere Religious Preference," in *Telling the Truth*, 157.

69. A similar conclusion is reached by Bauckham, "Kerymatic Summaries," *History, Literature and Society in the Book of Acts*, 216–17.

Chapter 4

PROCLAIMING JESUS IN A HOSTILE WORLD

The Lordship of Christ as Bold Confession

by Bryan Litfin

America is not a Christian nation. Judeo-Christian values no longer drive the culture in the United States. We are a post-Christian nation. So the church of the twenty-first century cannot expect to operate from a general Christian baseline within our society.

Within the Northern Hemisphere, Christianity is in decline. This is not to suggest it is about to die out, but only that its future growth lies in what recent commentators are calling the "global South." Philip Jenkins has spotlighted the shifting demographics of Christianity in *The Next Christendom: The Coming of Global Christianity.*

CHANGING REALITIES IN THE CONTEMPORARY WORLD

Demographic Trends

Jenkins, a professor of history and religious studies at Penn State University, draws from the reams of sociological and demographic data available in the *World Christian Encyclopedia* to chart the future of global Christianity. He argues that Christianity's centers of gravity are moving to Latin America, sub-Saharan Africa, and the Pacific Rim countries of Asia. These "newer churches" are marked by pronounced supernaturalism, traditional morality, and a communal emphasis. That is to say, they are receptive toward miracles, healings, exorcisms, and ecstatic experiences; they reject the liberal/secular value systems of the West; and they provide a communal-social infrastructure in the absence of such structures within impoverished nations. The next Christendom belongs to these churches.

What of America? Jenkins argues that Christianity is changing in the United States, but not as radically as in Europe, where "over the past century or so, massive secularization has seriously reduced the population of European Christians."[1] Most professed Christians in Europe are nominal practitioners at best, and if it were not for the immigration of practicing Christians from the global South, vibrant Christianity would be all but nonexistent there. The United States, in contrast, will not experience that same stagnation[2] and will remain the country with the greatest number of Christians. Yet their faces will be less often Anglo, and more often Latino, Asian, and Caribbean- or African-American. Latino Christians will be predominantly Roman Catholic, rather than evangelical Protestant. So while the United States will continue to be a majority-Christian nation in the coming decades, the particular expressions of American Christianity will be increasingly "Southern." Jenkins predicts that "Christianity should enjoy a worldwide boom in the new century, but the vast majority of believers will be neither white nor European, nor Euro-American."[3]

Cultural Shifts: A New Hostility and a Postmodern Perspective

Demographic changes are not the only forces at work in the American church. Profound changes are occurring in the dominant political, educational, and media elites in the United States—changes that do not always bode well for evangelical believers. Diana Eck, a Harvard professor of comparative religion and director of The Pluralism Project, argues that a new religious pluralism has emerged from heavy immigrations since a 1965 law opened the floodgates to the world. This diversity must result in acceptance of all faiths as equal. When Southern Baptists pray for Hindus who "worship gods which are not God," Eck castigates them for being "ill-informed and ignorant," and for bearing "false witness against our neighbors of other faiths."[4] Eck argues for "a new multireligious America" in which something "far more valuable than a Christian or Judeo-Christian nation" is realized: "a multireligious nation, the likes of which the world has rarely seen."[5]

Despite her anti-Christian rhetoric, Eck does have a point. There are many ways in which people of different faiths should cooperate. Tolerance, rightly understood, is a core Christian value. But sometimes "tolerance" can take an ominous turn. In *The Trouble with Jesus*, Joseph Stowell discusses the rise of what he calls a "New Paganism" that embraces a "wide-open spirituality, with a multiplicity of gods and no central moral authority."[6] Claims about Jesus being the only way to salvation are as unwelcome in the twenty-first century as they were in the first. Today our culture has a lot of trouble with Jesus—and those who believe in Jesus may soon find themselves in a lot of trouble.

Many social commentators suggest Christians in America are facing something beyond a benign religious tolerance that simply wishes to make room for all faiths. The problem is broader than just having to endure inclusive ecumenical public prayers or insipid politically correct "holiday celebrations" at Christmastime. Some parts of our contemporary culture display a hostile and aggressive opposition to the very name of Jesus and the religion He founded. In *Persecution: How Liberals Are Waging War Against Christianity*, David Limbaugh chronicles the systemic discrimination against Christians in American society today. Unfortunately, Limbaugh's use of prowling lion images and the language of persecution exaggerates what we Americans face compared with believers who truly have been, or are being, persecuted. Nonetheless, his well-documented book paints a frightening picture of anti-Christian sentiment in our public schools and universities, in Hollywood and the media, in the judicial system, and throughout the halls of government.

Of course, such opposition is not happening everywhere or at all times. But there is no question some Americans are fiercely dedicated to excluding the message of Jesus from the public square.

The seismic shifts rocking the American church are not limited to demographic changes or increased hostility toward the faith. A profound transformation is occurring in the way the average American views the world. This will inevitably affect the perspective from the pew as well. The new outlook goes under the catchall term *postmodernism*, and it manifests itself in various ways in churches today.

Brian McLaren, one of the leading figures in the emergent church, has called for a "new kind of Christian" for the postmodern age. Disenchanted with what he describes as an "industrial age faith" that is "rapidly aging," McLaren suggests many people are "disembedding" from the old paradigm for understanding God, Jesus, and faith.[7] Today's pastors must find a way to meet the needs of these new Christians. Instead of following the "modern" paradigm of detached, rationalistic, individualistic, and domineering leadership, pastors must learn to become co-journeyers walking with the congregation on the road of life.[8] The emergent churches are just one of many attempts to engage postmodern culture. Many Christians today clearly are looking for something different from what was available in previous generations.

How should Christian leaders respond to this situation? Let us imagine we are like a canoeist who has found himself swept up in a turbulent stream. The currents are strong. The leisurely float has taken a potentially dangerous turn. At least three options now confront us.

We could pretend these events are not really happening and go on living life in blissful ignorance. Perhaps the warm sun will lull us into a good doze. And if there is a waterfall up ahead . . . well, we can worry about that another day. On the other hand, if we recognize the powerful currents swirling about us and the dangers they present, we could fight against them with all our might. We could paddle furiously as we try to get back upstream. Perhaps some are strong enough to accomplish this difficult task. But most of us would probably find ourselves paddling to no avail. The conclusion seems obvious: We do our canoe and its passengers no favors by trying to fight the inevitable.

So what is left? The wisest option (and let's face it, the most exhilarating) is to ride the rapids through to the end. But should we be passive about it? Should we simply watch ourselves get sucked into the whirlpools or be smashed on the deadly rocks the river presents? Or should we paddle with great effort and river smarts, avoiding the dangers and navigating the hazards, always ready to dig in with hard strokes to shoot through a narrow gap?

This is how we must engage twenty-first-century culture: not by ignoring or denying the changes swirling about us, but by bringing biblical and theological insight into how we ought to proceed downstream. We must constantly scan the river for the best way forward. We paddle here and not there, guiding our canoe with wisdom and experience. We might even get hit in the face with an ice-cold wave. But through it all we are boldly confident, and we lend that confidence to our fellow canoeists. With courage we say to our people, "Come on. Let's go. It'll be a great ride!"

The purpose of this chapter is to suggest that as we navigate the river ahead, we ought to draw upon the wisdom of some river guides who have already made it downstream. I am referring the fathers of the early church, whose insights may prove beneficial to us as we ride the rapids ourselves. For one thing, *they lived in a hostile pagan culture much like our own.* Joseph Stowell writes,

The premier example of success in the midst of a hostile paganism is the story of faithful followers of Jesus in the first three centuries. In fact it is uncanny how the issues they faced are so parallel to ours . . . It was clear to everyone who paid attention that Jesus and His Father did not fit among the gods of the empire.[9]

Christian values were absent from the government, schools, civic institutions, and mass entertainment in the Roman Empire. The same is largely true today. Perhaps the church fathers provide a good example of how to live Christianly in an unfriendly society.

Another reason to draw upon the riches of the early church is that *our sense of solidarity with other believers can encourage us.* The writer to the Hebrews exhorted his readers that "since we have so great a cloud of witnesses surrounding us, let us also lay aside every encumbrance and the sin which so easily entangles us, and let us run with endurance the race that is set before us, fixing our eyes on Jesus, the author and perfecter of faith" (Heb. 12:1–2). For the original recipients of the epistle, that "cloud of witnesses" referred to the Old Testament saints. For us, it might very well include the great heroes of the Christian church as well. If they can run the race with conviction, so can we. The Ancient Church encourages us to persevere in the midst of difficulties.

But perhaps the most important reason to look for inspiration to the fathers of the early church is *their unequivocal proclamation of the lordship of Jesus Christ into the teeth of vicious culture.* Their victorious cry was "Jesus is Lord!" The ancients knew that Christianity did not center on abstractions, but on mighty deeds the Son of God had accomplished in human history. This is what the apostles preached and the Spirit-inspired Scriptures recorded. To help us understand the cosmic and life-changing power of the victorious Christ, we should explore the writings of the ancient Christians—those whose memory of Him was still fresh, new, and undimmed by the passage of time.

"JESUS AS LORD"
AS THE PROCLAMATION OF THE EARLY CHURCH

The word "Lord" (*kurios* in Greek) is often used to describe Jesus in the Gospels. The evangelists attest to this usage frequently by saying, "Then the Lord [did such and such] . . . " Likewise, the characters in the Gospel narratives commonly refer to Jesus by this title. Often the use is generic, akin to our term "sir." But other times it refers to His position of divine power and authority. A good example is doubting Thomas's confession in John 20:28, "My Lord and my God."

When Jesus Himself used the word "Lord," He was usually referring to the Father. However, in a few instances He embraced the title for Himself. For example, Jesus instructed His disciples to tell anyone who questioned their untying of the colt for the triumphal entry, "The Lord has need of it," (Matt. 21:3; Mark 11:3; Luke 19:31). He also applied Psalm 110:1 to Himself when He quoted, "The Lord said to my Lord, sit at My right hand," (Matt. 22:44–45; Mark 12:36–37; Luke 20:42–44). Or again, at the foot-washing in the upper room, Jesus said, "You call Me Teacher and Lord; and you are right, for so I am," (John 13:13).

Yet we must note that not one of these verses uses the exact formula "Jesus is Lord" or "the Lord Jesus." While the words "Jesus" and "Lord" are often used in the same verse, and while the title "Lord" certainly is ascribed to Jesus frequently, the specific designation "Lord Jesus" appears only twice in the Gospels:[10]

"So then, when the Lord Jesus had spoken to them, He was received up into heaven and sat down at the right hand of God." (Mark 16:19)

"But when they entered [the tomb], they did not find the body of the Lord Jesus." (Luke 24:3)

Is it significant that both of these examples occur *after* the resurrection? Perhaps. That, coupled with doubting Thomas's post-resurrection profession in John 20:28, might incline us to believe the phrase "the Lord Jesus" became a kind of confessional formula that proclaimed His deity on the basis of the resurrection.

Outside the Gospels, many refer to Jesus as Lord. Generally speaking, we find two main uses of *kurios* to describe Him: in the apostolic preaching in Acts, and as a formulaic confession of faith in Paul. Some examples:

"Therefore let all the house of Israel know for certain that God has made Him both Lord and Christ—this Jesus whom you crucified." (Acts 2:36)

"The word which He sent to the sons of Israel, preaching peace through Jesus Christ (He is Lord of all)." (Acts 10:36)

"They said, 'Believe in the Lord Jesus, and you will be saved, you and your household.'" (Acts 16:31; cf. 11:17, 20)

"If you confess with your mouth Jesus as Lord, and believe in your heart that God raised Him from the dead, you shall be saved." (Rom. 10:9)

"No one can say, 'Jesus is Lord,' except by the Holy Spirit." (1 Cor. 12:3)

"For we do not preach ourselves but Christ Jesus as Lord . . . " (2 Cor. 4:5)

"Every tongue will confess that Jesus Christ is Lord, to the glory of God the Father." (Phil. 2:11)

"Therefore as you have received Christ Jesus the Lord, so walk in Him . . . " (Col. 2:6)

In context, most of these verses link Christ's lordship with a proclamation of His entrance into human history, His death on the cross, and His triumphant resurrection, which makes life available to all. For the first Christians, "Jesus is Lord" was a statement grounded in the mighty act of power and divine approval that raised the Savior from the dead.[11]

Scholars have long recognized the confessional or creedal nature of the statement, "Jesus is Lord." J. N. D. Kelly (in what remains the best English-language book on the subject of creeds) points out that the earliest church had an incentive to summarize its faith into "one-clause Christologies" for the purposes of catechesis, baptism, liturgy, evangelistic preaching, and apologetics.[12] As part of the apostolic proclamation in Acts, "Jesus is Lord" summarized the faith-content to be believed by the Christian. Paul likewise envisioned a verbal expression of faith: "confess with your *mouth*," "no one can *say*," "every *tongue* confess," etc. The expression "Jesus is Lord" can therefore be understood as a summary of the ancient Christian proclamation.[13] It was the Gospel in a nutshell: Jesus Christ has triumphed over sin, death, and the forces of the evil age.

In his classic work *The Apostolic Preaching and Its Developments*, C. H. Dodd has carefully extracted from Scripture the essentials of the earliest Christian proclamation—known as the *kerygma* (the Greek word for "preaching"). According to Dodd, it differs markedly from "teaching," which refers to Christian exhortation and the communication of ethical precepts.[14] In contrast, *kerygma* was what we would call evangelistic preaching or gospel proclamation. Dodd demonstrates that the main elements of the New Testament gospel are as follows: Christ has fulfilled the Old Testament prophecies and has inaugurated a new age by His coming; He was born of the line of David, did miracles and ministered to Israel, died according to the Scriptures to deliver us from evil, and was resurrected; He has been exalted as Lord to the right hand of God by the resurrection; the Holy Spirit dwells in the church to empower it with Christ's present power; and Christ will return soon as Judge of the living and dead.[15]

Anyone who has ever recited the Apostles' Creed will likely recognize that it has the same basic contours as the apostolic *kerygma* noted by Dodd. This is because the fathers of the ancient church who passed on the apostolic preaching eventually formalized it as an official creed. In doing so, they continued to place a high emphasis on the idea of Jesus' lordship in their proclamation.

In the second century, before these ideas had hardened into a creed, the essential message of the Christian faith came to be called the "Rule of Faith." Contemporary scholars refer to this entity by the Latin term *regula fidei*. The Rule of Faith appears in several Christian writers such as Irenaeus, Tertullian, Hippolytus, Clement of Alexandria, Origen, and Augustine.[16] The *regula fidei* did not have fixed wording. Instead, it covered the same essential ideas but with variation in its phraseology. This fact reminds us that in the second and third centuries it was still a proclaimed message, rather than a creed *per se*. It could vary in each author's recitation of it.[17]

The Rule of Faith (*regula fidei*) always made Jesus Christ its central focus. After beginning with a brief statement about the Creator God, the Rule typically spoke of the prophetic predictions of the coming Son, then moved to His virgin birth, His ministry, His death, His resurrection, and His ascension. The Holy Spirit and the church were frequently mentioned together, and then there was the promise of Christ's return to judge wickedness and reign supreme. The *regula fidei* articulated the essential elements of Christian belief—centered on the mighty deeds of Jesus the Lord.

Eventually the ideas in the *regula fidei* coalesced into more concrete forms that we can think of as genuine creeds. Perhaps the most obvious and earliest example is the Old Roman Symbol. (The word *symbolum* means "creed.") Scholars debate its precise origins, but it was certainly being used in the fourth century as the established summary of the faith of the church in Rome. The Old Roman Symbol has given rise to our familiar Apostles' Creed. The received text of the Apostles' Creed used in churches today comes from an eighth-century manuscript written by a Benedictine missionary to Germany named St. Priminius. Scholars now recognize that direct apostolic authorship of the Apostles' Creed is impossible. Nevertheless, experts on the ancient creeds agree that the medieval Apostles' Creed emerged directly from the Old Roman Symbol, which in turn encapsulated the apostolic preaching itself.

We must not miss the important thread of commonality in all these confessions of faith from the early church. From the preaching of Peter in Acts, to the gospel summaries of Paul, to the early Rule of Faith proclaimed by the church fathers, to the Old Roman Symbol, to the Apostles' Creed still used by our congregations today, we discover a universal intent to proclaim Jesus Christ as Son of God and Lord of all. He was sent from the Creator God, born of the Virgin Mary, crucified for our sins, and raised again from the dead. His resurrection has exalted Him to the right hand of God. While His Spirit now indwells the church, He Himself will one day come again as Judge and rightful King of the world. This is indeed the universal and necessary teaching of the catholic Christian church.

THE ANCIENT CHRISTIAN MEANING OF "JESUS IS LORD"

We have seen that the proclamation "Jesus is Lord" encapsulated the ancient church's understanding of the gospel message. How then did this message function for the early believers? We will look at four key meanings of this sentence in the ancient church.

A Statement of Fact, a Promise of Victory

First, "Jesus is Lord" was, above all else, a *simple statement of fact.* It expressed a concrete reality that was objectively true in the world.

Therefore, the early Christians always thought it necessary to "confess" this truth: to make it known with the mouth, or to write it down as a record for posterity. It was a propositional truth, well-suited to verbal expression. Indeed, it became something of a necessary formula as it made the transition from biblical proclamation to Rule of Faith and then to a fixed creed. Furthermore, it was a statement of fact based on evidence. Direct testimony, recorded by authoritative eyewitnesses and passed on by reliable transmitters, attested to the veracity of the event that proved Jesus' Lordship true: His resurrection. The expression "Jesus is Lord" ably summarized what Christians believed to be objective truth.

But it was more than this. When Christians uttered, "Jesus is Lord," they were also heralding *a triumphant cry of victory*. The theme of "Christ the Victor" came to particular prominence through a series of 1930 lectures by the Swedish Lutheran bishop Gustaf Aulén, published as *Christus Victor: An Historical Study of the Three Main Types of the Idea of the Atonement*. Aulén argued that the atonement is God's own act of cosmic victory over the forces of evil. Salvation is a drama in which the protagonist resoundingly defeats the antagonist through the victorious resurrection of Jesus the Lord.

One of the clearest proponents of the *Christus Victor* theme in the ancient church was Irenaeus, the bishop of Lyons in Gaul during the late second century. Bishop Irenaeus is known for his theology of "recapitulation," whereby the sin of the world is undone through the obedience of Jesus Christ. God had to become man so that the work of man's enemy, the devil, would be defeated.[18] Irenaeus' understanding of Christ's victory is theology on a cosmic scale. He sees Calvary situated not merely in Jerusalem in the time of the Roman Empire, but against the backdrop of the great conflict between God and Satan. In the resurrection, Jesus the Lord utterly destroyed the devil's power. The theology of victory that Irenaeus hammered out would become part of the ancient church's essential proclamation of the gospel.

A Profession of Allegiance

In addition to being a statement of fact and a promise of victory, the expression "Jesus is Lord" also served as *a profession of the early Christians' personal allegiance*. It was a political statement with strongly partisan overtones. In the Roman Empire, "lord" often referred specifically to the emperor himself. Thus the confession "Jesus is Lord" stood in sharp contrast to the expression, "Caesar is lord." During the first century AD, the Roman emperor had come to be worshiped as a god in what was known as the Imperial Cult.

One of the primary manifestations of the Imperial Cult was the requirement to make a token offering at an altar. The offering was made to the "genius" of the emperor, the divine power that gave him success and strength. In the ancient church, sacrificing to the emperor was viewed as worshiping demons because it acknowledged Satan as lord instead of Christ. Many martyrs died because of their refusal to offer a pinch of incense in the sacred brazier before the governing authorities. The Christian martyr Polycarp was urged by the authorities, "What harm is there in saying 'Caesar is Lord?' . . . Swear by the genius of Caesar! . . . Revile Christ!'" His noble reply was, "Eighty and six years have I served Him, and He never did me any injury: how then can I blaspheme my King and my Savior?" For the ancient Christian, the statement "Jesus is Lord" was not just a mental belief but a concrete action that expressed undivided allegiance to the Savior—a decision that carried inherent risks.

A Narrative of a Community

Finally, the proclamation "Jesus is Lord" must be understood as *a communal metanarrative that distinguished Christianity from false religion*. In this proclamation, the early believers defined who they were, what they believed, and what history was their own. One of the most obvious places we can observe this communal self-definition at work is the ancient practice of baptism. New converts were baptized "into the name of the Lord Jesus."[19] Early Christian baptism declared to all who observed it the identity of the Lord to whom the Christians belonged.

In the early church, the baptismal service was held at dawn and began with a prayer over the font. The Christian discarded his or her clothes, as well as any gold ornament or other alien object; women were also supposed to loosen their hair. Two oils were blessed, one for exorcism and the other for thanksgiving. The initiate declared, "I renounce thee, Satan, and all thy service and works," and then was anointed with the oil of exorcism. Next he descended into the water accompanied by a deacon.

Baptism was performed in the threefold name of the Father, the Son, and the Holy Spirit, corresponding to the structure of the creed. Coming up from the font, the individual was anointed with the oil of thanksgiving, put on a new robe, and became a full member of the assembly. After being confirmed by the bishop, he was welcomed by the kiss of peace and partook of his first Eucharist.

The elements of this ritual served to place the baptized individual into a new community with a new worldview. In shedding his clothes and all ornamentation, he left behind all vestiges of his former life.[20] Likewise, in renouncing Satan and being exorcized of evil spirits, he showed his rejection of competing loyalties because of his newfound allegiance to Christ. In the ancient church, baptism was not (as it is for some Christians today) an addendum to the regular worship service that can be accomplished in short order and with relatively little ado. Instead it was the culmination of a long process of catechesis. It involved an elegant ritual in which water immersion served as the crux linking the period of preparation to the new benefits enjoyed in Christ's body. The baptismal creed rehearsed for the gathered faithful the great Christian story. Therefore, the convert's formal acceptance of the church's creed in baptism must be understood as his being incorporated into that very story. By being baptized "into the Lord Jesus," Christians celebrated their community's sacred history and glorious future. Those so baptized embraced a meta-narrative that marked them off from those who denied Jesus.

PROCLAIMING JESUS' LORDSHIP IN THE CHURCH TODAY

What insights might we draw from the "river guides" who have successfully navigated the treacherous currents of their hostile world? What does the early church have to say to us as fellow-Christians living in a similarly inhospitable culture? I offer four suggestions here, based on the four meanings of Christ's lordship discussed above.

1. Embrace propositional truth statements that express the core Christian doctrines.

Nowadays it often seems that the proclamation of truth is unwelcome —even within our churches. We are told that people today want to hear your "story" and are not interested in doctrine. Anything that smacks of propositional truth is said to be "modern" or enslaved to an outdated, Cartesian way of thinking. *Christianity Today's* November 2004 cover article on the emergent church describes the "visceral sense of disillusionment among evangelical pastors" with traditional approaches to Christianity.[21] Modernism is thought to represent "values like objectivity, analysis, and control," as opposed to "postmodern values like mystery and wonder."[22] But sometimes in their desire to display an authentic humility or a lack of domineering knowledge, emergent church leaders often appear reluctant to confess any truth at all. Says one: "I grew up thinking that we've figured out the Bible, that we knew what it means. Now I have no idea what most of it means. And yet I feel like life is big again—like life used to be black and white, and now it's in color."[23] Another leader comments, "I don't think the liberals have it right. But I don't think we have it right either. None of us has arrived at orthodoxy."[24] Really? Is there no longer a church that can be described as orthodox? Are there no more pastors who know what the Bible means?

In our haste not to be dogmatic or rationalistic, are we perhaps guilty of throwing out the baby with the bathwater? Reasoned discourse about truth—employing verbal assertions and rational evaluation—was not invented by Rene Descartes in the seventeenth century. It was carried out by the ancients and medievals long before the Enlightenment. Let us not be so postmodern that we become skeptical of reason itself, or shrink from making theological truth claims. Truth is absolute. It is found especially in the Bible, and it can be understood by all rational people. As D. A. Carson puts it: "If the emerging church movement, or conversation, wishes to remain faithful to Scripture, it must speak of truth and our ability to know it as sweepingly and confidently as Scripture does . . . [P]art of a faithful Christian witness insists that there *are* truths to be believed and obeyed."[25]

"Jesus is Lord" was the central component of the gospel in the ancient church. It was (among other things) a propositionally true statement based on demonstrable evidence. It served as a foundational premise that allowed further truth claims to be built upon it. The ancient Christians constructed from it an entire body of doctrine, which today we call "historical theology." This body of thought is not infallible, yet it is the received product of many stellar minds reflecting upon the truth, assessing it by reason, and expressing it in human language. We are by nature rational and verbal people. Certainly this is a divine gift. May we embrace the core doctrines of the received Christian faith. May the church today be the best example of a godly rationalism: one that respects verbal statements of truth and seeks to critically engage theology in each new generation through Spirit-led human reason.

2. Recognize the truth of Jesus' cosmic lordship by seeking to realize His victory in our society.

The ancient church understood that Jesus' death and resurrection accomplished more than simply guaranteeing benefits for Christians in heaven, or allowing Jesus to "come into our hearts" to give us inner peace. The Lord Christ has triumphed over the forces of Satan and his demons at the cross and delivered the cosmos from the devil's grip. In the setting of Greco-Roman paganism, the first believers were daily reminded of their ever-present struggle with what the apostle Paul calls "the spiritual forces of wickedness in the heavenly places" (Eph. 6:12). In this struggle, hope had finally arrived when Jesus conquered the grave. Though Jupiter and Artemis loomed large over the streets with their towering marble statues and impressive temples, the ancient Christian knew that Jesus Christ, and He alone, was truly the Lord.

Today the devil is but a caricature: a movie character, a team mascot, an innocuous bearded fellow with a pitchfork. But the truth is far more diabolical. Satan and his minions are entrenched in world religious systems and in the intractable forces of social injustice, repression, tyranny, and anarchy. Into this present darkness, the church must shout "Jesus is Lord!" as a cry of victory—a victory already won but not yet fully realized.

Churches must be involved in making Jesus Christ's victory real in our world by getting seriously involved in politics, social justice, environmentalism, outreach to the needy, and advocacy for those whom Jesus calls the "least" (Matt. 25:40, 45). As an example, the emergent community places heavy emphasis on the missional, real-world aspect of Christian living. Indeed it is one of its four core values. A leading Web site states,

> We believe the church exists for the benefit and blessing of the world at large; we seek therefore not to be blessed to the exclusion of everyone else, but rather for the benefit of everyone else. We see the earth and all it contains as God's beloved creation, and so we join God in seeking its good, its healing, and its blessing.[26]

Of course, this is a tall order. At times the seemingly infinite neediness of our world overwhelms our sense that we have anything to contribute. How could one American evangelical church possibly respond to such pressing global needs as AIDS, poverty, hunger, terrorism, environmental abuse, natural disasters, religious oppression, and a host of other societal ills? There is an old saying, "You can't bail the ocean with a teacup." True enough. Yet perhaps the point is not to bail the ocean. Perhaps what matters is that each one of us, as best we know how, takes a teacup in hand and starts scooping seawater. The Lord Christ does not call us to usher in the kingdom; that is His job, and it will be achieved when He returns. Instead we must proclaim His victory—already accomplished but not yet fully realized—by actions in our world that testify to His rule. For example, my church (College Church in Wheaton, Illinois) offers an outstanding ministry of inclusion and servanthood to the physically challenged, welcoming them in a society that often doesn't know what to do with them. In concrete ways like this, we gain a sneak preview of the coming kingdom.

3. Boldly profess our allegiance to Christ, while expecting opposition from the culture.

When I was in college, I once displayed a kind of boldness by spearheading a patriotic rally in opposition to a group of Gulf War protesters on our campus. Slogans were shouted, tears were shed, and not a few rounds of Lee Greenwood's "I'm Proud to Be an American" were sung.

It was only later that I had a chance to reflect critically on those events. I was forced to ask myself, "Had I ever proclaimed my allegiance to Jesus as boldly as I did to America?" To be sure, I had witnessed to many people over the years. But did I do so with the same passion and devotion that had swept me up that night at college? Today I recognize I am called only to wave the banner of Christ and to pledge my ultimate allegiance to Him alone. Yet whenever we make a bold profession of allegiance in a culture that has "trouble with Jesus," we can expect opposition. So we will do well to remember Jesus' words: "If you belonged to the world, it would love you as its own. As it is, you do not belong to the world, but I have chosen you out of the world. That is why the world hates you" (John 15:19 NIV). When this hatred is based on our unashamed proclamation of Jesus Christ (and not on rudeness, bigotry, narrow-mindedness, or intellectual sloppiness), then it is a badge of honor worthy of Him.

At times I have sensed within emergent church literature a desperate desire to appeal to postmodern American culture. Often this takes the form of creating as much distance as possible from politically conservative evangelical churches. A good example is the popular book *Blue Like Jazz*, in which Donald Miller continually indulges in the young man's delight of tweaking (and sometimes bashing) the institutions in which he was reared.[27] The message seems to be that if the emergent church can just show it is *different*, or that it is not the "Religious Right," it will gain a hearing among postmoderns.

Unfortunately, this protest often comes close to buying into a non-Christian worldview—watering down the gospel with a supposed "love" that is actually cowardice. For example, Miller tells of living in the woods with non-Christian hippies who were real and authentic, in stark contrast to the Christians who seemed like cardboard cutouts. "They were cute, these little Christian people. I liked them," he says patronizingly.[28] But then he gets angry. Why can't all the Christians just leave the hippies alone? "I wondered whether any human being could be an enemy of God," he says. (Psalm 68:21; Philippians 3:18; and James 4:4 provide the answer.)

What is Miller's solution? Pour on the love. Grant unlimited, non-judgmental approval to anything a person may be doing, for only when people sense this "love" will they hear your message. Of course we always want to be winsome and relevant in a postmodern world. But is it really "love" to offer approval always, to "tolerate" all lifestyles, and never speak prophetically into the culture as a voice for truth? If the emergent church truly wants to draw upon ancient wisdom, it must grapple with the fact that Christ and culture often conflict. There are enemies of the cross. Church leaders must be willing to take a stand for Jesus—and then be willing to face hostility from those who oppose His purposes. The early church certainly understood this.

4. Recognize our solidarity with the historic Christian community.

The Christian faith, at its heart, is a divine saga of creation, fall, redemption, and consummation. While I have argued above that the church ought not reject rational thought and truth claims (for to seek the truth reasonably is part of being human), I believe we are justified in using the postmodern categories of *narrative* and *community* when it comes to the church. We are a people who tell the story of God. This God is the One who created the world and everything in it; who sent His Son to be born, to die, and to rise again; and who incorporates us into the Spirit-filled church until Christ shall return in triumph. It is time for twenty-first-century Christians to view the church as a community bound by a shared narrative, with all the implications for our ecclesiology that this entails. In particular, it will mean that we must restore a connection with our ancient heritage in a critically appreciative way. United by the narrative of Jesus the Lord, we can recognize our solidarity with the historic church.

Robert Webber has been a leader in making the case for what he calls an "ancient-future faith." He suggests:

> The primary reason to return to the Christian tradition is because it is truth that has the power to speak to a postmodern world. Early Christian teaching is simple and uncluttered, it cuts through the complexities of culturized Christianity, and allows what is primary and essential to surface. Furthermore, the classical tradition is sorely needed because so many people have come to an end of their patience with the modern version of evangelical faith and with current innovations that have no connection with the past.[29]

Webber indeed understands where the trends are going. As a professor teaching college students, I too can attest that the authority of the past and the mystery of a premodern Christianity carries great appeal to the upcoming generation.

In what specific ways, then, can we discover a point of connection with the first believers? For one thing, we can read Scripture in the context of the interpretive tradition. This is not a call to place "man's doctrines" over the Word of God. Rather, it is a humble recognition that we are but dwarves seated on the shoulders of giants; that is, we are men and women who can see a little farther when we depend on the work of those who went before us. The great tradition of the received faith can help us interpret Scripture by providing boundaries and terminology for us as we seek to do exegesis. Some practical new resources give us access to the exegesis of the church fathers. InterVarsity Press has led the way with its very useful *Ancient Christian Commentary on Scripture*, edited by Thomas Oden. Eerdmans likewise has joined the task of making ancient exegesis available to a wider audience with its weighty *The Church's Bible* series, edited by Robert Louis Wilken. These resources are offered with the recognition that today's pastor may find it just as useful to consult St. Augustine on a Bible verse as some German higher critic or university-trained exegetical virtuoso.

Another way to connect with the church fathers is to pay closer attention to ancient worship forms. Robert Webber has blazed new trails in attempting to incorporate the liturgies of the early church into contemporary worship. He advocates making baptism and the Lord's Supper more central to the church's experience and suggests Christians ought to live according to the cycle of the liturgical year. Similarly, emergent churches have recognized the need to "embrace historic spiritual practices such as prayer, meditation, contemplation, study, solitude, silence, service, and fellowship, believing that healthy theology cannot be separated from healthy spirituality."[30] In the realms of Scripture and worship—of written word and ritual action—we would do well to look to the past to gain insight for the future.

But when it comes down to it, perhaps the most obvious point of connection between the ancient church and today is our shared experience of living in a hostile world. Wisdom counsels us to strive for the same no-holds-barred proclamation of Christ that the early church displayed. Granted, we will never be compelled to offer incense at Caesar's altar. But there are plenty of other altars at which the gods of the contemporary world are daily worshiped. All of us could use more of the courage exhibited by the martyr Polycarp who refused to "blaspheme my King and my Savior." Urged to swear loyalty to Caesar, he replied, "Hear me declare with boldness, 'I am a Christian!'" When the crowd cried out for his death, Polycarp was led to a pile of wood to be burned. As the soldiers moved to bind the old man, he admonished them not to do so; for the One who would suffer with him would give him the strength to remain in place. Polycarp went to his death on that dark day in AD 156, and on to his reward.

The person who chronicled Polycarp's martyrdom made a noteworthy observation about the crowd's response. "All the people," the narrator tells us, "wondered *that there should be such a difference between the unbelievers and the elect.*" These words ring out as a call to us as well. We will go to the stake if we must. And may everyone know that there is indeed a profound difference between the followers of the Lord Jesus Christ and the watching world.

Bryan Litfin is associate professor of theology at the Moody Bible Institute. He has earned the Ph.D. degree from the University of Virginia as well as degrees from Dallas Theological Seminary and the University of Tennessee in Knoxville.

NOTES

1. Philip Jenkins, *The Next Christendom* (Oxford: Oxford Univ. Press, 2002), 94–99.

2. Ibid., 99–105.

3. Ibid., 2. Jenkins even suggests, "Soon, the phrase 'a White Christian' may sound like a curious oxymoron . . . The era of Western Christianity has passed within our lifetimes, and the day of Southern Christianity is dawning. The fact of change itself is undeniable."

4. Diana Eck, *A New Religious America* (San Francisco: HarperSanFrancisco, 2001), 24.

5. Ibid., 384.

6. Joseph M. Stowell, *The Trouble with Jesus* (Chicago: Moody, 2003), 34–35.

7. See McLaren's discussion of his own personal journey in his introduction to *A New Kind of Christian* (San Francisco: Jossey–Bass, 2001), ix–xviii.

8. McLaren offers Dorothy from *The Wizard of Oz* as a good leadership model because, while she does not know very much and does not fit the leader's typical mold, she has true passion for her journey down the Yellow Brick Road with her imperfect comrades. See especially the chapter on leadership in Brian D. McLaren and Tony Campolo, *Adventures in Missing the Point:* (Grand Rapids: Zondervan, 2006), 140–148.

9. Stowell, *The Trouble with Jesus*, 36.

10. In Luke 2:11, the phrase "Christ the Lord" does appear. This is the only occurrence of this formula in the Gospels.

11. For discussion of this well-known fact of earliest Christology, see the article on *kurios* in Gerhard Kittel, *Theological Dictionary of the New Testament* (Abridged), trans. Geoffrey W. Bromiley (Grand Rapids: Eerdmans, 1985), 1088ff. There is a substantial body of scholarship on the subject of Jesus as Lord. See for example: Werner Kramer, *Christ, Lord, Son of God*, trans. Brian Hardy (London: SCM Press, 1966); John F. O'Grady, *Jesus, Lord and Christ* (New York: Paulist Press, 1973); F. F. Bruce, *Jesus: Lord & Savior* (Downers Grove, Ill.: InterVarsity, 1986); Eduard Schweizer, *Jesus Christ: The Man from Nazareth and the Exalted Lord* (London: SCM Press, 1987); and Markus Bockmuehl, *This Jesus: Martyr, Lord, Messiah* (Downers Grove, Ill.: InterVarsity, 1994). In addition, see the discussion of Bousset and Hurtado (note 13).

12. J. N. D. Kelly, *Early Christian Creeds* (New York: David McKay, 1972), 13–14.

13. Did the very first Christians believe in Jesus as Lord? One of the most influential books ever written on Jesus is Wilhelm Bousset's *Kyrios Christos: A History of the Belief in Christ from the Beginnings of Christianity to Irenaeus*, trans. John E. Steely (Nashville: Abingdon, 1970, orig. pub. 1913). Bousset argued that the original and earliest church was comprised of Palestinian Jews for whom Jesus was the prophetic Son of Man who pointed the way to an earthly kingdom made up of those who had discovered the love of God. But in a second stage of development, a foreign, Hellenistic, Gentile element was added to Christian belief, in which Jesus became a divine "lord" on the model of pagan veneration of gods, heroes, and civil rulers. Therefore, the idea of "Jesus is Lord" is viewed as an interpolation introduced into Christianity especially by the apostle Paul. For Bousset, this meant, "the Son of Man will be more or less forgotten and will remain as an indecipherable hieroglyph in the Gospels," (152). Bousset's view has been challenged by Larry Hurtado, especially in his book *Lord Jesus Christ* (Grand Rapids: Eerdmans, 2003). Hurtado argues that Christ-devotion included veneration of Jesus as Lord from the very beginning. "Contra Bousset, the *Kyrios* title does not represent some major terminological or christological innovation among Gentile Christians who supposedly appropriated the title

from pagan cults. Instead, the term goes back to the devotional life of Jewish Christian circles," (20–21). My discussion here concurs with Hurtado that "Jesus is Lord" was essential to the Christian proclamation from the very beginning.

14. Dodd's distinction between preaching and teaching has been challenged by Robert C. Worley, *Preaching and Teaching in the Earliest Church* (Philadelphia: Westminster, 1967). The debate is an important one, but is beside the point for our purposes here. We are interested in the content of the *kerygma*, not its relationship to other forms of oral communication.

15. C. H. Dodd, *The Apostolic Preaching and Its Developments* (London: Hodder & Stoughton, 1936), 17, 21–23.

16. The general reader probably will have easiest access to the writings of the church fathers in the widely available *Ante-Nicene Fathers* series edited by Alexander Roberts and James Donaldson, most recently reprinted by Hendrickson (1994). The *ANF* can also be found online at http://www.ccel.org/fathers2/. For some of the better examples of the Rule of Faith, see Irenaeus, *Against Heresies* 1.10.1 and 3.4.2 (*ANF* 1:330–31; 1:417); and Tertullian, *Prescription Against Heretics* 13, *Against Praxeas* 2, and *On the Veiling of Virgins* 1 (*ANF* 3:249; 3:598; 4:27).

17. Paul Blowers suggests that in the *regula fidei* the early church was committed "not to a universally invariable statement of faith, but to variable local tellings of a *particular* story that aspired to universal significance." Paul M. Blowers, "The *regula fidei* and the Narrative Character of Early Christian Faith," *Pro Ecclesia* (Spring 1997): 208. Similarly, L. William Countryman brings out the Rule's "oral-social" characteristics by showing that it was not a "document" with concrete wording. Like a performer recounting a narrative, the Rule could embrace different dramatic expressions while retaining the same essential form and content. L. William Countryman, "Tertullian and the *regula fidei*," *Second Century* 2 (1982): 208–227.

18. Irenaeus, *Against Heresies* III.17.6–7 (*ANF* 1:447–448).

19. See Matthew 28:19; Acts 8:16; 19:5. The formula "in the name of" (Hebrew, *l^eshem*) has been thought by scholars to derive either from the banking world, when a sum was credited to someone else's name, or from a Jewish cultic context by which it was made clear "in whose name" a given ritual action was being performed (Deut. 10:8; Mal. 1:11; m.Zeb 4.6). For a discussion of these perspectives, see Lars Hartmann, '*Into the Name of the Lord Jesus': Baptism in the Early Church* (Edinburgh: T&T Clark, 1997), 37–44.

20. Modern Christians may find it strange that nude baptism was practiced in the early church. The custom is widely attested in both the written and iconographical sources. For the ancients, it carried great theological significance as an expression of rejecting old things and "putting on the new." It is possible that the genders were sometimes kept separate, or that "nudity" did not preclude a loose garment being worn for modesty's sake. For a discussion of this matter, see Laurie Guy, "Naked Baptism in the Early Church: The Rhetoric and the Reality," *Journal of Religious History* 27 (2003): 133–142.

21. Andy Crouch, "The Emergent Mystique," *Christianity Today*, November 2004, 39.

22. Ibid., 38–39.

23. Ibid., 38.

24. Ibid., 40.

25. D. A. Carson, *Becoming Conversant with the Emerging Church: Understanding a Movement and Its Implications* (Grand Rapids: Zondervan, 2005), 193.

26. http://www.emergentvillage.com.

27. D. A. Carson has noted that emergent is very much about reactionary protest. See *Becoming Conversant*, 14–41.

28. Donald Miller, *Blue Like Jazz* (Nashville: Nelson, 2003), 211.

29. Robert Webber, *Ancient-Future Faith* (Grand Rapids: Baker, 1999), 29.

30. http://www.emergentvillage.com/Site/Belong/Order/index.htm

Chapter 5

PROCLAIMING JESUS IN WATER, BREAD, AND WINE

The Place of Baptism and Communion in the Gospel

by Gregg Quiggle

The church's one foundation is Jesus Christ her Lord,
She is His new creation, by water and the word . . .
One holy name she blesses, partakes one holy food . . .

The above words, written by Samuel Stone in 1868, express a profoundly Christocentric understanding of the church. The hymn also addresses the important role baptism and Communion[1] play in the life of the church and her relationship to Jesus. As I have grown older, this hymn, "The Church's One Foundation," has become one of my favorites. I find myself moved not only by the powerful, moving melody, but primarily by the words. The hymn expresses lyrically what I have come to believe is a thoroughly biblical understanding of the church.

As I have thought about church, I have found myself thinking of her relationship to Christ and of the role Communion and baptism play in church life. It appears I am not alone; two recent developments have generated a renewed interest in the subject of ordinances/sacraments[2] among some evangelicals.

THE ORDINANCES/SACRAMENTS AND ECT

One development has been the various documents and discussions surrounding ECT—Evangelicals and Catholics Together. In April 2002, I was attending a theology conference at Wheaton College jointly sponsored by InterVarsity Press and the Theology Department of Wheaton College. The conference was exploring the way Roman Catholics and evangelicals have related to each other over the past two decades, as well as the potential for future dialogue and cooperation.[3] It was, to say the least, a provocative several days.

A lecture delivered by Richard John Neuhaus particularly struck me. Neuhaus had converted to Roman Catholicism from Lutheranism and has become a central figure in the dialog between Roman Catholics and some evangelicals. At the end of his lecture, came a period for questions and answers. During the lecture, Neuhaus had talked about the role of the Eucharist in Roman Catholic life. After his comments, a gentleman from a Baptist church asked him several questions about the Roman Catholic Mass. Neuhaus again pointed out how, from his perspective, the Roman Catholic Eucharist is core to Christianity, and he praised its beauty and meaning. He reiterated the things evangelicals shared with Catholics and encouraged cooperation between them. At this point the Baptist gentlemen invited Neuhaus to come to his Baptist church to share in a Communion service. At first Neuhaus seemed startled, then he declined the invitation.

As I listened to the exchange, two thoughts passed through my mind. First, was the importance of Communion. I have taught for over twenty years at Moody Bible Institute, and during that time have been struck by the rather cavalier attitude many of my students had demonstrated toward both Communion and baptism. They seemed to have given little thought to the importance or meaning of either ordinance/sacrament. The conversation that April afternoon reminded me that Communion and baptism are critically important matters worthy of our attention. I also believe that if the ECT discussion continues, evangelicals will have to start thinking very carefully about this issue. As Roman Catholics and evangelicals continue this conversation, the issue of Communion will remain critical.

Second, I was struck that the conversation I was listening to had its origins centuries before during the period we now call the Reformation. The Reformation was the event in the sixteenth century that led to the church's division into the Protestant and Roman Catholic churches. One of the crucial questions debated in the sixteenth century was the meaning of ordinances/sacraments. In fact, more people were put to death for their beliefs concerning Communion or baptism than any other single issue. These issues were deemed so critical that Protestants even executed other Protestants because of their convictions concerning the ordinances/sacraments.

THE ORDINANCES/SACRAMENTS AND BIBLICAL SCHOLARSHIP

A second development has been in the field of biblical scholarship. Over the past three decades, certain scholars have questioned some of the traditional Protestant interpretations of Paul's writings. What is now referred to as "the New Perspective on Paul" has been spearheaded by the work of E. P. Sanders, James D. G. Dunn, and N. T. Wright.[4] These scholars are arguing that first-century Judaism must be understood on its own terms. They argue that since the time of the Reformation, the issues confronting the medieval Catholic Church have been read back into first-century Judaism. In short, the New Perspective is arguing that first-century Judaism was not a religion of self-righteousness whereby humankind seeks to merit salvation before God. Therefore,

Paul's argument with the Judaizers was not about Christian grace versus Jewish legalism. Rather, his argument was about the status of Gentiles in the church. Paul's doctrine of justification, therefore, had far more to do with Jewish-Gentile issues than with questions of the individual's status before God.[5]

As a corollary to this main point, many of the New Perspective thinkers are reevaluating their understanding of the ordinances/sacraments.[6] Bryan Chapell is the president and a professor of practical theology at Covenant Seminary in St. Louis. He has described this position in the following manner:

> They argue the New Testament sacraments are about *more than remembering* what Christ did in our behalf and that through the sacraments believers identify with the covenant community that God has elected for salvation and glory. Thus, the sacraments not only establish one's identification with the community, they are also the means by which God conveys aspects of His grace to individuals. The sacraments establish the boundaries of the saved community and, as a consequence, identify those within the boundaries as possessors of God's pledge of salvation. The sacraments are not magical, and few of the New Perspective advocates (or related groups) are willing to say that the sacraments actually cause the grace they signify apart from faith. Still, these groups perceive grace as so integrally related to identification with the covenant community that its boundary signs (sacraments) are being treated with an importance unparalleled in recent generations.[7]

Chapell's comments reflect the effect of the New Perspective on Presbyterians. Not surprisingly, among this group, the meaning of infant baptism has become a particularly contentious point.[8] But, as you can see from the above quote, there are implications for other evangelical Protestant denominations as well. What is clear is that evangelicals are likely to face continuing conversations about the ordinances/sacraments for the foreseeable future.

In this chapter, we will investigate the ordinances/sacraments with the goal of exploring their role in a Christocentric evangelical ministry. We will begin by taking a close look at the critical debates during the Reformation, paying careful attention to relevant biblical passages. We will conclude by considering some implications for current evangelical practice.

THE REFORMATION REVISITED

The turmoil that emerged in the European church during the sixteenth century would indelibly mark Christianity. The church had already suffered a schism in the eleventh century, leading to the emergence of Eastern Orthodoxy and Western or Latin Christianity. Now the Latin church would divide into Roman Catholicism and Protestantism.

As we have noted, one of the central issues that emerged during the sixteenth century concerned the sacraments. Three distinct questions emerged. First, how many ordinances/sacraments exist and what do we look to in order to answer this question? Second, what is the relationship of Jesus to the elements in Communion? Third, what makes a sacrament/ordinance valid and what makes it efficacious?

Seven Sacraments for Reconciliation to God

The medieval church recognized seven sacraments (affirming the Council of Florence), arguing these seven were either given directly through Christ's commands or indirectly through the apostolic tradition. The seven were:

1. Baptism, designed to remove original sin while infusing the recipient with sanctifying grace.
2. Penance, in which one confesses his/her sins to a priest.

3. The Eucharist, considered the reception and consumption of the actual body and blood of Christ (transubstantiation).

4. Confirmation, a formal acceptance into the church along with special anointing of the Holy Spirit.

5. Anointing of the sick or Extreme Unction, performed on a dying person for spiritual and physical strength as preparation for heaven. When combined with confession and the Eucharist, it is called the Last Rites.

6. Holy Orders, the process by which men are ordained to clergy.

7. Matrimony, which provides special grace to a couple.

The sacraments directly given by Christ are baptism and the Eucharist. The five indirect sacraments (meaning no explicit biblical reference was given by Jesus) are confirmation, penance, marriage, ordination, and extreme unction. Two of the seven, marriage and ordination, of course, were mutually exclusive in the medieval church.

These seven sacraments were largely understood as the means by which sinful men and women became reconciled to God. Underlying this system was the concept of *"ex opere operato." Ex opere operato* means that if the nature of the Christian sacraments is acknowledged, a sacrament properly performed conveys God's grace somewhat independently of the faith or moral character of either the priest or the recipients. The value of the sacrament comes from its divine institution, "from the work already done" (Latin *ex opere operato*), in which the sacrament participates. To oversimplify, the sacraments work automatically, that is, they do what they are intended to do because God instituted them.[9]

The Challenge by Luther

As the sixteenth century unfolded, this belief increasingly came under questioning. The most notable of the criticisms came from a young German Augustinian monk named Martin Luther. Luther, after undergoing a profound period of personal spiritual angst, began aggressively questioning the sacramental system. He grounded his questions in his newfound conviction that humans are justified by faith alone in Christ alone. In a provocative work he wrote in 1520 titled *The Babylonian Captivity of the Church*, Luther asserted there are not seven sacraments and that the Roman Church has held the sacraments captive.[10] Part of what Luther questioned was what he saw as a works righteousness. Specifically, he increasingly came to believe that the medieval sacramental system was a false gospel because it led to the belief that one was saved by the sacrament rather than by faith in Christ.

As Luther's thinking developed, his critique broadened. He began to question the criteria used to determine a sacrament because of his conviction that the Bible alone was the ground for faith (what one believes) and practice (how one exercises one's beliefs). He dramatically stated this conviction before the emperor of the Holy Roman Empire and the leaders of the Roman church at the Diet of Worms in 1521. At this meeting Luther was told to recant his teachings, as they conflicted with the teachings of the Roman Church. His response was telling, "Unless I am convinced by Scripture and plain reason—I do not accept the authority of the popes and councils, for they have contradicted each other—my conscience is captive to the Word of God. I cannot and I will not recant anything, for to go against conscience is neither right nor safe. God help me."

The contexts that would shape Luther's understanding of the sacraments were now in place. For Luther, faith in Christ as He is revealed in the Scriptures is the core of Christianity. Therefore, Luther concluded, a sacrament consists in the combination of the word of promise with a sign, that is, of a promise of Scripture tied to a sign or symbol instituted by Christ. He wrote, "For it is not a sacrament unless it is expressly given with the divine promise which demands faith, since apart from the word which promises and faith which receives we are not able to enter into any kind of relationship with God."[11]

In some ways Luther would set the agenda for later Protestants on this issue. Following his lead, later Protestants would settle the question of ordinances/sacraments by appealing to Scripture alone and guided by the conviction that justification comes from faith alone in Christ alone. However, as we shall see, other Protestants would disagree strongly with Luther's definition of a sacrament, and even his use of the term "sacrament."

The Issue of Communion/Eucharist

The second issue, the relationship of Jesus to the elements in Communion, would prove to be particularly contentious, among Protestants as well as between Roman Catholics and Protestants.

The generally accepted position in the late medieval church was that Jesus was literally present in elements of Communion. This teaching was known as "transubstantiation." The formation of the doctrine paralleled the emergence of scholasticism. Scholastic theologians sought to reconcile classical philosophy with medieval Christian theology. Many scholastics were influenced by Aristotelianism and used those philosophical catagories to try to explain how and in what way the bread and wine become the body and blood of Christ. What emerged was the notion of "transubstantiation," officially adopted in 1215 at the Fourth Latern Council. The Roman Church would reaffirm this teaching at the Council of Trent (1545–1563).

This doctrine holds that the elements are not merely symbols or even just spiritually transformed, but are actually transformed in their *substance* into the body and blood of Christ—thus, "trans*substan*tiation." While the elements retain the appearance (what was referred to as "accidents") of bread and wine, they are truly, literally the body and blood of Christ. In essence this means Jesus is actually, physically present in the elements of the Eucharist.

The key to understanding this doctrine is understanding the terms "substance" and "accidents." "Substance" is a philosophical term that describes what a given object is, that is, the properties of the object that are essential to making it it, as opposed to something else. "Accidents" on the other hand, are the nonessential properties; they are those things that are not essential to make the object what it is. For example, a tail is an accident of lizards, while being a reptile is substantial. If a lizard loses its tail, it is still a lizard. But if a lizard stops being a reptile, it is no longer a lizard, because being a reptile is essential to being a lizard. So, transubstantiation asserts that when the elements are consecrated, the substance of the elements change into the body and blood of Christ; while the nonessential properties or accidents (shape, taste, color) stay the same.

In defense of this position, the Roman Church often cites three texts. First, Matthew 26:26–28, where during the Last Supper Jesus says, "This is My body . . . this is My blood." Second, John chapter 6, especially verse 53, "Unless you eat the flesh of the Son of Man and drink His blood, you have no life in yourselves." Third is 1 Corinthians 11:27 (ESV), where Paul writes, "Whoever, therefore, eats the bread or drinks the cup of the Lord in an unworthy manner will be guilty of profaning the body and blood of the Lord."

A critical corollary to transubstantiation was the assertion that the Mass was a sacrifice. The Roman Church proclaimed the Mass was a true bloodless sacrifice that was propitiatory for both the living and the dead. The Council of Trent put it this way,

> And forasmuch as, in this divine sacrifice which is celebrated in the mass, that same Christ is contained and immolated in an unbloody manner, who once offered Himself in a bloody manner on the altar of the cross; the holy Synod teaches that this sacrifice is truly propitiatory and that by means thereof this is effected, that we obtain mercy, and find grace in seasonable aid, if we draw nigh unto God, contrite and penitent, with a sincere heart and upright faith, with fear and reverence. For the Lord, appeased by the oblation thereof, and granting the grace and gift of

penitence, forgives even heinous crimes and sins. For the victim is one and the same, the same now offering by the ministry of priests, who then offered Himself on the cross, the manner alone of offering being different. The fruits indeed of which oblation, of that bloody one to wit, are received most plentifully through this unbloody one; so far is this (latter) from derogating in any way from that (former oblation). Wherefore, not only for the sins, punishments, satisfactions, and other necessities of the faithful who are living, but also for those who are departed in Christ, and who are not as yet fully purified, is it rightly offered, agreeably to a tradition of the apostles.[12]

Luther objected to a number of these ideas. First, he rejected transubstantiation, noted in the previously referenced *Babylonian Captivity of the Church*. He began by dealing with the three biblical texts the Roman Church cites to support transubstantiation, John 6, Matthew 26, and 1 Corinthians 11. Luther argued John 6 is irrelevant to any discussion about Communion. He wrote, "John 6 is to be entirely excluded from this discussion, since it does not refer in a single syllable to the sacrament. For not only was the sacrament not yet instituted, but the whole context plainly shows that Christ is speaking of faith in the Word made flesh."[13] However, he granted the validity[14] of Matthew 26 and 1 Corinthians 11. Here his critique took a new tack.

Luther then asserted the Roman Church had arbitrarily inserted Aristotelianism and in doing so had denied the doctrine of the incarnation. This was a continuation of his commitment to *sola scriptura* and justification by faith alone in Christ alone. Luther conceded the Bible teaches Christ is truly present in the elements. His criticism was that transubstantiation is completely derived from Aristotelianism metaphysics. As noted Luther scholar Paul Althaus puts it, "He (Luther) felt that the church had in this dogma confused a metaphysical scholastic theory about the miracle of the real presence with an article of faith; furthermore, the metaphysical theory in the dogma of transubstantiation was completely dependent on the philosophy of Aristotle."[15] Since transubstantiation cannot be grounded in Scripture, it is simply not defensible—the principle of *sola scriptura*.

Further, transubstantiation led to the assertion that the Mass is a sacrifice with propitiatory properties—for both the living and the dead. This, in Luther's view undercut the principle of justification by faith alone. As he saw it, the Mass becomes a work. And following the principle of *sola scriptura*, Luther argued the idea of the Mass as sacrifice violates the plain teaching of Hebrews 10:12–14.[16]

However, Luther has conceded the Bible teaches some sort of presence of Christ relative to the elements. In fact he described Christ's body as being, "in, with, and under" the elements. Luther at this point, turned to the incarnation to help solve this problem. In essence, Luther argued that the incarnation provides the model for understanding the real presence of Christ in the elements. In fact he maintained his concept of real presence is an exact analogy to Christology. In Christ, two natures—one human, one divine—were united at the incarnation. Neither nature is in any way transformed. If anything, this was a consubstantiation—two substances residing side by side—for Luther. So, in Communion, we cannot and should not talk of a transformation of substance. Exactly how Christ is present, he did not know. But he maintained Christ is truly present, and it is certainly not a transubstantiation.[17]

Transubstantiation: Zwingli

All Protestants would join Luther in rejecting transubstantiation; however, Luther would soon face severe criticism from his Protestant brethren as well. Early on, the criticism would come from a fellow German speaker, but of Swiss origins, named Ulrich Zwingli. Zwingli had begun another reformation, independent of Luther, centered in the Swiss city of Zurich. By the late 1520s, the Reformation in Zurich faced a serious military threat from surrounding Swiss cantons. Zwingli sought aid from his fellow critic of Rome, Luther. In 1529 the two reformers met in the German city of Marburg. This event is now referred to as the Marburg Colloquy.

The ill-fated Marburg Colloquy was brokered by the German prince, Philip of Hesse, with the hope of aligning Lutherans and Zwinglians. In preparation for the meeting, Luther drew up fifteen articles for debate. Surprisingly, Luther and Zwingli agreed upon fourteen of the points. The problem area was Communion. While they both rejected the Catholic doctrines of transubstantiation and the sacrificial Mass, Zwingli's interpretation of the Lord's Supper as symbolic was unacceptable to Luther. Therefore, the colloquy failed to achieve the hoped-for alliance.

Specifically, the failure was due to Zwingli's belief that Jesus' words, "This is My body," and "This is My blood," must be understood spiritually rather than literally. Thus Zwingli conceived the whole ceremony of Communion as a memorial of Christ's death for us. For Zwingli, Christ was present, but His presence was in the hearts of believers. Consequently, Zwingli believed that when Jesus said, "This is My body" or "This is My blood" at the Last Supper, He was not speaking any more literally than when He said, "I am the vine" or "I am the door." Still Zwingli maintained Communion was in some sense a means of grace, and thus a sacrament.

By this time, Zwingli faced his own set of critics. The Anabaptists, many of whom were early disciples of Zwingli, questioned his interpretation.[18] While they were sympathetic to the basic trajectory of Zwingli thought, they objected to any notion of sacraments or presence. The Anabaptists argued the Lord's Supper was purely memorial and the elements were pure symbols. Baptists in England and North America would adopt this view later.[19] The Baptist would come to refer to Communion as an "ordinance," rather than a "sacrament."

Transubstantiation: Calvin

A generation later, another Protestant voice would emerge. John Calvin, an ethnic Frenchman, would become famous for his work in the French-speaking Swiss city of Geneva. Calvin would reject both Luther's and Zwingli's positions. Calvin rejected Luther's real presence/consubstantiation for reasons similar to Zwingli's. As did Zwingli, Calvin concluded Jesus' words, "This is My body" and "This is My blood" should not be interpreted literally. However, he broke with Zwingli's memorial view. Calvin writes:

> For there are some who define the eating of the flesh of Christ, and the drinking of his blood, to be, in one word, nothing more than believing in Christ himself. But Christ seems to me to have intended to teach something more express and more sublime in that noble discourse, in which he recommends the eating of his flesh, viz., that we are quickened by the true partaking of him, which he designated by the terms eating and drinking, lest any one should suppose that the life which we obtain from him is obtained by simple knowledge. For as it is not the sight but the eating of bread that gives nourishment to the body, so the soul must partake of Christ truly and thoroughly, that by his energy it may grow up into spiritual life.[20]

Calvin is admittedly a little unclear on this subject. However, by carefully reading him, it becomes apparent he was arguing for a spiritual presence. He argued Christ is spiritually present and that by faith we feed on Him. He cited Paul in 1 Corinthians 10:16 (ESV), where Paul talks of a "participation in the body of Christ" to ground his understanding.

The fundamental difference between Luther and Calvin lay in their understanding of the reality of Christ's body. Calvin, like Zwingli, maintained that Christ's body is in a place, heaven. Luther meanwhile argued that Christ's body has the same omnipresence as His divine nature. Calvin argued that through the Holy Spirit the believer is able to partake of Christ, while Christ is bodily in heaven. So for Calvin

Communion is a true Communion with Christ, who feeds us with His body and blood. Calvin's position would be adopted by the Church of England, Methodists, and the Westminster Confession that is used by several denominations.[21]

By the end of the sixteenth century, a Roman Catholic and three different Protestant views have emerged. They are illustrated in the chart below.

SUMMARY OF MAIN POINTS	
VIEW	AND SCRIPTURE REFERENCES
Roman Catholic	The Lord's Supper (Eucharist) is a sacrament wherein the consecrated bread and wine are changed in substance (transubstantiation) into the literal body and blood of Christ. Baptized persons who receive the Eucharist receive spiritual food for the soul (John 6:55). Christ is sacrificed in the Eucharist to atone for the sins of the recipient (1 Cor.10:18). Like baptism, the Eucharist is efficacious *ex opere operato*.
Lutheran	The bread and wine do not become the body and blood of Christ, but Christ's body is literally present in, with, and under the elements (consubstantiation). The sacrament brings Christ to us not in the elements, but by the Word of God which promises that Christ's body is "for you" (1 Cor. 11:24) and "for the forgiveness of sins" (Matt. 26:28). Faith in these promises is necessary for the sacrament to be efficacious.
Reformed	Christ is spiritually present in the celebration of the Lord's Supper. It is a memorial done "in remembrance" of Christ's sacrificial death (1 Cor. 11:24–25), but is

	more than a mere memorial. The Lord's Supper confirms the faith of the one partaking of it, and is a "participation in the body of Christ" (1 Cor. 10:16 ESV). This is only true for those partaking in faith, however.
Anabaptist Baptist	The Lord's Supper is an ordinance, a symbolic act of obedience whereby members of the church, through partaking of the elements, memorialize the death of Christ and anticipate His second coming (1 Cor. 11:26). Christ is not present in the elements of the Lord's Supper either literally or spiritually. The Supper is thus not a sacrament or a means of grace.

SOURCE: Ted Dorman, *A Faith for All Seasons,* 2nd ed., (Nashville: Broadman & Holman 2001), 300.

Making the Ordinances Valid and Effective

The final question has to do with the validity and efficaciousness of ordinances/sacraments. Actually there are two distinct questions here. First, the validity question, or what makes the ordinances/sacraments valid? Stated another way, When is the eating of wafers and drinking of wine or grape juice Communion, as opposed to a snack? This question explores ordinances/sacraments from the objective perspective. The efficaciousness question is subjective. It asks, What is it that causes the ordinance/sacrament to have an effect on the recipient?

On the question of validity, as might be expected, there was sharp disagreement between Roman Catholics and Protestants. The Roman Church argued that the validity of the sacrament is not a function of the morality of the priest or the faith of the recipient, but it is rather a function of the rite; that is, when it is done after the manner the church prescribes, it is valid. This means the morality or even orthodoxy of the priest is not the determining factor. The *Catechism of the*

Catholic Church teaches, "From the moment that a sacrament is celebrated in accordance with the intention of the Church, the power of Christ and his Spirit acts in and through it, independently of the personal holiness of the minister" (#1128). This statement also emphasizes the role and power of the church.

Probably the position most antithetical to the Roman Church is the one proposed by the Anabaptists. In the Schleitheim Confession of 1527, the early Anabaptists articulated a position that would be later embraced by many Baptists and independent churches. The Confession states:

> Baptism shall be given to all those who have learned repentance and amendment of life, and who believe truly that their sins are taken away by Christ, and to all those who walk in the resurrection of Jesus Christ, and wish to be buried with Him in death, so that they may be resurrected with Him and to all those who with this significance request it (baptism) of us and demand it for themselves. This excludes all infant baptism, the highest and chief abomination of the Pope. In this you have the foundation and testimony of the apostles. Matt. 28, Mark 16, Acts 2, 8, 16, 19. This we wish to hold simply, yet firmly and with assurance.[22]

This article outlining the Anabaptists' views on baptism demonstrates clearly their conception of validity. Specifically, for the Anabaptist personal faith and a profession of faith were necessary for a baptism to be valid. Because infants cannot profess faith, they cannot be baptized, a point the article clearly states. The salient point is this: Without personal faith on the part of the recipient, the ordinance is not valid. The typical Baptist baptism service makes this point clear. Generally the person being baptized is asked to give a testimony or state his or her commitment to Christ. At this point, the minister says something on the order of, "Upon your profession of faith, I baptize you in the name of the Father, the Son, and the Holy Spirit." The point is that the baptism rests on the profession of faith. Further, in direct opposition to the Roman Church, the Anabaptists argue the purpose of the ordinances is primarily to allow the recipients to communicate their faith to God and the congregation. So, in a sense, it is best understood as a "bottom up" event.

Since Luther and Calvin continued the practice of infant baptism, they obviously saw things differently from the Anabaptists. Both rejected the notion that faith on the part of the recipient is what makes the sacraments valid. Instead, reflecting their commitment to *sola scriptura*, they argued it is the Word of God that makes the sacrament valid. Luther wrote in his Small Catechism, "Baptism is not simple water only, but it is the water comprehended in God's command and connected with God's Word. . . . For without the Word of God the water is simple water and no baptism. But with the Word of God it is a baptism, . . ."[23] For Luther and Calvin, sacraments were the Scriptures in the form of water (baptism) or bread and wine (Communion). Calvin explained that God created sacraments to support our faith. It is not that the Scriptures alone are insufficient, but God, knowing the weakness of human beings, provided concrete aids to our faith—sacraments. So, without the Scriptures, the sacraments mean nothing.[24]

The sacraments, then, are primary "top down." They are primarily designed to communicate something from God to us. For example for Calvin, baptism has a God-manward meaning and a man-Godward meaning. Of course, God's action toward man has primacy:

> Now baptism was given to us by God for these ends (which I have taught to be common to all sacraments): first to serve our faith before him; secondly, to serve our confession before men. . . . Accordingly, they [e.g., the Zwinglians and Anabaptists] who regarded baptism as nothing but a token and mark by which we confess our religion before men, as soldiers bear the insignia of their commander as a mark of their profession, have not weighed what was the chief point of baptism.[25]

This is why both Luther and Calvin continued to baptize infants. If the validity of baptism does not rest on making a personal profession of faith, which infants cannot do, but on the Scriptures, then an infant can be validly baptized. This view of course raises the question, How is it compatible with their view of justification by faith alone? Or, how are they not still Roman Catholic? They answer is found in the question of efficacy.

Efficacy is the subjective question, that is, What is it that causes the sacrament to be effective in the life of the recipient? We have already seen the Roman position—*ex opera operato*. As you recall, this means, the sacraments work somewhat "automatically" in a sense because God instituted them.

All Protestants rejected this on the grounds of justification by faith alone. In short, they see *ex opera operato* as a kind of works salvation. Since Anabaptists reject the whole concept of sacraments and argue that faith is a prerequisite for an ordinance to even be valid, their rejection of *ex opera operato* is easy to understand. Things are a bit more complicated in the case of Luther and Calvin.

Luther makes his position clear in his discussion about baptism. In the *Small Catechism* Luther states it is faith in the promise of baptism that saves, not the act of baptism. Or, stated another way, faith in the promise of the Scriptures contained in the waters of baptism that saves. Thus, Luther is arguing that the efficacy of baptism depends on faith. Calvin is very similar. For Calvin baptism does not guarantee salvation. As one commentator puts it, in Calvin's view, "Its efficacy is objective, but also conditional. In other words, baptism puts us under covenant obligation to the Lord. The sign is effectual, because God works in it, but the reception of God's work requires faith."[26]

Consequently, for both Luther and Calvin, no salvation is possible without faith. It is faith in the promise of the gospel, seen in the person and work of Christ as the Scriptures present Him, that saves. The sacraments are means whereby Christ and His promises are presented.

Twenty-First Century American Evangelicalism

Thus far we have concentrated on the events of the sixteenth century. Now the logical question is, How is any of this relevant to a modern American evangelical? The most obvious application is that it helps us understand Protestant/Roman Catholic differences, as well as differences among various Protestants.

But a far more interesting question is, How does this affect the life of the average American evangelical church? Regarding that question I think there are at least three salient points.

First, the ordinances/sacraments matter. They matter if for no other reason than Jesus said so! Most of us are aware of the so-called Great Commission found in Matthew 28:18–20. In verse 19 Jesus says, "Go therefore and make disciples of all the nations, baptizing them in the name of the Father and the Son and the Holy Spirit." Regardless of how you think baptism should be done, or what baptism means, or who should be baptized, what is clear is that Jesus commanded it as something we should be doing. It seems discordant with Jesus' teaching simply to see baptism as optional or no big deal. Throughout the book of Acts, commitment to Christ involved baptism. In virtually all cases, it was the first step of obedience by new believers.

Christ also established Communion. Paul reinforces its importance in 1 Corinthians 10 and 11, where he reminds the Corinthians how seriously God takes Communion. He notes that the Corinthians have been abusing Communion and have suffered God's wrath. There are two lessons for us.

First, we must understand the seriousness of Communion. Do we honor and respect Christ in the manner in which we celebrate it? It is interesting that Paul does not command the Corinthians, in light of their abuse, to stop or limit the practice of Communion. That indicates the importance of Communion to the life of the church and the individual believer's life. Jesus did not command Communion for us to then decide whether or not we ought to do it. I wonder how many evangelicals suffer in their own spiritual life because they rarely if ever if ever partake of the Lord's Table.

Here's a second lesson: Communion has historically been the place where the church has exercised discipline. Specifically, disobedient members have often been closed off from the table till they repent. The problem of discipline in the American evangelical church deserves an entire additional book, but it maybe worth revisiting discipline in light of the Lord's Supper.

Second, the ordinances/sacraments point back to the Scriptures. Whether one sees baptism and Communion as "sacraments" or "ordinations," it is clear they uniquely reinforce the Bible by affirming and personalizing its promises.

Calvin probably surmises this best when he says:

In this way God provides first for our ignorance and sluggishness and, secondly, for our infirmity; and yet, properly speaking, it does not so much confirm his word as establish us in the faith of it. For the truth of God is in itself sufficiently stable and certain, and cannot receive a better confirmation from any other quarter than from itself. But as our faith is slender and weak, so if it be not propped up on every side, and supported by all kinds of means, it is forthwith shaken and tossed to and fro, wavers, and even falls. And here, indeed, our merciful Lord, with boundless condescension, so accommodates himself to our capacity, that seeing how from our animal nature we are always creeping on the ground, and cleaving to the flesh, having no thought of what is spiritual, and not even forming an idea of it, he declines not by means of these earthly elements to lead us to himself, and even in the flesh to exhibit a mirror of spiritual blessings.[27]

Baptism and Communion help us to "see" the Scriptures; they give us something to grab on to. As such, they show us to what lengths God will go to get us to grasp His Word. We should use these divinely instituted tools to help our congregations deeply ingrain the Bible in their lives.

They also personalize the promises of the Bible. Specifically, while preaching is something we experience corporately, the ordinances/ sacraments are something we experience personally. To illustrate, when I receive the bread in Communion, I am reminded in a graphic personal way that Jesus gave His body for me! And that just as bread sustains my life, in the same way I totally depend on Jesus. He is my life. We all need to be reminded again and again what Jesus did for us personally.

Third, the ordinances/sacraments remind us of the center of our faith. The washing away of sins that baptism symbolizes is actually accomplished by the blood of Christ. And just as I draw sustenance from bread and wine for my physical body, it is in Christ that I live. As Paul puts it in Galatians 2:20, "I have been crucified with Christ; and it is no longer I who live, but Christ lives in me; and the life which I now live in the flesh I live by faith in the Son of God, who loved me and gave Himself up for me." We are ultimately about Jesus. He alone gives us life. He alone sustains our life. He alone is worthy.

> He is the image of the invisible God, the firstborn of all creation. For by Him all things were created, both in the heavens and on earth, visible and invisible, whether thrones or dominions or rulers or authorities— all things have been created through Him and for Him. He is before all things, and in Him all things hold together. He is also head of the body, the church; and He is the beginning, the firstborn from the dead, so that He Himself will come to have first place in everything. For it was the Father's good pleasure for all the fullness to dwell in Him, and through Him to reconcile all things to Himself, having made peace through the blood of His cross; through Him, I say, whether things on earth or things in heaven. (Col. 1:15–20)

Ultimately, this is what we say in the water, and in the loaf and cup. And ultimately, this is what the water, and the loaf and cup say to us. God grant us the grace to understand and celebrate these truths to the praise of our Lord and Savior Jesus Christ.

Gregg Quiggle is professor of theology at the Moody Bible Institute, where he teaches church history, historical theology, philosophy, and apologetics. He is completing studies for a Ph.D. degree at the Open University, Milton Keynes, Great Britain. He holds degrees from Wheaton College, Wheaton, Illinois, and Marquette University, Milwaukee, Wisconsin.

NOTES

1. There are a number of terms used for *Communion* including *Eucharist* and *The Lord's Supper*. Without getting into the various arguments surrounding the terms, for the purpose of this chapter I will use them synonymously.

2. Protestants have never agreed among themselves on the terms for baptism and Communion. Most low and Free church traditions prefer *ordinances*, while most confessional churches use *sacraments*. To avoid this debate, I will simply refer to them as ordinances/sacraments.

3. For a sympathetic look at this movement, see Charles Colson and Richard J. Neuhaus, *Evangelicals and Catholics Together: Toward a Common Mission* (Dallas: Word Publishing, 1995). See also, Mark A. Noll and Carolyn Nystrom, *Is the Reformation Over?: An Evangelical Assessment of Contemporary Roman Catholicism* (Grand Rapids: Baker, 2005). For a critique, see R. C. Sproul, *The Evangelical Doctrine of Justification* (Grand Rapids: Baker, 1995).

4. For Sander's take, see *Paul and Palestinian Judaism* (Philadelphia: Augsburg Fortress Publishers, 1977). Sanders has been immensely successful in convincing New Testament scholars. Sanders has coined a now well-known phrase to describe the character of first-century Palestinian Judaism: "covenantal nomism." By "covenantal nomism" he means that human obedience is not construed as the means of entering into God's covenant. That cannot be earned. Inclusion within the covenant body is by the grace of God. Rather, obedience is the means of maintaining one's status within the covenant. And with its emphasis on divine grace and forgiveness, Judaism was never a religion of legalism. For Dunn's interpretation see *Jesus, Paul, and the Law: Studies in Mark and Galatians* (Louisville, KY: Westminster/John Knox Press, 1980). Finally, N. T. Wright position appears in *What Saint Paul Really Said* (Grand Rapids: Eerdmans, 1997).

5. For additional information about "The New Perspective" online see http://www.thepaulpage.com. Portions of the summary come from this Web site.

6. The best accessible brief discussion I am aware of is by Bryan Chapell, president and professor of practical theology at Covenant Theological Seminary, at http://www. covenantseminary.edu/news/newperspective.asp. Much of the discussion that follows is derived from Dr. Chapell's comments.

7. Bryan Chapell, http://www.covenantseminary.edu/news/newperspective.asp

8. Ibid. Chapell explains it as follows. "The baptism of children has become a particular point of tension because the sacramental emphasis discussed above also means greater significance is being attributed to this rite than has been the case in typical expressions of American Presbyterianism. By their baptism children are identified with the Christian community. They, too, come within the boundary markers of the covenant community by the administration of the sacrament. Thus, some who are advocates of the New Perspective—particularly from the Federal Vision and Auburn Avenue groups—say that baptism 'makes a child a Christian.' By this kind of wording New Perspective advocates do not typically (there are exceptions) mean that the child is automatically made regenerate by the baptism, but rather that the baptism gives the child identification with the covenant community. What this means precisely is hotly debated and variously expressed. For instance, some have argued that baptism is so conclusive a sacrament that it is improper for a person who was baptized as a child to speak of a later conversion by saying something like, 'I became a Christian in college.' The argument is made that the person became a Christian (i.e., was identified with the covenant community) in his infant baptism, and simply confirmed his Christian status as a young adult.

"So much confusion is being created by this terminology that New Perspective advocates are finding themselves pressed very hard to define the spiritual status of the baptized child, the benefits that are actually conferred by the baptism, the relation of the baptism to the parents' profession of faith, the nature of the child's (and/or the parents') profession, and even the nature of regeneration. This has led some ministers to make statements before presbyteries that sound almost indistinguishable from the Roman Catholic view of baptismal regeneration."

9. The Council of Trent put it this way, "If anyone says that by the sacraments of the New Law grace is not conferred *ex opere operato* but that faith alone in the divine promise is sufficient to obtain grace, let him be anathema."

10. Luther writes, "At the outset I must deny that there are seven sacraments, and hold for the present to but three—baptism, penance and the bread. These three have been subjected to a miserable captivity by the Roman curia, and the church has been deprived of all her liberty. To be sure, if I desired to use the term in its scriptural sense, I should allow but a single sacrament, with three sacramental signs. But of this I shall treat more fully at the proper time." Notice, Luther early in his career argued for three sacraments. As his thought evolved he reduced that to two, eliminating penance (1.18). See *Three Primary Works of Dr. Martin Luther*, ed. Henry Wace, and C. A. Buchheim (London: John Murray, 1883), 147.

11. Fourth Lateran Council, S-J 1, 264; see http://www.fordham.edu/halsall/basis/lateran4.html

12. See Council of Trent session 22, chapter 2. See also the following from session 22, CANON I: "If any one saith, that in the mass a true and proper sacrifice is not offered to God; or, that to be offered is nothing else but that Christ is given us to eat; let him be anathema." CANON II: "If any one saith, that by those words, Do this for the commemoration of me (Luke xxii. 19), Christ did not institute the apostles priests; or, did not ordain that they, and other priests should offer His own body

and blood; let him be anathema." CANON III: "If any one saith that the sacrifice of the mass is only a sacrifice of praise and of thanksgiving; or, that it is a bare commemoration of the sacrifice consummated on the cross, but not a propitiatory sacrifice; or, that it profits him only who receives; and that it ought not to be offered for the living and the dead for sins, pains, satisfactions, and other necessities; let him be anathema." CANON IV: "If any one saith, that, by the sacrifice of the mass, a blasphemy is cast upon the most holy sacrifice of Christ consummated on the cross; or, that it is thereby derogated from; let him be anathema."

13. The full quote is: "In the first place, John 6 is to be entirely excluded from this discussion, since it does not refer in a single syllable to the sacrament. For not only was the sacrament not yet instituted, but the whole context plainly shows that Christ is speaking of faith in the Word made flesh, as I have said above. For He says, 'My words are spirit, and they are life,' which shows that He is speaking of a spiritual eating, whereby whoever eats has life, while the Jews understood Him to be speaking of bodily eating and therefore disputed with Him. But no eating can give life save the eating which is by faith, for that is the truly spiritual and living eating. As Augustine also says: 'Why make ready teeth and stomach? Believe, and you have eaten.' For the sacramental eating does not give life, since many eat unworthily. Therefore, He cannot be understood as speaking of the sacrament in this passage. These words have indeed been wrongly applied to the sacrament, as in the decretal *Dudum* and often elsewhere. But it is one thing to misapply the Scriptures, it is quite another to understand them in their proper meaning. But if Christ in this passage enjoined the sacramental eating, then by saying, 'Except you eat my flesh and drink my blood, you have no life in you,' He would condemn all infants, invalids and those absent or in any way hindered from the sacramental eating, however strong their faith might be. . . . John 6 does not belong here. For this reason I have elsewhere written that the Bohemians have no right to rely on this passage in support of their use of the sacrament in both kinds." Martin Luther, *Babylonian Captivity of the Church*, Sacrament of the Altar 2.3 and 2.4.

14. He writes, "Now there are two passages that do clearly bear upon this matter—the Gospel narratives of the institution of the Lord's Supper, and Paul in 1 Corinthians 11. Ibid., 2.5.

15. Paul Althaus, *The Theology of Martin Luther* (Philadelphia: Fortress, 1963), 376.

16. Luther makes this point in another work from 1520, *Treatise on the New Testament*.

17. Again Althaus is helpful. See chapters 25–27 in *The Theology of Martin Luther*.

18. For a detailed and sympathetic look at the Anabaptist movement see, William R. Estep, *The Anabaptist Story*, 3rd ed. (Grand Rapids: Eerdmans, 1996).

19. *The New Hampshire Confession* 10, states that the bread and wine "commemorate together the dying love of Christ."

20. Calvin's *Institutes*, Book IV.17.5. See all of IV.17 for his complete thoughts on the subject.

21. For the Church of England (Anglican) see *Thirty-Nine Articles of Religion*, 28. Methodists, see *Twenty-Five Articles of Religion*, 18. *Westminster Confession*, 29.

22. See the Schleitheim Confession dated February 24, 1527. It consists of seven articles. The above quote is taken from article #1 on "Baptism."

23. Martin Luther, *The Small Catechism* (1529). See the section on Baptism.

24. John Calvin, *Institutes*, Book 4, chapter 14.3–4. Calvin puts it this way: "From the definition which we have given, we perceive that there never is a sacrament without an antecedent promise, the sacrament being added as a kind of appendix, with the view of confirming and sealing the promise, and giving a better attestation, or rather, in a manner, confirming it. In this way God provides first for our ignorance and sluggishness and, secondly, for our infirmity; and yet, properly speaking, it does not so much confirm his word as establish us in the faith of it. For the truth of God is in itself sufficiently stable and certain, and cannot receive a better confirmation from any other quarter than from itself. But as our faith is slender and weak, so if it be not propped up on every side, and supported by all kinds of means, it is forthwith shaken and tossed to and fro, wavers, and even falls. And here, indeed, our merciful Lord, with boundless condescension, so accommodates himself to our capacity, that seeing how from our animal nature we are always creeping on the ground, and cleaving to the flesh, having no thought of what is spiritual, and not even forming an idea of it, he declines not by means of these earthly elements to lead us to himself, and even in the flesh to exhibit a mirror of spiritual blessings. For, as Chrysostom says, (Hom. 60, ad Popul.) 'Were we incorporeal, he would give us these things in a naked and incorporeal form. Now because our souls are implanted in bodies, he delivers spiritual things under things visible. Not that the qualities which are set before us in the sacraments are inherent in the nature of the things, but God gives them this signification.'"

25. Ibid., chapter 15.

26. See http://www.hornes.org/theologia/content/rich_lusk/calvin_on_baptism_penance_absolution.htm#40a. Lusk writes, "In addition to what is provided above, in 4.15.16 and 4.15.17, Calvin gives two further lines of evidence for sacramental objectivity. First, he sides with Augustine in the Donatist controversy, arguing that baptism retains its validity apart from the worth of the minister. He says baptism has "enclosed in itself, the promise of forgiveness of sins, mortification of the flesh, spiritual vivification, and participation in Christ." Then, secondly, there is the way he interprets the experience of reformers like himself who were baptized as infants in the Roman Church but "converted" to Protestantism as adults: "To this question we reply that we indeed, being blind and unbelieving, for a long time did not grasp the promise that had been given us in baptism; yet that promise, since it was of God, ever remained fixed and firm and trustworthy. Even if all men are liars and faithless, still God does not cease to be trustworthy. Even if all men are lost, still Christ remains salvation."

27. Calvin's *Instititutes* Book IV. 14. 3; http://www.reformed.org/books/institutes.

Chapter 6

Proclaiming Jesus Through the Life of the Mind

Thinking as An Act of Worship

by Bryan O'Neal

A generation ago, Harry Blamires wrote, "There is no longer a Christian mind."[1] By this Blamires did not mean that Christians are stupid, or that there are no Christian *minds*. Such an assertion would be immediately self-refuting. Instead, Blamires claimed that Christianity had become significant only in privatized, individualized respects, concerned only with religious ritual or personal ethical decisions.

The thinking Christian was "lonely"—alienated from those with whom he shared a biblical faith and an eternal hope. There was "no public pool of discourse fed by Christianly committed thought on the world we live in . . . ; no common field of discourse in which we can dispute either harmoniously or inharmoniously."[2] He concluded: "In short we have, both at the public level and at the private level, a positively nurtured negative attitude towards ideas, ideals, and theories."[3] "Christian mind" is, or was, an oxymoron.

Some Christians might exult in Blamires's characterization of our "intellectualism" (or the lack thereof), agreeing with the hostile non-Christian that our faith is foolishness, and making our boast accordingly. These people may boldly proclaim the Christian faith, finding in the mockery of the world confirmation of their privileged spiritual (if not intellectual) status. Other believers might respond with defeatism, sighing that the world suffers from dark hearts and minds, that it will never understand the things of Christ, and that the proper Christian recourse is to withdraw and entrench into further Christian separation and ghettoization. We should, they contend, form our own communities—social, artistic, intellectual—and hope that the world "out there" will just let us live in peace. Others, however, might accept the challenge that Blamires puts forth—to reclaim the life of the mind as a distinctively Christian practice, one to be initiated and nurtured within the church, and to serve as a basis of confident Christian engagement with the world at large.

In this chapter, I will (1) comment upon the some of the progress of the Christian mind (at least in the English-speaking West) since Blamires offered his challenge forty years ago, and (2) assess the current state of the Christian mind, particularly as we determine what it is to live, think, and reason Christianly in a postmodern age. Then I will offer something of a prescription for individuals and churches to develop and sustain the practice of Christian thought.

A RECENT HISTORY OF THE CHRISTIAN MIND

As the commercial used to say, "You've come a long way, baby." Christianity, at least in America, seems to have enjoyed a resurgence of power and popularity. Politicians actively court "the evangelical vote," and evangelical leaders have "seats at the table" in positions of advisors to presidents and legislators of both major parties. Christians can overwhelm the White House switchboard or clog congressional e-mail boxes in a matter of hours. Cal Thomas's unabashedly Christian perspective appears in articles syndicated in newspapers nationwide. Christians are active in the music, film, and television industries, and a few evangelical authors even appear on *The New York Times* best-seller lists. Churches of five or ten thousand or more members serve large metropolitan areas of this country.

It is not my present task to evaluate the appropriateness or effectiveness of these developments, but I mention them to provide a context for the question at hand: Has the Christian mind enjoyed a similar resurgence? Though its prevalence is yet far from universal, I will argue that in significant respects the answer is "yes."

Francis Schaeffer and the Modern Christian Intellectual

Perhaps the first of the modern Christian intellectuals was Francis Schaeffer, missionary to Europe, counselor of troubled flower children, and founder of L'Abri Fellowship. Legions of contemporary Christian thinkers confess him as their intellectual forefather. Taking his stand for absolute truth (what he called "true truth") in an age of public relativism, Schaeffer demonstrated that Christian faithfulness and humility could be effectively coupled with intellectual rigor and social engagement—that Christians could study, understand, and respond to historic writers, artists, and thinkers, and do so in a way that neither compromised theological orthodoxy nor diminished what it is to be a fully rational human created in the (mental) image of God. He taught and modeled "how should we then live" (also the title of his best-selling book); for many people, that came to include a vibrant life of the mind.

The ministry of L'Abri continues around the world in study centers in England, continental Europe, and the United States, and its spokespeople and products include Dick Keyes, Os Guinness, and Jerram Barrs, among many others. Indeed, Schaeffer's overt impact continues through the ministry of the Francis Schaeffer Institute, affiliated with Covenant Seminary in St. Louis and under the direction of Luke Bobo.

Understanding Different Worldviews

The last thirty years have also seen the increasing prominence of the term "worldview,"[4] due in no small part to former Schaeffer associate James Sire and his book *The Universe Next Door: A Catalogue of Worldviews*, first published in 1976. This book has introduced millions of college students and Sunday school classes to the competing truth-claims of the religions and philosophies that surround the church, as well as provided the initial steps to a Christian assessment of and response to alien ideas: deism, naturalism, existentialism, the New Age, and—beginning with the 1997 edition of *The Universe Next Door*—postmodernism. The Christian with the courage to engage his neighbor "next door" has discovered that the Christian mind is fully capable of understanding, communicating, and transforming the world around us.

Sire's work has placed him in the vanguard of Christian thinkers encountering the world at the popular and semipopular level. Such engagement is occurring at the highest echelons of American academia as well.

The following discussion of the Christian mind at work in American academia focuses on the discipline of philosophy, for at least two reasons. First, my own graduate training is in that field, so this is the area to which I speak with least ignorance. Second, philosophy is the scholarly discipline most attentive to the life of the mind, and indeed here we have seen significant advances made by evangelicals, both in professional representation and professional contribution. Similar observations could be made about the work of evangelicals in other fields, including history, sociology, and the various sciences.[5]

A BUDDING RESURGENCE OF CHRISTIAN THINKING AT AMERICAN UNIVERSITIES

It is no secret that the last half century has seen the increasing and near complete secularization of the university. Even in disciplines and departments where evangelicals have been present, it has been hard to see their work as distinctively Christian or influenced by their faith. That is, the fact that a professor of engineering, English, or chemistry at an American university is an evangelical has been regarded as an accidental feature of that person, but it certainly has no influence on his work. Such a person might be recognized as a "nice" or "helpful" person, but such things are irrelevant to professional competence. In a thoroughly secularized setting, it is held that there is no distinctively Christian way to "do" engineering, English, or chemistry, or any other such "neutral" disciplines. And American universities have seen a systematic marginalization of religious thought, particularly Christian thought, for several decades.

The tide is turning, however. Rather than taking the cowardly option of loudly decrying our "victim status" as a persecuted people group, Christians ought instead to take heart by looking to the evangelical resurgence in philosophy as evidence of a vibrant Christian mind. Indeed, in a recent article in *Philo*, ("the official publication of the Society of Humanist Philosophers"), Quentin Smith chides his philosophical colleagues as having the distinction of being the only academic discipline that has actually ceded ground back to the evangelicals. He writes, "Today perhaps one-quarter or one-third of philosophy professors are theists, with most being orthodox Christians."[6] Smith notes that much of the credit for philosophy's Christian resurgence goes to Alvin Plantinga.

The Influence of Alvin Plantinga

The influence of Alvin Plantinga, noted professor of philosophy at the University of Notre Dame, extends not just to Christian philosophy and philosophers, but to contemporary Western philosophy as a whole. To illustrate his impact, consider the three perennial problems in philosophy: (1) the supposed inconsistency of evil and suffering in a world created by a loving God, (2) the failure of the ontological argument to demonstrate the existence of God, and (3) our ultimate skepticism about the world around us (as we always lack sufficient justification to claim to "know" that anything is true). For a working philosopher today to make a significant contribution to *any one* of these questions, not to mention to resolve the question, would be to secure his future in academia—tenure, fame, and security would follow as a matter of course.

In baseball terms, a player would be destined for the Hall of Fame if he completed his career among the all-time home-run leaders, or the all-time hits leaders, or the all-time batting-average leaders; rare is the player who is among the leaders in all three areas. Plantinga has more than "made a contribution," not by merely engaging a single issue, but by demonstrably settling *each* of these three questions, and by doing so in a way not only consistent with Christian principles but indeed by grounding his defense in Christian conviction. By analogy, he is among the lifetime leaders in home runs, hits, *and* batting average.

This is not to say that everyone agrees with Plantinga today, and that there are no atheists in philosophy departments (quite the contrary!). But those atheists and skeptics find in Plantinga—who is but a representative of a whole evangelical cadre of, by now, senior members of philosophy departments all over the country, and in Christian philosophy more generally—a formidable conversational partner, who can no longer be summarily dismissed and ignored as residing at the fanatic fringe.

Plantinga is merely modeling the agenda he set before Christian intellectuals twenty years ago. At his inauguration in 1983 as the John A. O'Brien Professor of Philosophy at Notre Dame, Plantinga delivered what has become "marching orders" for a whole generation of Christian thinkers in all academic disciplines: his "Advice to Christian Philosophers." Christian philosophers, and by extension Christian intellectuals of any stripe, ought to pursue their vocations with autonomy, integrity, and courage.[7]

Autonomy, in the sense of not taking our direction from the agenda of the secular world around us, means that we see ourselves as first of all called to the service of the church and its Lord. We cannot serve two masters, so we must be about our Father's business. *Integrity* (or *integrality*, as Plantinga also calls it) means that we bring to bear our Christianity on the questions at hand: There is a distinctively Christian way to think about the world, a Christian way to do engineering, English, chemistry, and philosophy. The compartmentalization in the minds of Christian academics as they "leave their faith at home" in the practice of their disciplines must stop—it is akin to "salt which has lost its saltiness," worthless as a seasoner or preservative.

Plantinga's Call to Courage

Such autonomy and integrity is risky, and will provoke opposition, which is why Plantinga also calls us to *courage*. It is risky to see and present yourself as a Christian first, who lives out his faith by teaching philosophy, programming computers, or driving trucks. But twenty years of faithfulness and inspiration on the part of Plantinga and others has brought us to the point that many college students may be wondering "What secularization?" when it comes to academic philosophy. It is very likely that their Introduction to Philosophy courses, whether at major research institutions, serene liberal arts schools, or local community colleges, will be taught by evangelical Christian professors or graduate students who unapologetically and professionally exemplify a Christian mind at work. To put it bluntly, you no longer have to "check your brain at the door" to be an intellectually robust Christian.

This quick survey has noted only a few representative figures, and predominately within the single academic discipline of philosophy. Though the evangelical mind has often evidenced "scandal"—see Mark Noll's critique with a similar title—it is a scandal under renovation and improvement, often in the very ways where Noll saw "hope" a decade ago.[8] Furthermore, the internal policing that Noll and others provide is actually additional evidence for a thriving Christian mind—and is a vast improvement over the exclusively external criticism so common only a few decades ago. It is ironic that as the Christian mind has gained a foothold, even credence, in the formerly inhospitable world of professional academia, we find its greatest threat now comes from within, as the church flirts with the uncritical assimilation of postmodern ideas and practices.

LOGOS, LOGIC, AND LOGOCENTRISM: THE POSTMODERN CHALLENGE TO REASON

A Helpful Critic of Modernism

Much of "postmodernism" includes a needful critique of modernism, the dominant philosophical and cultural worldview in the West since the time of the Enlightenment. Stanley Grenz characterizes modernism and the "Enlightenment project" as including the centrality and autonomy of the individual, the confidence in technology and science to manage and improve human life, the tenet that knowledge is "certain, objective, and good," and the determinative role of reason in adjudicating truth claims.[9] Postmodernism, by contrast, proffers an emphasis of community over individuality, an eclectic mixture of the technological and the traditional, the subjectivity of knowledge, and the role of factors like emotion and intuition in belief formation.

This is not the place to offer a full analysis of the postmodern critique, except to note that the proffered alternatives are not the exclusive province of the postmodern, and the most helpful aspects of postmodernism are but a recapturing of the premodern. For example, modernism is fairly and rightly castigated as advancing the interests of the autonomous individual over the good of the collective whole. The call to community is actually a regression to the premodern ideas of interdependence and holistic living. Postmodernism in practice is actually "hypermodern" in that the individual is radically autonomous in his self-identification, metaphysical commitment, and community participation (or lack thereof).

A Discomfort with Logic and Metanarrative

Particularly troubling to Christian postmoderns is the church's perceived abdication to classical Greek philosophy, especially Aristotelian logic. Carl Raschke is typical when he writes, "Aristotelianism was never compatible with the biblical faith perspective . . . and neither was deductive reasoning";[10] "'the Christian-moral view of the world' . . . was really ancient Greek metaphysics";[11] and "many contemporary theologians subscribe to 'pagan' logocentrism, . . . [which] is the obsession of metaphysics with the logical, or representational, side of language."[12] The bulk of Raschke's critique appears in a chapter entitled "The New French Revolution," wherein he calls the church to reject the influence of the ancient Greeks like Plato and Aristotle (though it has come to us filtered through Christian giants like Augustine and Aquinas), and turn for instruction instead to contemporary thinkers like Michel Foucault, Jacques Derrida, and Gilles Deleuze.[13] I fail to see how the rejection of pagan Greeks in favor of atheistic Frenchmen counts as a theological advance. It is not my goal here to offer a complete assessment of postmodernism and its impact in the church. My concern in the remainder of this section is limited to examining the cost and consistency of the postmodern turn from reason.

As noted, postmodernism is marked by its rejection of logic in general, as well as its incredulity toward metanarratives. (A "metanarrative" is a "big story," a worldview or framework for understanding all the "little stories" and pieces of our lives. For example, Christianity and atheism are both metanarratives.) These features make an uncritical Christian embrace of postmodernism particularly difficult. It is well known that the Greek word that John uses to introduce Christ to us in his gospel is *logos* (John 1:1–3), which is connected to our English word "logic." While it is a mistake to put too much emphasis on this connection, it would be equally erroneous to put too little. John's readers knew the word *logos* through various contexts, including the work of the pre-Socratic philosopher Heraclitus. "You can never step into the same river twice"[14] because the whole world, including that river, is in a state of constant change, or flux, according to Heraclitus. This change, however, is not random, but orderly and determined, according to a ruling principle he terms the *logos*. Heraclitus declared that the *logos* is an impersonal force, the unifying principle of the universe, in which all things hold together and by which they are all intelligible. He offers the logos as the metanarrative—the story that explains all the stories.

As offensive as an identification of logic with the mind of Christ might be to the postmodern, just as difficult is John's declaration that Jesus is Himself the *logos*—the supreme metanarrative. Against those who reject all metanarratives, Christianity is a call to submit to *the* Metanarrative—Christ the *logos*—by whom all things were created and in whom "all things hold together" (Col. 1:15–20). To brand reason and logic as mere "logocentrism" is to reject something fundamental about the person of Jesus as revealed in the Gospels, what it is for us to be created in God's image, and something basic about the created order (including that it is, well, orderly).

The Cost of Rejecting Logic

Before we accept the postmodern critique and dismiss logic as either "one way of doing things," or worse, some sort of oppressive Greco-Western imposition as an obstacle to pure spirituality, we ought to count carefully the cost of such a rejection.

Logic is at least as old as Aristotle and the ancient Greeks (I will argue below that it is much, much older than that). As a well-defined and defended science, certain patterns of reasoning have been identified as common, and either reliable (valid) or unreliable (invalid). For example, the most famous and most common "argument" (present in almost every beginning logic text) is the following:

Premise: All men are mortal.
Premise: Socrates is a man.
Conclusion: Therefore, Socrates is mortal.

Beyond establishing Socrates' mortality, this argument offers us a pattern, or skeleton, of reasoning, which has a broader application than this single instance. We recognize that any argument that "looks like" this argument shares the following "shape":

All As are Bs.
X is an A.
Therefore, X is a B.

This particular pattern of reasoning is well known to logicians, and goes by the designation, broadly speaking, *modus ponens*. Much as a veterinarian knows he is dealing with a cat by the examination of an X-ray, we know we are dealing with a well-reasoned argument if it conforms to this pattern. Though there are an infinite number of valid reasoning patterns, about six patterns are so prevalent that they merit particular attention, as are a similar number of unreliable (invalid, fallacious) patterns. I submit that an attention to our patterns of thought is a God-honoring human endeavor, which bears critically upon our interpretation, evaluation, and expression of both God's revelation and our own communication.

There are in fact two aspects of an argument subject to our evaluation: the validity of its structure and the truth of its premises. A proper engagement of an argument allows us to commend and condemn arguments regarding each aspect. As a contemporary example, some advocates of legalized abortion might argue:

Only human beings can be "murdered."
The fetus is not human.
Therefore, abortion is not murder.

If the pro-life Christian is completely dismissive, or worse, volatile, in response to this argument, he misses a genuine opportunity to commend his conversational partner, to advance the discussion, and to present his own worldview. He ought instead to say, without sarcasm or condescension, "Your argument is well considered and well reasoned, but unfortunately depends upon a premise that I think is false. Could you explain or defend for me the claim that the fetus is not human?" In so doing, he affirms the shared imprint of God, by our joint dependence upon words and logic for thought and communication, and also refocuses the conversation in a way to bring to bear a genuinely distinctive Christian voice—the issue at hand is really the ontological status of the fetus.

So, Christians need to avoid this first error of characterizing all aspects of non-Christian mental activity as corrupt, noting instead that even fallen men and women can reason well, though they often reach false conclusions because of their faulty premises and presuppositions.[15] The more popular (and more egregious) mistake common among Christians is to reject logic altogether, regarding its origin as merely human, and specifically Greco-Western. A common refrain among pietistic types is "God is not bound by any system of logic—He is above logic." This view is spiritualized by appeal to either "the mystery of God's ways" or a desire to protect God's sovereignty. To such people, I assert that, though your salvation may not hinge upon logic, your hope of salvation certainly does.

Many Christians are familiar with Evangelism Explosion, and in particular its motivating questions. Let us suppose that God is as well. That said, it would be no surprise if, at your death, you were to appear before God and He were to ask you, "Why should I let you into

My heaven?" Fortunately, you've been well prepared for this question, so you answer confidently, "Because on January 12, 1978, at 12:05 p.m., in First Church of Hometown, I called upon Jesus Christ and trusted Him for my salvation—I've got a card around here validated by the associate pastor."

If God Rejected Logic . . .

All is well, but what if God replies, "So?" You may get nervous, but recalling your years in AWANA (or some other children's Scripture memory program) you quote for Him, "Well, Lord, Acts 2:21 says 'Everyone who calls on the name of the Lord will be saved.'" What will be your recourse if God asks again, "And so?"

You might say (remembering Socrates and his deducible mortality), "Well, Lord, let me lay this out for you as a syllogism:

All who call on the name of the Lord will be saved. (Acts 2:21)
I called on the name of the Lord (see supporting documents, attached).
Therefore, I will be saved."

What will you say at this point if God replies with a snort, "Ha! Why in the world do you think I am bound by your way of thinking— your *modus ponens*? Don't you know that I am above logic?" Would you not think that God had been fundamentally deceptive, and unjust, in His revelation and judgment? To repeat, though your salvation may not hinge upon logic,[16] it is clear that your hope of salvation—what John calls *knowing* that you have eternal life (1 John 5:13)—as well as your understanding of God's revelation more broadly, depends in great part on traditional, syllogistic, "Aristotelian" logic.

Postmoderns Use Logic Too

In the rejection of logic, the pietist and the postmodern find common ground. The irony is particularly pointed in the case of the postmodern, because he is doubly dependent upon logic. In the first place, as with the rest of us, the postmodern depends upon logic for basic communication. When he says, for example, that we must reconsider the exclusive claims of traditional Christianity because they are excessively narrow,[17] he relies, parasitically, upon the syllogistic reasoning postmoderns explicitly reject:

> Exclusive-truth claims are wrong.
> Traditional Christianity makes exclusive-truth claims.
> Therefore, traditional Christianity is wrong.

If I were to tell the postmodern that I agreed with both his premises, but still adhered to every narrow tenet of the historic faith, he would no doubt grow very frustrated, and with good reason. Anyone who argues against logic is like the anarchist who defends his right to publicly oppose the Constitution by appeal to the First Amendment—he is free to do so, but his position is transparently self-refuting.

Postmoderns Embrace Technology (with Its Absolutes)

A second postmodern irony is telling as well. In addition to a rejection of traditional categories of learning and logic, postmoderns are positively marked by a preference for the practical and a love of technology. In the first place, the standard of truth is "whatever works (for you) is true (for you)."[18] In the second, all of us who live in the postmodern era know, and often appreciate, the decisive role technology plays in our everyday lives—our various electronic tools and toys. For those who reject logic, as well as the absolute categories of true and false, it is time to trash the technology. Because deep down in the computer code, under the magic goblet, the URL link, and the emoticon, at the primary level of technological "reality," there is nothing more than a series of 1s and 0s (read "true" and "false") without shades of gray or ambiguity, linked together in relationships characterized only by "and," "or," "not," and "if . . . then."

If the standard of reality is "what works," there is nothing *more real* in our postmodern technological utopia than classical categories of logic and true/false. The postmodern who blogs against logic and absolute truth is completely dependent upon the logical consistency of his word processor and Internet provider.

This realization ought not threaten us, nor diminish God, because logic is not in fact a human invention—it is a human discovery. Aristotle and the Greeks (or any other logical forefathers) no more invented logic than Isaac Newton invented gravity. Logic and rationality are a part of the stamp of the divine image on the human race: When we reason well, we think as God thinks.[19] Thinking well (logically) speaks to the *how*, if not the *what*, of thinking God's thoughts after Him. Furthermore, it is an act of worship. In *Chariots of Fire*, Olympic runner Eric Liddle says, "God made me fast, and when I run, I feel His pleasure." The Christian ought to say, "God made me rational, as He is, and when I reason well, I feel His pleasure."

HOW SHOULD WE THEN THINK?

What should we do, as individuals, churches, and institutions, to forge a Christian mind? In this section I will outline several specific activities in diverse realms—the church, the home, the individual mind. This list is neither exhaustive nor exclusive, but rather an illustration of the kinds of things to include in a healthy intellectual diet and exercise regimen. Just as an athlete may adjust the weight or repetitions in an exercise routine, it may be appropriate to "scale" my suggestions to a particular circumstance. Finally, beyond these paragraphs, I need not restate the standard—and correct—admonitions to read our Bibles, pay attention to the news, and be socially and politically engaged.

Think Biblically

Our minds are structured and renewed most decisively by the Scriptures—the Word of God—and all evangelicals, by definition, hold the Word in high esteem. At a practical level, however, this esteem is often diminished. *Preachers and congregations must commit themselves to the expositional proclamation of the Bible*, particularly in the face of internal and external pressures to move away from such preaching. Failure to do so results in pietistic platitudes concerned with external behavior instead of internal transformation.

Recently I heard a sermon on Luke 5:1–11—the miraculous catch of fish and Peter's call to discipleship—focusing almost entirely on a single phrase in verse 5, NIV, "because you say so." The theme of the sermon was that we are just to obey Jesus and see what will happen. But why was Peter able to say, "Because you say so"? The answer, of course, is in the context. Chapter 4 details a series of miraculous healings, including Peter's mother-in-law, but no mention of those verses was made in the sermon. Neither was mentioned the primary point of application, the one Jesus makes in the text: Just as you caught fish only through the miraculous power of God, now you will catch men in that same miraculous power. Instead we are left with another empty injunction to obey Jesus and try harder—exactly the opposite of the gospel writer's theological intent. It's a nice story, though.

We see the results of a steady diet of narrative, topical, non-theological, application-oriented preaching each fall when our new students arrive on campus. I am fully convinced that we get the cream of the evangelical crop at Moody Bible Institute—our students are intelligent (as attested by various objective measures) and passionate about God and ministry (every applicant must detail a very specific ministry orientation as a prerequisite for admission). And they know their Bibles, in a sense; that is, they know the stories. They know about Noah, and Jonah, and the feeding of the five thousand, and Jesus calming the storm. However, if asked to locate these accounts in their Bibles, or to put them in chronological order, or to explain their significance, historical or theological, they are often less successful.

In this I do not blame the students—they are after all the products of homes, churches, and Sunday schools around the country. Thus, I can't help but wonder, if these are the young people who are so passionate about God, His church, and His Word that they come to us to study for vocational ministry, what is the level of biblical and theological literacy among the rest of evangelical young adulthood? For this reason, biblical and theological studies have been and will be the core of every course of studies at a Bible school like Moody. These matters, however, are too important, too foundational, to be the province of only the "professionals" like pastors and missionaries.

The Christian mind cannot be formed or nourished apart from a clear and systematic understanding of the Scriptures. As noted before, pastors and congregants must jointly value the careful exposition of the Word. A steady diet of topical, issue-oriented preaching may "tickle the ears," but it leaves us susceptible to every wind of doctrine; we end up being unable to stomach "sound doctrine" and must settle for very thin milk indeed (2 Tim. 4:3; Heb. 5:12–14). In simple terms, pastors must regularly preach through entire books, and in doing so, must demonstrate the contextual and theological integration of the text. This responsibility does not fall to preachers alone, however. It is the responsibility of every mature Christian and household to be biblically and theologically equipped. As a practical means to that end: *Read Bible commentaries.* The next time you begin a time of personal or small-group study, set aside the topical fill-in-the-blank booklet filled with questions that begin "How do you feel about . . . ?" and read, in coordination with the Scriptures, a commentary instead.

Good commentaries are available at almost every ability level—one might begin with John Stott's commentary on the Sermon on the Mount in the series *The Bible Speaks Today.* Do not just accept Stott's word, or any other commentator's, but ask yourself and your study partners, "Is he right when he says . . . ?" This kind of critical engagement with the Bible and its teachers is what earned the Bereans the commendation of "more noble-minded" (Acts 17:11). In this admonition, and those that follow, I am consciously speaking to ministers as well as laymen: Commentaries are not written to be read in two-paragraph increments corresponding to this week's sermon passage, and theological texts have a higher purpose than decorating our office shelves.

Think Theologically

In pursuit of the Christian mind, we build on the foundation of biblical literacy by shaping a theological integration of the Scriptures. This used to be common in the evangelical church, by the extensive use of catechisms in discipleship. From Luther to Calvin to the Westminster divines through the present day, it has been understood that Christian maturity requires at minimum *the ability to articulate and explain the basics of Christian doctrine*, and to begin to do so at a young age. The disappearance of the catechism has been a tragedy for the modern church, and is no doubt traceable to a combination of factors, including a general anti-intellectualism in some evangelical traditions, a reluctance to say that some things are "true" (such claims divide, after all—anathema in an age of inclusion), and a common preference for the easy, the comfortable, and the vague (memorization is so demanding and precise). Its fruit is all too obvious, however, and can be observed in the fuzzy thinking of students heading off to college each year, as well as the popularity of certain books and television programs. Too many Christians are theologically underequipped to recognize and refute false doctrine, or to give a coherent defense of the hope that lies within them (1 Pet. 3:15).

In actuality, of course, catechizing is not hard at all, even (especially) for children. The *Westminster Shorter Catechism* (1647) was formulated explicitly for children and those young in the faith, as the

Larger Catechism was thought too extensive for beginners.[20] Ideal for family study of the catechism is *Training Hearts, Teaching Minds: Family Devotions Based on the Shorter Catechism*, by Starr Meade.[21] For those who might have a few doctrinal quibbles with Westminsterian theology, John Piper has also revised and annotated a Baptist catechism to serve similar ends.[22] Is this too hard, or does it take too much time? Of course not, though it may require an altered allocation of time or resources. We may need to watch less television, or intend to meet together more regularly for discipleship and accountability. In a former church, we had over fifty men who met weekly in groups of three to six, reading and discussing among other things portions of Alister McGrath's *Christian Theology*[23] and every chapter of Millard Erickson's *Christian Theology*.[24] Of course, it took two years of meeting weekly at 6:00 a.m., but the task held a high value to those men.

The development of a theological structure should be an ongoing intentional priority. I rotate theology texts beside my bed (currently Wayne Grudem's *Systematic Theology*) that I read in the ten or fifteen minutes by which I precede my wife to bed each night. I recall Os Guinness's words to me one night over dinner, "It is amazing how much you can read over a year if you devote fifteen minutes a night to it."

Think Logically

Given that I defended at great length above the discipline and application of logic, it stands to reason that I would recommend its study and application here. If it is indeed a basic feature of the world in which we live, think, and communicate, then it behooves us to *attend carefully to the study of logic and critical thinking*. You can find in almost every used-book store several inexpensive copies of logic texts (or new copies online and in college bookstores).[25] Get a book, read a chapter, do the exercises, attend to your thinking. You will be amazed at the relevance and frequency of application of your studies.

Mastery of the *identification of fallacies* (mistakes in reasoning) is especially needed in the church today. A few years ago, I had provided my students with a list of over twenty different fallacies, complete with made-up examples, enough to span several class discussions. One day, we attended an on-campus "debate" (the content of which is not relevant). I was able to move from that assembly into a classroom ten minutes later and say, "Put away your notes—almost every fallacy on the list was just illustrated for us today in your hearing." We then proceeded to reproduce the exchange, and very few fallacies were unaccounted for. My crusade to get Christians to think well was reinforced, not so much by the illogic on display by the Christian "leaders" on stage that day, but by the factious cheering from the student body as one point or another was illicitly defended.

After their training, these students, as well as young people who have completed similar studies in schools around the country, now sit in our churches and measure our preachers on the strength of their reasoning as but one facet of the exposition of the Scriptures. Christians in general, and preachers in particular, are people of the Word, and need to attend to the meaning and relationships of words—whether it is the appropriate use and interpretation of *or* or *if . . . then*, or the manipulative attempt to replace argumentation with emotional appeals or distracting red herrings.

Think Holistically

Upon the biblical and theological foundation, the Christian mind continues to build by adding a superstructure of what might be called holistic classical and contemporary cultural literacy. Our biblical and theological understanding provides the basis for understanding and engagement with the world at large, and it is here that a genuine Christian mind really shines (like a light on a lamp stand). Do you want to be relevant? Then say something interesting, instead of merely parroting back whatever is currently in vogue. The Christian mind is not afraid of the broader culture, but seeks instead to understand and engage it, even when the world "out there" does not appreciate or understand the Christian mind (1 Cor. 2:14–16). I call Christians to lifestyles of learning and engagement. An education is not something we have, but something we pursue, throughout a well-lived life.

The world in which we live is an amazing place, created by our good God, as a reflection of His mind and character. We ourselves and the society in which we live have been significantly shaped by the events and ideas that have preceded us. And, confident in the sufficiency of the truly Christian mind to appraise all things, we have nothing to fear from the study of or engagement with the world—indeed we are called to exactly that (cf. 1 Pet. 3:15; Col. 4:6).

Educate and Exercise Your Mind

How will we achieve this? The first thing to do is to *value education and truth broadly*, in the home, church, and school. *Everything* is interesting to the Christian mind.

The subset of evangelicalism that seems to do the best job of pursuing and developing the Christian mind is the homeschool crowd, and not just the children. Many an adult has lamented, "I should have paid attention in school." Home schooling often provides a second chance to repentant adults. Home-schooling parents often claim that they are the ones getting an education, from the studies of ancient Egypt to the American Revolution, to reading all those books you do not remember from high school. It turns out that they were interesting after all. So, if you want to understand the world in which we live and how to think Christianly about it, I recommend home schooling. In addition to the familial, spiritual, social, and education benefits (all of which are well documented), you get a personal refresher course in cultural understanding. I recognize that many of my readers cannot opt for home schooling. They may lack the requisite children, for example. However, that does not preclude them from obtaining the catalogs or one of the many helpful guides, and continuing their personal journeys of self-education.[26]

In addition to the radical course of home schooling, there are other avenues available to those who see education as a lifestyle. Like many Americans, I spend hours in the car every week, usually with the radio on. (Many others spend additional such time on treadmills, or in kitchens, etc.) I have discovered the products of The Teaching Company[27]—college-level lectures on nearly every topic under the sun, delivered by the most knowledgeable, articulate, and even entertaining experts in their respective fields. In the last year, I have heard entire courses on economics, ancient Egypt, Greece, Rome, Saint Augustine, World War II, Understanding Great Music, and the Search for Extraterrestrial Life—all in the flow of my regular routine, and all in the context of thinking Christianly.

For the further exercise of the Christian mind, I recommend that you *discover and pursue a passion* as a context and vehicle for thinking Christianly and engaging culturally. One of the most careful Christian thinkers I know is a Civil War re-enactor, and his knowledge of that conflict is encyclopedic. This passion is pivotal in his Christian understanding of both the past and the present (as we still wrestle with issues of power, racism, economics, and politics), and also serves as common ground for evangelism and defense of the Christian worldview. One of my graduate school professors, a world-class scholar on the work of Gottfried Leibniz, also collects and displays antique hand tools, in particular wood planers—all as an expression of his Christian faith. Christianity, and the pursuit of the Christian mind, is not only interesting in itself—it makes us interesting, and, yes, relevant!

Full-blooded discipleship involves not only equipping in the Word, but also equipping for the world. Churches, families, and schools need to see themselves preparing Christians for competence in both arenas, that we might *engage the popular culture* as thinking Christians. In our church, the pastor hosts a movie night almost monthly, at which participants not only watch a recent release but then also discuss the movie, its message, and how to engage it as Christians. I meet with a friend regularly, and among the things we discuss are books—Christian or "secular"—we choose to read in common. Others join or lead book discussions at a local library or Barnes & Noble. This twofold task is reflected in the structure of our curriculum at a Bible school: As an instructor in the Introduction to Philosophy class,[28] I must help my students to understand the significant role Western philosophy has had in the expression of Christian theology, as my course is a prerequisite for further studies in theology. I am also aware of what their old high school friends are learning in their liberal arts courses at the public or private college, so I must help them to understand the discipline more broadly as well—these are the people with and to whom my students will be ministering in years to come.

Contrary to ancient and contemporary monastic movements, the Christian mind is not a means to escape the world, but the way to be in the world without being of it. To be clear, in all of this I am not advocating education for its own sake, or the mere stockpiling of facts, but rather the intentional Christian act of worship by which we exercise our minds to the service and glory of God, as befitting those who enjoy a privileged status as image-bearers of the divine mind.

Concluding Practicalities

Almost every discussion of the Christian mind includes a discussion of those things that retard its development, and *indiscriminate media consumption* always leads the list. In our day, that usually means television and Internet. For the record, we have a television, and we watch it; we have Internet access, and we use it. But, their use is limited, and I respect very much those who eliminate them altogether. The absence of the Christian mind, however, is most noticeable among Christians (and their children) who mirror the culture at large—watching hours of television, playing hours of video games, endlessly talking on cell phones, e-mailing, chatting, and text messaging, web-surfing, reading formulaic books, and listening to formulaic music. If we want to be different from our culture, distinctively Christian, we must be different and intentional in our foundational lifestyle choices. If you were to conduct a survey, I think you would find happier, healthier, and more well-rounded children and families, not in the homes with a television and computer monitor in every bedroom, but in the homes with maybe one in the entire house.

Christians have a well-earned reputation for being naïve and reactionary, and the prevalence and anonymity of the Internet have only exacerbated the stereotype. I regularly receive, from no-doubt well-intended persons, forwarded announcements that Madelyn Murray O'Hair is trying to outlaw Christian broadcasting, that role-playing games are responsible for innumerable teen suicides, and that NASA scientists have proven the truth of the Bible by discovering Joshua's missing day. To be fair, these reports are not typically all included in a single message. An appropriate understanding of the Bible, theology, logic, science, and the general culture in which we live is sufficient to make us doubt the veracity of these sensationalistic "updates." That each of these accounts, and countless others, is demonstrably false is evident upon even the most cursory research,[29] but their continued circulation among Christians serves for me as a barometer of the current status of the Christian mind and the work that remains to be done. We have come a long way, to the glory of God, but we each remain confronted with the challenge to offer our priestly service of worship through the ongoing "renewing of [our] mind" (Rom. 12:1–2).

Bryan O'Neal is assistant professor of theology at the Moody Bible Institute. He is completing studies for the Ph.D. degree at Purdue University, West Lafayette, Indiana. He holds degrees from Purdue University and Moody Bible Institute.

NOTES

1. Harry Blamires, *The Christian Mind* (New York: Seabury Press, 1963), 1.

2. Ibid., 13, 16.

3. Ibid., 18.

4. Though the term itself dates back to at least Immanuel Kant, and has been variously appropriated by thinkers of varying philosophical stripes, the contemporary popular usage has come to serve as almost a Christian "buzzword," as a topical book search at Amazon.com will reveal—a significant if not dominant percentage of the resulting books are of a broadly Christian nature. As to the history of "worldview," see David Naugle's definitive work *Worldview: The History of a Concept* (Grand Rapids: Eerdmans, 2002); also James Sire's *Naming the Elephant: Worldview as a Concept* (Downers Grove, Ill.: InterVarsity, 2004).

5. In history, Mark Noll; sociology, Michael Emerson; almost all the leaders of the contemporary intelligent design movement in biology, physics, mathematics, astronomy, and other disciplines are operating within a Christian, if not always evangelical, paradigm.

6. Quentin Smith. "The Metaphilosophy of Nature," *Philo* 4, no.2; www.philoonline.org/library/smith_4_2.htm

7. This address is widely available on the Internet; it is also reprinted in *The Analytical Theist: An Alvin Plantinga Reader*, ed. James Sennett (Grand Rapids: Eerdmans, 1998). This book contains much of Plantinga's seminal work in philosophy's varied subdisciplines, is highly accessible, and is an excellent general introduction to Plantinga's thought.

8. Mark Noll, *The Scandal of the Evangelical Mind* (Grand Rapids: Eerdmans, 1994), 211–253.

9. Stanley Grenz, *A Primer on Postmodernism* (Grand Rapids: Eerdmans, 2004), 2–4.

10. Carl A, Raschke, *The Next Reformation: Why Evangelicals Must Embrace Postmodernity* (Grand Rapids: Baker, 2004), 94. One wonders what those who say "Christianity must do X or else" (see John Spong's *Why Christianity Must Change or Die* [San Francisco: HarperSanFrancisco, 1999]) do with Jesus' assurance in Matthew 16:18. Isn't the church assured of perseverance against even the "gates of Hell?"

11. Ibid., 46.

12. Ibid., 54.

13. Ibid., 35–68; see also Grenz, *Primer,* 123–50.

14. See, for example, *A Presocratics Reader*, ed. Patricia Curd, et al.; (Indianapolis: Hackett 1996), 36.

15. As often does the Christian, by the way.

16. God could, in principle, dispense saving grace arbitrarily.

17. Rob Bell, pastor of Mars Hill Church in Grand Rapids, in newspaper interview in *The Grand Rapids Press*, 30 July 2005.

18. John Dewey was instrumental in the initial characterization of the "pragmatic school" at the beginning of the twentieth century; Richard Roty advanced a postmodern version of pragmatism by the end of the century.

19. Not, of course, exhaustively or infallibly, as the truth of many propositions remains unknown to us, and many reasoning patterns are too complex for us to contemplate— but properly, as befitting our rational condition.

20. Many moderns and postmoderns like to regard our present age as much more sophisticated and intellectually advanced when compared to those who have gone before, but they balk at suggestions such as mine here as "unrealistic." How do you imagine a lay elder or deacon in a contemporary American church faring in a biblical or theological discussion with his counterpart in sixteenth-century Geneva or Puritan New England?

21. Starr Meade, *Training Hearts, Teaching Minds* (Phillipsburg, N.J.: P& R Publishing, 2000).

22. Available through www.desiringgod.org.

23. Alister McGrath, *Christian Theology: An Introduction* (Oxford: Blackwell, 1994).

24. Millard Erickson, *Christian Theology* (Grand Rapids: Baker, 1998).

25. Standards in the field include Irving Copi's *Introduction to Logic* (now in its 11th edition) and Patrick Hurley's *A Concise Introduction to Logic* (recently released in its 9th edition).

26. Resources include Veritas Press catalog (www.veritaspress.com). For a comprehensive overview of strategy for providing a classical education see Susan Wise-Bauer's *The Well-Trained Mind* (New York: Norton, 1999). Those who feel ill-equipped even to begin such a journey will profit from Bauer's prequel *The Well-Educated Mind: How to Acquire the Classical Education You Never Had* (New York: Norton, 2003).

27. http://www.teach12.com.

28. For example, these ideas apply to history, psychology, and English literature as well.

29. As a challenge and exercise in my own development and maintenance of a Christian mind, I sometimes try to time myself as to how quickly I can debunk various myths and urban legends. Internet resources like www.snopes.com usually make this task easy.

Chapter 7

PROCLAIMING JESUS THROUGH INTELLECTUAL DEFENSE

A Response to Both Modernism and Postmodernism

by Kevin D. Zuber

At first glance, the task of "proclaiming Jesus" and the idea of "intellectual defense" might seem an improbable combination. Indeed, some would suggest they are inimical and Christians should *eschew* "intellectual defense" and just "preach Jesus." I frankly have some sympathy with that notion but will note in a moment that it is not a viable option. Others would suggest that we must *first* launch an "intellectual defense" in order to get a hearing from unbelievers that would then allow us to "preach Jesus." I find myself somewhat perturbed by that view. It smacks of the notion that *we*, by our efforts and ingenuity, must get people intellectually prepared for the work of the Holy Spirit!

Still others view the matter of "intellectual defense" in martial terms —a "battle," "struggle," or "contest"—and engage in it as if the unbeliever were an opponent or belligerent rather than a mission field, a lost person in need of the saving message of the gospel of Jesus Christ.

They speak in terms of "winning" and of getting the unbeliever to capitulate. In such instances "proclaiming Jesus" is marred by an arrogant spirit and condescending tone, and the love and grace of Jesus Christ are largely lost in the heat of the "debate."

I suggest that we combine the two concepts of "proclaiming Jesus" and "intellectual defense." My approach is to make the "proclaiming" the key element of what amounts to an "intellectual defense." I suggest that we as Christians begin by acknowledging Jesus Christ as the intellectual (epistemological) foundation of the Christian worldview. He *is* the "Light which . . . enlightens every man" (John 1:9)! He *is* "the truth" (John 14:6)! Then, *from* that foundation, *as* we "proclaim Jesus," we engage unbelief with the love and grace of Jesus Christ. With that foundation and by humble yet honest and bold proclamation of the gospel, we will be "destroying speculations and every lofty thing raised up against the knowledge of God, and we are taking every thought captive to the obedience of Christ" (2 Cor. 10:5).[1]

The "defense of the faith" as a part of the "proclamation of Jesus" is, of course, technically known as "apologetics." While the term and the field of study have had a long history, and while the books and debates about the theory, the methods, the procedures, and the practical application of apologetics are many, it is still a term and a field of study of which many evangelical Christians are largely ignorant. As Douglas Groothuis writes, "The evangelical world today suffers from apologetic anemia."[2] Those who do venture into the field soon discover that sharp disagreements exist about the procedure and the method of Christian apologetics.[3]

Nevertheless, such "defense" is necessary for many reasons. Here are just two: First, because the culture around us is "relativistic" and "pluralistic"[4] and prefers what is "politically correct" over any truth claim (no matter how well that claim may be supported objectively, logically, or even biblically), we will have to answer for the claim "Jesus Christ is *the* way of salvation."[5] Second, we must engage in intellectual defense in order to obey the Scriptures. Scripture has both direct admonitions urging us to give an answer for the hope that is within us (1 Pet. 3:15) and examples of engagement with unbelief (for instance Paul's encounter with the philosophers of Athens in Acts 17).

Main Intellectual Challenges That Christian Apologists Face

This bit of "intellectual history" has been told many times. I will provide just a summary overview. The main issue we are dealing with is called "epistemology."[6]

Modernism

Modernism may be defined as the cultural offspring of the combination of Cartesian rationalism plus British empiricism yielding a Kantian *Aufklarüng*, or Enlightenment. By many accounts modern philosophy and modern epistemology began with the work of René Descartes.[7] Descartes sought to establish his epistemology on the foundation of something "certain and indubitable," metaphorically equivalent to that of "Archimedes [who] wanted just one firm, immovable point in order to shift the entire earth."[8]

Descartes and Other Rationalists

Descartes figured he could get to that one thing if he began by doubting everything until he came to at least one thing he could not doubt.[9] This "one thing" he believed he had found in the famous formula, *Cogito ergo sum*: "I think, therefore, I am."

Other rationalist philosophers (Spinoza, Leibniz) also sought a foundation in human reason. Some key assumptions (!) underlie this "foundation." First, while Descartes satisfied himself that "he must *be* if he is a thinking thing" he assumed "*be-ing* in the first place." That is, he just assumed "ontology" or "being itself." Now, you might say that that is an obvious assumption to make, but remember that Descartes was going to doubt everything until he could find a reason not to doubt it. Apparently, he forgot to doubt the existence of "being"! He, and the other rationalists tried to address this problem by positing arguments for the existence of God. (Usually the ontological argument in some form was prominent.[10]) Yet the attempt to prove the existence of God assumes that "existence" or "being-in-general" is just "out there" ready to be true of God.

Furthermore, Descartes assumed that the "I" in this formula participates in the "existence" he assumes is just "out there." James Sire points out that if the formula " 'I think therefore I am' is taken as an argument, it is circular and therefore invalid. The conclusion ('I') is already in the premise." But Sire notes Descartes probably meant the formula not as an argument but as "the description of an intuition."[11] Nevertheless, this "I" is assumed to have some basic or prior relationship to "being." In a word, this "I" assumes "autonomy." The point is this: Even if Descartes does get around to "proving God's existence" (he's still assuming "being in general" is just "out there"), he does so from the standpoint of the "autonomous I." "This means that for the modern thinker, God is not the 'given,' but at the best the conclusion of the argument. . . . We are no longer dependent on God for all our knowing."[12]

Locke and Empiricism

Returning to the survey of modernism, after Descartes we should note the work of John Locke in particular and British empiricism in general. Locke rejected the rationalist notion that there are innate ideas in the mind, which one could discover by applying the "methods" of rationalistic thought as Descartes had done. He sought to ground epistemology in experience. "Here then is a foundationalism of a different sort from that of Descartes. Rather than beginning with indubitable first principles obtained introspectively and drawing inferences from them, the basic starting point is sense experience."[13] However, Locke also assumed the standpoint of the "autonomous I." Accordingly he wrote, "But yet nothing, I think, can under that title (of revelation) shake or overrule plain knowledge, or rationally prevail with any man to admit it for true, in a direct contradiction to the clear evidence of *his own* understanding."[14]

Kant and the Turning Point

The quest for rationality lead to "the Enlightenment," also known as the "Age of Reason." During this period of eighteenth-century intellectual history, philosophers and others argued that human autonomous reason should be the sole authority for what counts as rationality. The Enlightenment reached a critical turning point in the work of Immanuel Kant. Kant recognized the impasse for epistemology created by the competition between the rationalists and the empiricists. He writes, "There can be no doubt[15] that all our knowledge begins with experience." However, to this very "empiricist" sounding comment he adds, "But though all our knowledge begins with experience, it does not follow that it all arises out of experience."[16] Kant is not trying to be clever here. His point (in what is perhaps the densest piece of literature in Western history)[17] is this: Our "thinking" needs input from sense experience, but that input is "processed" by concepts (he called them "categories") already present in the mind. His famous dictum is: "Percepts without concepts are empty; concepts without percepts are blind."[18] In other words, the empiricists were partly right, for we cannot even begin to think without sense experience. However, the rationalists were also partly right, Kant held, in that the mind "re-works" the experiences according to some "pre-programmed" categories. The mind brings concepts like "cause and effect," "numerical succession," and even "time and space." It is through these "concepts" that the "percepts" of sense experience must pass. Of course, this means that for Kant we never really know "the-world-out-there" (the noumenal); we only know "the-world-out-there-having-been-processed" by the mind (the phenomenal). Basically Kant said all our knowledge is conditioned.[19]

One final point about Kant: He rejected the traditional proofs for the existence of God. God could be "postulated" as a principle of "practical reason" (God needs to "be there" for there to be some basis for "morality"), but it was not possible to know by pure reason that "God was/is there." In short, with Kant, any "knowledge" of nonempirical reality is sacrificed to maintain autonomous human reason.

The Role of Isaac Newton

One final contributor to the modern viewpoint is the towering figure of Isaac Newton. His stature in Western culture and science is huge, but his contribution as far as our discussion is concerned is fairly simple. Newton's explanation of the physics of gravity could be considered an example, and a successful instance, of Kant's call for man to "think for himself." But Newton and some of his followers tried to employ the thinking in this case in support of theism. If unseen forces such as "gravitation" could be explained by man's reason, then perhaps it is not true that man cannot know that "God is there." "For Newton, gravity is a power emanating directly from God. . . . Matter, motion, and the mathematical laws of nature, in so far as we can determine them, consequently originate in the will and power of the Almighty."[20]

Although this might seem a positive development,[21] what Newton's argument actually did was to reinforce the notion that the most reliable foundation of knowing (even knowing of the providence and power of God) was autonomous human reason.

Two other features of Enlightenment thinking are noteworthy. One is the idea of "progress" or the notion that by the application of autonomous human reason to questions and problems man could continually find answers and bring resolutions to the improvement and advancement of mankind. ("Better Living Through Chemistry!") The continual accumulation of knowledge was always "upward" and was inherently good. Modern medicine is usually held up as the paradigm here. The other feature of modernism to note is the idea (perhaps largely inherited from the premodern Christian worldview drawn from the Bible) that there is a "story" to history, that is, a "story with a point to it." "From Kant to Hegel to Marx, modern thinkers have attempted to tell the story of humanity, usually in terms of the progress of the race."[22] The point here is that there *is* some "meaning" or "objective" to history, a metanarrative into which all events "fit" and by which all events are explained.

Postmodernism

As the term suggests, postmodernism conscientiously sees itself as the successor to modernism. Beyond that, the movement or "condition" defies simple definition. Many authors have undertaken to describe and interact with "the postmodern condition" from an evangelical perspective,[23] and we will have to leave much unsaid. (A helpful introduction to and critique of postmodernism appears in chapter 6.) Nevertheless, at the risk of oversimplification we may begin with this from D. A. Carson, who suggests "The majority view, however, is that the fundamental issue in the move from modernism to postmodernism is *epistemology*—i.e. how we know things or how we think about things."[24] Dan Kimball, a leader in the "emergent church" movement[25] agrees that epistemology is a key factor in the "cultural shift" we are now experiencing.[26]

What then is the "epistemology of postmodernism?" Largely, it is a negative reaction to the epistemology of modernism. Kevin J. Vanhoozer summarizes the key elements.[27] First, "postmodernists reject the epistemological foundationalism" of modernism.[28] The postmodernist is not irrational. "They do not reject 'reason' but 'Reason.' They deny the notion of universal rationality." For the postmodernist, "reason is rather a contextual and relative affair."[29] Carson notes that the postmodernist argues that the modernists' epistemological "'foundations' are not secure, because they are 'self-evident' only within *cultures*."[30] They are the product of finite humans and, using Vanhoozer's descriptive words are "always *situated* within particular narratives, traditions, institutions, and practices. This situatedness conditions what people deem rational."[31] In short, truth is "local," it is found only in reference to the community, be it a regional one, religious one, scientific one[32] a gender-oriented one, or some other preferred or chosen one. For postmoderns what is rational, what is truth, even language itself[33] is "socially constructed." For postmoderns there is no access to any extralingusitic reason or any "real world."

Furthermore, postmoderns are suspicious of the notion of an all-encompassing, grand, historical narrative. They are equally suspicious of all metaphysical claims.[34] These projects suggest a capacity for human reason that postmoderns deny is possible. Simply put, autonomous human reason is inadequate to "know" there is one grand narrative or to "know" that the metaphysical claims it makes are so. "Postmoderns are suspicious of truth claims, of 'getting it right.' Upon hearing the assertion, 'That's the way things are,' postmoderns are likely to respond 'that's the way things are for you.'"[35] "Truth under the regime of postmodern epistemology cannot partake of 'a historical universality.' All truth claims are merely true for some people, even if not for all people at all times and places."[36] And since they "reject the premise that history moves according to a unified linear logic"[37] postmoderns are also suspicious of any notion of "progress."

IMPEDIMENTS TO AN INTELLECTUAL DEFENSE
OF JESUS AND CHRISTIANITY

We should note that in spite of the ubiquity of the term and mindset of postmodernism (and in spite of certain exaggerated assertions to the contrary[38]) the worldview of modernism is by no means completely dead. And just as "modernism" lives, so the various evangelical responses to it continue to be exhibited. And just as postmodernism can impede the proclamation of Jesus and the gospel, even so modernism, wrongly handled, can impede the proclamation of the gospel.

Rise of Modernism: Two Evangelical Responses

Anti-intellectualism

Unfortunately, one of the early evangelical responses to the Enlightenment was a self-conscious anti-intellectualism. This response has appeared sporadically ever since the advent of the Enlightenment. It was the response of many late nineteenth- and early twentieth-century evangelicals to modernism in biblical studies in particular, and in the scholarly/intellectual arena in general. With the "triumph" of the worldview of modernism, many evangelicals withdrew from intellectual engagement. "The faith" was proclaimed as "truth," and "modernism" was condemned straightaway and inexorably, without further deliberation, as it was simply not "the faith."[39]

Naïve intellectualism

Seeing anti-intellectualism as a "scandal," more sophisticated and culturally engaged (and academically zealous) evangelicals began to attempt an "intellectual defense" of the faith. Actually, the practitioners of naïve intellectualism[40] had role models among those who were the first to confront the impact of the Enlightenment. I am thinking here of men like Joseph Butler (1692–1753) who attempted to defend the faith by arguing for the "plausibility of Christianity in terms of the analogy between revealed and natural religion."[41] Also William Paley (1743–1805) came up with the classic "watchmaker" formulation of the teleological argument.[42] These men essentially accepted the underlying premise of Enlightenment thinking (start with yourself) and attempted to employ its epistemology (sometimes wittingly and sometimes not; the latter often just accepting this epistemology as "the way careful thinkers do their business") in defense of the faith.[43] This approach to apologetics has had, and continues to have, many followers.[44] If historical studies had tended to undermine confidence in the history of the Bible, then a more rigorous use of the tools of historiography and the deliverances of archeology would prove that the biblical history was reliable. If the canons of "scientific inquiry" demanded "neutral observation" and "objective examination of the evidence" then evangelical scholars would employ such canons and from them provide skeptics with "evidence that demands a verdict" favorable to the faith. Since Enlightenment epistemology was predicated on the notion that autonomous human "reason" must and could find a "foundation" of indubitable certainty from which all other "thinking" could proceed, then evangelicals would accept the starting point of autonomous human "reason" and from that demonstrate the "reasonableness of the Christian faith."

However, neither response to modernism has proved to be quite satisfactory. Anti-intellectualism has had profoundly negative effects on evangelical faith.[45] And the reliance upon Enlightenment epistemology has produced a sort of "divided mind" and an inconsistency among evangelicals so far as concerns the relationship of apologetics and evangelism on the one hand, and theology and Christian life on the other hand. In my opinion, those who practice this approach are guilty of trying to win unbelievers to the Christian worldview by standing with unbelievers in their non-Christian worldview! In short, they not only permit, but also seek to use, autonomous human reason to get a hearing (or victory!) in defense of the faith. This is an unnecessary (and potentially harmful) concession to autonomous human reason and, frankly, a compromising of the necessity, clarity, sufficiency, and authority of God's self-authenticating Word in Scripture.[46]

Rise of Postmodernism: Three Evangelical Responses

It is somewhat ironic that, with the rise of postmodernism, many evangelicals find themselves defending the canons of modernism! And this is not just in the ranks of those who adopted the naïve intellectualism noted above.

Defending foundationalism

A number of evangelical philosophers, theologians, and apologists have attempted to defend foundationalism against its postmodern critics. In its philosophical sense, *foundationalism* is the idea that the human mind has access to basic or self-evident beliefs or truth that do not need to be justified or given support by argument or evidence. Such foundational beliefs or truths provided the basis or foundation on which other beliefs may be developed. Thus foundationalism is at loggerheads with postmodern thought. As Moreland and Craig concede in the very large volume *Philosophical Foundations for a Christian Worldview*, "In some ways, this entire book is a critique of and an alternative to postmodernism."[47]

In a book with the subtitle *Defending Christianity Against the Challenges of Postmodernism*, Douglas Groothuis affirms the need for, and asserts the possibility of "some foundations for knowledge."[48] While he wants to affirm a "minimal foundationalism," Groothuis nevertheless finds these foundations in "logic" and "objective truths" that "can be known by those who presently hold another worldview."[49] Groothuis asserts, "There are basic forms of reasoning that are nonnegotiable and are universally valid; they are not matters of contingent social construction or personal taste."[50] In other words, there are the forms of reasoning necessary for all "rational discourse, Christian or otherwise."[51]

While this may seem to the reader quite sound and persuasive, the underlying premise of these assertions is exactly what postmodernism denies is possible and what Christian epistemology *should* want to avoid, namely autonomous human reason. Bruce Ellis Benson helps to explain this point. He argues that by adopting the premises of modern philosophy, evangelical thinking has actually fallen into a form of idolatry! "Modern idolatry (of an epistemological variety) has three characteristics: an emphasis on the autonomy of the individual, a 'strong confidence in the powers of human reason in general and the rationality of the individual,' and the 'objective' character of reason itself."[52]

These points must be seriously considered. On the one hand, they cannot be dismissed by a reassertion that, in spite of it all, there just *is* objective reality out there, and we will establish it even if we have to resort to the syllogisms of logic to prove it! On the other hand, the Christian should carefully consider the "idolatrous" element in the commitment to the "autonomy of the individual" and "strong confidence in the powers of human reason." Paul said our objective should be "destroying speculations and every lofty thing raised up against the knowledge of God" (2 Cor. 10:5). I honestly fail to see how shoring up what amounts to little more than Enlightenment foundationalism escapes the postmodernists' critique. Nor does it help to defend the faith when it essentially confirms to the unbeliever that he *can trust his own fallen mind*! (recall Jer. 17:9.)

Making the Postmodern Turn

On the other hand, sensing the weight of the postmodernists' critique of foundationalism, a number of evangelicals have advocated a move "beyond foundationalism" to embrace "the postmodern turn." Prominent among this number is (the late) Stanley J. Grenz. Grenz and coauthor John R. Franke write, "In the cultural setting 'after modernity,' many theologians continue to pursue the modernist theological agenda. They routinely either discount the significance of the intellectual and cultural changes transpiring in our society or view such changes as largely negative." Grenz and Franke point out however, that "a growing number of theologians are convinced that Christians ought to take seriously the church's context within the contemporary postmodern cultural milieu."[53] These authors are amenable to this suggestion and undertake to present a postmodern theology based not on Enlightenment foundationalism but on a "chastened rationality."[54]

Another author who advocates embracing postmodern thought is Carl Raschke. Raschke suggests many evangelicals fail to see that postmodern thought is amenable to evangelical thinking because much modern evangelical thought "has unwittingly bought into the Cartesian assumption about the nature of truth" and sought to maintain the foundationalism that goes with it.[55] Raschke attempts to demonstrate how genuine "reformation faith" and postmodern thinking are alike and agreeable, and that evangelical faith is actually at more odds with Enlightenment foundationalism (even though many evangelicals are now the ones attempting to shore up foundationalism!). Although he does a good job of exposing the weaknesses of the evangelical attempt to shore up foundationalism, Raschke does not offer a compelling argument "why evangelicals must embrace postmodernity."[56]

A popular manifestation of this embracing of postmodern thought in service to evangelical faith is "the emerging church movement."[57] A prominent advocate of this perspective is Bruce McLaren.[58] The "emergent church" like postmodernism rejects foundationalism (and so rejects those forms of conservative Christianity, like fundamentalism, that retain this feature of modern thinking), embraces the concept "community over individuality," and promotes tolerance and "authenticity" over what it perceives to be the rigidity and inauthenticity of "organized religion."

A number of fine and detailed responses have emerged to these initiatives—acknowledging the positives of the critique of modernism and challenging the embrace of the postmodern mind-set.[59] For our purposes here I will suggest only that the postmodernists have made at least one very huge mistake. They have equated Enlightenment foundationalism and its epistemology with any form of foundationalism or any foundation. Admittedly, when they examine those evangelicals who defend foundationalism they see (as we have noted above) that in fact those evangelicals *are* defending a form of Enlightenment foundationalism (e.g., Groothuis in *Truth Decay*). Nevertheless, we should be prepared to consider a foundation that is not based on autonomous human reason.

Finding a middle way

Finally, another response to postmodernism takes its critique of foundationalism seriously but eschews the "postmodern turn"—"Postfoundationalist Theology." One of its most prominent exponents is Princeton Theological Seminary professor J. Wentzel Van Huyssteen, who argues that postfoundationalist theology is a "middle way" that "acknowledges contextuality, the epistemically crucial role of interpreted experience, and the way tradition shapes the epistemic and non-epistemic values that inform our reflection about God."[60] Essentially the postfoundationalist is saying what Vanhoozer said about postmodernism epistemology earlier: "Reason is *situated*." "At the same time, however, a postfoundationalist notion of rationality in theological reflection claims to point beyond the confines of the local community, group, or culture toward a plausible form of interdisciplinary conversation."[61]

The task, in other words, is to acknowledge the postmodern situation of incommensurate epistemologies, various and conflicting truth claims, and different forms of rationality, but through cross disciplinary dialogue (e.g., theology and the sciences) "to identify the shared resources of human rationality in different modes of reflection."[62] In short, postfoundationalist theology attempts, by critical conversation with other modes of knowing, to reach some point of epistemological agreement. My read is that this is a sort of "epistemic triangulation" which hopes to find "an epistemic location" (i.e., "truth claim") on which more than one community can agree.

This is not yet a widely held, or well-developed position, but I will make a couple of pertinent observations. First, the "interdisciplinary dialogue" approach assumes that by comparing "different modes of reflection" there may appear "the shared resources of rationality." But is there any reason to think that what appears to be "shared" will indeed be shared and not be merely "resemblances" that are not actually referring to the same thing? In other words, what looks to be the same "one something" in one paradigm, in another paradigm may not, and I would suggest probably is not, the same "one something"—simply because every "one something" is what it is only in relation to the paradigm of which it is a part.[63] Furthermore, even if the method refines the "epistemological process," it remains a process dependent on autonomous human reason.

THE PROBLEM AND A PROPOSAL

Autonomous Human Reason Is *Not* a "God's Eye Point of View"

The main problem with modernism, we have seen, is the hubris of "autonomous human reason." Autonomous human reason is biblically "unacceptable" to say the least (Isa. 55:8–9; Jer. 17:9; Rom. 9:20)! However, the problem of postmodernism is likewise "autonomous human reason." D. A. Carson notes that postmodernism, despite its critique of the "modern self" also "begins with the 'I,' the finite self."[64] Vanhoozer summarizes:

> Modernity cultivated autonomous knowing subjects . . . If one had to associate the spirit of modernity with one of the seven deadly sins, surely it would be pride: pride in human reason, pride in human goodness, pride in human accomplishments. It is precisely at the prideful constructions of modernity . . . that postmoderns direct their iconoclasm and ideology critique. Postmoderns aim to *situate* reason, reminding modern pretenders to a God's-eye point of view that they are in fact historically conditioned, culturally conditioned, and sexually gendered finite beings.[65]

So much for the pride of "modernity." But Vanhoozer continues, "Are there idols particular to postmodernity? The preference for the creature over the Creator no doubt takes many forms . . . Yet the besetting temptation of the postmodern condition is not pride, I submit, but *sloth.*"

So modernity's attempt to provide a foundation is effectively critiqued by postmoderns: "Postmodernism has powerfully exposed the Achilles' heel of modern epistemology: the finiteness of the 'I' means that the path to certainty about almost everything is far more difficult than many Enlightenment thinkers have supposed."[66] But in its place the postmodernist offers the hard antithesis between "absolute knowledge" and "the limited and situated perspective" of community or tradition. As Carson summarizes, "The antithesis demands that we be God, with all of God's omniscience, or else be forever condemned to know nothing objective for sure."[67] In other words, the postmodernist, having dispensed with Enlightenment foundationalism due to its lack of a "God's eye point of view" has concluded there is no "God's eye point of view."

It remains only to be noted that such a conclusion, to be fully accepted, itself requires a "God's eye point of view." The postmodernist has arrived at his position not by the rigors of the modernists' method but by the "shrug of the shoulder,"[68] or what one author calls "the knowing smirk."[69] But even while postmoderns exhibit outwardly a "perceptive cynicism," it merely masks both intellectual sloth and another manifestation of the "finite self."

A Modest Proposal to "Proclaim Jesus" as "Intellectual Defense"

The reader may be asking at this point, "How does all this relate to 'Proclaiming Jesus?'" Just this: The weakness of modernism is the attempt to find a foundation for epistemology in autonomous human reason. Postmodernism effectively exposes that weakness by showing that among other things, modernism pretends to but does not actually possess a "God's eye point of view." But postmodernism is, as Carson and others have shown, in no better position, for it too ultimately pretends to have but does not actually possess a "God's eye point of view."

It is into this situation the Christian should "proclaim" his or her foundation, which *does provide us with* a God's eye point of view in the person of the incarnate Christ! Jesus Christ is our foundation! "For no man can lay a foundation other than the one which is laid, which is Jesus Christ" (1 Cor. 3:11). At this point I caution the reader from thinking that I have slipped from philosophy to piety. This is not an attempt to "proof text" my way out of the philosophical corner. I am proposing that we consider seriously this epistemological foundation: the incarnate and risen Christ!

As understood by the rationalist, this may seem like naked fideism. But I would suggest that unlike the rationalist who posits epistemology before ontology (remember Descartes's error noted above), the Christian does not think his or her thinking is the foundation for the existence of God but that God's existence is necessary for his or her thinking (not to mention *being*) in the first place. In other words, the Christian *acknowledges* (that is a key word!) that ontology precedes epistemology.[70] Our being and our thinking are not *ours* in the first instance, but both are derived and dependent on God's!

Of course we acknowledge that the only way we could know even this is if One with the God's eye point of view *tells* us that this is so! But that *is* the Christian claim!

We make the claim because of epistemological necessity.

In the first sentence of the preface to the first edition of *Critique of Pure Reason,* Kant writes, "Human reason has this peculiar fate that in one species of its knowledge it is burdened with questions which, as prescribed by the very nature of reason itself, it is not able to ignore, but which, as transcending all its powers, it is also not able to answer."[71] To my mind this sounds akin to Solomon's admission in Ecclesiastes 3:11 that God "has also set eternity in their heart, yet so that man will not find out the work which God has done from the beginning even to the end." We are created with the capacity to know, but we cannot know it on our own! The "it" is God's ways in Ecclesiastes 3, and the "questions" reason must ask but cannot answer, says Kant, have to do with "metaphysics." In other words, autonomous human reason tries to "find out God" but no amount of searching (Job 11:7) that relies on autonomous human reason will do, because man is "built" as receiver not a maker of foundational truth! The Christian claim I suggest is this: Jesus Christ is the only foundation; we must receive Him.

We make the claim because of the self-authenticating Christ.

Again, I assert this as an epistemological axiom. Jesus Christ is *the Logos*, the Word (John 1:1). Whatever else John might have meant by using this term, he surely knew the philosophical background extending to the Stoics who used it to express "the rational principle by which everything exists, and which is of the essence of the rational human soul."[72] This Word became flesh (1:14) and coming into the world He "enlightens every man" (1:9). He is the Revealer of God (1:18), the only One who can reveal Him (John 6:46)! He is the image of the invisible God (Col. 1:15), the exact representation of His character (Heb. 1:3). In Jesus Christ we have the epistemological foundation for the God's eye point of view!

In Jesus Christ we have "the way, and *the truth* [!], and the life" (John 14:6). Whatever else this declaration may indicate about Christ primarily, at the least it is commensurate with the idea that He, in His person (and the valid implications of His historical presence on earth) is the ground of the believer's epistemology: we can know there is Truth (only) because Jesus Christ "is."

Theologian Thomas F. Torrance can help make the point here.

Torrance argues that "if we try to reach knowledge of God from some point outside of God, we cannot [later claim to] operate with a point *in God* by reference to which we can test or control our conceptions of Him, but are inevitably flung back on ourselves."[73] Applying the point, we cannot try to find a foundation outside of God by which we may discover a foundation *in God* (as the rationalists attempted to do), for then we are inevitably flung back on ourselves (that is, we are flung back to autonomous human reason). If we are to have a truly Christian epistemology, we must have a God's eye point of view revealed to us. Do we have such a God's eye point of view? Torrance offers this in *Space, Time and Resurrection:*

> I make no apology for taking divine revelation seriously. If God really is God, the Creator of all things visible and invisible and the Source of all rational order in the universe, I find it absurd to think he does not actively reveal himself to us but remains inert and aloof, so that we are left to grope about in the dark for possible intimations and clues to his reality which we may use in trying to establish arguments for his existence.[74]

Later Torrance suggests:

> The framework of objective meaning which concerns the theologian here is bound up with the Incarnation of the Son of God to be one with us in our physical human existence . . . and therefore it is bound up with the Resurrection of Jesus Christ in body . . . Thus the incarnation and the resurrection, bracketing within them the whole life and activity of Jesus Christ, constitute together the basic framework within which the New Testament writings for all their rich diversity are set.[75]

In short, the incarnation and the resurrection are, in Torrance's terms, *ultimates* of the framework of knowledge upon which the objective meaning of the New Testament is based. Torrance writes, "As such, then, the incarnation and the resurrection together form the basic framework in the interaction of God and mankind in space and time, within which the whole gospel is to be interpreted and understood."[76] And I would, therefore, add, within which the task of apologetics must be done. "But," he stresses, "they are *ultimates*, carrying their own authority and calling for the intelligent commitment of belief and providing the irreducible ground upon which continuing rational inquiry [epistemology] and theological formulation [and apologetic activity] take place."[77]

What I am suggesting from these points from Torrance is this: Christians should not be defending "foundationalism" but *proclaiming the foundation, namely, Jesus Christ!* Cornelius Van Til rightly said, "If Christ is who He says He is, then all speculation is excluded, for God can only swear by Himself. To find out what man is and who God is, one can only go to Scripture. Faith in the self-attesting Christ of the Scriptures is the beginning, not the conclusion, of wisdom"[78] Our epistemological foundation is Jesus Christ! Our task is not to defend a foundation from the position of some purported neutrality, for that is a concession (capitulation!) to another form of autonomous human reason. Rather we are to proclaim the self-authenticating Christ and the self-authenticating Word of God!

Carson's comments in critique of postmodernism support this approach:

> An omniscient, talking God changes everything. It does not change the fact that I will always be finite and that my knowledge of him will always be partial. But once I know he exists, that he is the Creator and my Savior and Judge, it is improper, even idolatrous, to try and think of my knowing things without reference to him. All of my knowledge, if it is true knowledge, is necessarily a subset of his.[79]

The question is, How do we come to know Him? Carson admits, "In every instance I have come to know him by his self-disclosure. I am a dependent being and my knowledge is dependent knowledge. For all the methodological rigor of modernism, and for all the useful recognition of the entailments of finitude in postmodernism, the fundamental starting point of these systems is disastrously mistaken."[80]

With this in mind, my approach to apologetics is twofold: "indirect" and "direct." When I engage either modernism or postmodernism, my objective is to "undermine," or "deflate," them by exposing "autonomous human reason" as intellectually pretentious (not to mention spiritually rebellious and disobedient to God!) and inadequate for the task of upholding either modernism or postmodernism. I will use postmodernism to "deflate" modernism, but then I will expose the "emperor's new postmodern clothes" as equally inadequate, for postmodernism itself does not escape from autonomy. Again quoting Carson, "For all its innovations, postmodernism . . . shares [modernism's] fundamental weakness: it begins with the 'I,' the finite self."[81]

"Autonomous human reason" is the problem. This is the very means Satan used to tempt Eve! After Satan's direct contradiction of God's Word (Gen. 3:4), Eve accepted the premise that she, the creature, was in a place to pass judgment on God's Word as opposed to the word of a mere creature. *This is the mistake that she made!* (Note too, she was unfallen here, and still she was inadequate to the tasks of judging God's Word!) Eve should have held to her epistemological high ground and replied to Satan, "No! This is God's Word, and so by epistemological necessity and ontological priority it must be the truth and you are a liar." (Or words to that effect!) How strange that some apologists today want to *foster* that sort of autonomous thinking in unbelievers. They want to find some "common ground," some mutually agreed upon (this with autonomous human reason!) epistemically neutral point from which an argument for the faith can be made. This is what Paul conscientiously avoided! "That your faith would not rest on the wisdom of men, but on the power of God" (1 Cor. 2:5).

Instead of trying to build a neutral common ground with an unbeliever, we should urge them to see the inadequacy and inconsistency of their own worldview; the untenability, on their own premises, of their own commitment to autonomous human reason. When unbelievers are faced with the uncertainty of their foundation in autonomous human reason, we should preach Jesus Christ and affirm our confidence in the self-authenticating Word of God.

SOME PRACTICAL APPLICATIONS

As thinking Christians we should learn enough of both modernism and postmodernism to be able to draw out from the unbeliever that his or her real "foundation" is "autonomous human reason." Expose it and realize this: Deep down we all know we are "not enough." We are not smart enough to think we have all the answers, or good enough to think our moral standard is "right." Deep down we all know we are creatures who live in a world that we did not create, and that we are dependent and frail. Neither modernism nor postmodernism has a satisfying answer for "sin and death" (or for a host of other "realities" like hatred between races, the destruction of the environment, the reality of evil itself). *But we Christians do!* And that answer is the truth about Jesus Christ! From the foundation of the incarnation and the resurrection, we preach the incarnation and resurrection!

Don't accept the burden of proof—you cannot "prove" the rightness of a worldview or even a truth claim in one worldview while you stand in another worldview.

Have Conversations, Not Debates!

If a person from a modernist/naturalistic worldview *knows* the dead *never* come back to life, no amount of evidence for the empty tomb, or arguments based on the canons of historic credibility, or complicated "probability theorems" will convince him that Jesus Christ, the Second Member of the Holy Trinity, rose again for our justification. In that situation we can press the individual to explain how she knows that dead do not come back to life. Here we are not trying to prove the person wrong. We are trying to make him realize that his claim to "know" is based on a worldview, the foundation of which (as the post-modernists are happy to point out) is really not the objective bedrock she has supposed it to be.[82]

Faced with a postmodernist who suggests he *knows* (or even *thinks*) that it's impossible to *know* the "real truth," we can agree with the post-modernist here: "On your presuppositions, from your worldview you are right! You cannot know real truth!" But then we should press him: "And yet you live everyday *as if you do have access to reality*![83] How is that? Furthermore, you seem to think you *do know* something about that "real truth" out there, namely you *know* it's unknowable; that's a contradiction."

Now a sharp postmodernist may say something like, "Oh, but I'm willing to live with contradiction!" Some postmodernists "embrace" contradiction, paradox, and absurdity. In such cases I ask them if they can spot the difference between a contradiction or some absurdity on the one hand, and consistency and rationality on the other hand. If they say they can, I ask them how that is. Their attempts to explain the difference will always be cast on the side of rationality. If they say they cannot spot that difference, then I ask them how it is we are hold-ing a conversation at all! (Actually, if they claim the latter they are just being obstinate and you can tell them that.)

Stick to Your Acknowledgment of Jesus as the Foundation

Never give up the epistemological high ground of the foundation, namely the incarnate and risen Christ. Never shift from your presup-positions of "He is there and He is not silent." I could get into some deep philosophical notions of "transcendental arguments" and the fact that God must exist for any predication anywhere to mean anything, but for this see the work of Greg Bahnsen[84] and his teacher Cornelius Van Til. Never concede that "autonomous human reason" actually brings a person to "true truth."

Often at this point someone suggests that we should try to find some common ground with the unbeliever. This person might argue that, after all, because of "common grace" the unbeliever knows some "truth." I understand the motivation and the point here. But in my opinion the problem with arguing that unbelievers can know things because of "common grace" is that *they* do not think they know things by "common grace" —*they* think they know them by the use of their own "autonomous human reason."

Now, we can try the method of "bait and switch." That is, we can ostensibly agree to their "truth claims" if those claims appear to be acceptable in our worldview or we have similar-sounding truth claims. But at some point we will have to address how we, the Christian and the unbeliever, each came to those claims. We will find at this point not "common ground" but a deep chasm as to the actual starting point of our thinking. And then we will have to say, "Oh, by the way, I made it seem as if I thought you knew something on your own and that we were agreed on this or that point, but actually my position is you only know things because of God's common grace." But that is likely to sound pretty hollow to an unbeliever, especially after the Christian apologist has virtually confirmed (as far as the unbeliever himself is concerned) the viability of the unbeliever's autonomous human reason. From the Scriptures, *I* know that *they* know *what* they know *only* because they are creatures made in the image of God and they live in the world God created. I really want them to come to admit this. So I will question not only what they know (especially if it is error) but also how they know it.

Use the Uniqueness of Jesus

Use the uniqueness of Jesus to make your case (but don't get sucked into thinking you have to defend it!). This is a subtle point. Am I saying "Never offer proofs for the resurrection"? No. I often rehearse the arguments for the resurrection with folks—the empty tomb, the record of appearances, the amazing change in the disciples from Good Friday's crucifixion scene to the triumph of Pentecost! But I do NOT use them to attempt to convince the unbeliever of the "historical fact of the resurrection" (which, I want it to be perfectly clear, I believe is a historical reality. I believe it because I firmly believe the [self-authenticating] Scriptures, which teach me what the thing called "historical reality" is *by* such historical events as the resurrection). I use such "evidences" to expose the worldview of the unbeliever to the unbeliever.

So a conversation might go like this:

Me: "These evidences are very convincing to me. How do they strike you?"

Unbeliever: "They are either made up, fictions, or can be explained by some other (natural) means."

Me: "You don't think the resurrection is the best explanation?"

Unbeliever: "No."

Me: "Why not?"

Unbeliever: "The idea that a dead person could come back to life is crazy! It's not possible!"

Me: "You seem pretty sure of that. How do you know that?"

And from here I zero in on this: ultimately this person thinks what she does because *she* thinks it. Even if she is a modernist following the deliverances of scientists or a postmodernist following the standards of her community, *she* has decided that these deliverances or standards are right from her own position of autonomy. But that is a very shaky position. The fact is, to have "true truth" human beings need a "God's eye point of view." We have it! The incarnation and resurrection of Jesus Christ are the ultimates, the foundation of our Christian epistemology.[85] So proclaim *the* Foundation! Proclaim Jesus Christ!

Kevin D. Zuber is professor of theology at the Moody Bible Institute. He earned his Ph.D. from Trinity Evangelical Divinity School, Deerfield, Illinois, and has degrees from Grace College and Grace Theological Seminary, both in Winona Lake, Indiana.

NOTES

1. This approach is essentially twofold: direct and indirect. Later on I identify this approach in these terms but they are reversed, indirect and direct.

2. Douglas Groothuis, "Six Enemies of Apologetic Engagement," www.leaderu.com/common/sixenemies.html.

3. See Steven B. Cowen, ed., *Five Views of Apologetics* (Grand Rapids: Zondervan, 2000).

4. These are elements of postmodernism. We will discuss the overarching intellectual environment of postmodernism below.

5. See Joseph Stowell, *The Trouble with Jesus* (Chicago: Moody, 2003), 17.

6. "Epistemology" is the study or theory of knowledge or the branch of philosophy that studies how knowledge is gained. It answers the questions, "How do we know what we know?" and "How much can we know?" It also deals with how we justify what we know.

7. See Roger Scruton, *A Short History of Modern Philosophy: From Descartes to Wittgenstein*, 2nd ed. (New York: Routledge,1995), 3, 12; also Millard J. Erickson, *Truth or Consequences: The Promise and Perils of Postmodernism* (Downers Grove, Ill.: InterVarsity, 2001), 53.

8. René Descartes, *Meditations on First Philosophy*, trans. John Cottingham (New York: Cambridge Univ. Press, 1968), 16.

9. That "one thing" could not come from his senses or his experiences because these could be, and often were, mistaken. His eyes might "deceive him."

10. See Norman L. Geisler, *Christian Apologetics* (Grand Rapids: Baker, 1976), 29–35.

11. James W. Sire, *Naming the Elephant: Worldview as a Concept* (Downers Grove, Ill.: InterVarsity, 2004), 59–60.

12. D. A. Carson, *Becoming Conversant with the Emerging Church* (Grand Rapids: Zondervan, 2005), 93.

13. Erickson, *Truth or Consequences*, 64.

14. John Locke, *An Essay Concerning Human Understanding* (1693; Amherst, N. Y.: Prometheus, 1995), 585; italics added.

15. I have always wondered, given what the rest of the sentence says, if this was a wry side-glance at Descartes!

16. Immanuel Kant, *Critique of Pure Reason*, unabridged ed., trans. Norman Kemp Smith, (New York: St. Martin's Press, 1965), 41.

17. Only Hegel could possibly rival Kant for sustained philosophical murkiness.

18. This is variously restated and translated; see Erickson, *Truth or Consequences*, 72.

19. This has a rather "postmodern ring" to it, but Kant did not mean that knowledge is "conditioned" in quite the same way postmoderns mean knowledge is "conditioned."

20. Jonathan I. Israel, *Radical Enlightenment: Philosophy and the Making of Modernity 1650–1750* (New York: Oxford University Press, 2001), 519. See also, Erickson, *Truth or Consequences*, 61–62.

21. "Newton had developed a natural theology, according to which the orderliness of nature required a God." Erickson, *Truth or Consequences*, 62. It should be noted that Newton was not a Trinitarian.

22. Kevin J. Vanhoozer, "Theology and the Condition of Postmodernity," *The Cambridge Companion to Postmodern Theology* (New York: Cambridge Univ. Press, 2003), 11.

23. The literature here is vast and growing. One of the best and most accessible introductions for evangelical students and pastors is Stanley J. Grenz, *A Primer on Postmodernism* (Grand Rapids: Eerdmans, 1996). Moving up the "scholarly ladder" is Erickson, *Truth or Consequences*. Another survey type treatment is Robert C. Greer, *Mapping Postmodernism: A Survey of Christian Options* (Downers Grove, Ill.: InterVarsity, 2003). Of course, one can consult the other footnotes in this chapter for further treatments.

24. Carson, *Becoming Conversant with the Emerging Church*, 27.

25. For a quick definition and overview of the emerging or emergent church see www.emergentvillage.org.

26. Dan Kimball, *The Emerging Church* (Grand Rapids: Zondervan, 2003), 42. Kimball's definition of epistemology (side box, p. 42) is brief but accurate, which makes his equation of the terms "epistemology" and "worldview" in his text somewhat mystifying.

27. Vanhoozer, "Theology and the Condition of Postmodernity," 10–12.

28. Ibid., 10. Carson notes, "Postmodern epistemology is profoundly suspicious of all foundationalism; one could even say it is passionately anti-foundationalist." Carson, *Becoming Conversant with the Emerging Church*, 96.

29. Vanhoozer, "Theology and the Condition of Postmodernity," 10.

30. Carson, *Becoming Conversant with the Emerging Church*, 96–97.

31. Vanhoozer, "Theology and the Condition of Postmodernity," 10.

32. Cf. Thomas S. Kuhn, *The Structure of Scientific Revolutions,* 3rd ed. (Chicago: Univ. of Chicago Press, 1962), 1996. Kuhn's premise that science does not make progress by the inexorable accumulation of scientific facts but by "revolutions," that is, by "shifts in paradigms," is predicated on the insight that what often passes for "knowledge" is just the "reigning paradigm" and its assumptions, which when challenged by a competing "paradigm" that can explain more "data," will fall. In such a perspective "truth" is what "fits" the paradigm; what is "true" in one paradigm may turn out to be "not true" in another "paradigm." This is why postmoderns are suspicious of "truth claims."

33. Vanhoozer, "Theology and the Condition of Postmodernity," 10–11.

34. Ibid., 11. Vanhoozer offers this from the important analysis of Steven Best and Douglas Kellner *The Postmodern Turn* (New York: Guilford Press, 1997), xi. "Postmodernists reject unifying, totalizing, and universal schemes in favor of new emphases on difference, plurality, fragmentation, and complexity."

35. Ibid.

36. Carson, *Becoming Conversant with the Emerging Church*, 97.

37. Vanhoozer, "Theology and the Condition of Postmodernity," 11.

38. See Stanley J. Grenz and John R. Franke, *Beyond Foundationalism: Shaping Theology in a Postmodern Context* (Louisville: Westminster John Knox, 2001). These authors refer to the "demise of foundationalism." See also, Stanley Grenz, *Renewing the Center: Evangelical Theology in a Post-Theological Era* (Grand Rapids: Baker, 2000), chapter 6, entitled "Evangelical Theological Method After the Demise of Foundationalism."

39. The whole subject of evangelical anti-intellectualism, what caused it, how it was fostered, and the problems it created for evangelical faith is much too vast to consider in more detail here. The magisterial study on the subject is the venerable work of Richard Hofstadter, *Anti-intellectualism in American Life* (New York: Vintage, 1963). For a more recent analysis from an evangelical perspective, see Nancy Pearcy, *Total Truth* (Wheaton, Ill.: Crossway, 2004), 260–93. And we should mention an important work on the subject by Mark A. Noll, *The Scandal of the Evangelical Mind* (Grand Rapids: Eerdmans, 1994).

40. This is my own characterization. I call this "naïve intellectualism" because it naively accepts the notion that man's autonomous human reason is adequate for the task not only of building a worldview but for defending the faith.

41. Norman L. Geisler, "Butler, Joseph," in *Baker Encyclopedia of Christian Apologetics* (Grand Rapids: Baker, 1999), 108.

42. Norman L. Geisler, "Paley, William," in *Baker Encyclopedia*, 574.

43. Van Til writes, "And it is at this point that the weakness of the method of the defense of Christianity as advocated by Butler appears most clearly. It was based upon the assumption of brute facts and man's ability, apart from God [autonomous human reason] to explain at least some of them. . . . We need to challenge man's ability to interpret any fact unless that fact be created by God and unless man himself is created by God." From Greg L. Bahnsen, *Van Til's Apologetic: Readings and Analysis* (Phillipsburg, N.J.: Presbyterian and Reformed, 1998), 379.

44. For the scholarly side of the spectrum see J. P. Moreland and William Lane Craig, *Philosophical Foundations for a Christian Worldview* (Downers Grove, Ill.: InterVarsity, 2003).

For the popular side of the spectrum see Lee Strobel, *The Case for Christ: A Journalist's Personal Investigation of the Evidence of Jesus* (Grand Rapids: Zondervan, 1998).

45. See Charles Malik, "The Other Side of Evangelism," *Christianity Today*, November 7, 1980, 40. And see Charles Malik, *The Two Tasks*, (Westchester, Ill.: Cornerstone, 1980), 29–34.

46. See Van Til's outline of the problems with the method I have called naïve intellectualism and he calls "the Traditional Method." Greg L. Bahnsen, *Van Til's Apologetic: Readings and Analysis* (Phillipsburg, N.J.: Presbyterian and Reformed, 1998), 727–30.

47. Moreland and Craig, *Philosophical Foundations for a Christian Worldview*, 149.

48. Douglas Groothuis, *Truth Decay: Defending Christianity Against the Challenges of Postmodernism* (Downers Grove, Ill.: InterVarsity, 2000), 176.

49. Ibid., 179.

50. Ibid., 177. If Groothuis is correct, then those "basic forms of reasoning" are not distinctively Christian either!

51. Ibid., 176. Of course, Groothuis might see these forms of reasoning as "intrinsic to the rational nature God has granted us" (176), but the unbeliever is likely to see them not as granted to him by God but intrinsically his own or at least humankind's own, possessed and employed without reference to or permission of God. Therein is the idolatry!

52. Bruce Ellis Benson, *Graven Ideologies: Nietzsche, Derrida and Marion on Modern Idolatry* (Downers Grove, Ill.: InterVarsity, 2002), 42.

53. Stanley J. Grenz and John R. Franke, *Beyond Foundationalism: Shaping Theology in a Postmodern Context* (Louisville: Westminster John Knox, 2001), 10.

54. Ibid., 22.

55. Carl Raschke, *The Next Reformation: Why Evangelicals Must Embrace Postmodernity* (Grand Rapids: Baker, 2004), 24. He cites Groothuis as a prime example of this (cf., 21–22).

56. Raschke's portraits of the Reformers and presuppositionalism (Schaeffer) are "idiosyncratic" to say the least; his portrait of the French philosophers of postmodernism (Derrida, Deleuze) is skewed by being a bit too laudatory; his prescription to eliminate "inerrancy" is flawed as to its basic analysis and simply a mistake.

57. Carson, *Becoming Conversant with the Emerging Church*, 9.

58. Bruce D. McLaren, *A New Kind of Christian* (San Francisco: Jossey-Bass, 2001). This movement, or whatever it is, is much too large to attempt to engage in this study. The reader is strongly urged to consult Carson's book, which has been cited herein frequently already.

59. See, for instance, Millard J. Erickson, Paul Kjoss Helseth, Justin Taylor, eds., *Reclaiming the Center: Confronting Evangelical Accommodation in Postmodern Times* (Wheaton, Ill.: Crossway, 2004).

60. J. Wentzel Van Huyssteen, *Essays in Postfoundationalist Theology* (Grand Rapids: Eerdmans, 1997), 4.

61. Ibid.

62. Ibid. See also F. LeRon Shults, *The Postfoundationalist Task of Theology* (Grand Rapids: Eerdmans, 1999).

63. All "facts" are "facts" only in relation to the system in which they are identified. See Geisler, *Christian Apologetics*, 95.

64. Carson, *Becoming Conversant with the Emerging Church*, 122.

65. Vanhoozer, "Theology and the Condition of Postmodernity," 23.

66. Carson, *Becoming Conversant with the Emerging Church*, 103.

67. Ibid., 105.

68. Vanhoozer, "Theology and the Condition of Postmodernity," 16.

69. Graham Johnson, *Preaching to a Postmodern World* (Grand Rapids: Baker, 2001), 50.

70. Space does not permit me to develop this key point but see Sire, *Naming the Elephant*, chapter 3, 51–73.

71. Kant, *Critique of Pure Reason*, 7.

72. D. A. Carson, T*he Gospel According to John* (Grand Rapids: Eerdmans, 1991), 114. See Bertold Klappert, "Word," in *New International Dictionary of New Testament Theology*, vol. 3, ed. Colin Brown (Grand Rapids: Zondervan, 1978), 1116.

73. Thomas F. Torrance, *The Trinitarian Faith* (Edinburgh, Scotland: T & T Clark, 1988), 51; quoted in Colyer, *How to Read Torrance*, (Downers Grove, Ill.: InterVarsity, 2001), 130. Brackets added.

74. Thomas F. Torrance, *Space, Time and Resurrection* (Edinburgh, Scotland: T & T Clark, 1976), 1. This may be understood as advocating the methodological principle "ontology precedes epistemology."

75. Ibid., 13–14.

76. Ibid., 20.

77. Ibid.

78. Cornelius Van Til, "My Credo," in *Jerusalem and Athens* (Phillipsburg, N.J.: Presbyterian and Reformed, 1980), 14.

79. Carson, *Conversant with the Emerging Church*, 123.

80. Ibid., 123–24. Vanhoozer strikes a similar note when he writes, "Christians . . . know something about the true end of humanity. They know it not because they discovered it but because they were told. The knowledge claim that Christians make about human nature and destiny is based neither on speculation [rationalism?] nor observation [empiricism?] but on apostolic testimony. . . . Ultimately what theology wants to say to postmoderns concerns wisdom: about living in accordance with the shape of the life of God displayed in the life of Jesus." Vanhoozer, "Theology and the Condition of Postmodernity," 24.

81. Ibid., 122.

82. See N. T. Wright, *The Resurrection of the Son of God* (Minneapolis: Fortress, 2003), 710–717.

83. It is said that even the one who denies the reality of the external world will get out of the way of the bus!

84. http://www.reformed.org/apologetics/index.html

85. Several recent books on preaching to postmoderns may help us to be scripturally sound and culturally relevant. Already referenced is Johnston, *Preaching to a Postmodern World*; in addition note Craig A. Loscalzo, *Apologetics Preaching: Proclaiming Christ to a Postmodern World* (Downers Grove, Ill.: InterVarsity, 2000); and David J. Lose, *Confessing Jesus Christ: Preaching in a Postmodern World* (Grand Rapids: Eerdmans, 2003).

Chapter 8

PROCLAIMING JESUS THROUGH PASTORAL INTEGRITY

The Role of Old Testament Imagery in Jesus' Temptation

by Andrew J. Schmutzer

Temptation is one of those words that's fast losing synonyms in the English language and may disappear altogether. What does remain of the word is being redefined. To be tempted by Krispy Kremes, for example, suggests that one is the *passive victim* of a highly delectable doughnut. In popular thought, *temptation* signals a shift in blame, a rationalization that reassigns responsibility. *Temptation* has become a loaded term to legitimize a desire, so as to get us off the hook—but also one that leaves us wondering why we were tempted at all.[1]

While temptation is a common reality for believers, it is also commonly unpopular to talk about it. What will attract the unsaved to our churches if we actually address the "ins and outs" of temptation? In reality, the devastation of *sin*, the most unpopular word, and the fact that the church's statistics on "moral ills" now run neck-and-neck with society's, should sound a call for integrity. What's at stake biblically has been traded for a *sense* of what's at stake practically. Value has dethroned virtue.

So what can integrity mean when temptation is practically a taboo discussion? Churches seem to avoid the very topic as much as its leaders try to avoid its assault. The truth is, *how we view temptation has enormous implications for how we define sin, pursue ethics, explain maturity, understand "joy," participate in discipleship, and warn the reckless.* Our view of temptation also will affect how we restore the "fallen" who actually do drop the integrity ball.

Our dire need for integrity means the church now lives in a desperate hour. Professor Emeritus Howard Hendricks is fond of saying, "The greatest crisis in the church today is a crisis of leadership, and the greatest crisis of leadership today is the crisis of character." The frightening thing is that he's been saying that for over twenty years! At stake are not only the maturity of those within the body (Eph. 4:1–16), but also the credibility of the gospel for those who are watching believers.

THE ANTIDOTE IN TWO PARTS

Our struggle for integrity, by its very nature, must face the fuller reality of temptation. My suspicion is that asking "What would Jesus do?" helps some orient their feet in the right direction, but participating in the *Pilgrim's Progress* and its "journey theology" actually describes the road. After three years with Jesus, even His disciples didn't know "what to do," with some in His inner circle returning to fishing! Certainly, we can no longer anesthetize ourselves with a facade of Christlikeness when our primary human relationships reveal sin's cancer (Col. 3:5–9). I'm proposing an antidote to our struggle for integrity as we face the fuller reality of temptation. This two-part antidote is actually a reemphasis of two truths every Christian must embrace.

1. The Certainties of Scripture

Part of the antidote lies in *a return to the certainties of Scripture.*[2] The jury is not "out" on the foundational truths—certainties *can* exist.

Indeed, dialogue must make room for these certainties at the post-modern table that often disputes ultimate truth.[3] This requires an intellectually honest discussion where synthetic Christian "images" and "denominational expressions" are laid aside for *triage discipleship*, that is, discipleship with "teeth." Who would dare ignore an irregular heartbeat or a decaying tooth? Yet the analogy fits the spiritual health of our church culture all too well. What we are ignoring *is killing us*—body-life inside and testimony outside (cf. 1 Tim. 3:7).

Triage discipleship acknowledges, teaches, and deals with the hard issues of integrity—on Sunday as well as the other six days. Both symbolically and practically, it would help to formally establish local church ministries dedicated to biblical integrity, forgiveness, and restoration of the body of Christ.[4] Instead, the covert "small group" has become a dumping ground for many things the little sheep need to hear taught through, see wept over, and observe lived out by their shepherds.[5] Such certainties that lie behind orthodox convictions and core-value statements will only reemerge when the congregation listens in submission and biblical teachers issue challenges with empathy.

The apostle Paul reminds us that the Scriptures are "useful for teaching, rebuking, correcting, and training in righteousness" (2 Tim. 3:16 NIV). According to Grant Osborne, New Testament professor at Trinity Evangelical Divinity School: "The problem lies not so much with a disinterested laity but with a leadership that has capitulated to a myth, the myth that people do not want to be fed . . . [but] 'if we feed them they will come.'"[6]

This "training in righteousness" includes an equipping and warning about the biblical role of temptation in the life of the believer *and his local church*. Extolling integrity requires tackling temptation afresh; yes, both as a local church and as individuals! Pastors and teachers must actually read, teach, and discuss those biblical stories that embarrass and perplex us—publicly. This is the arena of sin's effect; it is also the arena of needed accountability. It's time to replace the "promise" of

Promise Keepers with "obedience." It's time to make good on all "pledges of purity" both by young and old. Doing so will restore the health of Christian families, the virtue of Christ's bride, and the respect of our ministries.

2. An Understanding of Temptation's Role in Our Lives

Second, the antidote also requires *an understanding of the function of temptation* within the broader scope of life. Scripture is utterly vital, but so is an awareness of our lives in the ongoing drama of God's work. This pertains to our "earthen vessels," as Paul describes our lives in 2 Corinthians 4:7. We must beware of lining up behind those who know more about the divine Bible than about the human struggle of living out that truth in "real time." The earthen vessels of broken, humble lives and the "treasure" of our salvation work together, even if some traditions shun the first and extol the second. When pastors and Bible teachers avoid discussion of pornography, eating disorders, and sexual abuse, they neither teach the young nor hold the older believer accountable.

Thankfully, *spiritual formation* is increasingly viewed as the believer's identity rather than a rescue. Yet preconversion habits of the heart take time to root out. Covering guilt and shame with spiritual things must give way to an honest evaluation and a change to Christ's righteousness.

This raises a significant truth. *Temptation presents believers with opportunities to display their stewardship and commitment to God's kingdom work.* Maybe we should reread the various facets in the "Disciples Prayer" (Matt. 6:9–13). Wrapped up in our daily experience of temptation are dynamic opportunities to make choices that either promote or default on our service in the life and program God has lain out for the church (Matt. 6:10a). Too long have we isolated and compartmentalized temptation as "my struggle," "my burden," or "my loss" as if personal-moral issues were *all* that's at stake. Consequently, any failure, if it's ever admitted, is strictly "mine." By far, this is how the contemporary church views temptation and, unfortunately, what many believe is all that's at stake.

Unfortunately, this view has not only lost sight of community, it has lost the perspective that our response to temptation also shapes our stewardship and effectiveness for God's present redemptive mission. The stiff upper lip of "image-keeping" tends to breed false humility, ignore relational accountability, and foster a critical spirit toward others who live differently. Biblical integrity, on the other hand, pertains to both heart-righteousness (vertical dimension) and ethical credibility among others (horizontal dimension). Biblical integrity also drives our stewardship for God; that is, how we carry out our *living role* in His redemptive drama, which will hurt or help our Lord.

Perhaps we can more keenly sense Paul's fear of being "disqualified" from his ministry (1 Cor. 9:27) for lack of appropriate control (9:24–26).[7] His imagery is that of an athlete's rigorous discipline, *in order to enable service rather than hinder it.*

The temptation that all believers experience mingles an "internal push" with an "external pull," inner lust with outer lure. The effect includes doubting God's goodness, unbelief toward His perfect plans, and rebellion toward His Word. The strategies Satan uses in temptation are tailor-made for the right external pull.[8] There is always a twofold result when one gives in to temptation: rejection of God's will as just and good, on the one hand,[9] and defaulting on one's role in the Redeemer's universal mission, on the other.

The "internal push," James reminds us, distinctly emerges from within: "Each one is tempted when, by his own evil desire, he is dragged away and enticed" (1:14 NIV). We need to stop blaming the Devil for so many choices we make. Our own internal lusts often prove to be the Devil's best ally against God's work and the unity of His people (cf. Gal. 5:13–21). However, Jesus' own temptation differs in this key area: He had no "internal push" toward evil. Yet, as we will see, the temptation was not only real for Jesus (Heb. 2:18), but the Devil's "external pull" worked in ways we need to be more aware of.

THE BAPTISM OF CHRIST AND
ITS OLD TESTAMENT IMAGERY (MATT. 4:1–11)

The Old Testament (OT) is the "theological dictionary" of the New Testament (NT).[10] Its writers used specific genres, key terms, topographical symbols, and a host of rich images to communicate to their audience.

John the Baptist's preaching is no different, capitalizing on the people's familiarity with OT themes in his stinging call to repentance (Matt. 3:1–12; cf. 4:17).[11] In Matthew's account, the temptation of Jesus is intimately tied to the language of John's baptism scene. A study of Jesus' temptation reveals these connections.

Images Associated with John and His Baptism of Jesus

As a person, John is presented as "Elijah-like" since he is offering renewal to Israel (cf. 1 Kings 18:21). His preaching is the final prophetic installment of covenant renewal (Mal. 4:5–6). His wilderness location calls the people to acknowledge their current state of "spiritual exile," for they must trek out to "see him" (Matt. 3:1; cf. 11:7–9).[12] John has in mind a "new exodus" built on Moses' work (cf. Psalm 114) and Isaiah's prophecy (40:3). Their repentance in the Jordan valley reenacts Moses' earlier covenant renewal at the edge of the Jordan (Deut. 9:1ff), for repentance in the OT can include a returning a place of origin to begin again.[13] It is here that Jesus emerges, at a new "Jordan crossing" with a purified remnant.

Jesus' baptism was not for repentance but to model for Israel true submission to and endorsement of John's words, fulfilling Israel's covenant requirements (Matt. 3:15; cf. 5:17).[14] Jesus would prove a model of obedience to God's law, the very law He would quote during

His temptation. The divine Son (3:17) will relive core experiences of the "national son" (Ex. 4:22; Deut. 8:5),[15] but succeed where Israel had failed.[16] Jesus is God's Son since He is David's heir.[17] It is vital for us to see how the Father's testimony plays into Jesus' ensuing temptation.

John's voice was one of preparation, but it is the Father's declaration that formally breaks the silence of four hundred years: "This is my Son, whom I love; with him I am well pleased" (Matt. 3:17 NIV). Their combined voices constitute the OT legal requirement of two witnesses. The "opened heavens" (3:16) signal a new era, marked by new revelation. Yet the actual words are not new; in fact, God the Father alludes to three OT texts in His witness. "This is my Son"[18] draws on Psalm 2:7, a king's personal testimony of his adopted "messiahship" and commission by the Lord. The Father's declaration officially commissions Jesus for ministry as *the* ultimate anointed Messiah (cf. Mark 1:1; Ps. 2:2).[19] According to contemporary rabbinic thought, the dove reflects Israel,[20] but more likely signals a new era of life analogous to Noah's dove (Gen. 8:8–11).[21] Regardless, it is the greater Son now in focus. Essentially, the Spirit anoints Jesus, authorizing His ministry (Acts 10:38).[22]

The second OT text in the Father's declaration (in Matt. 3:17 NIV) signals that the kingly reign of this Messiah will indeed be different: "my Son . . . with him I am well pleased" alludes to Isaiah 42:1.[23] The tenor of the Servant Songs (Isa. 40–55) portrays a role of affliction and personal sacrifice, but coupled with Psalm 2:7, Matthew's point becomes clear —Jesus will be a suffering King!

Third is a more opaque reference in the middle phrase: "my Son, whom I love"—probably an echo of Genesis 22:2, a text Paul similarly uses (Rom. 8:32; cf. Matt. 12:18). Abraham's profound obedience and submission to God's command to sacrifice Isaac had an acute effect on Israel's theological imagination. Jesus is the only Son, whom the Father loves, yet whom He is willing to sacrifice for the sake of the world. Similarly, Jesus is being called to imitate Isaac's quiet availability.[24]

We can now grasp the weight of the Father's pronouncement, for it gives Jesus His "fundamental theological orientation for His ministry,"[25] His guidelines to undertake His mission. In the end, the declaration of the Father combined divine Sonship of the royal Messiah with the Spirit's endowment of the Servant of the Lord.

Kingship Language

All this emerges from the OT Scriptures and progressively raises the status of Jesus to both audience and reader. Not surprisingly, the cross event will find kingship language reemerging: "This is Jesus the King of the Jews" (Matt. 27:37). [26]

As Dumbrell observes, "The office of messiah is thus not one that grows out of disappointment with the empirical monarchy . . . but rises with the advent of kingship itself."[27] Notions of kingship came early, beginning with the patriarchs and uniquely defining David.[28] With Jesus' temptation, a four-step "process" is achieved. Note the following pattern:

1. *Selected* by God (1 Sam. 16:1—David; cf. Matt. 3:17—Jesus)
2. *Anointed* by God's prophet (1 Sam. 16:13—David; cf. Matt. 3:16–17—Jesus)
3. *Endowed* for office by the Spirit (1 Sam. 16:13—David; cf. Matt. 3:16—Jesus)
4. *Attested* by public military act(s) (1 Sam. 17—David; cf. Matt. 4:1–11ff.—Jesus)

Amazingly, these four elements that distinguished David (and Saul) are not associated with another king until we arrive at the ideal kingship manifested in the ministry of Jesus.[29] With Jesus' temptation, cosmic hostility erupts on the redemptive stage.

THE TEMPTATION OF CHRIST AND
ITS OLD TESTAMENT IMAGERY

For Matthew, the parallels to Jesus' temptation focus on Israel's wilderness experience[30] and Moses' life. The exodus imagery forms a strong Christological reflection.[31] Broadly speaking, Jesus also "passes through" water, moves into a wilderness, and experiences the core tests of hunger, self-denial, and idolatry that Israel did. In fact, Matthew capitalizes on themes from Deuteronomy 6–8 where Moses explained how a series of tests would determine Israel's devotion to the Lord. Jesus will be tested as the ideal Israelite. As Israel's champion He will fight on behalf and as a representative of His people, using the law as a greater Moses.[32] Additionally, the texts Jesus quotes are all taken from the passages where Moses explains the significance and very goal of Israel's wilderness testing (cf. Deut. 8:1–5).

We can better appreciate the context of the temptation by observing in Matthew's gospel the geographical orientation of Jesus' ministry.[33]

A   Genealogy, birth, and the infancy narrative of Jesus (1:8–2:23)

B   Jesus in **Judea**: baptism, *temptation*, and preparation (3:1–4:17)

C   Public ministry around **Galilee**; preparing the disciples (4:18–10:42)

X   Response to Jesus' public ministry—the kingdom parables (11:1–16:20)

C' Private ministry in **Galilee**; preparing the disciples (16:21–18:35)

B' Jesus in **Judea**: from Palm Sunday to Passover (19:1–26:13)

A' Suffering, death, and resurrection of Jesus (26:14 –28:20)

In this concentric pattern, the outside pertains to Judea, recounting Jesus' baptism and temptation, on the one hand, and His passion and death on the other (A, B, B', A'). The inner portion reveals Jesus' ministry in Galilee (C, C') with the central core being Jesus' seven parables on the kingdom (X).

The Account: Disputation and Dialogue

The actual temptation account is triadic, composed of three separate units (Matt. 1–4, 5–7, 8–11). Each unit is highly stylized, reflecting a literary genre of rabbinic *disputation* or debate.[34] These scenes are unified through an increase of geographical elevations: "up . . . into the wilderness" (4:1), "on the pinnacle of the temple" (4:5), and culminating with "a very high mountain" (4:8).[35] Each encounter begins with the narrator's note of a key location and is then followed by a confrontational dialogue. As for the characters, the Devil is the resourceful initiator and Jesus the vigorous responder. With each temptation the Devil issues a proposition that brings a swift and climactic retort from Jesus, formally closing that "exchange."

In fact, it is *dialogue* that makes this temptation scene unique as Jesus and the Devil wage war with words.[36] While the Devil uses "Son of God" (4:3, 6), Jesus will twice respond with "Lord your God" (4:7, 10). Twice the Devil states: "If [since] You are the Son of God" (4:3, 6), a statement that builds on the Father's earlier pronouncement of Jesus' identity as "My beloved Son" (3:17).[37] The Devil's first two propositions ("if You are") conclude with a bald temptation (4:3, 6; cf. v. 8), a movement from personal to universal as the issue of sovereignty culminates Jesus' temptations.

The Issue: Self-Seeking or Submissive Son

The issue is not whether Jesus is God's Son, but what *kind* of Son He will be—a self-seeking Son or submissive Savior. The fact that Jesus includes a direct reference to "God" in all three responses reveals His submission to His Father (4:4b, 7b, 10b). Jesus is under authority, tested by authority before He can assert His own authority.[38] This language and dialogue add a personal flavor to Jesus' encounter. While

Jesus' temptations do not occur in a public forum, the didactic lessons are clear, nonetheless. What transpires is richly typological,[39] deeply Christological[40], and highly supernatural.[41] The narrator opens with the Holy Spirit leading and closes with angels ministering (4:1, 11). The following diagram shows the structure and content of Matthew's account, along with the OT allusions in Jesus' temptation.

	TEMPTATION 1	TEMPTATION 2	TEMPTATION 3
Synoptic Texts:	Matt. 4:3–4; Luke 4:3–4; cf. Mark 1:12–13	Matt. 4:5–7; Luke 4:9–12; cf. Mark 1:12–13	Matt. 4:8–10; Luke 4:5–8; cf. Mark 1:12–13
Location:	Wilderness	Temple	Mountain
Devil's Proposition:	"feed Yourself"	"throw Yourself"	"worship me"
OT Precedent:	Ex. 16:2–8 (Israel's hunger)	Ex. 17:1–7 (Israel's rebellion)	Ex. 32:1–35 (Israel's idolatry)
Jesus' Quotation:	Deut. 8:3 "not live by bread alone"	Deut. 6:16 "shall not put the Lord your God to the test"	Deut. 8:13 (NIV) "serve Him only"
"Shema" Correspondence:	Deut. 6:5a (NIV) "all your heart"	Deut. 6:5b (NIV) "all your soul [life]"	Deut. 6:5c (NIV) "all your strength"
Related NT Texts:	John 6:35; cf. 1 John 2:15–17	Heb. 4:14–15; cf. 1 Cor. 10:1–13	Heb. 1:6; cf. 2:18; James 4:7

The Encounter: Meeting with the Devil

"*Then* Jesus was led up" (4:1; italics added) reflects one of several connections between His baptism and temptation, involving "the Spirit" again (cf. 3:16). Isaiah noted earlier that God had "led" His people in the wilderness (63:14; cf. Psalm 107:7). Moreover, mention of the Spirit's agency ultimately marks the entire temptation as God's doing,[42] expressly for Jesus' testing.[43] Jesus shows that He is the archetypical "man of the Spirit."[44]

"Devil" means "accuser," as does "Satan" in the OT (cf. 4:10). "Satan" was more title than name, but increasingly was viewed as Israel's prosecuting attorney (cf. 1 Chron. 21:1; Zech. 3:1).[45] In Scripture, testing often functions as a rite of confirmation, much as Abraham had experienced a "proving" (Gen. 22:1).[46] In other words, God *tests* to prove the quality of commitment and obedience, while the Devil *tempts* to destruct and derail (cf. Deut. 13:3; Psalm 81:7; Job 2:3–4). Matthew shows the reader that the Devil is operating under God's control (cf. Job 1:11–12).

The Encounter: The Locations

Reflecting Israel's experience, Jesus is ejected into the wilderness by God (cf. Ex. 5:3; 8:27). Moses had reminded the nation: "Remember how the LORD your God led you all the way in the desert these forty years, to humble you and to test you in order to know what was in your heart, whether or not you would keep his commands" (Deut. 8:2f NIV). The wilderness (4:1) is one of three topographical locations Matthew stipulates, adding "temple" (4:5) and "mountain" (4:8). All three sites function as OT eschatological locations, that is, major points of divine contact and revelation in Israel's history and Jesus' teaching of the kingdom.

Israel's exodus became synonymous with their wilderness travels, but also tension with God.[47] Between Egypt and the Promised Land, God used the wilderness as His crucible for spiritual and national development.[48] The antithesis of safety and supply, the wilderness was essentially negative,[49] a place of hunger and the haunt of evil spirits (Ps. 107:4–5; Matt. 12:43).[50] The wilderness was "a precondition for both covenant and land,"[51] prompting submission and trust to God. But devoid of resources for life, the wilderness highlighted vulnerability—Israel's and Jesus'.

Matthew capitalizes on this wilderness motif as the place where Jesus' call must be tested.[52] Abraham's test previewed Israel's experience, providing a dramatic analogy for Jesus' testing. In contrast to Israel, however, Jesus depends on God's direct care.

The "temple" was the center of Jewish faith, elevating YHWH— God Jehovah—above all competing deities and, therefore, linked to political rule. The core function of the temple was worship, assuring any person of YHWH's presence at the temple (1 Kings 8:12–13). Moreover, the temple was the cosmic "center" of the world, guaranteeing order, justice, and life itself (Pss. 46; 48; 84; 87).[53]

Although Matthew's "high mountain" was symbolic and visionary (4:8a), it forms a thematic extension from the temple (4:5b), since temples were built atop mountains.[54] Zion, and the temple built there, are the "cosmic mountain," replicating the heavenly mountain of YHWH at Mt. Horeb/Sinai (cf. Ps. 48:1–4).[55] In OT imagery divine councils occurred on mountains (Isa. 14:13; cf. Ex. 24:12–18). Matthew's mountain imagery draws numerous analogies to Moses' life and Israel's own worship. Theophanies occurred at Mt. Horeb/Sinai (Ex. 3–4; 32–34) and divine decrees were made there (Ex. 19–20). When Jesus views the "kingdoms of the world and their glory" (Matt. 4:8), the event echoes Moses' climb of Mt. Nebo to survey the Promised Land (Deut. 32:49–52; 34:1–8). But imagery related to Moses doesn't stop here.

The Timing of the Temptation

Jesus' fast recalls the same experience of Moses and Israel (Ex. 24:18; 34:28; Deut. 8:2–3).[56] With Jesus' fasting "forty days and forty nights," Matthew emphasizes the typological number (i.e., "forty") in its correspondence to Moses and Israel rather than Jesus' growing state of hunger. By adding "forty nights," Matthew clearly conforms Jesus' fasting to Moses' forty-day-and-night fast.[57] Jesus' fast is preparatory for ministry, reflecting appeal for divine assistance in a time of danger (cf. Est. 4:15–16)[58] and even preparation for "war" (cf. 1 Sam. 7:6).[59] Engaging the Devil, Jesus fights a "new Canaanite"[60] and emerges as the triumphant champion on behalf of His people.[61]

According to Matthew, the Devil tempts Jesus *after* His forty-day fast (cf. Luke 4:2). In this way the Devil's approach capitalizes on Jesus' physical weakness (first temptation), then moves to the insecurity of life (second temptation), climaxing with the attraction of idolatry as a solution (third temptation).[62] Just how Jesus overcomes the "tempter" (Matt. 4:3a) requires another look at the makeup of these temptations.[63] We'll briefly consider the Devil's proposals, then the substance of Jesus' answers.

The Nature of the Temptations

Throughout the three temptations it is the *nature* of Jesus' Sonship that's at stake, not its fact.[64] What is often misunderstood, however, is the actual goal of these temptations. The Devil's ploy is to construct scenarios that tempt Jesus to rely on His Sonship in self-serving ways.[65] External seduction rather than internal lust is the Devil's ploy here.[66] Yet because we tend to read these as isolated moral tests, we fail to appreciate the gravity of what's really at stake: a redemptive mission extending beyond Jesus' personal moral fortitude, though requiring it. In essence, the Devil is attempting to lure Jesus away from His redemptive messianic mission. While we might assume that serious temptations would, at some level, involve "money, sex, and power," the Devil's attack is more sophisticated than that. What, for example, was so treacherous about Jesus' making bread (4:3)?

The Devil's propositions amount to three different "paths" Jesus could take as messianic deliverer; that is, each temptation reflects a popular expectation of the messianic role within the prevailing culture of that time.[67] We could call the first temptation *the way of the populist* (4:3–4).[68] Would the messianic Son provide for His own physical needs or trust His Father's provision? Making bread would not only satiate

Jesus' hunger, as a social strategy it would also give the masses what they want (cf. Matt. 14:17; John 6:7, 26).[69] But grateful masses of people would come at the cost of Jesus' self-satisfaction. So Jesus refuses to be a messianic magician, creating a "new manna" for Himself.

The second temptation is *the way of the wonder worker* (4:6–7). Would the messianic Son place Himself in mortal danger and force God to deliver Him since His Father does dwell in the temple? As a strategy, forcing His Father into a spectacular deliverance at an international location would surely galvanize the crowds. But dazzled crowds at the sacred site would not justify divine protection merely for Jesus' self-vindication. So Jesus refuses the role of deluded visionary and the demonstration of divine authorization for His ministry in this manner.

The final temptation could be termed *the way of the political opportunist* (4:9–10). Would the messianic Son use instant wealth, profile, and even militaristic shortcuts to attain power? As a strategy such influence could liberate an oppressed nation. But redemption is for relationship and not social revolution or self-promotion.[70] So Jesus refuses this means of universal recognition in exchange for "all the kingdoms of the world" (4:8).

The Devil's temptations use external *seduction*: from dependence to self-assertion (i.e., bread), from trust to coercion (i.e., danger), from allegiance to betrayal (i.e., power). Giving in to these temptations was not about Jesus' personal piety, but His recognition of an unacceptable detour from His redemptive mission. The Devil's temptations were intended to remove the cost of sacrifice and the necessity of self-denial, thereby derailing Jesus from *the way of the cross* (cf. Heb. 2:18; 4:15; 5:8).

In each successive temptation Jesus not only responds with Scripture ("It stands written . . . " [Matt. 4:4, 7, 10]), He uses texts exclusively from Deuteronomy (i.e., bread [Deut. 8:3], danger [Deut. 6:16], power [Deut. 6:13]). More than citing proof texts from the law, Jesus shows His penetrating grasp of Scripture by referencing key portions rooted in the wilderness experience of Israel's own testing (Deut. 6–8). God had desired *humility* from the nation's testing (Deut. 8:16). Jesus' parry with the Devil reveals His commitment and obedience to the covenant as a new Moses. Yet as with an iceberg, more is happening beneath the surface than merely a duel with the Devil through use of Scripture.

References to Deuteronomy

Jesus' references to Deuteronomy come from Moses' "second address" (4:44–28:68)—the very heart of the book, with its call to love God.[71] Here Moses' tone is one of exhortation, calling for covenant loyalty to God. Jesus strategically uses Moses' Deuteronomy "preaching" to Israel about their past rather than citing the historical events themselves from the book of Exodus. In this way, Israel's demand for food (Ex. 16:2–8) and God's provision of manna (Ex. 16:13–31) stand in the background in Jesus' claim that "man does not live on bread alone, but on every word . . . " (Matt. 4:4 and Deut. 8:3 NIV).

Whereas Israel had shown an untrusting heart, Jesus illustrates how covenant obedience to God's eternal *Word* is more important than temporal bread. Moreover, Israel's rebellion at Massah and Meribah (Ex. 17:1–3) and God's provision of water (Ex. 17:4–7) is the backdrop for Jesus' claim not to "put the Lord your God to the test" (Matt. 4:7 and Deut. 6:16). Whereas Israel tested God by doubting His presence with them, Jesus emphatically refuses to test God's rescuing presence.

Finally, Israel's idolatry with the "golden calf" (Ex. 32:1–35), resolved only by Moses' intercession (Ex. 32:11–14), is the backdrop for Jesus' retort: "Worship the Lord your God, and serve Him only" (Matt. 4:10 and Deut. 6:13).[72] The people's actions brought God to the brink of canceling His covenant with them (Ex. 32:8–10).[73] In a parody of the tabernacle construction (Ex. 25:1–9), the people had built a golden calf (Ex. 32:1–6) and in so doing broke the first two commandments. Jesus, on the other hand, makes no concession and refuses any substitute for God's presence, proving His loyalty and love for God.

Jesus' allusions to the exodus while citing Deuteronomy raise some important observations. First, Jesus achieves a symbolic second "preaching" of Deuteronomy as a new Moses for a purified remnant. If these covenantal texts defined Israel's mission, how much more for the eschatological Son. Second, Matthew arranges Jesus' Deuteronomy quotations (Deut. 8:3; 6:16; 6:13) to preserve the chronological order of the Exodus events (Ex. 16:2–8; 17:1–7; 32:1–6). This, in turn, highlights Matthew's rich themes and the typology he draws between the national son and the divine Son. Typologically, the significance of Jesus' obedience in the wilderness is a study in contrasts, since it was there that Israel had enraged God with her rebellion and apostasy.[74]

Third, and most significant, Matthew has set the order of Jesus' temptations to reflect the form of the *Shema* (Deut. 6:5).[75] By implication, loving God with one's *heart*[76] meant the refusal to make bread in self-interest; *life* ("soul")[77] meant the refusal to jump and capitalize on divine protection; *might*[78] was tied to idolatry and the refusal to worship the Devil in exchange for the kingdoms of the world. Viewing the temptations in light of the Shema explains the movement beginning with the inner being, adding the whole person, and concluding with all one claims as one's own. For his part, the Devil quotes Psalm 91:11–12 out of context, omitting "in all your ways" since a deliberate throwing does not correspond to accidental stumbling.[79] The temple was a place of refuge, not presumption, and the Son was to serve the Father, not vice-versa. "He who dwells in the shelter of the Most High" (Psalm 91:1) began precious words in a psalm of protection, but the Devil twisted it for a dare! While the Devil's use of Psalm 91 was Christ-centered, it was not *God*-centered![80]

Following Jesus' second refusal and His mention of "God," the Devil cunningly substitutes *himself* for God in the final temptation, offering Jesus the whole world in exchange for His submission.[81] Because this last temptation attacks the foundation of the covenant relationship that bound Israel to God, Jesus counters with the core theme of Deuteronomy—exclusive covenant commitment to the Lord.[82] Satan is, after all, representing the interests of his own kingdom (Matt. 12:26). Significantly, Jesus was already committed to His Father's redemptive mission and could cite commands and their context to defend His calling. For Jesus to know was to obey. No additional reasoning was necessary.[83] So the only extemporaneous words of Jesus are reserved for Satan's banishment: "Go, Satan!"

Seeing beyond the personal moment, Jesus rightly viewed His temptations as redemptive distortions and stayed on the path of pain and suffering to follow His Father's will. There simply could be no messianic kingdom without the cross.[84] Having rejected food and angelic assistance, He receives both at the end (4:11).[85] Hailed as king (Matt. 2:2), He chose the crown of thorns, and the divine King finally *reigned from the cross* under the title "King of the Jews" (Matt. 27:37).[86] Unlike Israel, He demanded neither food nor miracle. Messianic expectations were not met on the triumphalist terms of the masses but through trust in His Father. Jesus' temptation clearly shows the cost of His Sonship.[87] As Evans states: "Having accepted God's rule for himself, Jesus has begun to proclaim the rule of God for all of Israel. By remaining loyal to God, *Jesus remains qualified*, as God's 'son' (Mark 1:11), to proclaim God's kingdom."[88]

His stewardship was complete, His mission accomplished, and one day He would even provide a "new manna" for His people (Matt. 14:13–21; 15:32–38). On another mountain, Jesus announces that all earthly power is His, but it came from God and *after* the cross (Matt. 28:18).[89]

INTEGRITY GUARDS CHRIST'S REDEMPTIVE MISSION

Cosmic Effects of Temptation

Temptation not only destroys, it also forfeits, with cosmic effects. Three months after 9/11/2001 and the surprise terrorist attacks on the United States, Peter Jackson's film *Fellowship of the Ring* released into theaters. As the first film in The Lord of the Rings trilogy, *Fellowship of the Ring* played worldwide to large audiences; yet in America it had a uniquely salve-like effect. The core reason, I believe, was that it brilliantly portrayed the struggle of good and evil with an honesty and clarity the public was craving to believe but could hardly admit. It was an epic picture of a cosmic battle. It helped realign a nation's moral compass as it taught a shocked society how to live with heavy burdens and face permanent losses.

In the film, we watched little people—Hobbits—doing big things on a cosmic scale, and we came away strangely comforted. We marveled with Lord Elrond that young Frodo withstood the evil power of the ring, initially. The presence of temptation and our fight against it can be viewed as a "celebration of self-denial" for the cause of Christ, which remains clear on the horizon. It is the upright who struggle and are tested.[90]

Stanley Grenz explains this irony:

> We repeatedly discover that the intensity to which we sense the force of the onslaught of temptation corresponds to the degree to which we are resisting it. In those areas where we are especially vulnerable, we know little of the power of temptation. In such situations we yield to the evil impulse without a struggle, sometimes even without perceiving our own defeat. In other areas—areas where we are gaining victory over the tempter—we have a greater sense of its power . . . [Jesus] was completely cognizant of what was at stake in the choices placed before him. And he was entirely conscious of the cosmic implications of the decisions he needed to make.[91]

However, the danger of defining temptation strictly in terms of personal integrity is that, ironically, self often gets enshrined in false humility. In this scenario some sterile image of righteousness has become the endgame, and shaming others squeezes out dependence and forgiveness. According to these rules, believers only speak of "those sins" they *don't* do, as if that makes their sins on the record less offensive.

Frankly, this illustrates the danger of pursuing a kind of "selective holiness": a malignant narcissism takes over that simply cannot see God's redemptive work occurring at a cosmic level. Deeds of sin and righteousness can have far-reaching effects in the lives of others, long after we're gone. Much as tree rings reveal drought and nourishing years that go back decades, so our acts of sin—and righteousness—can have a lasting impact.

Don't misunderstand; integrity is absolutely crucial, but it was never meant to function alone, merely preserving self. As Jesus' temptation illustrates, it's not about one individual seeking personal holiness, far more is actually at stake.[92] Beyond one's personal trial, temptation threatens to sever a lifeline of dynamic relationships—in the way the liver "catches and disposes of" toxins, relationships can snag integrity issues and purify us. The result of not being honest about sin is a damaged reputation, marred relationships, or a corruption of responsibilities.[93]

A Worthy Model: Jesus' Response to Temptation

Jesus' temptation and His response reveal a biblical pattern: *temptation → integrity → stewardship*. That temptations will come in life and ministry is a given; that integrity will be there to stare them down is another matter. With integrity, the battles are spiritual, the vision is eternal, and the reputation at stake is Christ's. The role of integrity is one of gatekeeper, interrogating each and every "option" that comes, probing for everything from the faddish to the false. Biblical integrity is what qualifies the believer to march in step with God's parade, pursuing kingdom aims on a far grander stage. Integrity that is conscious of stewardship is both heart-righteous (vertical dimension) and ethically credible (horizontal dimension).

Observing this pattern (*temptation →integrity →stewardship*) helps us face temptation at deeper levels. We must not only internalize Scripture's standards, we must avoid the Devil's example of "selective application." Particular sections of Scripture must be handled in a manner that is faithful to that context. The full counsel of Scripture is our aid, giving us discernment with the "mind of Christ."[94] Temptation is often a grand distortion of an essential good: *relevance*—but for sheer demonstration?; the *spectacular*—but for applause?; or *influence*—but for my empire or Christ's kingdom?[95] Can we see through the physically full, physically safe, and politically powerful, to kingdom implications?[96] Like Jesus resisting the tempter's call to make bread to satisfy personal hunger, we must be able to see beyond the possible, and even the fair, to the issues of stewardship on a redemptive horizon. Put another way, temptation can involve "the desire for a good thing, but in a wrong way."[97] Biblically speaking, our struggle with temptation is essential in the process of our character formation and maturity.

We are perplexed by His temptation and embarrassed by ours. We must train heart and hand for cosmic battle—there lies the battleground of stewardship. Jesus doesn't model the mechanical quotation of Scripture, but grasps the implications of the text. If we do not commit to the program of Scripture, and have a re-texting of our hearts, we will increasingly struggle to sort out the life-giving from the death-giving voices;[98] and temptation, along with suffering, will become entirely unpalatable. We will forget that suffering precedes glory. We will forget His example of devotion to the Father.

Spiritual maturity, moral character, and social accountability may be the strands of the integrity rope, but the larger goal is obedient *stewardship* in the redemptive mission of Christ. Temptation is testing within a community, a community we must lean on and learn from. As Dietrich

Bonhoeffer wrote, "[He] who can no longer listen to his brother will soon be no longer listening to God either."[99] Integrity keeps us "on course," effectively participating in God's kingdom work. Embracing this stewardship helps us gain victory in temptation. In this context, temptation can indicate strength rather than weakness. "The greater one's capacities, the greater one's temptations can be."[100] But such stewardship for God is not possible if we have in mind mere human concerns, rather than the concerns of God (Matt. 16:23). We must remember that we've been called to obedience, not success.

If we lose such words as "temptation" and "evil," it will increase the distance between language and reality. We will exchange *Pilgrim's Progress* for *Pollyanna*, and surrender the cosmic for the cute.[101] Maybe more than ever, the church needs shepherds with a vision of moral clarity. Without the language of temptation, we cannot even be honest with ourselves. Without a cosmic vision of stewardship, all of us will be impoverished.[102] Temptation truly has a "bigger picture," and Jesus didn't mince words when He taught us to pray. Concern for kingdom work, the Father's will, evil, and even bread reappear—all in the context of community.[103]

> *"Our Father in heaven,*
> *hallowed be your name,*
> *your kingdom come,*
> *your will be done,*
> *on earth as it is in heaven.*
> *Give us today our daily bread.*
> *Forgive us our debts,*
> *as we also have forgiven our debtors.*
> *And lead us not into temptation,*
> *but deliver us from the evil one."*[104]

Andrew J. Schmutzer is associate professor of Bible at the Moody Bible Institute. He has earned the Ph.D. degree from Trinity Evangelical Divinity School, Deerfield, Illinois, and degrees from Dallas Theological Seminary and Moody Bible Institute.

NOTES

1. Harry Lee Poe, *See No Evil: The Existence of Sin in an Age of Relativism* (Grand Rapids: Kregel, 2004), 152.

2. D. A. Carson, and John D. Woodbridge, *Letters Along the Way* (Wheaton, Ill.: Crossway, 1993), 90.

3. For an excellent discussion of postmodernism's struggle with truth in general and correspondence theory in particular, see J. P. Morland, "Truth, Contemporary Philosophy, and the Postmodern Turn," *Journal of the Evangelical Theological Society* 48, no. 1 (2005): 77–88.

4. Helpful essays can be found in *God and the Victim: Theological Reflections on Evil, Victimization, Justice, and Forgiveness*, ed. L. B. Lampman (Grand Rapids: Eerdmans, 1999); and R. L. Brosning and R. A. Reed, *Forgiveness, Reconciliation, and Moral Courage* (Grand Rapids: Eerdmans, 2004).

5. See the excellent discussion of pride and humility in leadership in C. Maki, "Gentile Giants: The Paradox of Authority and Humility in Christian Leadership," *Evangelical Journal* 18, no. 1 (2000): 29–48.

6. "Christianity Challenges Postmodernism," *Evangelical Journal* 15, no. 1 (1997): 15; see also E. A. Martins, "Moving from Scripture to Doctrine," *Bulletin for Biblical Research* 15, no. 1 (2005): 77–103.

7. Paul's appeal to his own behavior (8:13) leads into an extended account of his apostolic practice in general; see S. C. Barton, "'All Things to All People': Paul and the Law in the Light of 1 Corinthians 9:19–23," *Paul and the Mosaic Law*, ed. J. D. G. Dunn (Tübingen, Germany: J. C. B. Mohr, 1996), 271–86.

8. Luther warned, "Don't argue with the Devil. He has had five thousand years of experience. He has tried out all his tricks on Adam, Abraham, and David, and he knows exactly the weak spots" (quoted by Carson and Woodbridge, *Letters*, 103).

9. C. G. Kromminga, "Temptation," *Evangelical Dictionary of Theology*, W. A. Elwell, ed. (Grand Rapids: Baker, 1984), 1072.

10. J. Goldingay, "The Old Testament and Christian Faith: Jesus and the Old Testament in Matthew 1–5, Part 2," *Themelios* 8, no.2 (1983): 5.

11. E.g., such notions/phrases as: "heaven is at hand," "flee the coming wrath," "the ax at the root of the trees," "harvesting," and "burning chaff." "Harvest" imagery is a common medium to describe judgment in the OT (Isa. 17:13; Jer. 13:24; 15:7; 51:33; Joel 3:12–14).

12. William J. Dumbrell, *The Search for Order* (Eugene, Ore.: Wipf & Stock, 2001), 182. John's animal-skin clothing and diet of locusts with wild honey is not only that of an "exiled" person, but of one avoiding unclean food (Matt. 3:4; cf. Gen. 3:21; Ex. 10:4; 2 Kings 1:8; 2 Macc. 5:27).

13. Ibid., 161.

14. Dumbrell, *The Search*, 163.

15. Cf. Hos. 11:1 with Matt. 2:15.

16. According to E. E. Ellis, "A case can be made out that Matthew has in mind Christ as the 'embodiment' of Israel," (*Paul's Use of the Old Testament* [Grand Rapids: Baker, 1981], 132).

17. Cf. 2 Sam. 7:14; Luke 1:32; Matt. 16:16; John Goldingay, *Old Testament Theology: Israel's Gospel*, vol. 1 (Downers Grove, Ill.: InterVarsity, 2003), 817.

18. The account in the NIV reads: "You are my Son" rather than "This is my Son" in the parallel accounts (cf. Mark 1:11; Luke 3:22), making Matthew's wording beneficial both to Jesus personally and to the crowd as a public pronouncement.

19. C. L. Blomberg, *Matthew*, New American Commentary (Nashville: Broadman, 1992), 82. Two Qumran texts connect the title "son of God" with the anticipated apocalyptic leader (messiah) to be sent by God (4Q246 [= 4QpsDan ar^a]; 4Q174 [= 4QFlor 10–14]; cf. Targum Isa 42:1).

20. H. L. Strack and P. Billerbeck, *Kommentar zum Neuen Testament aus Talmud und Midrasch,* vol. 1 (Munich: C. H. Beck, 1922), 123–25.

21. Goldingay, *Old Testament Theology*, 816; cf. Ps. 55:6–8.

22. Ibid.; Craig S. Keener, *Bible Background Commentary: New Testament* (Downers Grove, Ill.: InterVarsity, 1994), 53.

23. For a discussion of Isaiah's "servant" (42:1–12), also energized by the Spirit, see Robert B. Chisholm Jr., *Handbook on the Prophets* (Grand Rapids: Baker, 2002), 99–101.

24. Goldingay, *The Old Testament*, 5.

25. Ibid.

26. See also Matt. 26:29; Luke 23:42, 51; John 3:5; esp. Mark 15:2, 9, 12, 18, 25, 32, 39.

27. William J. Dumbrell, *The Faith of Israel: A Theological Survey of the Old Testament*, 2nd ed. (Grand Rapids: Baker, 2002), 85.

28. Cf. Gen. 17:6, 16; 35:11; 49:10; 2 Sam. 7:12; cf. Ps. 105:15, etc.

29. R. Knierim, "The Messianic Concept in the First Book of Samuel" in *Jesus and the Historian*, ed. F. T. Trotter (Philadelphia: Westminster, 1968), 43–44.

30. See Keener, *Bible Background*, 137.

31. Cf. Matt. 2:16–18 w/ Jer. 31:15; Ex. 1:15–22; Matt. 26:17, 26–28 w/ 1 Cor. 5:7; 11:25; Ex. 17:6 w/ 1 Cor. 10:4.

32. Keener, *A Commentary on the Gospel of Matthew* (Grand Rapids: Eerdmans, 1999), 138. For examples of representative characterization in epic literature, see: 1 Sam. 17; 2 Sam. 2:14–16; Homer, *The Illiad* 3.69–70, 86–94, etc.

33. Adapted from Duane L. Christensen, *The Unity of the Bible* (New York: Paulist Press, 2003), 199–200.

34. R. F. Collins, "Temptation of Jesus," *Anchor Bible Dictionary*, 6:382 [382–83]. "Disputation" is an overarching genre found in legal, wisdom, and prophetic texts (cf. Isa. 10:8–11; 28:23–28; Jer. 2:23–28; 2:1–5; Amos 3:3–4a, 5a, 6–8; 9:7; Mic. 2:6–11).

35. Luke's reversed order of temptations two and three reflect his thematic emphasis on Jerusalem. For Matthew, the final temptation corresponds the climax of his account, Matt. 28:18. (G. H. Twelftree, "Temptation of Jesus," in *Dictionary of Jesus and the Gospels*, ed. Joel B. Green, Scot McKnight [Downers Grove, Ill.: InterVarsity, 1992], 823.

36. L. Schiavo, "The Temptation of Jesus: The Eschatological Battle and the New Ethic of the First Followers of Jesus in Q," *Journal for the Study of the New Testament* 25, no. 2 (2002), 144–46.

37. This is a first-class condition, assumed true for the sake of argument, but here used manipulatively by the Devil (see Daniel B. Wallace, *Greek Grammar Beyond the Basics: An Exegetical Syntax of the New Testament* [Grand Rapids: Zondervan, 1996], 690–94). Throughout Jesus earthly ministry, the demons never question Jesus' identity; they recoil, cognizant of His mission.

38. F. Kermode, "Matthew," *The Literary Guide to the Bible*, ed. Robert Alter, Frank Kermode (Cambridge, Mass.: Harvard Univ. Press, 1987), 397.

39. For a discussion of typology and its use in early apostolic tradition, see W. W. Klein, C. L. Blomberg, R. L. Hubbard Jr., *Introduction to Biblical Interpretation*, (Nashville: Nelson, 1993), 31–34.

40. Literarily, Jesus' encounter with Satan essentially brackets the book of Matthew with the antagonism of the Jewish leaders closing Jesus' ministry, thereby defining a *cosmic conflict*. Cf. E. M. Boring, "Matthew," in *The New Interpreter's Bible*, vol. 8 (Nashville: Abingdon, 1995), 162.

41. For the Devil to walk Jesus from his wilderness location to the summit of the Jerusalem temple in his famished state is highly unlikely; but to find a mountain peak from which all the kingdoms of the earth could be viewed is impossible. Thus, some use of vision is evident.

42. Luke strengthens the role of the Spirit by mentioning Him twice at the outset (4:1).

43. "To be tested/tempted" (*peirosthenai*), aorist inf. pass., stresses *purpose*. Blomberg's observation is helpful: "Matthew warns against two common errors—blaming God for temptation and crediting the Devil with power to act independently of God" (Blomberg, *Matthew*, 83).

44. J. I. Packer, *Keep in Step with the Spirit*, 2nd ed. (Grand Rapids: Baker, 2005), 73.

45. G. B. Gibson, "Satan," *Dictionary of the Bible* (Grand Rapids: Eerdmans, 2000), 1169.

46. Frederick D. Bruner, *The Christbook* (Waco, Tex.: Word, 1987), 100.

47. Cf. Ex. 15:22–26; 16; Lev. 10; Deut. 1:19–46; Jer. 7:24–26; Ezek. 20; Psalms 78; Neh. 9; Acts 7:38–43; 1 Cor. 10:5–12; Heb. 3–4, etc. See the helpful discussion by D. W. Baker, "Wilderness, Desert," *Dictionary of the Old Testament: Pentateuch*, ed. T. D. Alexander, D. W. Baker (Downers Grove, Ill.: InterVarsity, 2003), 893–97; and W. H. Propp, "Wilderness," *The Oxford Companion to the Bible*, ed. Bruce M. Metzger and Michael David Coogan (Oxford, England: Oxford Univ. Press, 1993), 798.

48. Walter Brueggemann, "*Reverberation of Faith: A Theological Handbook of Old Testament Themes* (Louisville, Ky.: Westminister/John Knox, 2002), 231.

49. Ironically, the wilderness is also a place of spiritual renewal (cf. Gen. 16:7; Ex. 3:1–4:17; Luke 5:16; John 11:54).

50. W. H. Propp, "Wilderness. The scapegoat tradition surrounding Aza'el (Lev 16) later represented the chief of wicked angels. Also called a "desert demon," this tradition may also lie behind the emphasis of Jesus' *wilderness* temptation (see A. Maurer, "Azazel," in *Encyclopedia of the Dead Sea Scrolls*, ed. Lawrence H. Schiffman and James VanderKam [New York: Oxford University Press, 2000], 1:70–71).

51. Ibid. Moses' intercession with God (Ex. 32:11–14) showed that he understood the Promised Land without God would miss the goal and, therefore, was not an option.

52. Keener, *Background*, 139.

53. C. Meyers, "Temple, Jerusalem," *Anchor Bible Dictionary*, 6:358.

54. For a helpful discussion of the temple and its apparatus, see J. M. Monson, "The Temple of Solomon," *Zion: City of Our God*, ed. Richard S. Hess and Gordon J. Wenham (Grand Rapids: Eerdmans, 1999), 1–22.

55. R. J. Clifford, *The Cosmic Mountain in Canaan and the Old Testament*, Harvard Semitic Monographs 4 (Cambridge, Mass.: Harvard Univ. Press, 1972).

56. Elijah also endured a forty-day fast enroute to Mt. Horeb/Sinai (1 Kings 19:8). Others also see the connection to Moses; see R. H. Gundry, *Matthew*, 2nd ed. (Grand Rapids: Eerdmans, 1994), 55; and W. D. Davies, Dale C. Allison Jr., *A Critical and Exegetical Commentary on the Gospel According to Matthew*, International Critical Commentary Series, vol. 1 (Edinburgh:T &T Clark, 2004), 165–72.

57. Gundry, *Matthew*, 54. Even the account of Moses' fast emerges in the context that Jesus will quote to the Devil (cf. Deut. 9:9–18; Ibid., 54–55). Additionally, only Matthew stipulates "fasting," followed later by further instructions (6:16–18).

58. Cf. Ezra 8:21–22, 31b; Dan. 9:3; 6:17–25. This is likely the rationale behind Jesus' comment that some demons are driven out "only by prayer and fasting" (Matt. 17:21).

59. D. L. Smith-Christopher, "Fasting," *Eerdmans Commentary on the Bible*, 456; cf. 1 Sam. 14:24; 2 Sam. 11:11–12; 1 Macc. 3:46; 2 Macc. 13:12.

60. G. K. Beale, *The Temple and the Church's Mission: New Studies in Biblical Theology* 17 (Downers Grove, Ill.: InterVarsity, 2004), 172–73.

61. Keener, *Background*, 138.

62. A. J. Saldarini, "Matthew" in *Eerdmans Commentary on the Bible*, ed. James D. G. Dunn and John W. Rogerson (Grand Rapids: Eerdmans, 2003), 1011.

63. Rather than viewing the temptations as exclusively (1) salvation-historical (recalling Israel), (2) Christological (against contemporary expectations of messiahship), or (3) parenetic (taking Jesus as a model for believers), Keener seems correct to see elements of all three functioning in Matthew's account (*Background*, 137).

64. Keener, *Background*, 139.

65. Gundry, *Matthew*, 55.

66. Stanley J. Grenz, *Theology for the Community of God* (Grand Rapids: Eerdmans, 1994), 276.

67. Keener, *Background*, 139; Bartholomew and Goheen, *The Drama*, 134.

68. These descriptive phrases are adapted from Keener, *Background*, 139–41, and from Bartholomew and Goheen, *The Drama of Scripture: Finding Our Place in the Biblical Story* (Grand Rapids: Baker, 2004), 133.

69. Keener notes a Jewish tradition expecting a new exodus from a new Moses with a new manna (*Background*, 54).

70. As practiced by the Zealots and the Jewish aristocracy (Matt. 26:55, 61; 27:11–12; John 18:36).

71. Gordon J. Wenham, *Exploring the Old Testament: A Guide to the Pentateuch*, vol. 1 (Downers Grove, Ill.: InterVarsity, 2003), 132–32.

72. Matt. 4:10 reflects the Septuagint (Deut. 6:13), though replacing "fear" (*fobevw*) with "serve/worship" (*proskunephobew*).

73. Wenham believes Moses' smashing of the tablets (Ex. 32:19) cancelled the covenant just made (*Exploring*, 78).

74. The well-articulated argument of W. H. Propp, *Water in the Wilderness: A Biblical Motif and Its Mythological Background*, Harvard Semitic Monographs 40 (Georgia: Scholars Press, 1987), 37–38, 68–69, 109.

75. Not only supported by rabbinic interpretation (*m. Ber* 9:5; Sipre Deut. #32), but noted by modern scholars as well: Gundry, *Matthew*, 56; D. H. Hagner, *Matthew 1–13*. vol. 33A, *Word Bible Commentary* (Dallas: Word, 1993), 66; Saldarini, "Matthew," 1011. Liturgically, the *Shema* is the greatest passage in the Pentateuch, the fundamental Jewish creed of faith.

76. The word "heart" (*leb*) refers to the seat of one's emotions and intellect, practically "inner being."

77. The word "life" (*hepes*) in this context refers to a person or "essential-self" (cf. Lev. 21:11). The translation of "soul" is misleading since it assumes body-soul dichotomy foreign to OT thought (Alter, *Five*, 912).

78. The word "might" (*meod*), usually an adverb meaning "exceedingly," is here a noun meaning "wealth" or "property" (so Qumran: CD 9:11; 12:10).

79. Gundry, *Matthew*, 57. Following Jewish practice, Jesus in turn quotes a more pertinent passage. Interpretively, He illustrates the danger of valuing wording over meaning (Keener, *Background*, 143).

80. Goldingay, *Old Testament*, 8.

81. Saldarini, "Matthew," 1011.

82. Ibid.; cf D. I. Block, "How Many Is God? An Investigation into the Meaning of Deuteronomy 6:4–5," *Journal of the Evangelical Theological Society* 47, no. 2 (2004), 193.

83. Keener, *Background*, 144.

84. Ibid., 142.

85. Angels had already protected Jesus (Matt. 2:1–23), and would again if summoned (Matt. 26:53).

86. Dumbrell, *The Search*, 256.

87. U. W. Mauser, "The Temptation of Christ," in *The Oxford Companion to the Bible*, 736.

88. C. A. Evans "Inaugurating the Kingdom of Good and Defeating the Kingdom of Evil," *Bulletin for Biblical Research* 15, no. 1 (2005): 66. Italics mine.

89. Boring, "Matthew," 164.

90. F. B. Craddock, "Testing That Never Ceases," *CC* 107.7 (1990): 211.

91. Stanley J. Grenz, *Theology for the Community of God* (Vancouver, Canada: Regent College Pub., 2000), 277.

92. Bartholomew and Goheen, *The Drama*, 133.

93. Poe, *See No Evil*, 153.

94. Goldingay, *Old Testament*, 8. Jesus counters Satan at the level of relationship with God: submission to God, trust in God's promise, and worship of God's name.

95. Henri J. M. Nouwen, *In the Name of Jesus* (New York: Crossroad, 1989), 16–17, 38–39, 58–59.

96. John Shea, *The Spiritual Wisdom of the Gospels for Christian Preachers and Teachers* (Collegeville, Minn.: Liturgical Press, 2004).

97. Poe, *See No Evil*, 153.

98. Walter Brueggemann, *Awed to Heaven, Rooted in Earth: Prayers of Walter Brueggemann*, ed. E. Searcy (Minneapolis: Fortress, 2003), 55.

99. Dietrich Bonhoeffer, *Life Together* (San Francisco: Harper & Row, 1954), 83.

100. Craddock, "Testing," 211.

101. Language borrowed from David Neff, "Naming the Horror." *Christianity Today* 49.4 (2005), 76 [74–76].

102. Ibid., 74.

103. Eight plural pronouns in the prayer (e.g., "our," "we") clearly define the individual within community.

104. Matt. 6:9b–13, NIV. The word for "temptation" (*pieravzw*) can also mean "testing" (6:13a). Keener translates the line, "Let us not sin when we are tempted" (*Background*, 62). Similarly, "And don't let us yield to temptation" (NLT). The request is rhetorical, asking God for protection.

Chapter 9

PROCLAIMING JESUS IN A CROSS-CULTURAL CONTEXT

Understanding the Trinity as a Model for Declaring the Gospel

by David Rim

To the question of what the Trinity is, Dorothy Sayers once commented, "The Father incomprehensible, the Son incomprehensible, and the whole thing incomprehensible. Something put in by theologians to make it more difficult—nothing to do with daily life or ethics."[1] James Pike portrayed the Trinity as a "heavy piece of luggage" that Christians should not have to tote along when doing church missions.[2]

It matters not whether it is in supposedly Bible-literate America or a culture steeped in animism—the Trinity is one of those key doctrines of God that people in most cultures stumble over. Even scholars who count the Trinity as part of their faith have lamented over the failure of the church to integrate Trinitarian theology into everyday life, into theology overall, and into missions. As we proclaim Jesus, this key doctrine has implications for presenting the Christ to other cultures.

PERSONHOOD AND THE TRINITY

Before we look at the implications of the Trinity for cross-cultural proclamation of Jesus the Messiah, it is good to ask why a doctrine that is supposed to shed light into the very nature of the God Christians worship fell into such disarray. Colin Gunton provides several reasons: an inability to demonstrate its practical relevance to the Christian life, the separation of the being of God and the actions of God in salvation history,[3] and the failure of articulating an adequate understanding of personhood within the doctrine of the Trinity. These failures have rendered the doctrine of the Trinity into a mathematical puzzle to be solved rather than a doctrine that should be lived.[4]

While all three reasons given above are significant, perhaps the most crucial is the last: the concept of persons. In the formulation of the doctrine of the Trinity—one being, three persons—the linchpin rests upon what we mean by "person."[5] In essence, "Trinitarian doctrine is therefore inescapably a theology of personhood, regardless of how this is formulated."[6]

Yet the importance of defining this term is matched only by the difficulty of the task. To say that a controversy exists over what it means to be a person is an understatement. Emmanuel Mounier notes that while man can define objects exterior to himself only by observation, personhood is the one reality of which we come to know from within: "Present everywhere, it is given nowhere."[7] Bishop Timothy Ware also expresses similar concerns in defining personhood. After asking the question, "What is my true self? Who am I? What am I?" he responds that the answers are not obvious: "In an important sense we do not know exactly what is involved in being a person."[8]

One can sympathize with the frustration of Augustine when he attempted to explain why the term "person" was not applied to "these three together," so that "one person" is equivalent to "one being" and "one God." The reason is, Augustine wrote, "that we want to keep at least one word for signifying what we mean by Trinity, so that we are not simply reduced to silence when we are asked three what, after we have confessed that there are three."[9] By failing to properly distinguish the plurality from the unity, Augustine seems to have unwillingly reduced the rich Trinitarian relations found within the Christian God into the one divine substance.[10]

Perhaps Gunton is correct when he writes that the concept of persons is a logically primitive concept. "Because it is both ontologically and logically primitive," he argues that the term *person* cannot be defined in other words, but rather, other realities take their meaning from this concept.[11] While we may not be able to adequately *define* the concept of personhood, we can sufficiently *describe* it to render the concept meaningful.

The revival of the doctrine of the Trinity over the last few decades has been fueled by a shift in how the term *person* was understood. Rather than characterizing personhood with individualistic connotations, as was done throughout the Enlightenment period (a person is a rational individual), a generation of scholars has embedded the concept of persons with communal notions (persons are constituted by relationships).[12] Fostered by the postmodern emphasis upon relationality in understanding who we are,[13] a relational view of persons has flourished in theology and in the academic disciplines.[14]

This chapter will briefly chronicle this conceptual shift, explore the moral implications of this shift, and then lay out the practical relevance of a relational understanding of persons to cross-cultural missions. It is my prayer that a renewed perspective on persons will inform the rest of our theology and the way we live our lives.

PERSONHOOD AS A RELATIONAL CATEGORY

Models of the Trinity have generally fallen into two categories: those that apply subjectivity to the one and those that apply it to the many. The former fall into the thought patterns of the Western/Latin world, where the emphasis has been upon the single divine essence;[15] while the latter fall into Eastern molds of thought, where the emphasis has been upon the plurality of persons.[16] Historically, those who have applied it to the one have been accused of modalism,[17] while those who have applied it to the three have been accused of tritheism.[18]

One of the primary proponents of a singular consciousness in the one divine being was Karl Barth. For him, the concept of person was intricately connected to the idea of individual centers of consciousness. Thus he refused to use the term *person* to reference the plurality within the Godhead.[19] To do so, he believed, would imply three subjects within the one God, a form of tritheism.

Assuming that the inner reality of God was the same as the God who revealed Himself, he believed that the doctrine of the Trinity could be generated by the single proposition: "God reveals himself through himself, and reveals himself."[20] The Father is the one who reveals Himself (Revealer), the Son is the one through whom this revelation occurs (Revelation), and the Spirit is the one who brings this revelation to light in the heart of fallen man (Revealedness). Rather than referring to the Father, Son, and the Spirit as persons, he preferred the term *modes-of-being*.[21]

In contrast to Barth, Wolfhart Pannenberg notes that Jesus in His obedience and submission to the Father, especially in His death on the cross, distinguished Himself from the Father with an awareness of the self that is distinct from, but dependent upon the Father.[22] Given that the Son's identity is different from the Father's, the Son must be a distinct person. Given that the Son's actions are distinct from the Father's, the Son must be a distinct subject. Because of this mutual distinctiveness, he reasons that the Father, Son, and the Spirit "must be understood not merely as different modes of being of the one divine subject but as living realizations of separate centers of action."[23] But since the concept of action demands a subject, and since the divine essence is not a subject, only the three persons of the Trinity can be "direct subjects of the divine action."[24]

There exists, however, a second way of categorizing models of the Trinity. Rather than focusing on which aspect of the Trinity to apply "subjectivity" (the one or the many), one can view the different proposals through the concept of person. When we do, models of the Trinity can be divided into those which view persons as *rational individuals* and those which view persons as being *constituted in relationships*. The rest of this section will further explore these two differing perspectives of personhood.

Persons as Rational Individuals

The modern understanding of persons as rational individual substances arose from within the philosophy of René Descartes.[25] Enlightenment-period discussions of personhood usually find their way back to him. In search of an "Archimedean point"—a fixed and unmovable point of reference—to construct a sure foundation for certain knowledge,[26] Descartes engaged in a process of systematically doubting all that can be doubted until he hit the one truth which could not be doubted: "I think, therefore I am."[27] The very act of doubting was a type of thinking. With this discovery, Descartes separated the person into a mind and a body, and identified the self with the mind. For him, a person was a thinking thing, the source of intellectual reality and the ground of all certain knowledge: "I am therefore precisely only a thing that thinks; that is, a mind, or soul, or intellect, or reason . . . a thing that thinks."[28]

The most penetrating criticism of Descartes' philosophy of personhood comes from the writings of John MacMurray. He faults Descartes for doubting that which there was no reason to doubt,[29] and for grounding his philosophy upon the self as a reflective individual in isolation.[30] Instead, MacMurray offers the self as an agent as the starting point for his philosophy of personhood. Both the self as thinker (mind) and the self as doer (body) are aspects of the self in action.[31] But action implies the presence of another. Now if the other is an immaterial object, the self can be viewed mechanically (composed of atoms). If the other is a living entity, the self can be viewed organically (differentiated but a harmonious functioning of parts for the whole). But if the other is a being with whom the self can enter into a relationship of being-for-the-other,[32] the self is and becomes a person.[33]

From this analysis, MacMurray concludes that "personal existence is *constituted* by the relation of persons" (italics his).[34] In other words, the personal self has "its being in relationships"[35] and, therefore, "the independent individual, the isolated self, is a nonentity."[36]

Persons as Parts of Relationships

John MacMurray's thoughts become an excellent point of departure for introducing the concept of persons as a relational category. While those in the rational substance category have no problems equating persons with individual human beings, those in the relational category view the equating of persons and individuals as a categorical fallacy.[37] The concept of personhood is organically linked to relationships. It is a communal category that emerges out of relationships of being-for-the-other. The two concepts—persons and relationships— are necessarily linked, for where you find a person you must necessarily find another. As Royce Gordon Gruenler writes: "The truth of the matter is, a person is never a person in isolation. He *becomes* a person *in relation*. To be is not to be alone. To be is to be together."[38]

The presence of a person is equivalent to the presence of a friend or a spouse. The concepts necessarily imply the existence of a relationship in which that person stands. It is this view of personhood that has enriched contemporary discussions of the Trinity, and which will be the basis of our discussion on cross-cultural missions in the last section of this essay, "Personhood as a Missionary Category."[39]

One can draw several implications from a relational view of personhood. First, as briefly noted above, to be a person is not equivalent to being an individual. The concept of personhood is a "between-ness" concept—one that emerges between individuals who possess the capacity of being for the other. But the concept of persons cannot be reduced to the concept of an individual, for persons differ from individuals "in the sense that the latter is defined in terms of *separation from* other individuals, the person in terms of *relation with* other persons."[40] Or in the words of MacMurray, "Individual independence is an illusion; and the independent individual, the isolated self, is a nonentity."[41]

Second, the concept of personhood is not reducible to the relationship itself, only necessarily linked. Perhaps one can argue that one of the major difficulties Aquinas, and perhaps Augustine,[42] experienced in their formulation of the doctrine is this very issue: a lack of differentiation between personhood and relationship. This very failure, according to Cornelius Plantinga, so flattened the distinctions between divine essence, person, and relation in Aquinas' theology of the Trinity that any robust sense of plurality within the Christian God was effectively eliminated.[43] T. F. Torrance helpfully notes that the persons of the Trinity are not merely relations, but rather, "the relations between the persons belong to who the persons actually are."[44]

Third, a person's identity can be discovered only in the presence of another. The answer to the question "Who am I?" can only be found in the presence of another who asks "Who am I?" In an "I-Thou" relationship, the "I" is defined by the "Thou."[45] The "who-ness" of the "Thou" defines the "who-ness" of the "I," and vice versa.[46] The defining is bi-directional. In this way, identity is a mutually dependent and mutually reciprocal concept. The First Person of the Trinity possesses the identity of Father only in the presence of the Second Person, who is the Son. The Father's "father-ness" defines the Son's "son-ness" and vice versa. But in the very act of the Father's defining of the Son, the Son's identity is itself defined.

Fourth and last, since human beings are created in God's image, some similarity must exist between the divine and the human. As to what that similarity is—whether it is dominion or relationship or representation or some type of structural likeness such as reason, we should be careful to adhere to Stanley Grenz's advice not to view the image language "from too narrow a perspective."[47] Perhaps the safest way to proceed in an article of this size is simply to say that through the concept of image we learn that human personhood is not only grounded in, but can also be understood by exploring, the biblical revelation concerning divine personhood.[48] Thus, we must seek to understand personhood not in terms of our experience of human persons or modern definitions of persons, but on the basis of the way the divine persons are understood in the Trinity.[49] What this means, notes Gunton, is that "anthropology stems from theology and not the other way around."[50]

PERSONHOOD AS A MORAL CATEGORY

Love Found in the Personhood of God

Personhood is a deeply moral category. The basis for this statement is John's proclamation that God is love (1 John). In this one glorious statement we not only find both the defining characteristic of God (God *is* love) but also the definitive call to the divine way of living (God *loves*). In this one statement we have divine ethics grounded in divine ontology: to *be love* is *to love*, or in the words of John, to *be* is to be *with* (John 1:1). In God, love functions both as a verb (the ethical) and as a noun (the ontological)—the former grounded in the latter—the "ought" derived from the "is." Thus, only in the perfection of God (Matt. 5:48) do we have the *being* of God fully reflected in the *actions* of God. For only in God is the love of God grounded in the God who is love.

As noted above, the truth that God is love necessarily implies mutual distinctions within God, for love requires the presence of another.[51] For God to be love there must exist a plurality of persons in relationships of being-for-the-other. The Trinitarian formulation "one being, three persons" is, therefore, an ontological statement concerning God, as well as the ethical ground for all of God's actions. The Father's love is grounded in His personhood (because it is constituted by relationships of being-for-the-other); but His personhood is grounded in God who is love (because love implies otherness). Just as divine love is both a verb and a noun, so also is divine personhood.

Perhaps no theologian has seen this truth more clearly than John Zizioulas. For him, personhood is not a "static entity," but one which can only be conceived dynamically as it "*relates to*"[52] (italics his). To be a person is to "relate to" another, since for him "the person cannot exist without communion."[53] Thus, personhood must imply the "openness of being," or an "*ek-stasis* of being," that is, "a movement toward communion which leads to a transcendence of the boundaries of the 'self' and thus to *freedom*"[54] (italics his). Only in this act of "transcending" does the noun of personhood (i.e., is love) fulfill its teleological ends in the verb of personhood (i.e., loves). Only in the act of transcending does the person truly experience freedom—the freedom *to be*. To be a person is to be open to every community by which one's personhood is constituted.

By being created in the image of God, all human beings are persons and called to be persons. The dignity and worth, as well as the ontological ground of human personhood, is found in divine personhood. In an absolute sense, only the divine is truly personal, and all created persons are so only because they have been "personalized" from above.[55] As persons (noun), we are called to be persons (verb). As LaCugna reminds us, "The achievement of personhood is the fulfillment of the *telos* (the proper end) of the [human] nature."[56]

But this openness to community cannot be accomplished from below, for the fall of Adam and Eve so disoriented humanity in such a way that their individuality preceded their community, leading to individualism. The image in which they were created became so marred that they became individuals seeking community rather than a community out of which one became aware of one's individuality (i.e., persons). Thus, all fallen beings experience the dynamic tension of being created to be persons without the ability to fulfill that "telos" for which they were created.

Love for Others Expressed Through Relationship with God

Only in the identification of the believer with the one true image of God (Jesus Christ) can created persons fulfill their calling to love the other by participating in the loving actions of the Son on behalf of the Father for us on the cross. In the "loving" of the Son, the sons and daughters can now "love." As "personalized persons," our calling is this: to call forth the person from the individual. Or to put it another way, in the words of Miroslav Volf, "Salvation must *consist in an ontological deindividualization that actualizes their personhood.*"[57] Only to the degree that we are open to the personhood of God can we become persons in the fullest sense, where community once again precedes individuality.

The irony here is that to the degree one reflects and focuses on the self, the self disappears—for in reflecting on the self, the other disappears. "When individual self-contemplation becomes the basis of self, rather than the relation to the divine and human others on which our reality actually depends," Gunton warns, "the self begins to disappear."[58] Without the other there is no person. But centeredness on the other brings life to the self, for the self becomes the person only in the light of the other. Love for the other brings life to the self. Love for the self apart from the other brings death. That is why Thomas Merton can write that "love not only prefers the good of another to my own, but it does not even compare the two. It has only one good, that of the beloved, which is, at the same time, my own." This occurs, he continues, only when the self, by "identifying" itself with the other, sees the self in the other and, therefore, the other's "good becomes my own."[59]

A warning: The call for persons to love the other does not mean the negation of the self. In other words, the kind of community that constitutes one's personhood is the kind that frees the person to be one's unique self. Just as the Father is for the Son while still remaining the Father, so human persons are to be for the other while still retaining their distinctive otherness. As Gunton insightfully reminds us, "Just as Father, Son and Spirit are what they are by virtue of their others-in-relation, so that each *particular* is unique and absolutely necessary to the being of the whole, so it is, in its own way, for our being in society."[60] Communities characterized by conformity are not true communities but merely totalitarian societies.

Thus, the freedom of transcending the self is a careful balance between the extremes of self-absorption and other-obsession. Truly free persons are free from the compulsion of pleasing those around them (thereby negating their uniqueness) and the need to dominate others with their wishes (thereby asserting their uniqueness). As LaCugna counsels us, "Personhood requires the balance of self-love and self-gift."[61] Rather than autonomy (naming oneself with reference to oneself) and heteronomy (naming oneself with reference to another), she urges theonomy—the naming of the human person in reference to God.[62] Only when the human person is fully personalized by the divine can he or she walk the fine balance of being for the other without negating the distinctiveness of the self. Only in Christ can we say that He lives in me, yet I live (Gal. 2:20). Christ liberates the self for the other without negating the self.

PERSONHOOD AS A MISSIONARY CATEGORY

Our Missionary God

Our God is a missionary God. John Thompson views Christ's incarnation as the center of God's missionary movement in human history as it unfolds from creation to its "renewal in glory."[63] God's longing to see people from all nations and all tribes come to Him through His Son appears throughout the biblical narrative. We find it in the central covenant of the Old Testament, where He promises that through the choosing of Abraham, all the nations will be blessed (Gen. 12:1–3). We see this in the reversal of the dispersal of the nations in the Tower of Babel episode when, during Pentecost, Jews from all the nations returned to Jerusalem and once again understood in one language. We see this in the Jerusalem Council, when through the Spirit the leaders of the emerging church learn that Gentiles did not have to become Jews to belong to the people of God (Acts 15:22–35). We see this in the final book of the Bible when we're given a preview of people from all nations and tribes wearing white robes and singing "Salvation belongs to our God who sits on the throne, and to the Lamb" (Rev. 7:9–10 ESV).

The biblical narrative points to the triune God as one intensely involved in missions. In fact, the divine missionary movement is a cross-cultural one, not only in the sense that God's heart beats for people of all cultures, but also in the sense that Christ has entered another culture to fulfill His missionary calling. Thus, the triune God becomes not only the inspiration but also the model for the church's participation in cross-cultural missions.

The Goal: Communal Oneness among Diversity

The goal of cross-cultural missions is to experience the communal oneness of the divine in the midst of cultural diversity without creating cultural conformity through the redemptive work of Jesus Christ on the cross. The task of the church is not to squeeze the richness of humanity into the mold of which we are most comfortable, but to foster a context in which the oneness of the divine can be given fuller, and thus richer, expression in culturally diverse settings.

The Example of the Trinity

The relational concept of personhood discussed above can provide the theological framework for such a philosophy of cross-cultural missions. The divine persons of the Trinity exist in such a way that the diversity of persons does not threaten their unity, but also in such a way that this unity is not preserved through conformity. The Father is distinct from the Son, and the Son from the Father, in that they are aware of their identities as being distinct from the other. They each give the other room to be unique. Moltmann affirms this truth when he writes that "the divine persons exist with one another, for one another, and in one another. They exist in one another because they mutually give each other space for full unfolding."[64] Personhood, therefore, being a relational category, is enriched in a fundamental way by the diversity of the other's "otherness."

Furthermore, the persons of the Trinity reflect their identity (who they are) in the roles they play in salvation history (what they do). The Father as Father decrees and sends; the Son as Son listens and obeys. The Spirit, as the Spirit of Christ (e.g., Rom. 8:9) and the Spirit of God the Father (e.g., 1 Cor. 2:10–14), brings to completion what the Father has decreed and what the Son has redeemed. Each has a distinct role because each possesses a distinct identity.

But their distinctiveness does not undermine their interdependence. As noted earlier, the distinctiveness of the Father's identity depends on the distinctiveness of the Son's identity, and vice versa. The Father needs the Son to be the Father, and the Son needs the Father to be the Son. By each giving room for the other to be the other, they allow the other to be the other; but it is precisely the other's "otherness" that constitutes the "I" who gives room in the first place. Both distinctiveness and interdependence flow out of a relational view of personhood.

Furthermore, their distinct roles in salvation history complement each other's, for the roles they play reflect mutually constituted identities. By the Father allowing the Son to reflect His identity as Son by playing the role of Son in the divine missionary task on earth, the Father is able to reflect His identity by playing the role of Father in that same task. In this way, the movement of the triune God in salvation history does not reduce itself to a boring monologue,[65] but comes to life as each person plays His part in the divine drama. And since their roles are mutually complementary, their glory is mutually shared.

Toward the end of His life, Jesus transferred the commission He received from the Father on to the church: "As the Father has sent Me, I also send you" (John 20:21). As the image of the triune God, Jesus calls the church to reflect that image in space and time by participating in the divine missionary task. The calling of the church, therefore, is the same as that of Jesus Christ: to call forth the person from the individual.[66]

Bringing Honor to the Triune God

As the members of the church fulfill their calling by reaching out to those in other cultures, they must do so in ways that honor the One they image. Since the triune God exists as a plurality in unity, the church must also carry out its cross-cultural mandate of preaching the gospel in ways that give room to those in other cultures to be their unique selves, without undermining the unity of the body. We learn from the writings of Paul that the unity of belonging to Jesus Christ transcends the diversity of ethnic background (neither Jew nor Greek) and of social class (slave nor free), as well as gender (male or female) differences (Gal. 3:28). But this unity does not arise at the cost of diversity, for it is precisely the diversity of persons within the community that enriches their unity. For if the "I" is born in the presence of the "Thou," perhaps we can say that it is the diversity of the "Thou" from the "I" that enables the "I" to become more fully a person.

A STRATEGY FOR REACHING EVERY CULTURE

How should the church go about fulfilling its call to reach people of all cultures and all tribes? Once again we look to the One we image and ask ourselves, How did Jesus reach out to a culture different from His own? The answer: through the incarnation. By combining the text of John 13:3–17 with Philippians 2:5–11, Gary Parrett draws several implications for what incarnational ministry looks like.[67] This section will rework some of his insights, along with those from other thinkers, to make several points concerning incarnational ministry.

Begin with the Calling

First, incarnational ministry begins with a calling. The Son understood that the Father had sent Him and that all power to accomplish His calling was given to Him (John 13:3). This call was grounded in the Father's love for the Son and in His desire to bring glory to the Son. Only in fully grasping the love behind the call will cross-cultural ministry be possible. For as Sherwood G. Lingenfelter and Marvin K. Mayers warn, "Becoming incarnate in another culture will be a trial by fire . . . and most of all a test of the veracity of one's love."[68]

Since our love for the other is only a reflection of our experience of God's love for us, the steadiness of our love for those who are different from us in times of difficulty will depend upon the steadiness of our faith in God's love for us.

Know the Culture

Second, we must know our culture. While this point may seem pedantic, failure here can derail one's cross-cultural ministry before full incarnation can take place. All of us live in a particular culture.[69] Knowing ourselves is a prerequisite to knowing others.

Cultural self-awareness is crucial for two reasons. First, just as Christ had to leave behind certain aspects of what it meant to be divine (i.e., the glory and privilege) while remaining divine (Phil. 2:7), those who enter into another culture must also leave behind aspects of their own culture that might hinder the communication of the gospel. Unless we are aware of the nuances of our culture, we will not know what to leave behind. Second, since the gospel is always spoken and heard in a particular cultural context, it is difficult to distinguish at times what aspects of the church's proclamation represent the gospel and what aspects reflect the particular culture in which it is proclaimed.

Lesslie Newbigin, missionary to India, humbly confesses that as he grew older he realized that many of his critical evaluations of Hindu beliefs and practices reflected more his own culture rather than Scripture.[70] Just as it is impossible to remove all of our presuppositions in interpreting the biblical text, it may not be possible to completely distinguish the cultural aspects of the gospel spoken and heard. But just as we are able to hear more of the text as we become more aware of our presuppositions, in the same way, we can speak and live more of the heart of the gospel in another culture as we become more aware of our own.

Identify with the Culture

Third, we must identify ourselves with the new culture. When the eternal Logos became flesh (John 1:1, 14; Phil. 2:7), He entered the Jewish culture of the first century as a baby. From the very beginning of His human life, Jesus became identified with that culture by learning and assimilating many of its values and practices (Luke 2:52). He worshiped in their manner, was trained as a carpenter, held beliefs consistent with the people of that time, and spoke their language. Thus, Lingenfelter and Mayers call Jesus the 200 percent person—100 percent divine and 100 percent Jew.[71] While such a statement may not be theologically precise, it does get its point across. Jesus remained who He was, yet was assimilated into another culture from birth. While it is not possible for human beings to be born into a second culture, it is possible for us to follow Christ's footsteps and take more of another culture upon ourselves for the sake of the gospel.

Only by identifying with the targeted culture can a missionary achieve truly persuasive communication.[72] It is not merely one's ability to use stories, figures of speech, images, and ideas to convey the biblical story—but also to adopt the culture's manner and attitude of speaking that determines one's success in persuasively communicating the gospel.

The manner is just as important as the message. The goal is not imitation; it is incarnation. Such immersion can occur only as one continually lives and breathes that culture.

Eugene Nida proposes four levels of communication.[73] In the first level, the message has no significant impact on behavior (e.g., two plus two equals four). In the second, it has significant impact, but only on the level of behavior and not in values (e.g., the dam has broken and the town is being flooded). In the third, the message affects the entire value system because it alters one or more of their foundational beliefs (e.g., gospel). In the last level, the receiver is so moved by the message that he or she moves from the receiving mode to the communicating mode—from convert to discipler (e.g., Samaritan woman in John 4). Persuasive communication on levels three and four can occur only when the speaker identifies himself or herself with the culture of the listener.

Cross-cultural missionaries must also remember, however, that just as the call for persons to love does not mean the negation of the self; incarnation into another culture does not mean the negation of one's own culture. This was not the case for the incarnate Christ, who belonged to two "cultures" or "communities"—the divine and the human.[74] Both "cultures" are allowed to maintain their distinctiveness in the one person of Christ; but at the same time, the two exist in harmony. Cross-cultural ministry is the addition of another culture, not the replacement of it. In maintaining both cultures without minimizing either (to the degree possible), they become channels by which the blessings of God's presence in one culture can be translated into symbols and stories of another.

Remember It's All about People

Fourth and finally, we need to remember that cross-cultural missions are all about people. It is very possible for us to get so caught up in learning the language and picking up the mannerisms of another culture that we miss the obvious. Jesus did not consider equality with God something to be held on to, but took the role of a servant to die on the cross for people (Phil. 2:6–8). He came to wash feet (John 13:5). Parrett offers a timely reminder for all who are involved in cross-cultural missions: "When all is said and done, the command that confronts us is not 'Love another culture as your own' but 'Love you neighbor as yourself.'"[75] Love covers a multitude of cultural infractions. Love knows no cultural barriers.

KNOWING THE CONTEXT AND THE CONTENT OF THE GOSPEL

This chapter intends to show how a relational view of personhood should impact cross-cultural ministries. As we consider such a context for the message, we must not forget the content of the message—the gospel of Jesus Christ.

Isaiah's Gospel

Paul defines the gospel in 1 Corinthians 15:3–4 as the death and resurrection of Jesus Christ for our sins. This is the gospel that we are most familiar with, the one that introduced us to the Christian faith, the one found in the Four Spiritual Law brooklets of Campus Crusade for Christ. But this is not the only definition of the gospel found in the Scriptures. The prophet Isaiah helps to clarify the gospel, using the term "gospel" four times. First, in 40:8–11 preachers of the gospel are told to proclaim without fear the message: Israel's God will come and reign with power and might, and gather the lamb in His arms like a mother sheep. Second, Isaiah 52:7 describes those who bring the gospel, who announce the coming of peace because Zion's God will reign. Third, in Isaiah 60:6, the Gentiles will come to proclaim the good news of the Lord, bearing gold and frankincense (see Matt. 2:1–12). Finally, in Isaiah 61:1–2 we learn that the Spirit of the Lord God will anoint the coming Savior so that He might bring the gospel to the oppressed.

Putting these passages together, we can summarize Isaiah's gospel as the proclamation that one day Israel's God will reign over all the world. Furthermore, in this reign Israel's faith in their God will be vindicated and the Gentile nations will find their hope in the Jewish King.[76]

The New Testament Gospel Writers on Isaiah's Gospel

When we come to the New Testament, we find the gospel writers connecting Jesus' message of the kingdom with Isaiah's gospel. Mark introduces the theme of his work as the good news concerning Jesus Christ (1:1). The good news Jesus preaches in Galilee is the proclamation that the kingdom is near (1:14–15). The arrival of John the Baptist to prepare the way for the one who brings good news (1:2–3; cf. Isa. 40:3), coupled with the Spirit's anointing of Jesus at His baptism (1:9–11), draws us back to Isaiah's gospel that the Spirit of the Lord will come upon His Servant who will preach good news to the oppressed (Isa. 61:1).

We find a similar connection in Matthew and Luke. When John the Baptist sends two of his disciples to see if Jesus was the one, he points to the fulfillment of Isaiah's prophecy found in 61:1–2 as a response: the oppressed have the good news preached to them. And what is the content of this message? Matthew writes that Jesus entered the synagogues preaching the "gospel of the kingdom" (4:23). Luke also has Jesus referencing the gospel found in Isaiah 61:1–2 as the first message he preached in his hometown of Nazareth (Luke 4:16–19). In Jesus Christ, the gospel writers seem to be saying, Isaiah's gospel has been fulfilled. As the anointed one of God, Jesus Christ will reign; and His reign will inaugurate the long-awaited kingdom.

A BALANCED GOSPEL FOR THE WORLD

In the light of these two "gospels," what can we say about them? First, the gospel is the message that Jesus, God's anointed Messiah, will fulfill God's promise of *shalom* through His reign (i.e., the kingdom).[77] But this reign will be established on the basis of the gospel that this messianic King has died and has risen for our sins. Jesus' message that "the kingdom of God is near" (Mark 1:15 NIV) is predicated upon His message that the Son did not come to be served but to serve and be a ransom for many. Rather than viewing one or the other gospel as "another" gospel, the one (i.e., He died for our sins) enables the fulfillment of the other (i.e., Israel's God reigns).

Second, if we focus primarily, or in some cases exclusively, on the gospel of Jesus' death, then we have unwittingly cultivated a spirit of individualism. For the implication of this gospel is that Jesus died for the sins of individuals. Certainly we as evangelicals do not reject this truth. But given the traditional Western view of the person as a rational substance, with our primary focus upon the gospel as Jesus' death, we have not only lost the ability to appreciate and apply the riches of God's relationality, but have failed to appropriate it as the theological ground for cross-cultural missions.

In recent days a number of voices have called the church back to what they believe is a more biblical model of personhood—a relational model derived from the plurality in unity of the one God whom Christians worship. Such a model provides a theological framework for bringing people of all nations and tribes into the church, while encouraging them to maintain their unique cultural identities. But it is also the gospel as the reign of God that calls the church into all the nations and tribes of the world.

A holistic emphasis is implied in God's reign—for His kingdom extends not only over all the nations, but also over land and over the demon powers. The church is called to participate in the *mission dei* of extending His reign across the boundaries of culture. Cross-cultural mission is built into the very heart of this gospel. The church not only preaches the gospel to the nations, but the gospel itself calls the church to the nations.

David Rim is associate professor of theology at the Moody Bible Institute. He holds the Ph.D. degree from Trinity Evangelical Divinity School, Deerfield, Illinois, along with degrees from Dallas Theological Seminary and Carnegie-Mellon University, Pittsburgh.

NOTES

1. Dorothy Sayers, *Creed or Chaos* (New York: Harcourt, 1949), 22.

2. James Pike, *A Time for Christian Candor* (New York: Harper & Row, 1964), 124.

3. The phrase "being of God" refers to the immanent Trinity (a way of speaking about the interior life of God apart from His activity in the world), and the phrase "actions of God" refers to the economic trinity (a way of speaking about God in terms of His work of redeeming the world through the sending of the Son and the Spirit).

4. In this regard, see also Roger Haight, "The Point of Trinitarian Theology," *Toronto Journal of Theology* 4, no. 2 (1988): 195.

5. There has been much discussion in the literature over whether the term *person* should even be used to reference the plurality within the one divine being. While a number of various proposals have been made, none has caught on. Surely Walter Kasper is correct when he writes that the term *person* is far more concrete than the other proposals (e.g., *mode of being, distinct manner of subsisting, identity*) that have been made in recent years, and that personhood "is the highest category we have at our disposal" when we speak of God. See Walter Kasper, *The God of Jesus Christ*, trans. Matthew J. O'Connell (New York: Crossroad, 1996), 154. Kasper also astutely points out that it is difficult to "adore and glory a distinct manner of subsisting." Ibid., 288.

6. Catherine LaCugna, "Trinitarian Mystery of God," *Systematic Theology*, ed. Francis S. Fiorenza (Minneapolis: Fortress, 1991), 1:180; cited by Ted Peters, *God as Trinity: Relationality and Temporality in Divine Life* (Louisville, Ky.: Westminister/John Knox Press, 1993), 37.

7. Emmanuel Mounier, *Personalism* (Notre Dame, Ind.: Univ. of Notre Dame Press, 1979), xvi–xvii.

8. Timothy Ware in Panayiotis Nellas, *Deification in Christ: Orthodox Perspectives on the Nature of the Human Person* (New York: St. Vladimir's Sem. Press, 1987), 9.

9. Saint Augustine, *The Trinity*, ed., trans. Edmund Hill (New York: New York Press, 1991), 228–229 (VII.3.11).

10. Ibid., 228. But if the person of the Son and the Spirit are nothing more than the substance of the Son and the Spirit, and there is only one divine substance, how does one distinguish the three persons? How does one understand relationships given this particular framework? For further discussions on issues surrounding Augustine's understanding of personhood, see William Riordan O'Connor, "The Concept of the Person in St. Augustine's *De Trinitate*," *Augustinian Studies* 13 (1982): 133–143.

11. Colin E. Gunton, *The Promise of Trinitarian Theology*, 2nd ed. (Edinburgh: T & T Clark, 1997), 11.

12. For example, Ted Peters sees the connections between individuality and relationality in the last half of the twentieth century as being crucial in the renewed discussions on the Trinity. See his *God as Trinity*, 15. While Peters offers a number of insights about the Trinity, his own views lean toward process theology.

13. Peters, *God as Trinity*, 15, 35. For a critical assessment of the postmodern view of persons, see Gene Edward Veith Jr., *Postmodern Times* (Wheaton, Ill.: Crossway, 1994), chapter 4. For a helpful introduction to postmodernism in general, see Stanley J. Grenz, *A Primer on Postmodernism* (Grand Rapids: Eerdmans, 1996).

14. For the doctrine of the Trinity and epistemology, see Bruce Marshall, *Trinity and Truth* (Cambridge, England: Cambridge Univ. Press, 1999); for spirituality, see Alistair I. McFadyen, *The Call to Personhood: A Christian Theory of the Individual in Social Relationships* (Cambridge, England: Cambridge Univ. Press, 1990), and F. LeRon Shults and Steven J. Sandage, *The Faces of Forgiveness* (Grand Rapids: Baker, 2003). For the implications of a relational view of persons and the development of the human being, see Jack Balswick, Pamela King, and Kevin Reimer, *The Reciprocating Self* (Downers Grove, Ill.: InterVarsity, 2005).

15. Besides Karl Barth, proponents of this view would include Augustine and Rahner. While Augustine used the term *person* to refer to plurality of the Godhead, the implication of his theology is that God is *one person*. See William Hill, *The Three-Personed God* (Washington, D.C.: Catholic Univ. of America Press, 1982), 61.

16. Besides Wolfhart Pannenberg, whose views we will detail later in the text, proponents of this view include Jurgen Moltmann, who rejects the term *monotheism* in reference to the Christian God because of its implication of a single subject. See Jurgen Moltmann, *The Trinity and the Kingdom* (Minneapolis: Fortress, 1993), 129–50. Millard Erickson sees God as a complex society of persons; see Millard Erickson, *God in Three Persons* (Grand Rapids: Baker, 1995), 221–225. See also Cornelius Plantinga Jr.'s significant essay "Social Trinity and Tritheism" in *Trinity, Incarnation, and Atonement: Philosophical and Theological Essays*, ed. Ronald J. Feenstra and Cornelius Plantinga Jr. (Notre Dame, Ind.: Univ. of Notre Dame Press, 1989), 21–47. From a liberation theology perspective, see Leonard Boff, *Trinity and Society* (Maryknoll, N.Y.: Orbis Books, 1988), 129–135.

17. For example, see Moltmann's charge against Barth in Moltmann, *Trinity and King-*

dom, 144; Walter Kasper's analysis of Rahner's rejection of the term *person* in his book, *God of Jesus Christ*, 289; and Robert Letham's belief that Barth cannot be completely exonerated from the charge of unipersonality, in spite of his denials of modalism. See Robert Letham, *The Holy Trinity: In Scripture, History, Theology, and Worship* (Phillipsburg, N.J.: P & R, 2004), 278.

18. Edmund J. Fortman sees Barth drawing this conclusion in his writing. Barth writes in this regard: "Three personalities in God . . . would be worst and most pointed . . . tritheism." See Barth's work, *The Doctrine of the Word of God*, trans. G. T. Thompson, 2 vols. (Edinburgh, Scotland: T & T Clark, 1960): 414–415; cited by Fortman, *The Triune God* (Grand Rapids: Baker, 1972), 261.

19. Barth rejected the use of the term *person* to reference the plurality within God because of possible confusion. In God, he believed, there is only one "nature, so there is one knowledge, one self-consciousness." Therefore, to speak of three persons within the one God implied tritheism. See Karl Barth, *Church Dogmatics* (Edinburgh, Scotland: T. & T. Clark, 1975), 1:358–9.

20. Barth, *Church Dogmatics,* 1:296.

21. Ibid., 1:279. For brief summaries of Barth's view of the Trinity, see Letham, *The Holy Trinity*, 271–290, and Stanley Grenz, *Rediscovering the Triune God* (Minneapolis: Augsburg Fortress, 2004), 34–54.

22. Wolfhart Pannenberg, *Systematic Theology*, trans. Geoffrey W. Bromiley (Grand Rapids: Eerdmans, 1988), 1:310, 314.

23. Ibid., 1:319.

24. Ibid., 1:384.

25. David Brown argues that the earliest traces of individualistic notions of personhood are actually found in the writings of Augustine. For this reason Augustine found within human psychology his strongest analogy of the Trinity, for the image of God in man is found in the mind. See his article, "Trinitarian Personhood and Individuality," in *Trinity, Incarnation and Atonement*, ed. Ronald J. Feenstra and Cornelius Plantinga (Notre Dame, Ind.: Univ. of Notre Dame Press, 1989), 58.

26. Rene Descartes, *Discourse on Method and Meditations on First Philosophy*, trans. Donald A. Cress (Indianapolis: Hackett Publishing Co., 1980), 61.

27. Ibid. The actual conclusion Descartes made in his *Meditations* was "I am, I exist," but the Latin form found in his *Principles of Philosophy* is used here because that is the most well known.

28. Ibid., 63. There are several implications to equating the self with the mind. First, we have a strongly dualistic and individualistic view of persons. For Descartes, relationships were at most secondary and peripheral. In fact, in his view the self was so isolated from the other that the question of other minds became a genuine problem in Western philosophy. Second, we have the belief that man is most personal when he is most self-reflective. See Brown, "Trinitarian Personhood and Individuality," 57.

29. John MacMurray, *Self as Agent* (New York: Humanity Press, 1991), 76.

30. Ibid., 31.

31. MacMurray believes that by beginning with action he has eliminated the mind-body

problem. For when the self acts, it must include the "bodily self" and the "mental self," which are in reality not two selves but two aspects of the self who acts. See his *Self as Agent*, 79.

32. By the phrase "a relationship of being-for-the-other," I am referring to relationships where the participants possess the capacity, or the potential capacity (e.g., babies), to make moral decisions where one's actions toward the other are for the other (i.e., the other is the end) rather than for the self (i.e., the other becomes a means).

33. MacMurray, *Self as Agent*, 104–126.

34. Ibid., 12.

35. John MacMurray, *Persons in Relation* (New York: Humanity Press, 1999), 17.

36. Ibid., 211.

37. A categorical fallacy is committed when a concept from one discipline is inappropriately applied in another discipline.

38. Royce Gordon Gruenler, *Jesus, Persons, and the Kingdom of God* (Bloomington, Minn.: Bethany, 1967), 19.

39. Several pieces of biblical evidence can be used to support a relational view of personhood: (1) the Hebraic worldview perceived persons as communal entities; (2) John's proclamation that God is love is best understood in relational categories (1 John 4:8); and (3) the opening statement in the gospel of John concerning the Word can be understood in a relational sense.

40. Gunton, *The Promise of Trinitarian Theology*, 11.

41. MacMurray, *Persons in Relation*, 211.

42. Gerald Bray argues that Augustine's understanding of the Trinity as the Father who loves (Lover), the Son who is loved (Beloved), and the Spirit as love seriously undermines the personal reality of the Holy Spirit, with the result that "the question of his personhood has become a major theological issue." See his book, *The Doctrine of God* (Downers Grove, Ill.: InterVarsity, 1993), 173.

43. Cornelius Plantinga, "The Threeness/Oneness Problem of the Trinity," *Calvin Theological Journal* 23 (1988): 47. Frame also finds Aquinas' idea of subsistent relations odd, cf. John Frame, *The Doctrine of God* (Phillipsburg, N.J.: P & R Publishing, 2002), 702. Because of the lack of distinction between divine essence, persons, and relations, both Plantinga and Frame accuse Aquinas of falling into the trap of modalism.

44. T. F. Torrance, *The Christian Doctrine of God, One Being Three Persons* (Edinburgh, Scotland: T & T Clark, 1996), 157.

45. The phrases and the way they are used come from Martin Buber, *I and Thou*, trans. Walter Kaufmann (New York: Touchstone Books, 1970).

46. Balswick, King, and Reimer write, "An individual recognizes his or her uniqueness in relationship with another. In a sense the other provides an orientation for the self to be made known." See their book, *The Reciprocating Self*, 34.

47. Stanley Grenz, *The Social God and the Relational Self* (Louisville: Westminister/John Knox, 2001), 200.

48. Torrance connects human "persons" with the divine through image language. See T. F. Torrance, *Christian Doctrine of God*, 160. So also does Todd H. Speidell, who writes that because of the *imago Dei*, "they are not self-sufficient or autonomous individuals but those who live 'humanly only in I-Thou-We relations.'" See his article "A Trinitarian Ontology of Persons in Society," *Scottish Journal of Theology* 47 (1994): 285.

49. Robert Letham writes: "Personhood is to be understood (insofar as we can ever understand it) in terms of the way God is three." See his book, *The Holy Trinity*, 462.

50. Gunton, *The Promise of Trinitarian Theology*, 91.

51. See endnote no. 39.

52. John Zizioulas, "Human Capacity and Human Incapacity: A Theological Exploration of Personhood," *Scottish Journal of Theology* 28: 407–408.

53. John Zizioulas, *Being as Communion: Studies in Personhood and the Church* (New York: St. Vladimir's Seminary Press, 1985), 18.

54. Zizioulas, "Human Capacity and Human Incapacity," 408.

55. Torrance speaks of God as the "personalizing Person" and ourselves as "personalized persons." See his book, *Christian Doctrine of God,* 160.

56. Catherine LaCugna, *God for Us* (San Francisco: HarperSanFrancisco, 1993), 289.

57. Miroslav Volf, *After Our Likeness: The Church as the Image of the Trinity* (Grand Rapids: Eerdmans, 1998), 83.

58. Colin E. Gunton, *The One, the Three and the Many* (Cambridge, England: Cambridge Univ. Press, 1993), 118.

59. Thomas Merton, *No Man Is an Island* (San Diego: Harcourt Brace, 1983), 4.

60. Gunton, *The Promise of Trinitarian Theology*, 13.

61. LaCugna, *God for Us*, 290.

62. Ibid.

63. John Thompson, *Modern Trinitarian Perspectives* (Oxford, England: Oxford Univ. Press, 1994), 71. For a detailed interpretation of God's movement in human history from a missions perspective, see Arthur F. Glasser, *Announcing the Kingdom* (Grand Rapids: Baker, 2003).

64. Jurgen Moltmann, *The Coming of God* (Minneapolis: Augsburg Fortress, 1996), 298.

65. Volf, *After Our Likeness,* 193.

66. Hans Urs von Balthasar, "On the Concept of Person," *Communion* 13 (Spring 1986): 25.

67. Gary Parrett, "Becoming a Culturally Sensitive Minister" in Elizabeth Conde-Frazier, S. Steve Kang, and Gary Parrett, *A Many Colored Kingdom* (Grand Rapids: Baker, 2004), 121–150.

68. Sherwood G. Lingenfelter and Marvin K. Mayers, *Ministering Cross-Culturally* (Grand Rapids: Baker, 2003), 25.

69. David J. Hesselgrave reminds us that there are no acultural persons, since we all as babies were born into a particular culture. In fact, he believes that culture is more important than race, nationality, and gender in determining our thoughts, desires, and values. See his book, *Communicating Christ Cross-Culturally* (Grand Rapids: Zondervan, 1991), 102–103.

70. Lesslie Newbigin, *Foolishness to the Greeks* (Grand Rapids: Eerdmans, 1986), 21.

71. Lingenfelter and Mayers, *Ministering Cross-Culturally*, 16.

72. A good illustration of this principle is the life story of Hudson Taylor. See Howard Taylor, *Faith's Venture* (London: China Inland Mission, 1960).

73. Eugene Nida, *Message and Mission* (New York: Harper & Row, 1960), 164–166.

74. The relational concept of personhood allows us to speak of the divine and human aspects of the one person Jesus Christ in ways that were not possible with the rational substance view of personhood. While clearly more work needs to be done in this area, is it possible for us to think of the two aspects of Jesus Christ as dual identities rather than dual natures? In the one person of Christ, we have two answers to the question, "Who am I?" The divine response is that Jesus Christ is the Son who identifies the First Person of the Trinity as Father. This identity belongs to no other human being except Jesus Christ. The human response is that Jesus Christ is the Savior who identifies the church as His body. This identity belongs to no other person of the Trinity except the Son. These comments are only tentative suggestions that require much more thought.

75. Conde-Frazier et al., *A Many Colored Kingdom*, 144.

76. For an introductory discussion on Isaiah's gospel, see N. T. Wright, *What Saint Paul Really Said* (Grand Rapids: Eerdmans, 1997), 40–44.

77. Robert Guelich, "What Is the Gospel?" *Theology, News and Notes* 51, no. 2 (Spring 2004): 5.

Chapter 10

PROCLAIMING JESUS IN GLOBAL MISSION

A Pauline Perspective

by Trevor J. Burke

Where in the world are Christian missions headed today? For sure, the mission enterprise is moving, but perhaps not in ways we had expected or anticipated. Within the last fifty years a seismic shift has occurred—no longer is the Northern Hemisphere the Jerusalem or sending church. Rather, the Southern Hemisphere and cities such as Jos in Nigeria or Seoul in South Korea are now sending out the majority of missionaries. Recent mission statistics show that Nigeria, for example, easily the most populous country in Africa, has sent 3,300 missionaries to serve with 110 different agencies, while South Korea has sent a staggering 12,000 missionaries with 116 agencies, 10,000 of whom are serving in 156 countries.[1]

This is surely a cause for giving thanks to God, but it is not a new phenomenon. For several decades now, power, leadership, and influence have been shifting away from Europe and North America to the burgeoning churches in Africa, Asia, South America, and the Pacific.

Today, the church in the Northern Hemisphere is slowly awakening to this fact. As Andrew Walls, emeritus professor at the Centre for the Study of Christianity in the Non-Western World, University of Edinburgh, points out: "The missionary movement from the West is only an *episode* in African, Asian, and Pacific Christian history—a vital episode, but for many churches an episode long closed."[2]

Nonetheless, my opening question is deliberately ambiguous, for global mission has not only to do with "geography"—it has also to do (as I shall show in the next section) with theology. Moreover, in light of the changing face of mission, the church in the Northern Hemisphere would do well to ask, What ought we to do to rise to the challenge of how to do mission in the twenty-first century?

RESPONDING TO THE
CHANGING FACE OF GLOBAL MISSION

The Method and the Focus of Missions

How should we respond? Should we panic,[3] throw up our hands in despair, or recognize this as a part of God's sovereign plan in redemptive history? One recent response by some evangelical missiologists has been to lay the blame for the decline in mission in the Northern Hemisphere at the door of a faulty *methodology*. In *Changing the Mind of Missions*, James Engel and William Dyrness call for a new "revolution" in our understanding of mission. The greatest need of mission today, they maintain, is *not* to seek to win people to faith in the Lord Jesus Christ. Rather, "the mission of Jesus" is much wider and more "holistic," as evidenced in Jesus' inaugural sermon in the synagogue: "The Spirit of the Lord is on me . . . he has anointed me to preach good news to the poor . . . to proclaim freedom for the prisoners . . . to release the oppressed" (Luke 4:18 NIV) "If this defines the agenda of Jesus," declare the authors, "it also must define ours"[4]

Now do not get me wrong. I can empathize with the issues that

Engel and Dyrness raise and the need to have Christ's compassion and love in our hearts as we respond to the plethora of needs in our world. Mission should be holistic. It does involve the need to relieve poverty through education, medical aid, etc. Yet in all this, the preaching of the gospel to change lives should not be sidelined. After all, the opening words of Jesus' sermon above are: "The Spirit of the Lord is on me . . . to *preach good news.*"

Over the years there has been a steady shift in emphasis, going right back to the early 1970s and the influence of ecumenism. As a result, the Great Commission (Matt. 28:19–20) has not only been redefined but has also taken on an ominous ring of liberation theology. Today, it seems, mission has more to do with justice for the poor and caring for the environment and less to do with making disciples and obeying the command of Jesus Christ to proclaim the good news and to proclaim Him who calls men, women, boys, and girls to turn from their sin and trust in Him alone for salvation.

But the changing face of global mission has brought another response from the church in the Northern Hemisphere, namely, a renewed awareness that it is not always necessary to send missionaries to Africa, Asia, South America, or the Pacific. Richard Mouw rightly observes, "The North American Christian community today is in a missionary location." Certainly this is a challenge as the church wrestles with a whole raft of missiological issues, including religious pluralism (e.g., the fantastic growth of mosques in North America), as well as increased experimentation with the occult, the practice of pre-Christian goddess religions, and consultation of astrological stars.

In light of this syncretistic melting pot, the great need of the hour, Mouw points out, is for the church to develop "missionary sensitivities while operating with a missionary vision in North America."[5] His observations are good, but he too blames the decline of mission in the Northern Hemisphere on a faulty *methodology.*[6] Moreover, his insights are not new, as recognized by Joseph Stowell who prophetically commented more than a decade ago: "In America today, the world is moving to our cities and to our neighborhoods. The mission fields are coming from all over the world to us." Stowell then added the following penetrating remark: "That sounds exciting . . . unless you live in a nice suburb, and four weeks later a big truck pulls up. As you look through the blinds, you notice that the people moving in aren't like you. They don't have the same color of skin."[7]

Stowell brings mission down to the personal level and puts his finger on the pulse of the issue: today in twenty-first-century North America (and the United Kingdom, I hasten to add). We do not have to cross the seas to be involved in mission. All we have to do, if we have the concern (or is it obedience?), is to cross the street. When mission presents itself in one's own backyard, then we need all the sensitivity and courage to share the good news of Jesus Christ. But then those involved in mission have always been known for daring to risk their necks for the sake of Jesus Christ and the kingdom of God, have they not?

The Ongoing Need to Proclaim the Gospel in Other Cultures

Don't misunderstand; I still think there is a need for those whom God has gifted and called to take the gospel of Jesus Christ to other parts of the world. The so-called "10/40 Window" where fifty-seven countries comprising 3.6 billion people, or 60 percent of the world's population, is evidence of this need. Right across the world's middle belt, from North Africa into the Middle East and right through Asia, the needs are greatest. Statistics "show that the vast bulk of people who have yet to hear a clearly communicated invitation to repent, turn to Christ, and worship God are those deeply embedded in cultures that largely, if not exclusively, follow a religion other than Christianity."[8] Clearly some serious evangelization is required if the Great Commission is to be fulfilled. The need is for sensitive cross-cultural missionaries who will learn the culture and language in order to meaningfully communicate the message of the gospel.

But perhaps the most compelling reason that I am persuaded of the need for missionaries to serve overseas is, as mentioned earlier, the phenomenal growth of the church in the Southern Hemisphere. New wine in Africa, Asia, South America, and the Pacific is flowing in abundance. In addition, our brothers and sisters in Christ need the continued support of the church in the Northern Hemisphere.[9]

Those needs were brought home forcibly to me when I was teaching New Testament in a theological seminary in West Africa a few years ago. Just prior to going for our annual two-week vacation and as the rainy season was about to begin, we planted a shrub at the side of the house. On our return as we drove into the campus we were amazed that this young shrub had grown almost to the height of the door. Astonished at this spurt, I got out of the car and went across to inspect this tender shrub only to discover when I tugged at the base of the plant the whole thing uprooted in my hand!

Symbolic? I think so. The spread of the church in the Southern Hemisphere has been rapid but the roots do not always go very deep.[10] Perhaps the greatest need for all those called to work in cross-cultural contexts is for "well-trained biblical scholars and adept, sensitive theologians . . . to establish a foundation—not *for* but *with* the Third World—grounded in the bedrock of God's unchanging Word."[11]

If the decline in mission from the Northern Hemisphere does not lie with a defective methodology, where then does it lie? According to David Hesselgrave and others,[12] the roots lie much deeper:

> Unfortunately, evangelicals in mission still tend to proceed as though their major problems were methodological. They are not. They are *theological*. It would be to their everlasting credit if evangelicals would devote themselves, their organizations, and their conferences to frequent and thorough studies on the Christian mission as set forth in the biblical text. By its very nature, biblical mission entails clear biblical priorities.[13]

The Perspective of the Apostle Paul

So where can we turn in God's Word for guidance? Who better than the apostle Paul! Why not Jesus, you may ask? For a start, "the Pauline Great Commission"[14] stands in line with the Great Commission given by Jesus (cf. Matt. 28:19–20; Rom. 15:20–22) who commissioned the apostle to take the gospel to all nations. Thus, "Paul's mission is nothing less than the outworking of *Christ's* own mission."

Second, Paul is helpful because the shift in the epicenter of missionary activity from the Northern to the Southern Hemisphere in the twenty-first-century world is akin to what Paul himself experienced. Remember, Paul was the vehicle for the changing complexion of the church in the first-century as it moved from being essentially Jewish in nature at its inception to one mostly Gentile in composition. Paul, therefore, serves as an excellent guide to the changing complexion of global mission today.[15]

Third, Paul was first and foremost a pioneer missionary[16] who had a burning passion to make Christ known: "It has always been my ambition to preach the gospel *where Christ was not known*, so that I would not be building on someone else's foundation" (Rom. 15:20 NIV). Paul was never complacent or reliant upon what had already been accomplished but always set himself new challenges, determined to break fresh territory and push across new frontiers with the gospel of the Lord Jesus Christ. Moreover, Paul was not only a missionary. He is more accurately described as a *cross-cultural* missionary—faced with the challenge and entrusted with the responsibility of taking the gospel of Jesus Christ across cultural barriers. Paul was the cross-cultural missionary *par excellence*. He was a Jew, "of the tribe of Benjamin, a Hebrew of the Hebrews . . . a Pharisee" (Phil. 3:5); he also wrote in Greek and could converse in Aramaic (cf. Acts 22:2); and he was a Roman citizen (Acts 22:29). Thus, Paul's multicultural background uniquely qualified him for the task of cross-cultural mission. Although a Jew,

Paul was called to be a missionary to the Gentiles (Gal. 1:14–16; cf. Acts 9:15), a point that "lies at the heart of Paul's work as missionary and pastor."[17]

But finally and most important, Paul was a theologian, as well as being a missionary. Paul's theology was beaten out on the anvil of his missionary travels and work and activity and is best described as "missionary theology."[18] "We cannot understand Paul's theology without integrating his perspective on mission into the larger interpretation of his theology."[19] Further, Paul's missionary message was christologically grounded, evident in the succinct summary of his missionary message: "I resolved to know nothing while I was with you except *Jesus Christ* and him *crucified*" (1 Cor. 2:2 NIV). The person and the work of Jesus Christ pervaded the apostle Paul's message.

These are all good reasons for considering Paul's writings for his *own* thinking on mission. Paul's role as missionary is one that needs to be reclaimed. But before we look at the content of Paul's missionary message, it is important to turn to the events that directly influenced what he was to preach: his conversion and call.

THE GROUND OF PAUL'S CONVERSION AND CALL AS MISSIONARY: THE REVELATION OF JESUS CHRIST

The basis of all Paul's missionary activity finds its origin in *the* epoch-making events in his own life: his conversion and call.[20] It is highly significant that at the outset of his missionary activity Paul describes his conversion and call on the road to Damascus in christological terms.[21] Paul makes this clear in Galatians 1:12, 15–16: "I received it [the gospel] through a revelation of Jesus Christ. . . . God . . . was pleased to reveal His Son in me so that I might preach Him among the Gentiles." Here Paul provides a twofold description of the nature of the revelation. First, he designated Christ as the agent through whom he receives the gospel: "I received the gospel through a revelation of Jesus

Christ."[22] As far as his conversion and call are concerned, Paul owed nothing to human intervention and everything to the living, risen, and exalted Christ whom he had encountered.

Second, Paul goes on to stress how through his conversion and call "God . . . was pleased to reveal His Son in me" (1:16). Paul's use of the term *Son* here (cf. Rom. 1:4; 1 Cor. 1:9; 2 Cor. 1:19; Gal. 2:20) is a central christological ascription for Jesus the Messiah. Paul's use of the verb *to reveal* in Galatians 1:16 together with the prepositional phrase *in me* underscores the objective (external) and subjective (internal) aspects of the revelation given to him. Regarding the former, this revelation was objective, having come from God and outside of himself. What happened to Paul was no mere fantasy nor premonition or even wishful thinking on his part; still less was it a mystical experience. Rather, the outward, visible aspect of the risen Lord who appeared to Paul on the road to Damascus was dynamic and real and life changing for the apostle. In respect of the latter, the revelation was subjective as the phrase *in me* denotes, having taken place within Paul, and not those who were travelling with him. This phrase underscores "the inwardness already implied by the verb 'reveal,' which connotes a disclosure involving perception and understanding on the part of the recipient."[23]

What is the purpose of this christologically defined revelation? Paul states that it is "that I might preach *Him* [i.e., Christ] among the Gentiles" (1:16b). It is instructive to note here the vital connection between revelation and proclamation: the risen and exalted Jesus Christ, the Son of God, who appeared to Paul was to be the sum and substance of his missionary message. Note that Paul's proclamation of Jesus as Son here in Galatians 1:16b finds corroboration in Acts 9:20, where Luke relates how Paul after his conversion on the road to Damascus "immediately . . . began to proclaim Jesus in the synagogues, saying, 'He is the Son of God.'" In Galatians 1:16b the verb *preach*, in the present tense, contrasts with the previous verbs in the aorist tense (*called, set apart*), thereby emphasizing the ongoing proclamation of a message that was not subject to alteration or change.[24]

THE CONTENT OF PAUL'S MISSIONARY MESSAGE:
THE PERSON AND WORK OF CHRIST

We often overlook the fact that Paul's letters are missionary letters, written by an itinerant missionary preacher whose goal was not only to bring people to Christ but also to establish churches in which those nascent converts could mature in the Lord. When Paul wrote his letter to the church at Rome, he had many reasons for doing so.[25] One of his reasons was his upcoming missionary plan to visit Spain and the need to have the support of the church at Rome. Moreover, Romans can be read is as a "missionary document"[26] in which Paul presents his missionary theology.

At the outset of the letter, the apostle states his missiological purpose for coming is that he "might have a harvest among" (Rom. 1:13 NIV) the Roman Christians. The central element of Paul's missionary preaching is, of course, the gospel (e.g., 1:1, 9, 15, 16, 17; 2:16; 15:16, 19), and the content of that good news is succinctly summarized in a highly compressed christological statement in Romans 1:3–4[27]: Jesus Christ, Son of David, risen Son of God and Lord. In Romans 1:3–4 Paul underscores Jesus' messianic credentials as one born of the seed of David (v. 3b) in fulfillment of the prophetic hopes of the people of Israel (e.g., 2 Sam. 7:12–16; cf. Isa. 11; Jer. 23:5–6). Romans 1:3–4 concurs with Galatians 1:16 concerning the content of Paul's gospel, where repetition of the noun *Son* (vv. 3, 4) emphasizes that Paul is delineating nothing less than "Son-christology."[28]

Some commentators see Paul as contrasting the two natures of Jesus Christ in Romans 1:3–4—Jesus' full humanity ("descendant of David") versus His divinity as evidenced in His resurrection from the dead.[29] It is more likely, however, that Paul is contrasting two eras or the two phases in Jesus' historical career where Christ's resurrection is the turning point. Prior to His resurrection Jesus was truly the Son of God, but after He was raised from the dead He entered a new phase of sonship by being appointed the Son-of-God-in-power. Crucially, for Paul, it is the vindicated and resurrected Jesus Christ, the Son of God, who not only ushers in a new era but who is also given power to save all who trust in Him.

This same christological note appears later in the letter when Paul states how God sent "His own Son in the likeness of sinful flesh and as *an offering for sin*" (Rom. 8:3, italics added). The purpose of the Son of God coming into the world was not only incarnational but also sacrificial: Jesus Christ, the Son of God, was born with the supreme purpose that He might die for our sins. Moreover, it is significant how Paul "explicitly connects . . . the sending of the Son of God in Romans 8:3 with . . . the . . . consequences of divine adoption" (Rom. 8:15, 23).[30] That is to say, the Son of God who stepped out of eternity into history, and who subsequently died on the cross, is the one through whom others are enfranchised to become the adopted sons of God.[31]

Paul's first letter to the Thessalonians also provides some of the earliest and vital evidence of his missionary preaching. In verse 1:9–10 (ESV), Paul reminds the Thessalonians how they had turned from polytheism to monotheism: "to God from idols to serve the living and true God."[32] Conversion stands at the heart of all of Paul's missionary preaching. In this text the monotheistic emphasis is clearly evident, but we should not overlook how Paul sounds an important christological note by recounting the life and ministry of Jesus, especially His death, resurrection, and glorious return. Paul states that the result of the Thessalonians' conversion was "to wait for His Son from heaven, whom He raised from the dead, that is Jesus, who rescues us from the wrath to come" (1:10). Once again a "crucified and risen Jesus Christ is the content of Paul's missionary preaching."[33] It is particularly instructive to note how Paul uses the name *Jesus* in verse 10 without the accompanying noun *Lord*. That is not only unusual but also emphasizes Jesus as a historical figure with respect to His humanity, i.e., life, death, and resurrection.

Interestingly, Paul's initial mentioning of the deliverance from the coming wrath (1:9–10) is repeated at the end of the letter (5:9–10) and functions as an *inclusio*, thereby underscoring that "Paul's Christology remains uniform throughout."[34] In 1 Thessalonians 5:9–10 (NIV), Paul writes: "For God did not appoint us to suffer wrath but to receive salvation through our Lord Jesus Christ. He died for us so that . . . we may live together with him." At the beginning of the letter Paul had declared that the church is "in . . . Christ" (1:1), a clear reference that only those who have been united with God's Son in His death, burial, and resurrection belong to Him. Paul sounds the same note later in the epistle when he discusses Jesus' vicarious death *for* (Gk. *huper*, 5:10) its members, which delivers them from eschatological wrath *through* (*dia*, 5:9) Him. Viewing 1 Thessalonians 1:9–10 and 5:9–10 as bookends to this letter reminds us that the alpha and omega of Paul's earliest missionary message to the Thessalonians are rooted christologically in the death and resurrection of Christ.

The Goal of Paul as Missionary-Pastor: Present Everyone Mature in Jesus Christ

Paul preached the gospel of Christ so that people might be converted. Conversion, however, was only part of Paul's larger missionary objective—the founding of Christian communities. But an even higher objective is in view because establishing churches was not Paul's final goal. According to Paul, the supreme end of the founding of communities was to present everyone mature in Jesus Christ on the last day. He writes to the church at Colossae: "Him we proclaim [i.e., Christ], warning everyone and teaching everyone with all wisdom, that we may *present everyone mature in Christ* (Col. 1:28 ESV, italics added).

Paul was no fly-by-night missionary or charlatan. There were plenty of those around in the first-century world who could spin a good sermon, charge an exorbitant fee, and disappear without trace. Rather, as W. P. Bowers points out, the "defining dimension of the Pauline mission [was] Paul's missionary commitment to . . . nurturing Christian communities as the central goal of his missionary endeavours in any particular region. . . . Paul's missionary commitment includes nurturing such communities toward mature stability."[35]

But just how did the apostle Paul go about bringing people to maturity in Jesus Christ? Let's consider this intriguing subject in a little more depth.

PAUL'S NURTURING OF HIS CONGREGATIONS

Paul used various means of pastoral care as a missionary to ensure that his churches grew in the Lord. One method was corresponding with them (and they with him, cf. 1 Cor. 7:1) by letter. Paul also regularly visited those communities he had founded to see how they were progressing and to resolve difficulties, divisions, and doctrinal problems. Further, he dispatched emissaries (e.g., Timothy, cf. 1 Thess. 3:6) to report on his converts' progress.

Another fascinating piece of evidence of Paul's continued pastoral care for the fledgling communities he had founded was in the personal and relational family language he used in his writings. The nurturing and caring for the communities he founded was as much part and parcel of Paul's missionary responsibility as his activity of establishing them in the first place. Paul demonstrated his responsibility toward his congregations, for example, by his use of paternal metaphors:

I do not write these things to make you ashamed, but to admonish you as my beloved children. For though you have countless guides in Christ, you do not have many fathers. For I became your father [literally "I fathered you"] in Christ Jesus through the gospel. (1 Cor. 4:14–15, ESV; cf. Philem. 10)

Many of Paul's letters contain much family terminology, but 1 Thessalonians contains the heaviest preponderance of such language where he describes his relationship to the Thessalonians as a father to his children (1 Thess. 2:10–12). Paul also uses maternal metaphors to underscore his desire to nurture the fledgling community for whom he felt responsible: "as apostles of Christ we might have asserted our authority. But we proved to be gentle[36] among you, as a nursing mother tenderly cares for her own children" (1 Thess. 2:6–7). And he portrays the Thessalonians' relations to one another as "brothers" no fewer than nineteen times (eg., 1 Thess. 1:4; 2:1, 14, 17; 3:2; 4:1, 6, 13; 5:1, 4), proportionately more often than any other letter.

Why does Paul use this family language? One suggestion is that it was only natural for Paul to use such terms—given the fact that not long after the founding of the Christian "family" the apostle was abruptly forced from his fledgling church, leaving him concerned and anxious to return (1 Thess. 2:17–3:6). But another reason for this familial emphasis in Paul's letters is that he is drawing from a whole raft of assumptions in the ancient world to regulate relationships between himself as father and his converts as children. That is to say, Paul as father expected obedience, love, honour, etc., from his spiritual offspring, and they also expected discipline, love, etc., from him. The relationship was a reciprocal one.[37]

Two points about this imagery are worthy of note. First, Paul is contextualizing his pastoral care: He is drawing from a common understanding of "family" in the ancient world, which he uses to instruct, guide, and care for this young community.[38] Second, Paul undergirds his pastoral care as missionary by his desire to see Christ glorified in his converts' lives. One example from the ancient world of Paul will suffice. One way in which children in the ancient world were expected to obey their fathers was through imitation. For example, Plutarch, the prolific Greek writer and contemporary of Paul writes: "Fathers . . . above all should make themselves a manifest example to their children, so that the latter, by looking at their fathers' lives as at a mirror, may be deterred from disgraceful deeds and words" (*De Lib.* 20/14B). Similarly, Jewish fathers expected no different. Josephus, the first-century historian, states, "The Law . . . enjoins sobriety in the upbringing from the very first. It orders that they [i.e., children] be taught to read and shall learn the laws and deeds from their forefathers, in order that they may imitate [*mimōntai*] the latter" (*Ap.* 1. 204; cf. 1 Macc. 2.51).

Paul's Personal Example

Paul is also not afraid to hold himself up as a personal example for his converts to follow. We see this in 1 Thessalonians 1:6, where Paul commends the Thessalonians for the manner in which they "became imitators of us and *of the Lord*," where Paul means that "he imitated Christ and the Thessalonians imitated him,"[39] and in imitating him they were following the example of Christ. Paul makes a similar point in his letter to the church at Corinth, one which he had also founded, and where he writes "I became your father through the gospel. Therefore I exhort you, be imitators of me" (1 Cor. 4:15–16).

Here again while Paul is keen for his converts to follow him, later in the letter he writes: "Follow my example, as I follow the *example of Christ*" (11:1 NIV, italics added). As a faithful missionary and pastor, Paul sets before the Corinthians Jesus Christ as the primary model for imitation, not only for himself and but for all believers to follow. Why? Simply because Paul was not only in the business of making converts but also in the business of ensuring they grew and matured in the Lord. Indeed, for the apostle the Corinthians' growing up into Jesus Christ is not a take-it-or-leave-it matter but a Pauline priority, clearly evident in his use of the imperative mood in verse 16.

THE CHALLENGE OF GLOBAL MISSION FOR THE CHURCH

In light of Paul's missionary message, what lessons can the twenty-first-century church glean in order to effectively communicate the gospel?

The Decisive Factor: the Message, *Not* the Messenger

A cursory reading of Paul's letters reveals that his overriding concern was not with his missionary work or even his theology but with the gospel as centered on God's Son, the Lord Jesus Christ. Jesus Christ was the promised Messiah, who in the last days had made God known by providing salvation through His death and resurrection. Christian mission for Paul was always Christ-centered. Paul had no desire to preach himself or his own message, because his message was the message of Jesus his Savior.

This matter of whether Paul's message was the message of Christ has been much debated in scholarly circles, because some have tried to drive a wedge between the two. The debate is well summarized in the title of David Wenham's (the British scholar's) monograph *Paul: Follower of Jesus or Founder of Christianity?* in which he concludes: "Paul would have been horrified at the suggestion that he was the founder of Christianity . . . Paul saw himself as the slave of Jesus Christ."

We have seen that Paul as missionary was the founder of churches, not of Christianity, and we have observed how he did this by preaching a message centered on Jesus Christ, the Son of God. Paul did not wish to start a new religion, nor did he wish to have a personal following. The latter was a particular problem in the church in Corinth (1 Cor. 3:1–5), where Paul sought to combat the cult of personality in which the *church members* were putting priority on man over the message. While different groups within the church were seeking to elevate Paul, Peter, and Apollos (cf. 1:10–13 and 3:3–9), the apostle responds, "What then is Apollos? And what is Paul? Servants *through* whom [not "*in* whom"] you believed" (3:5, emphasis added). To be sure, Paul was God's agent through whom the church was brought into being, but he always deflected attention from himself by seeking to elevate and glorify the Lord Jesus Christ (1 Cor. 2:2).

It is a simple but important point, and missionaries and pastors would do well to follow Paul's example and words when he states, "We do not preach ourselves but Christ Jesus as Lord" (2 Cor. 4:5).

The Prepared Missionary: Grounded in Scripture and Theology

We have observed that Paul was both missionary *and* theologian. These two do not contradict but rather complement each other. It is instructive to note how the church in Antioch sent two of its members, Paul and Barnabas (Acts 13:1–3), who had been involved in the ministry of the church, overseas to engage in mission. What is particularly important here is that Paul and Barnabas were especially gifted teachers. Luke records in Acts 11:26 how after a great number had turned to the Lord (11:21), Barnabas sent for Paul and brought him to Antioch and "for a whole year Barnabas and Saul met with the church and taught great numbers of people" (11:26 NIV).

Note that the church at Antioch did not send novices overseas to engage in mission but dispatched two of its most spiritually gifted and involved members. Likewise, the church today should send people who are already serving in the church, the arena where gifts and calling have been identified, tested, fostered, and developed. This means that pastors-elders, along with the church body, have a vital role to play in looking for gifted people in their congregations who believe God may be calling them to go overseas. The church then tests this calling by providing opportunities for them to preach, teach, or engage in short overseas missions trips.

In light of the importance of theology in Paul's understanding of mission, missionaries should be as well qualified and trained theologically as pastors.[40] We sometimes think that theological training is required only for the latter and that the former are somehow exempt.

This is erroneous thinking. Think of it this way: If it is foolhardy to let loose into an operating theatre a surgeon with only a little training, how much more dangerous is it to allow a missionary to go overseas with only a little theological training when the eternal destiny of people are at stake? "Of all the people who are engaged in the Lord's work, the missionary is probably in greatest need of sound, thorough, theological training."[41]

This raises a related issue, namely, that those training for the pastoral ministry should be given exposure to the church overseas. The fruits of this initiative will pay off in the long run because if a pastor has a healthy interest in mission, you can rest assured his church will also. Working and living in another culture will not only change the way a person looks at the world (and how one is perceived *outside* one's own country); more important, the experience will change values and widen one's understanding of what God is doing in other parts of the world. It is worth remembering that those training for pastoral ministry will probably one day be sending others overseas to engage in mission. If they have some exposure to a cross-cultural context they will have some idea of the joys and struggles of serving in another country and be able to help their churches pray more intelligently.

Clear Communication: Presenting the Gospel *in the Cultural Context*

As we have seen, Paul was the consummate communicator, contextualizing his message by taking his readers from what they knew to what they didn't know. Of course, in doing so, Paul was only following Jesus' example of teaching His disciples by parable (e.g., seed, goats). Paul was a master of metaphor and used the image of the ancient family to communicate Christ to his congregations.

Contextualization and biblical mission are as much the agenda of the local pastor as of the cross-cultural missionary. We can all too easily employ clichés and slip into using "the language of Zion" without thinking about whether our preaching is really resonating with our hearers. People may hear, but do they understand what is being preached?

There has never been a more appropriate time in the life of the Christian church than today for an innovative proclamation and contextualization[42] of a biblically based message to meet the needs of a lost world. "Connect and relate" should be the church's battle cry. Yet do not become irrelevant!

"But the gospel *is* relevant," you reply. It most certainly is, but missionaries, pastors, and church workers under the guidance of the Holy Spirit need to articulate that message clearly so that others will understand how Jesus can meet their deepest need—their salvation. The gospel message is always the same, but the context in which we serve will determine how we present it.

Byang Kato, the late visionary Nigerian leader, described contextualization simply as "making concepts or ideas relevant in a given situation." It is, he continued, "an effort to express the never-changing Word of God in ever-changing modes of relevance. Since the gospel is inspired but the mode of its expression is not, contextualization of the modes of expression is not only right but necessary."[43]

For the cross-cultural missionary to connect meaningfully is a particular challenge—a lesson brought home to me early in my teaching career. While in Nigeria, teaching an exegesis class to seminary students on 1 Timothy, we had reached chapter 4:11–16 where Paul provides instructions for young Timothy as pastor. On three occasions in this chapter the apostle underscores Timothy's responsibility not only to preach but also to teach (vv. 6, 11, 13) the Word. In short, Timothy was to offer instruction to those under his care.

This resonated with me in the context in which I was working. Many new converts were in the churches in Nigeria, and I was especially keen that my students learn not only to preach but also to teach. As I thought about this, I remembered the hens and chicks (preaching fees!) we kept at the back of our house and recalled the many lessons I had learned from observing animal behavior during my undergraduate days of studying psychology. After the lecture I decided to invite my seminary students over to the back of our house where I had watched these birds.

Then I threw down a large hunk of bread for the hens. They quickly started to do what they always did, namely, break off small pieces and drop them on the ground for their young offspring to eat. A smile began to break over the students' faces as my contextualized message hit home: "Here is what you are to do as pastors in your teaching," I concluded. "Break the Word of God into easily digestible pieces so that the believers under your care can grow up into the Lord Jesus Christ. By your so doing, Christ will truly be glorified in His church."

Trevor J. Burke is professor of Bible at the Moody Bible Institute. He has earned the Ph.D. degree from University of Glasgow, Scotland, as well as degrees from the University College of North Wales, Bangor; Queen's University, Belfast, Northern Ireland; and the New University of Ulster, Coleraine, Northern Ireland.

NOTES

1. These statistics are taken from Patrick Johnstone, *Operation World, 21st Century Edition* (Carlisle, Pa.: Paternoster Press, 2001).

2. Andrew Walls, *The Cross-Cultural Process in Christian History* (Maryknoll, N.Y.: Orbis Books, 2002), 45 (italics added).

3. Some hold the view that there is a crisis in global missions evident by the title of an excellent collection of essays edited by Russell L. Penney: *Overcoming the Missions Crisis: Thinking Strategically to Reach the World* (Grand Rapids: Kregel, 2001).

4. James F. Engel and William Dyrness, *Changing the Mind of Missions* (Downers Grove, Ill.: InterVarsity, 2000), 23.

5. Richard J. Mouw, "The Missionary Location of the North American Churches," ed. Craig Van Gelder, *Confident Witnesses—Changing the World* (Grand Rapids: Eerdmans, 1999), 3–15.

6. Ibid., 3, 7.

7. Joseph Stowell, *The Dawn's Early Light* (Chicago: Moody, 1990),173.

8. A. Scott Moreau, Gary R. Corwin, Gary B. McGee, *Introducing World Mission* (Grand Rapids: Baker, 2004), 295.

9. Even as I write, an article has been posted on the Web site of the Society of Biblical Literature in which a Chinese professor who introduced a course on Scripture into the curriculum was inundated with students wanting to take the course. Later in his letter he goes on to make a plea to the West, asking "for help from all of international biblical studies scholars who will keep an eye on the development . . . The following difficulties are . . . lack of books in this field, lack of multimedia materials, rarity of national and international conferences in this field held in China." See www.sbl.org.

10. See David F. Wells, *God in the Wasteland: The Reality of Truth in a World of Fading Dreams* (Grand Rapids: Eerdmans, 1994), 195, who questions whether the roots are any deeper in some of the churches in North America today. He states, for example, that students coming to Bible colleges and seminaries in North America are not as biblically literate as their counterparts thirty years ago.

11. J. Ronald Blue, "The Necessity of Missionary Training for the Missionary," *Overcoming the Missions Crisis*, ed. Russell L. Penney (Grand Rapids: Kregel, 2001), 183.

12. David Hesselgrave "Evangelical Mission in 2001 and Beyond," *Trinity World Forum*, Spring 2001: 1–3; cf. Samuel Escobar, "The Global Scenario at the Turn of the Century," *Global Missiology for the 21st Century*, ed. William D. Taylor (Grand Rapids: Baker, 2000) asserts that what we need to do is to get back to basics because "it has become evident that the new century will require a *return to biblical patterns of mission* . . . it is time for a paradigm change that will come from a salutary *return to the Word of God.*"

13. Hesselgrave, "Evangelical Mission in 2001 and Beyond," 3.

14. This phrase is the title of chapter 5 of T. O'Brien, *Gospel and Mission in the Writings of Paul: An Exegetical and Theological Analysis* (Grand Rapids: Baker, 1995).

15. Andrew F. Walls, *Cross-Cultural Process in Christian History* (Maryknoll, N.Y.: Orbis Books), 30, writes: "The first change in the center of gravity of the Christian world, entirely representative of what was to follow, took place within the first century of the Christian era, and its pathway is marked within the New Testament itself. Within a remarkably short time, Christianity ceased to be a demographically Jewish phenomenon centered in Jewish Palestine and expressed in terms of the fulfillment of God's promises to Israel. It moved toward a new expression as a demographically and culturally Hellenistic one, dispersed across the Eastern Mediterranean and then beyond it . . . That Christianity was itself not swept away was due to the cross-cultural diffusion that had already begun, and the consequent emergence of a new Hellenistic model of Christian expression."

16. Eckhard J. Schnabel, *Early Christian Mission: Jesus and the Twelve*, vol. 1 (Downers Grove, Ill.: InterVarsity, 2004), 6, rightly laments the fact that "the body of literature on the early Christian mission is not large. This is true even for Paul's missionary work." The reason is that while Paul is important today as a theologian, during the early church he was primarily viewed as a missionary. Schnabel concludes that the apostle's missionary enterprise has been downplayed to the extent that "Paul's missiological work is almost completely ignored in . . . descriptions of Paul's life."

17. Stephen C. Barton, "Paul as Missionary and Pastor," *The Cambridge Companion to St. Paul*, ed. James D. G. Dunn (Cambridge: Cambridge Univ. Press, 2003), 35.

18. Andreas J. Köstenberger and Peter T. O'Brien, *Salvation to the Ends of the Earth: A Biblical Theology of Mission*, New Studies in Biblical Theology 11 (Downers Grove, Ill.: InterVarsity, 2001), 164.

19. Ibid., 164.

20. In recent times Paul's experience on the Damascus road has been understood as a call and not a conversion. Yet it is not a case of one or the other but both/and; see the most recent defense for both by Peter O'Brien, "Was Paul Converted?" *Justification and Variegated Nomism: The Paradoxes of Paul*, ed. D. A. Carson, Peter T. O'Brien, and Mark A. Seifrid, vol. 2 (Grand Rapids: Baker, 2004), 361–91.

21. Richard N. Longenecker, *Galatians,* Word Biblical Commentary, vol. 41 (Nashville: Nelson, 1990), 31–32.

22. The phrase "Jesus Christ" can be understood as an objective (Jesus as the content) or subjective genitive (Jesus as the agent).

23. Murray J. Harris, "Prepositions and Theology in the Greek New Testament," ed. C. Brown, *The New International Dictionary of New Testament Theology*, (Grand Rapids: Zondervan, 1978), 1191.

24. Seyoon Kim, *The Origin of Paul's Gospel* Wissenschaftliche Untersuchungen Neuen Testament (Tubingen, Germany: Mohr, 1981) has argued that Paul received all of his theology, i.e., soteriology, Christology etc., at his conversion on the road to Damascus.

25. See A. J. M. Wedderburn, *The Reasons for Romans* (Edinburgh: T & T Clark, 1988).

26. Eckhardt J. Schnabel, *Early Christian Mission: Paul and the Early Church*, vol. 2 (Downers Grove, Ill.: InterVarsity Press, 2004), 1472.

27. For one of the most cogent defenses for Pauline authorship of these verses see James M. Scott, *Adoption as Sons: An Exegetical Investigation into the Background of Huiothesia in the Pauline Corpus* WUNT 2.48 (Tubingen, Germany: Mohr, 1992), 229–36.

28. Kim, *Origin of Paul's Gospel,* 111

29. There is a host of exegetical issues here. For guidance see Douglas J. Moo, *The Epistle to the Romans* NICNT (Grand Rapids: Eerdmans, 1996), 44–51.

30. L. W. Hurtado, "Son of God," *Dictionary of Paul and His Letters*, ed. Gerald F. Hawthorne, Ralph Martin & Daniel G. Reid (Downers Grove, Ill.: InterVarsity Press, 1994), 905.

31. See further Trevor J. Burke, *Adopted into God's Family: A Study of a Neglected Pauline Metaphor*, New Studies in Biblical Theology (Leicester, England: InterVarsity, 2006).

32. Charles A. Wanamaker, *Commentary on 1 and 2 Thessalonians*, New International Greek Testament Commentary (Grand Rapids: Eerdmans, 1990), 84–89, for a defense of this text as the authentic missionary preaching of Paul in Thessalonica.

33. Schnabel, *Early Christian Mission*, vol. 2, 981.

34. Paul W. Barnett, *The Birth of Christianity: The First Twenty Years*, vol. 1 (Grand Rapids: Eerdmans, 2005), 44.

35. W. P. Bowers, "Mission" in Gerald F. Hawthorne, Ralph Martin, and Daniel G. Reid, eds., *Dictionary of Paul and His Letters* (Downers Grove, Ill.: InterVarsity, 1994), 608–19 (610).

36. This verse has an important textual problem that centers on the inclusion (*nepioi*, "infants") or omission (*epioi*, "gentle") of one Greek letter.

37. See Trevor J. Burke, "Paul's Role as 'Father' to His Corinthian 'Children' in Socio-Historical Context," *Paul and the Corinthians: Studies on a Community in Conflict, Essays in Honour of Margaret Thrall,* ed. Trevor J. Burke and J. Keith Elliott (Leiden, England: Brill, 2003), 95–114. For a similar approach in 1 Thessalonians see Trevor J. Burke, *Family Matters: A Socio-historical Study of Kinship Metaphors in 1 Thessalonians,* Journal for the Study of the New Testament Series 247 (London: T & T Clark International, 2003).

38. For all the primary source material, see Burke, *Family Matters,* chaps. 2 and 3.

39. Abraham J. Malherbe, *The Letters to the Thessalonians: A New Translation with Introduction and Commentary,* vol. 32B (New York: Doubleday, 2002), 114.

40. For a strong argument in favor of missionaries being as theologically well qualified as pastors, see Ron Blue, "The Necessity of Theological Training," 173–188.

41. Blue, "The Necessity of Theological Training," 173.

42. The term *contextualization* can mean different things to different people; missiologists distinguish between linguistic contextualization and contextualization of thoughts. For a working definition of contextualization see, for example, David Hesselgrave, *Contextualization: Meanings, Methods, and Models* (Grand Rapids: Baker, 1989).

42. Byang H. Kato, "Contextualization and Religious Syncreticism in Africa" *Biblical Christianity in Africa* (Nairobi: African Christian Press, 1985), 23.

Chapter 11

PROCLAIMING JESUS THROUGH DISCIPLESHIP

A Look at the Discipling of Thessalonian Believers

by Ron Sauer

In an issue of *Focus on the Family* magazine, the late Reggie White, former football great and ordained Baptist minister, told of how, after becoming a Christian, he sometimes fell into sexual immorality. While not excusing himself, he lamented, "The problem was I had no mentor. I had nobody to keep me accountable, to tell me I was wrong."[1] Having a Christian mentor was no guarantee that Reggie would have remained sexually pure, but it would have increased the likelihood.

Some years ago a student enrolled at Moody Bible Institute whom I will call "Jack". He struggled with pornography and asked me to help him deal with it. We met for some time outside of class regarding this vice. But he continued to struggle, and so asked for more of my time. Due to a busy schedule, I did not give him additional time. Soon afterward he began dating one of our students, "Jill." Initially their relationship was pure and disciplined. But because he was unsuccessfully struggling with pornography, their relationship gradually became sexually impure, and they were dismissed from the Institute. Some of their failure can be placed at my doorstep. Had I given Jack the extra assistance needed, perhaps he could have overcome his pornography habit and maintained a healthy relationship with his girlfriend.

I have not always made mistakes with students. Not long ago Dustin was on the verge of graduating from Moody. He told me, "My fiancée, Natalie, and I have done everything correctly in our relationship. . . . For instance, in physically expressing our affection for one another, not once have we exceeded proper boundaries." Then he reminded me: "A year and a half ago I came to your office saying that I had a girlfriend, and as the man I wanted to lead the relationship correctly. For one hour you gave me suggestions from things you had done both incorrectly and correctly. Later I told my girlfriend I wanted to incorporate these suggestions into our relationship, and she agreed. We followed your suggestions." A dating couple can do things properly. But they have a better chance with the help of a third party.

When my wife and I began dating, and even soon after marriage, we jumped off into deep water and thrashed around, trying to learn how to swim romantically. We almost drowned in the process. Many couples who try it this way do indeed drown—their romance fails. There is a better way. Had I known at the commencement of my courtship and marriage what I know now, Susan and I would have humbled ourselves and put our relationship under an older, godly couple who were decades further down the path of romance. This older couple would have already made their mistakes, learned what works and what does not, and gotten it together romantically. They could have speeded up our learning curve, saving us from making some mistakes, or lessening the intensity of those mistakes we would have inevitably made.

We should all stand on the shoulders of other people and learn from what they already know. The topic of this chapter is discipleship or mentoring, and I will use these two terms synonymously. In their book

As Iron Sharpens Iron: Building Character in a Mentoring Relationship, Howard and William Hendricks borrow the definition of mentoring from Paul Stanley and Robert Clinton: "Mentoring is a relational process [in which a] mentor, who knows or has experienced something . . . transfers that something (resources of wisdom, information, experience, confidence, insight, relationships, status, etc.) to a mentoree, at an appropriate time and manner, so that it facilitates development or empowerment."[2]

From a close look at 1 Thessalonians, it seems the apostle Paul willingly gave his time to believers not only inside but also outside the church. He was willing to minister to the congregation as a whole, as well as to individuals or small groups within that congregation. The apostle served as preacher to the entire church and mentor to certain persons within it. This becomes evident as we now consider the Thessalonians' *deficiencies* in 3:10, their *instruction* in 4:1–2, and their *discipleship* in 2:1–20. In examining these passages, all the translations I used for them are my own, made from the original Greek text, unless otherwise indicated.

THEIR DEFICIENCIES (1 THESSALONIANS 3:10)

Day and night we are praying most earnestly that we may see you face-to-face and that we may [lit., complete] *remove the deficiencies in your faith.* (1 Thessalonian 3:10, author's translation)[3]

Paul had modeled Christ before the Thessalonian converts during his earlier time with them, and they in turn modeled Christ for other believers. Paul's imitators, in turn, were being imitated by other Christians. Discipleship proclaims a Christlike way of life to a convert, teaching him or her how to live it. As this convert grows more into this new way of living, he can teach still others the very same way of life (see 2 Tim. 2:2).

Now Paul wants to return to Thessalonica and have more time with his children in the faith to finish his ministry among them. And he wants "to remove the deficiencies in your faith." The word rendered "remove" actually means "to supply, equip, to complete," and thereby put something or someone in proper condition.[4] Paul's second prayer request can be translated literally, "and to supply the things that are lacking (i.e., deficiencies) in your faith"—truths and doctrines in which they are not yet instructed, and certain moral disciplines they have not yet formed and cultivated. This must be done for every person who comes to faith in Christ. It is done, in part, by sermons from the pulpit, by the convert's own personal Bible reading and praying, and by his interaction and fellowship with other Christians. But it can also be achieved, in large part, by mentoring—that is, an older believer spends time instructing the younger in the Word, assisting him or her with problems, frustrations, and relationships, including his relationship with Christ, teaching him how to resist temptations, how to pray, how to witness, how to walk in the Spirit, etc.[5]

THEIR INSTRUCTION (1 THESSALONIANS 4:1–2)

As for the rest, then, brethren, we request you—in fact, we strongly urge by the Lord Jesus' authority—that, just as you learned [lit., received] *from us how you ought to* [lit., walk] *live so as to please* [such a Being who is] *God— just as you actually are now living—[we strongly urge] that you would progress more and more.* (4:1)

Paul's petition, "We request you" is followed by a second verb, "We request you—in fact we strongly *urge* . . ." The former verb *request* is that of a friend to a friend;[6] the second verb *urge* is stronger, turning the request into an appeal from an authoritative person. Paul's requesting and urging come not merely by his own authority but "by the authority of the Lord Jesus."[7]

"We request . . . that you would progress more and more." What does this requested progression concern? In the comparative clause, "just as you learned from us . . ." the verb translated "learned" means to receive spiritual truth as it is handed down from others to the recipient.

What, exactly, did the Thessalonians learn from Paul and his fellow evangelists? They learned "how you ought to live. . . ." The word rendered "live" literally means "to walk," but Paul uses it metaphorically to signify living.[8] This is the fundamental meaning of discipleship and mentoring: it is teaching a new or immature convert how to rightly and successfully live the Christian life. The "so as to please God" expresses a result of living the spiritual life correctly. The comparative clause "just as you actually are now living" indicates they were faithfully complying with the indoctrination the apostle had passed on to them. Still, Paul is requesting that his converts "would progress more and more." The Christian can never rest content with spiritual progress made. So Paul "requests and strongly urges" them to make even greater strides than heretofore.

Yes indeed, you know what commands we gave you by the authority of the Lord Jesus. (4:2)

The Thessalonians "know what commands we gave you." As an example of such commands, verses 3–8 remind the Thessalonians of the apostle's instructions on sexual purity.

An engaged couple, business people from Chicago and both in their early thirties, asked me and my wife to give them premarital counseling. I said to them, "Mutual friends have informed me and Susan that you two are living together. Is that correct?" They answered yes. I further inquired, "Are you sleeping together and having sex?" They again answered yes. I gave them both a Bible opened to 1 Thessalonians 4:3–8, and explained this passage on sexual purity to them.

Just as the explanation of the last verse concluded, the businessman began to weep and, holding up his hand, said, "Wait!" Turning to his fiancée, he said, "I am so sorry for morally tainting you and leading you away from the Lord. Will you, can you, forgive me?" She replied in the affirmative. Then turning to me he said, "Today I will move out of her apartment, and we will not have sex again until married." He was true to his word on both accounts: He moved out that day, and they maintained a pure, disciplined relationship till married months later.

All new converts and immature believers have deficiencies in their Christian knowledge and gaps in their moral character and practical conduct. Paul's converts had such deficiencies. But a mentor can remedy some of these academic and practical gaps.

THEIR DISCIPLESHIP (1 THESSALONIANS 2:1–20)

The second chapter of 1 Thessalonians is special and unique. For it reveals insights into Paul's pastoral heart and into the keys to his ministry's success. But the catalyst for all this is an unhappy one, namely, false accusations by his adversaries. Yet these charges against him became by divine providence like torches flung at an unpopular figure. They surprisingly served to illuminate and reveal his sterling character and conduct.[9] One of the keys of the apostle's Thessalonian service is that he spent time with some of his new converts outside the pulpit in a mentoring relationship.

Indeed, you yourselves know, brethren that our ministry [lit., entrance, visit] *to you was not empty.* (2:1)

What the writer affirms of his ministry is that it "was not empty."[10] This word *empty* is to be understood in two ways: Paul did not come to their city with nothing to give them. Rather, he came with the truth, power, and pure motives, and he gave them the gospel, thus changing their lives. And neither did the apostle come empty-handed so as to get something from them, such as their money, possessions, etc. He came not to get, but to give. The tense of *was* signifies that all the facts of his Thessalonian ministry are in and stand on record, so the readers can assess them,[11] thus refuting the adversaries' charges against him.

> On the contrary, although we had previously physically suffered and been verbally insulted in Philippi, just as you know, we were emboldened by our God to speak to you the gospel of God amidst an intense struggle. (2:2)

Paul definitely had something to impart to the Thessalonians. What he had to impart is the word translated "gospel" (*euaggelion*), and it literally means "good news." In this clause the word "gospel" is modified by "of God." This means that while Paul is the immediate speaker, God is the ultimate speaker of the good news contained in the gospel. God Himself speaks through the apostle's lips.

The Role of Adversity in Ministry

Paul was divinely emboldened to preach, "although we had previously physically suffered and been verbally insulted." This adversity happened "in Philippi," and the story is recorded in Acts 16:19–40. But these Philippian persecutions did not prevent Paul from preaching that same "gospel" elsewhere. That same message preached in Philippi brought fresh but similar persecution in Thessalonica—"amidst an intense struggle." Such adversity is divinely used to enrich the servant's ministry, enhance his relationship with Christ, keep him humble and dependent on the Lord, and keep him sympathetic with those whom he serves, for they, too, are wrestling with their own struggles.

Can adversity enhance a servant's ministry? Yes, for it can serve as one of the defining moments in the lives of those being ministered to, as they observe how the minister is being sustained and "emboldened . . . by God."

Recently our daughter Jan Naomi unexpectedly and tragically died. My wife and I went through "an intense struggle" of grief and sorrow. This tragedy was not divorced from our ministry. Rather, it accompanied our service to the students of Moody Bible Institute. Sue and I were quite open about it, letting the classes in on our sorrow, our questions, and our continuing confiding in an all-wise, sovereign, and loving God. According to their remarks, not a few students were encouraged by seeing Sue and me being divinely sustained. They were taught and convinced that God's grace really is sufficient for whatever may befall us in life.

The Thessalonians observed up close and firsthand how Paul responded to the severe persecution and adversity. That is why he adds, "just as you know." Similarly, Sue and I let our students walk with us through our own "intense struggle."

Exhorting without Error or Impurity

For our exhortation does not come from error nor impurity nor in deceit. (2:3)

The word rendered "exhortation" appeals to the will[12] and urges others to spurn sin, embrace the gospel, and adopt a new course of action. Paul denies this appeal or "exhortation" springs "from error" and "impurity." The former concerns a wandering from the right doctrinal path. His preaching does not come from theological error. The latter, "impurity," pertains to impure motives, such as money, longing for ease, praise, or desire for fame, and it includes sexual impurity as well.

Many of my students are young men preparing for Christian ministry. Not a few exclaim, "Dr. Sauer, I struggle with sexual lust and impure thoughts." So we talk about it. I tell them, "Fellas, you and I are going to struggle with sexual temptation until this life is finished. So we must get really good at this struggle—skilled and progressively victorious in it. Many of the people whom God will give you to minister to are females. Let me tell you what I do when a woman walks into my office for counsel: I get hold of myself and control my thoughts and attitude. I am careful with my words and hands, viewing her as a child of God, and so I treat her as a daughter of heaven, mindful of the Lord's presence and watching eye. I make sure that everything in my office happens just as it should, so that when she walks out, the Lord has been pleased. If I do that, so can you. And I expect you to do just as I do!" Then the young men and I discuss practical steps to take to deal with temptation and to grow in moral purity. And we pray about it.

All of the apostle's motives in ministry were proper. Paul's third denial is that his appeal was "in deceit." Greek literature uses this noun for bait to catch fish. Here it applies to deceitful ways to gain converts, such as inducing conversions by promising fraudulent blessings, prosperity, by hiding the cost of discipleship, etc.[13]

But just as we have been approved by God to be entrusted with the gospel, so we speak, not as pleasing people, but God, who constantly examines our hearts. (2:4)

A correspondence exists between Paul's commission and his performance: He is executing his ministry in accord with, and due to, his divinely given commission to the gospel service. The divine examination of Paul has found him worthy, and so he has been approved "to be entrusted with the gospel." God chooses His messengers and examines them prior to committing the truth to them.[14]

It is sometimes a temptation to gear one's message to what pleases people and to avoid displeasing them in any way. The apostle refuses to do this. He attempts to please God. A trait of Paul's service was to declare God's truth and please heaven, whatever people might think of it.

God's examining a person's worth for ministerial service is not a once-for-all exam. It is continual. "Our hearts" here represents one's hidden thoughts, motives, and desires.[15] Paul might deceive people, but not God, who sees and "continually examines" what people cannot. Paul may not always have God's consent to preach. It is conceivable for the apostle to fall into sin or misconduct. That is why he strives daily to please the Lord rather than man.

One of the best students I ever had at Moody was "Ted." After graduating, he attended a fine theological seminary, where he rose to the top of his class. Upon finishing seminary he pastored a church, where initially his ministry was fruitful. But he imprudently fell into an unhealthy relationship with a woman in the congregation. The Lord, "who constantly examines our hearts," eventually found Ted no longer fit for the pulpit. Consequently, he lost both his wife and ministry.

Three Cautions: No Flattering Speech, Seeking Greed, nor Seeking Praise

For we did not ever employ flattering speech, as you know, nor pretense for greed, God is witness. (2:5)

The verb in this verse, *egenēthēmen*, means entering[16] a condition and partaking of it.[17] The *William's New Testament* translates it, "We never indulged in." Similar is my "We did not ever employ . . ." The apostle denies using two things in his Thessalonian service: "Flattering speech" and a "pretense for greed." Paul adds the clause, "as you know" inviting the readers to assess what they can, knowing his ministry as they do. He adds, "God is witness," calling on heaven to assess and bring to light what only God can.

Nor were we seeking praise from people—neither from you nor from others, although we could have wielded our authority as apostles of Christ. (2:6)

Paul's third disclaimer[18] is he refused to seek "praise from people." Paul does not deny having obtained the Thessalonians' esteem, but rather that he did not set out to get it "from you nor from others."

Paul and his evangelistic colleagues possessed, "as apostles of Christ," enormous authority. That notwithstanding, these divine envoys did not seek, let alone demand, praise from the Thessalonians or from any others.

Susan and I run the risk of letting students get close to us. It is easy to look good from a distance. But when people draw near, then they can spot flaws and shortcomings and realize that she and I do not do everything right. One day after classes a Moody student came home with me to spend the night with us, so she and my wife could have some time together. When this young woman and I walked through the front door of our home, our then-eighteen-year-old son Jeff was in the middle of throwing a hissy fit, spewing his displeasure all around. At first, I was mortified, wondering what kind of home this student would think we had. Then I reasoned, *This is OK. In fact, this student needs to see that our children are not perfect, because when she later has her own kids, they won't wear haloes either. It may be helpful to this future mother to see how Jeff's parents respond to and handle his angry outburst.* Even should this impressionable student from the Institute come away from that episode with a lower opinion of our family life, the experience may still be profitable for her.

Modeling Gentleness and One's Very Life

Instead, we were gentle in your midst, as a nursing mother tenderly cares for her own children. (2:7)

In teaching, mentoring, and influencing others, firmness and rebuke are sometimes necessary. But for the most part, gentleness is required. Accordingly, Proverbs 16:21 (ESV) claims, "The wise of heart is called discerning, and sweetness of speech increases persuasiveness."

In my early years of teaching, I was a ferocious tiger in the classroom. As a particular semester wore on, I noticed that one of my students, "Bill," appeared lazy and undisciplined. One day in class I called on him to answer a question. He confessed to not knowing the answer. "Why?" I asked. "Because," he replied, "I didn't do my homework." At that, my fangs and claws came out, and in the presence of his classmates I verbally skinned him alive. Bill did not utter a word in defense. But after class he went straight to the registrar's office and dropped my class. I forever lost any further chance to teach him and leave a positive influence on him. Paul avoided making my mistake. He was "gentle . . . as a nursing mother tenderly cares for her own children." This adjective *gentle* (*nepioi*) occurs in 2 Timothy 2:24 as a mark of the Lord's servant: he must be gentle even in his dealings with heretics. That is the disposition the mentor must display toward those mentored.

And so, longing for you, we were delighted and remained determined to share with you not only the gospel of God but also our own souls as well, because you had become dear to us. (2: 8)

"And so . . . we were delighted and remained determined [*eudokoumen*]." Although this translation uses two verbs in English, it renders but one in Greek, the verb *eudokoumen*. This word here combines two ideas: resolve and being pleased or taking delight. It conveys, then, willing purpose.[19] This verb's form can be a present tense, but the majority regards it as imperfect, which expresses continuous action. Putting all this together it is translated, "We were delighted and remained determined."

But in what was the apostle delighted and what was he resolved to do? "To share with you not only the gospel of God but also our own souls as well." The word *share* signifies not giving all one has to others, but imparting some to others, yet keeping some for oneself.[20] The missionaries were both pleased and determined to share two valuable assets with the Thessalonians, the truth—here called "the gospel of God," and themselves—here called "our own souls." Preaching the gospel involves a total commitment of the messenger to the task.[21] So he was just as determined to share his soul, which refers to his inner life:[22] his feelings, emotions, experiences, time, talent, and energy—the whole personality.

I once visited a church that formerly had been pastored by a nationally renowned preacher. I asked an elderly man, who had been under the ministry of this pastor, what he was like. He said, "I have to answer in two ways. First, my former pastor was an outstanding preacher of the Scriptures, none better. But second, he did not know your name, and he did not want to know it. He spent no time with people outside the pulpit. All he wanted to do was preach, then retreat to his study to prepare next Sunday's sermon. He was a preacher, not a pastor—an expositor, not a shepherd!"

Paul is claiming he was not like that pastor. The apostle did not just indoctrinate his converts, but also got his hands dirty with their needs and problems. In discipling others the mentor has to impart truth and be just as willing to give of himself, and often the latter is the harder to do. "We . . . remained determined" denotes that giving others one's time and fund of experience is not easy, convenient, or automatic. The mentor must continually resolve to be available and give of himself to others in a pastoral or shepherding manner.

"Longing for you" expresses the manner in which Paul carried out his ministry—he longed for his spiritual children. They had become "dear" to him. This Greek word means "beloved"—they were the objects of his affection. The mentor must love his disciples. In addition, the ideal mentor longs after and yearns for his spiritual pupils.

You are witnesses and so is God, that we conducted ourselves devoutly and uprightly and blamelessly toward you who believe. (2:10)

One Sunday at church a woman in her early thirties told me, "I like watching your wife. She continually approaches women in the congregation—expressing affection, encouraging them, or holding someone's baby so the mother can give full attention to the sermon." The Thessalonians constantly had their eyes on Paul. He taught them not only with his lips but also with his life. He lived out the gospel before them.

Verses 10–12 form one sentence[23] in Greek, which summarizes and concludes the review of the missionaries' ministry in Thessalonica. This lengthy sentence contains but one main or independent clause, "You are witnesses and so is God." The emphatic personal pronoun *you* strongly conveys the thought "you—the very ones we gave ourselves to, the recipients of all our love and labor and sacrifice!" as mentioned in verse 8. His converts are witnesses because Paul did more than just preach to them. He spent time with them, opening up and sharing his own soul with them (v. 8). They heard the truth from his mouth and saw the truth incarnated in his life. So here the writer calls on his readers to bear witness to and verify what he is about to say from the remainder of verse 10 through verse 12.

The verb here translated "conducted" means "to be," with the nuance of possessing certain characteristics—thus, "prove to be, turn out to be." The three adverbs describing the apostle's conduct are: *devoutly*, concerning a proper attitude and duty toward God; *uprightly*, pertaining to Paul's commendable relations toward his fellow man; and *blamelessly*, having to do with himself—Paul was beyond reproach in his behavior as observed publicly. The nuance of the Greek indicates that it was to the benefit of those who observed the apostle's holy behavior.

After "Melissa" graduated from Moody she returned home to Kansas and married. She kept growing and maturing as a fine Christian. Her church liked what they saw in her Christian life and committed a "flock group" of twelve younger women to her for mentoring. She mentors in the same way Paul did, by lip and life, by meeting with them as a group, and by spending time with them one-on-one. She is a skilled shepherdess.

Caring like a Father . . . like a Mother

As you know, every single one of you, like a father does his own children.
(2:11)

This verse continues the long sentence begun in verse 10 but not completed until verse 12. "As you know" appeals to their knowledge of his ministry to verify what he now recalls.

"Every single one of you," is the direct object of the three verbs in verse 12: "we were *exhorting* and *encouraging* and firmly *insisting*." This direct object, strongly constructed, points to the importance of each person in the church. It would have been sufficient had the author written that the missionaries were exhorting "each of you." But to the direct object *each*, Paul adds the emphatic numerical adjective *hena*, which literally means "one" and marks the importance of each and every church member. So the full direct object is rendered "every single one of you."

Ideally a pastor should not just teach the congregation as a whole, and only from the pulpit. He also ought to give, in privacy, individual instruction and guidance suited to each person's particular needs and problems, "like a father does his own children." Believers need fatherly advice as well as motherly care. So to the figure of a mother (v. 7) is added that of a father. In the ancient world the father was responsible for the birth, education, instruction, and behavior of his children, as well as for socializing them into the current socioeconomic and cultural way of life. So Paul, like a father, re-socialized his spiritual children as new Christians to life and the world.[24] A dad loves and trains all of his children as a group. But he also loves and instructs each of his children as individuals. So the apostle did the Thessalonians.

Last semester "Bob" and "Beth" walked into my office. They planned to marry in a few months. But Bob's personal life was falling apart—he was losing confidence in himself, unsure of marriage, plagued by doubts, and struggling with an unfulfilling job. He wanted to postpone the wedding six to twelve months to deal with his own struggles, thereby hoping to gain more assurance about marriage. But Beth was adamant that they should hold to the wedding date, since they had decided to marry, and so should implement it and make it work. Some months earlier my own son Joseph had asked my advice on the timing of his marriage. With Bob and Beth I now endeavored to impart, from the same concerned parental heart, counsel suited to their own situation and circumstances. I recall beginning, "Beth, if you were my daughter, this is what I would advise you." Then they followed my advice. This was the Pauline philosophy of ministry, and the Thessalonians knew it because they had observed it firsthand in him.

Living the Christian Way of Life

We were (1) exhorting and (2) encouraging and (3) firmly insisting that you [lit., walk] *lead lives* [lit., worthy of] *consistent with the nature of God, who is continuously calling you into his own kingdom and splendor.* (2:12)

This verse finishes the lengthy sentence begun in verse 10 and completes the review of the author's Thessalonian ministry. The three independent participles[25] spell out how Paul dealt with "every single one of you" in the congregation:

(1) "We were exhorting [*parakalountes*]" you. Appealing to the will,[26] this word urges a person to adopt a certain conduct and way of living. It exhorts the inquirer about Christianity, or the hesitant, pleading with them to embrace the gospel and the Christian way of life.

As a student at Dallas Theological Seminary, I worked part-time as an assistant apartment manager. Off the street into our office walked "David." Divorcing his wife and leaving her in Denver, he was moving to Dallas to make a new start. After showing him vacant apartments, he and I returned to the office for an application form. Noticing my Bible lying on the desk he inquired if I were a Christian. He asked, "Do you have a few minutes to talk?" A few minutes turned out to be two hours. David was hurting and searching. He later moved into our apartment complex, and we often read Scripture and discussed the validity of Christianity. Sue and I encouraged him to attend our church's midweek Bible study. He did, and they eventually led David to Christ. Afterward, he returned to Denver, reconciled with and remarried his estranged wife, brought her to Dallas, and later led her to the Lord. David was "exhorted" to embrace the gospel, and he did so. He was also "exhorted" to adopt a new way of life—the Christian life, and he did that too.

(2) "And [we were] encouraging [*paramuthoumenui*]" you. This participle concerns the feelings and emotions. It is addressed to the fainthearted[27] who need soothing comfort and encouragement due to trying circumstances, difficulty, and failure. Currently I'm mentoring three of our male Moody students, meeting with each weekly. These are such fine lads. God's hand is evident upon them, and clear is His call summoning them into Christian ministry. Obvious is their being divinely gifted for this service. But they struggle with various issues (such as sexual lust) and periodically fail. They occasionally get down on themselves, wondering if they should forget their ministerial plans. They require encouragement from an older person who is further down the path of life, who himself recalls the idealism and struggles of his own youth, and so has a more realistic perspective.

(3) "And [we were] firmly insisting [*marturovmenoi*]." This Greek word concerns duty and is directed toward slackers and waverers.[28] Using authority, one solemnly charges a slacker to do his Christian duty and to do it rightly. We do not always enjoy victories here at Moody. Sadly, occasional failures occur. "Phil" and "Penny" were planning to marry. My wife and I gave them premarital counseling to help prepare them for taking this step. After our nine-week course, Sue and I sensed they were not ready for marriage and so suggested they wait a year. They chose not to wait. Not long afterward Penny ended up in

another man's bed. My wife and I "firmly insisted" that she sever the illicit relation with this other man and reconcile with her own husband. Our appeal fell on deaf ears, and her marriage disintegrated. There will be casualties in the Christian life. Paul had his share, as, for example, Demas fell in love with the world and deserted him (2 Tim. 4:10).

The bottom line of Paul's appeal was "that you lead lives consistent with the nature of God, who is continuously calling you into his own kingdom and splendor." Since the readers are citizens of heaven, they should behave as such. Since they will share in God's own *splendor*, their lives should reflect some of that now.

Recognizing the Word as Divine

And we, too, thank God unceasingly for this reason: when you received the [lit., word] *message heard* [immediately] *from us* [but ultimately] *from God, you accepted not a mere human message but, as it really is, a divine message, for it definitely works in you who persist in believing.* (2:13)

This verse turns from Paul's ministry to the Thessalonians' response to it.[29] They "accepted"—personally embraced—the data they had intellectually received. Elsewhere it is translated "You took it to your hearts"[30]

The "message" Paul's audience "received" and "accepted" was divine revelation given through Christ and His messengers.[31] The Thessalonians did not view the gospel they embraced as the word of frail man, "but, as it really is, a divine message." Paul had the conviction that he was simply heaven's mouthpiece, and that what he spoke was God's true Word. His converts shared this same conviction.

"Julie," a woman in her mid-thirties, phoned me to make an appointment to talk in person. "I've been dating a wonderful, handsome man with a sparkling personality, suitably employed, spoken well of by everyone. He accompanies me to church and is everything I'm looking for in a husband, except for one thing—he's not a Christian.

Don't you think that it is OK with God that I date an unbeliever?" I briefly cited 2 Corinthians 6:14, which prohibits a Christian becoming romantically involved with a non-Christian. Julie's response was, "If that is what God's Word says, you need not say another thing!" Afterward she told her boyfriend that she would like to pursue a relationship with him, but that heaven does not give her permission to do so. Why? Because, like the Thessalonians, Julie views Scripture not so much as the word of man, but rather as the Word of God Himself.

What makes the Christian community view the gospel as the Word of God? It is that the Scripture "definitely [*kai*] works in you." The word translated here as "definitely" stresses that the Word is surely at work changing sinners into saints, the wicked into righteous people. The gospel's transforming power authenticates its divine origin.

THE JOY OF DISCIPLESHIP

For what is our hope or joy or crown of rejoicing—or is it not you, too— in the presence of our Lord Jesus at his coming? (2:19)

The apostle knows his work will be divinely assessed on judgment day to determine his reward. His *hope* for a divinely spoken "well done" and for heavenly recompense lies, in large part, in his converts. *Joy* is the apostle's inner gladness of heart over their conversion and persistence in faith, despite their trials. This joy is both current and future. "Crown of rejoicing" is not a ruler's crown but a victor's wreath awarded in triumph, like that given an athlete for winning a race. Such a "crown" will bring him "rejoicing," over the Thessalonians, along with his other converts and disciples "in the presence of our Lord Jesus," and "at his coming." That's when Paul's joy climaxes and his heavenly reward is given.

Yes indeed, you really are our pride and joy![32] (2:20)

291

Paul calls his converts "our pride and joy." So his source of joy was the salvation and maturing of the Thessalonian converts. They were a source of current gladness and his hope for future joy.

"Alicia" was a Chicago public school teacher. She said to my wife, "I see your joy, observe your peace in the midst of trials, take note of how you love your husband, and I'm impressed with your servant's attitude toward the needy. Would you teach me how to do these things?" So every Thursday night Sue and Alicia would get together for two hours of Bible study, prayer, and discussion of life, needs, struggles, how to trust God, etc. Alicia bloomed and blossomed spiritually. Later she was led to Bolivia where she now is mentoring her own female disciples on the mission field. Such a person is Sue's "pride and joy."

THE CALL TO DISCIPLE AND BE DISCIPLED

To sum up: Nothing will ever suitably replace either the professor's lecture in a classroom or the pastor's sermon from a pulpit. These are necessary means of imparting instruction and moral guidance to people. But there can be and really should be more. Supplementing the lecture and sermon is discipleship. Jesus did it with the Twelve, training a handful of common, ordinary men who later turned the world upside down for Christ (Acts 17:6). True, Christ ministered to masses and multitudes of people. But He also "appointed twelve, so that they would be with Him and that He could send them out to preach" (Mark 3:14).

Paul mentored his missionary colleagues and converts. The apostle instructed Timothy, "The things which you have heard from me in the presence of many witnesses, entrust these to faithful men, who will be able to teach others also" (2 Tim. 2:2). And women are not exempt. The same apostle directs Titus that "older women likewise are to be . . . teaching what is good, so that they may encourage [Gk.

sōphronizōsin, which means 'to train'] the young women" (Titus 2:3–4). Every Christian school and church needs some older, mature believers who can take younger ones by the hand and teach them truth, training them how to live correctly, walk with God, minister to the needy, cope with adversity, and maintain a healthy romantic relationship. Most can benefit from the steady hand, encouraging voice, and wise counsel of an older person who is further down the path of life where the younger believer is now headed.

The younger believer can certainly learn as a part of a class of students or member of a congregation. But quite often that younger person needs the personal, face-to-face guidance that mentoring affords. In either a one-on-one or smaller group context, the mentoree can pour out his private struggles that he may hesitate to reveal in the larger setting. And the mentor can provide advice and guidance personally tailored to the individual's own needs. Usually there are young or immature Christians consciously looking for a mentor. They know their need for one. Other young people need a mentor but are not consciously aware of their need. And usually there are older people in both the church and on the campus to whom heaven has given a fund of knowledge and experience that can help younger believers enormously.

Often the older Christians underestimate themselves, thinking they cannot mentor others. Sometimes they fear that any who get close to them will see their own flaws and weaknesses. The younger believers need to see the blemishes of the older ones to realize that no one is perfect, and no one should be set on a pedestal. When the older believers reveal their imperfections, they can encourage the younger. The younger reasons, "If my mentor has grown spiritually and matured so well morally, his flaws notwithstanding, then maybe there's hope for me. Maybe I, too, can do that, despite my imperfections."

Not infrequently the older feels intimidated by a younger person getting too close to him or her, thinking, "I don't have it all together yet!" One of our Moody students, "Rachel," disciples high school girls in her church. Rachel told me, "I'm not much older and don't know much more than these high school girls. And I'm afraid of them." I replied, "You are not much older, but you are a bit older than they. You don't know much more than they do, but you do know a little more. You are not very far down the path of life, but you are somewhat further than they are down that path. You are exactly what those younger girls need now. So go ahead and be afraid of them, and let this fear work for you, by humbling and driving you to the feet of God for His help in ministering to them. When those high school girls have a problem, you will probably be the first person they turn to for help. Don't abandon them!"

Sometimes an older person thinks he cannot disciple others because he is not very good at it. The best way to get good at it is by doing it. Practice makes perfect. There was only one perfect mentor. All the rest of us are imperfect. So allow yourself to make mistakes. You will sort those out, learn from blunders, and find out better ways to mentor others. Do not underestimate yourself. God has given you knowledge and experience that other people need. As stated earlier, no one need invent the wheel. It has already been done. No one need learn everything from scratch all alone. We should instead all stand on the shoulders of others. Should you need it, find an older person's shoulders to stand on. And consider letting a needy, younger person stand on yours.

Paul puts it this way: "We proclaim Christ, admonishing every [*panta*] person and teaching every person with all wisdom, that we may present every person mature, due to his relationship with Christ" (Col. 1:28). Did you notice that three times the word "every" (*panta*) occurs in this one verse? That word, among other things, points both to the importance of each believer, and to the individual, personal ministry that is necessary on occasions to each believer. As my wife puts it, "Walk alongside others, showing them the way." Like this, we proclaim Christ to others with lip and with life.

Ron Sauer is professor of Bible at the Moody Bible Institute. He holds the Ph.D. degree from the University of Manchester, England, along with degrees from Dallas Theological Seminary and Mississippi College.

NOTES

1. Tom Neven, "Fighting the Good Fight," *Focus on the Family*, October 1999, 7.

2. Howard and William Hendricks, *As Iron Sharpens Iron: Building Character in a Mentoring Relationship* (Chicago: Moody, 1995), 165.

3. Our various English translations, such as the New American Standard Bible and New International Version, are excellent. But as a teacher of Greek, I train and encourage my student to translate the Greek text for themselves. Hence, as a matter of integrity I translate the original text in all the key 1 Thessalonians passages in this essay. As in mentoring others, one must practice what he preaches.

4. Walter Bauer, *A Greek-English Lexicon of the New Testament and Other Early Christian Literature*, trans. W. F. Arndt and F. W. Gingrich, 3rd ed., rev. F. W. Danker (Chicago: Univ, of Chicago Press, 2000), 526.

5. William Hendriksen, *Exposition of 1 and 2 Thessalonians*, New Testament Commentary (Grand Rapids: Baker, 1955), 88–90.

6. W. E. Vine, *An Expository Dictionary of New Testament Words* (Old Tappan, N.J.: Revell, 1966), 79.

7. I. Howard Marshall, *1 and 2 Thessalonians*, New Century Bible Commentary (Grand Rapids: Eerdmans, 1983), 104.

8. Bauer, *Greek-English Lexicon*, 803.

9. James Moffatt, "The First and Second Epistles to the Thessalonians," *The Expositor's Greek Testament*, vol. 4, ed. W. R. Nicoll (Grand Rapids: Eerdmans, 1961), 6.

10. Hendriksen, *1 Thessalonians*, 60.

11. Marshall, *1 and 2 Thessalonians*, 62.

12. Robert L. Thomas, "1 Thessalonians" in *The Expositor's Bible Commentary*, vol. 11, ed. F. E. Gaebelein (Grand Rapids: Zondervan, 1978), 251.

13. John Stott, *The Gospel and the End of Time* (Downers Grove, Ill.: InterVarsity Press, 1991), 50.

14. Leon Morris, *The First and Second Epistles to the Thessalonians,* The New International Commentary on the New Testament (Grand Rapids: Eerdmans, 1973), 72.

15. Bauer, *Greek-English Lexicon*, 508.

16. George Milligan, *St. Paul's Epistles to the Thessalonians: The Greek Text with Intro-duction and Notes* (New York: Macmillan, 1908; reprint ed., Minneapolis: Klock & Klock Christian Publishers, 1980), 19.

17. Charles J. Ellicott, *A Critical and Grammatical Commentary on St. Paul's Epistles to the Thessalonians* (Boston: Draper and Halliday, 1854; reprint ed., Minneapolis: James Family Publishing, 1978), 33.

18. Ernest Best, *The First and Second Epistles to the Thessalonians*, Black's New Testa-ment Commentary (Peabody, Mass.: Hendrickson Publishers, 1986), 98.

19. John Eadie, *Commentary on the Greek Text of the Epistles of Paul to the Thessalonians* (New York: Macmillan, 1877; reprint ed., Grand Rapids: Baker Book House, 1979), 67.

20. Marshall, *1 and 2 Thessalonians*, 71.

21. Morris, *First and Second Thessalonians*, 79–80.

22. Bauer, *Greek-English Lexicon*, 1099.

23. Marshall, *1 and 2 Thessalonians*, 72.

24. Charles A. Wanamaker, *The Epistles to the Thessalonians: A Commentary on the Greek Text*, The New International Greek Testament Commentary, ed. I. H. Marshall and D. A. Hagner (Grand Rapids: Eerdmans, 1900), 106.

25. See this use of the participle discussed by A. T. Robertson, *A Grammar of the Greek New Testament in the Light of Historical Research* (Nashville: Broadman, 1934), 1132–35.

26. Milligan, *St. Paul's Epistles to the Thessalonians*, 25.

27. D. Edmond Hiebert, *1 & 2 Thessalonians* (Chicago: Moody, 1992), 109.

28. Morris, *First and Second Thessalonians*, 84.

29. Best, *First and Second Epistles*, 109.

30. F. F. Bruce, "The First Epistle to the Thessalonians," *An Expanded Paraphrase of the Epistles of Paul* (Exeter, Devon, U.K.: Paternoster Press, 1965), 47.

31. Bauer, *Greek-English Lexicon*, 599.

32. I borrowed most of my translation of this clause from the *Today's English Version's* "You are our pride and joy."

Chapter 12

PROCLAIMING JESUS THROUGH WORSHIP

A Theology of Genuine Worship

by Richard M. Weber

In his popular song, "The Heart of Worship," songwriter and worship leader Matt Redman proclaims that the center of Christian worship—the "heart" of worship—is "all about . . . Jesus."[1] In his song, Redman laments the emphasis placed on secondary issues, and he vows to make Jesus the hub of his worship.

In contrast, Ronald Allen and Gordon Borror describe worship as a celebration of *God*. It is, they say, "an active response to God whereby we declare His worth."

"Because of who God is and what He does," they write, "we attribute to Him the glory that is due His name. . . . When we worship God, we celebrate *Him*: We extol Him, we sound His praises, we boast in Him."[2]

Allen and Borror say nothing here contrary to Scripture, but do they say enough? As Christians, we must ask how *Jesus* fits in with our understanding of worship. What is it about *Christian* worship that differs from the Hebrew worship of God portrayed in the Old Testament? With the incarnation, what, if anything, changed in the way human beings approach God—or at least in the way we *understand* our approach to God?

CHRISTIAN AND HEBREW WORSHIP

The worship expressed by the Christian church is not identical to that expressed by Israel. C. F. D. Moule writes, "Distinctively Christian worship bears the same sort of relation to Jewish worship as the distinctively Christian writings do to the Jewish Scriptures."[3] The Christian Scriptures do not *contradict* the Hebrew Bible; rather, taken together they represent the totality of the written revelation of God— what Robert Rayburn describes as the "composite whole" of God's message to humanity.[4] In the same way, Christian worship grows out of Hebrew worship. The Christian worship that emerges out of the temple and synagogue does not nullify or contradict the Jewish cult, but it *fulfills* it—it provides a "transcendent meaning" for understanding Old Testament ritual.[5] However, while it is continuous with Jewish worship, Christian worship is nonetheless *distinctively Christian.*

In ancient Israel, worship was a celebration of God's deliverance of Israel from captivity in Egypt. God redeemed the nation and established a covenant with them, instructing them as to how they were to interact with Him. Worship, expressed through a clearly defined system of sacred rituals, servants, and places, was the fundamental means of expressing their relationship to God.[6]

Christian worship is also a celebration of divine redemptive activity. Thus, the Old Testament *concept* of worship as a celebratory remembrance of redemption translates to the New Testament. However, the deliverance presented in the New Testament relates not to the deliverance of a national people from slavery in a foreign land but to the message of salvation displayed in the life, death, and resurrection of Jesus Christ.

We must recognize, then, that the worship of the church differs from the worship of Israel as antitype differs from type. The worship of Israel found its roots in the Exodus; the heart of Christian worship is in the Christ event.

UNDERSTANDING THE COMMUNITY OF GOD

According to Allen and Borror, true worshipers are those who "feel that they are a part of a *worshiping community*." They are "those who hold Him [God] in reverence and who practice His presence as a way of life."[7] True worshipers comprise the community of God. But what is the *"community of God"*?

The New Testament "community of God" is the believing church—every individual who will confess, "Jesus is Lord," believing that God has raised Him from the dead (Rom. 10:9). John Stott writes:

> The Christian community is a community of the cross, for it has been brought into being by the cross, and the focus of its worship is the Lamb, once slain, now glorified. So the community of the cross is a community of celebration, a eucharistic community, ceaselessly offering to God through Christ the sacrifice of our praise and thanksgiving.[8]

The worshiping community is comprised of the redeemed, and the center of its worship is the Lamb of God. Apart from the Christ, there can be no worship. Indeed, without the cross, there is no "community of God" that is distinctly Christian! "Christian worship," says Terry Wardle, "is a celebration of Jesus Christ—God the Son, our living Redeemer. There is no legitimacy to meeting as worshipers if we do not lift Him up."[9]

The contemporary church's obsession with matters of *style* in regard to worship has grown to epidemic proportions. In *The New Worship*, Barry Liesch launches into his opening chapter, "Hymns or Choruses," without first developing an understanding of the *function* of hymns or choruses. Tom Kraeuter's *Developing an Effective Worship Ministry* focuses almost exclusively on the formation and rehearsal of a contemporary worship band, neglecting the more fundamental issue of the biblical and theological basis for what an "effective worship ministry" is.[10] Personally, I have interviewed in churches where I was asked for my *philosophy of worship* (i.e., issues of musical style, hymns vs. choruses, whether or not I would use a worship team and, if so, how large it would be), but was never asked about my *theology of worship* (i.e., what I believe biblical worship to look like, its focus and its goal).

Any activity of the church must have a theological basis. "A person is not free to worship as he or she wishes, but only in 'truth,' that is, according to God's commands,"[11] notes Russell Shedd. If we hope to approach God as worshipers, we must understand *how* we are to approach God, and for what purpose. Regardless, then, of musical styles, instrumentation, or the precise number of hymns that should be sung, *worship must have a theological basis.*[12]

In this chapter, we will consider the theological basis for Christian worship, which I see as uniquely Christocentric. In the process, we will consider three central facets of Hebrew worship—the sacrificial system, the priesthood, and the temple. Each of these I see as foundational to the Jewish cultic approach to God—and fulfilled in the person and work of Jesus Christ. The Jews worshiped God through sacrifices, which appointed priests offered in unique locations. Christian worship, in every way, focuses on Jesus Christ. We will see that Jesus is, indeed, the heart of worship.

HOMAGE AND SERVICE:
THE BIBLICAL TERMINOLOGY OF WORSHIP

Urban legend claims that Eskimos have fifty words for "snow." Even English uses several words to describe the cold white stuff. I'm more concerned about reports of an approaching blizzard than an early winter flurry. The hardpack a climber might encounter on Everest is certainly more substantial than the powder I might scoop off my driveway on a cold February morning. Unless I understand the nuances associated with each of these terms, their distinctions would be lost.

The Hebrew and Greek Scriptures use various terms, all of which are translated by the single word "worship" in most English versions. But should we generalize the writers' vocabulary in this way, our understanding would be, at best, limited! As we seek to understand the Christocentricity of worship, we must first consider the specific terms that the biblical writers used, noting the particular nuance of each. In this section, we will consider two groups of terms, noting how the New Testament uses them to place Christ at the center of all true worship.

Showing Homage and Reverence

The first set of terms revolves around the general concept of *homage* or *reverence*. The Hebrew term *hištaḥᵃwâ* speaks of the act of "bowing down" or "bending oneself over at the waist." In Genesis 18:2 (NIV), when Abraham rushed to greet his three mysterious visitors, he "bowed low to the ground" as a sign of deference to them. In the same way, the woman from Tekoa "fell on her face to the ground" to pay King David honor (2 Sam. 14:4). In these (and other) cases, the act of one individual bowing before another demonstrates reverence and respect.

When the translators of the Septuagint chose a Greek term to translate *hištaḥᵃwâ*, they selected the Greek term *proskynein*, a compound of the preposition *pros* ("toward") and verb *kynein* ("to kiss"). *Proskynein*, therefore, suggests a "kiss" offered "toward" another. Because a kiss, in the ancient world, was a sign of one's esteem or reverence for another, *proskynein* connotes the same meaning as the Hebrew term. Forms of *proskynein* are used of the Israelites, who, when construction began on the temple, "bowed low and fell prostrate (*prosekynēsan*) before the Lord and the king." Later, when construction was completed, they "knelt on the pavement with their faces to the ground, and they worshiped [*prosekynēsan*] and gave thanks to the LORD" (2 Chron. 7:3 NIV).

The New Testament use of *prosekynēsan* shows that the Son of God receives homage and reverence. People regularly "bow down" in worship to Christ. Not long after Jesus' birth, the magi "saw the Child with Mary His mother; and they fell to the ground [*prosekynēsan*] and worshiped Him" (Matt. 2:11). On the first Easter morning the women "took hold of His feet and worshiped [*prosekynēsan*] Him" (Matt. 28:9).[13] Ultimately, in John's vision of heaven, he saw "the four living creatures kept saying, 'Amen.' And the elders fell down and worshiped (*prosekynēsan*)" (Rev. 5:14). In the New Testament, Jesus Christ is the object of reverent worship!

Giving Faithful, Dedicated Service

A second group of terms signifies the notion of *faithful, dedicated service.* The Hebrew term *'abad* speaks of the total fidelity and allegiance that were to characterize Israel's worship. "Serve the Lord your God with all your heart and with all your soul," (Deut. 10:12), they were commanded. Indeed, we repeatedly read that the very purpose for their deliverance from Egypt was that they might *serve the Lord*![14]

The Septuagint translates this term using forms of the Greek word *latreuō.* This term was generally used to speak of service rendered by a slave, as opposed to that of a hired servant. Imagine the level of commitment implied in this simple term! A hired servant is free to come and go, having a life outside the household in which he or she serves. A slave, on the other hand, is the absolute possession of the master and has no commitments beyond pleasing him. When the Septuagint applies a form of *latreuō* to Israel's worship, it implies that Israel was to be the veritable possession of God. Its worship was to be a service of total commitment to the Lord.[15]

The New Testament reiterates the Old Testament notion of the totality of one's commitment to God, but it insists that the believer is enabled to offer such exclusive service only by means of the work of Christ. Paul, for example, instructs Christians to present themselves as "living sacrifices, holy and pleasing to God" (NIV). He declares that this commitment of oneself is a "spiritual service of worship [*latreien*]" (Rom. 12:1).[16] Later in the New Testament, however, we learn that only "the blood of Christ . . . [will] cleanse our consciences from acts that lead to death, *so that we may serve* [latreuein] *the living God!*" (Heb. 9:14 NIV). Zechariah foresees this when, upon the birth of the one who was to "prepare the way" for the Lord, he avows that the whole purpose of messianic redemption is that God's people might be enabled to "serve Him without fear" (Luke 1:74). Worship is still described in terms of service to God in the New Testament, but Christ is the necessary and central means to such service.

THE CENTRAL OBJECT OF CHRISTIAN WORSHIP: JESUS

Considering the terminology, therefore, we affirm that the New Testament makes Jesus central to Christian worship.[17] The writers readily employ terms that the Septuagint used for the worship of God, focusing them specifically on the Son. Jesus becomes, therefore, the central object of Christian worship.

For example, Paul writes that "God exalted [Jesus] to the highest place and gave him the name that is above every name, that at the name of Jesus every knee should bow, in heaven and on earth and under the earth, and every tongue confess that Jesus Christ is Lord, to the glory of God the Father" (Phil. 2:9–11 NIV). Even the *angels* are instructed to worship the risen Christ in Hebrews 1:6. It is easy to recognize that this Jesus—now crowned "with glory and honor" (Heb 2:7 NIV)—is the object of Christian worship.

But Christian worship is not a matter of recognizing the glory of Christ and worshiping Him from afar; rather, it is the recognition of the covenant bond that exists between the head and the body, between the vine and the branches. Because of the federal relationship existing between the Second Adam and His people, believers may be said to have died with Him, been raised with Him, and are seated with Him at the right hand of the Father. Being united to the Savior, believers "have come to Mount Zion and to the city of the living God, the heavenly Jerusalem"—not because they have obeyed God's commands and merit acceptance by God, but because of "Jesus, the mediator of a new covenant" (Heb. 12:22, 24). Christians worship at the "heavenly Jerusalem" because Christ has brought us there.

Furthermore, Christ enables Christian worship in that, in the corporate gathering of the congregation, Christ Himself stands as a co-worshiper with His brothers and sisters. Hebrews 2:11 declares that Christ is not ashamed to be of the same family as those He is making holy, and to call them "brothers" (NIV). Immediately after this statement, we read the words of Psalm 22:22, but as coming from the mouth of Jesus: "I will declare your name to my brothers; in the presence of the congregation I will sing your praises" (NIV). From this, we learn that Jesus Himself sings the praises of God in the corporate worship of His brothers and sisters. In the midst of the worshiping people of God, Jesus announces, "Here am I, and the children God has given me" (Heb. 2:13 NIV; cf. Isa. 8:18). In other words, as Jesus declares God's name to His brothers and sisters and sings the Father's praise, He does so amidst the worshiping children of God. Christian worship must, therefore, be Christ-centered, for it is Christ-enabled.

THE HEART OF WORSHIP:
CENTRAL FEATURES OF HEBREW AND CHRISTIAN WORSHIP

When God desires worshipers, He does not go looking in search of people who fit the bill, who are qualified to come before Him. When God desires worshipers, He *makes* worshipers!

The Bible stresses that "acceptable worship does not start with human intuition or inventiveness, but with God's action."[18] God acts, redeeming a people to be His own, calling them into covenantal relationship with Himself. Robert Webber states, "God's people are the people of a saving event. And it is this event, and all that it represents, that lies at the heart of biblical worship."[19] This is the distinctive feature of worship for both Hebrews and Christians, setting them apart from every other religion in the world: namely, that those who truly worship God are those whom He has redeemed![20] This relationship between the Redeemer and the redeemed provides the basis for all acceptable worship.

Redemptive Events in the Old and New Testaments

In the Old Testament, the key redemptive event providing the foundation for Israel's relationship with the Lord was the exodus. If we consider the Ten Commandments, for example, we note that prior to charging the Israelites with these ten basic laws, God reminds them of what He has done for them, thereby highlighting the event that established the basis for His claim on their lives. "I am the Lord your God," He says, "who brought you out of the land of Egypt, out of the house of slavery" (Ex. 20:2). Only after establishing this principle does God then proceed to instruct them on the proper way to honor Him.

As we read through the rest of the Pentateuch, we observe the detailed cultic instruction that God prescribes. He had taken the initiative, delivering them from captivity and gathering them at Mt. Sinai to be the *q'hal Yahweh* ("assembly of God"). Now, He demands their exclusive devotion. He delineates precisely *how* they are to worship Him, dictating the procedures of the sacrificial system. He imposes restrictions on *who* may actually carry out the worship that He will accept, limiting cultic activity to a select priesthood. He outlined precisely *where* worship was to take place, restricting the offering of sacrifices first to the tabernacle and later to the temple. Considered in its entirety, then, the exodus shaped Israel's worship from beginning to end. It provided the rationale for Israel's special relationship with the Lord, and it culminated in a series of mandates telling the people how to approach God.

The redemptive event that determines the faith, practice, and worship of the church is the life, death, and resurrection of Jesus Christ. Because of His finished work on the cross, Jesus has laid claim to the exclusive devotion of His people. Late in the eleventh century, Anselm of Canterbury reasoned that the savior of men and women had to be God, for "supposing any other person were to rescue man from eternal death, man would rightly be judged his bondslave."[21] And men and women, he contended, are properly the bondslaves of none but God. If we follow this reasoning, agreeing that men and women properly find themselves bound to their redeemer, we conclude that they are Jesus' bondslaves and they owe all their worship to Christ.

But the New Testament lacks the clear cultic instruction that we find in abundance in the Old Testament. Robert Webber bemoans the "fragmentary nature of the sources" regarding New Testament worship."[22] Gone are the meticulous instructions about sacrifices, the specialized ministers who enjoy a privileged access to God, and the geographical specifications that make worship acceptable. In short, the New Testament offers very little instruction for Christian worship. In his massive analysis of Pauline theology, Herman Ridderbos observes,

> The New Testament knows no holy persons who substitutionally perform the service of God for the whole people of God, nor holy places and

seasons or holy acts, which create a distance between the cultus and the life of every day and every place. All members of the church have access to God (Rom. 5:2) and a share in the Holy Spirit; all of life is service to God; there is no "profane" area.[23]

What, then, are we to do? Is the church left to wander in the wilderness with no map to guide it into God's presence? Or are we to assume that "anything goes" when it comes to New Testament worship? Are we to excise Leviticus and Deuteronomy from the canon of Scripture, relegating it to material useful in days gone by, but pointless for the church?

Appropriate worship, whether in the fifteenth century BC or the twenty-first century AD, depends on adherence to God-given directives. Although we don't find lists of rules and regulations in the New Testament, the necessity of an atoning sacrifice, a priestly intermediary between God and the people, and an approved site for encountering God was never abrogated. Rather, Jesus is the atoning sacrifice, Jesus is the great high priest, and the believer encounters God only in Him. For the New Testament believer, *every detail that is central to the worship God requires has been fulfilled exclusively in Jesus Christ.*

Sacred Sacrifices: How to Draw Near to God

To speak of the sacrificial system is to speak of the *how* of Hebrew worship. How were the Israelites to approach the Lord? What sort of worship would He find pleasing? Indeed, how were sinful people to offer any worship to a holy God at all? The answer was found in the Old Testament concept of sacrifices.

Shortly after the fall, people began bringing sacrifices to God. The children of Adam and Eve brought offerings to the Lord, Cain bringing "some of the fruits of the soil" and Abel bringing "fat portions from some of the firstborn of his flock" (Gen. 4:3–4 NIV). After Noah and his family emerged from the ark, he "built an altar to the LORD and, taking some of all the clean animals and clean birds, he sacrificed burnt offerings on it." This sacrifice, we are told, produced a "pleasing aroma" to the Lord (Gen. 8:20–21 NIV). How, then, did people worship God? From earliest times, they worshiped Him through sacrifices.

These sacrifices were frequently associated with the covenants that God made with His people, functioning as "visible signs that expressed the relationship between God and his people."[24] When God smelled the pleasing aroma of Noah's sacrifice, He blessed Noah and promised never again to destroy the world by a flood (Gen. 8:20–9:17). The covenant God established with Abram was sealed through the ritualistic slaying of "a three year old heifer, and a three year old female goat, and a three year old ram, and a turtledove, and a young pigeon" (Gen. 15:9–21). Likewise, when God confirmed this same covenant with Isaac, promising to bless him and increase the number of his descendants, Isaac worshiped God by offering a sacrifice—he "built an altar . . . and called upon the name of the Lord" (Gen. 26:25).[25] Even the covenant between God and His people, Israel, is ratified with a sacrifice. In Exodus 24:5–6, we find Moses employing the newly given instructions regarding the sacrificial system, taking the blood of a sacrifice and putting half of it in bowls, sprinkling the other half on the altar.

Having been ratified by a sacrifice, the covenant with Israel was also *maintained* by an elaborate system of sacrifices. Sin continued to be a problem among God's people, and if Israel was to relate to the Lord and approach Him in worship, it must be addressed. In the blood of the sacrifice, atonement was made vicariously for the sins of the people. God Himself explains this gory aspect of worship, saying, "The life of a creature is in the blood, and I have given it to you to make atonement for yourselves on the altar; it is the blood that makes atonement for one's life" (Lev. 17:11 NIV). The sacrifice, then, enabled sinners to approach a holy God in worship. Without the atonement found in the sacrifice, there would be no legitimate worship in Israel.

God ordained various types of sacrifices, each accompanied by specific instructions. Burnt offerings, for example, involved the sacrifice of an unblemished animal burned whole upon the altar (Lev. 1:4, 9; cf. 1:13, 17; 6:8–13). The peace offering (or fellowship offering) symbolized the restoration of fellowship between the Lord and the one bringing the offering. Described in Leviticus 3, this offering saw part of the slaughtered animal being consumed in a fellowship meal, while other parts were burned on the altar. God Himself appears as an honored guest at the fellowship meal, as the "pleasing aroma" of the burning flesh ascends from the altar.[26]

The sin offering (or guilt offering) was required by all, to make atonement for transgressions and to provide access to God.[27] It stands in stark contrast to the burnt offering and peace offering, for these yielded a sweet-smelling aroma, pleasing to the Lord. The focus of the sin offering, on the other hand, was not so much about God's *pleasure* as about the *expiation of God's wrath*. Symbolically bearing the sins of the nation, the sacrificial victim was under God's curse. Vividly symbolizing the odiousness of sin, the victim was then removed from the midst of God's people and burned outside the camp (Lev. 4:12). This sacrifice made atonement for Israel's transgressions, maintaining the possibility of worship even in their ongoing sinfulness.

With the inauguration of the new covenant, the necessity of an atoning sacrifice in the worship of God's people remains. In both the Old and New Testaments, then, the sacrifice is fundamental to worship, for it met both the righteous requirements of a holy God and the deep-seated need of human beings.

In the New Testament, the sacrificial system is fulfilled in the person and work of Jesus Christ. Paul proclaims, "God presented [Jesus] as a sacrifice of atonement, through faith in his blood" (Rom. 3:25 NIV). "Just as the old covenant was inaugurated by blood," writes Australian theologian David Peterson, "so the new covenant order is consecrated by the blood of Christ and his death suffices to purify his people and bring them ultimately into the presence of God."[28] He is the believer's "burnt offering," having "loved us and [given] himself up for us, a fragrant offering and sacrifice to God" (Eph. 5:2 ESV). He is our unblemished offering, for He who had no sin was made sin for us, "so that in him we might become the righteousness of God" (2 Cor. 5:21 ESV). He is our peace offering, having restored communion between God and humanity; when we sit at table with God, we do so "in remembrance of [Him]" (Luke 22:19; cf. 1 Cor. 11:24), looking to the sacrifice of the body and blood of Christ "Himself [who] is our peace" (Eph. 2:14). Finally, He is our sin offering, having "suffered outside the city gate to make the people holy through his own blood" (Heb. 13:12 NIV). He is our sacrificial victim, and has "redeemed us from the curse of the law by becoming a curse for us" (Gal. 3:13 ESV).

In Christ, though, God has provided an abiding solution to the problem of sin. The epistle to the Hebrews frequently contrasts the typical sacrifices of bulls and lambs with the antitypical sacrifice of Christ. "It is impossible," the writer tells us, "for the blood of bulls and goats to take away sins" (Heb. 10:4). However, the sacrifice of Jesus Christ has "made perfect forever those who are being made holy" (Heb. 10:14 NIV). The believer's sin has been dealt with by means of a sacrifice that need not be repeated daily; God has established a lasting solution for the sin problem.

The sacrificial system was the key to Old Testament worship. Without it, Israel would have been entirely unable to offer any acceptable worship to God, for their sins would have severed their relationship. We must acknowledge, then, that Jesus Christ is central to Christian worship, for it is in His sacrificial death on the cross that this fundamental requirement for worship has been met. And it is *His* sacrifice that Christians look to when they gather to worship.

Sacred Servants: By Whom to Draw Near to God

If I want to invest one thousand dollars in that latest sure thing the stock market offers, I would not put on my best suit, drive to the stock exchange, and fight my way across the crowded floor to purchase my shares. Instead, a stockbroker would function as my liaison, handling all aspects of the trade that I am not qualified to perform myself. It is important to recognize *by whom* the act may be accomplished.

Now that we have considered how Israel was to worship, we must consider *by whom* it was to be performed. In Israel, specific individuals —*priests*—brought the people's sacrifices to God so that they might be accepted. They stood between a holy God and a sinful people, representing them before God and providing them access to His presence. These descendants of Moses' brother Aaron (himself descended from Levi) acted as "living bridges," bringing would-be worshipers to God.[29]

Priests gave their lives entirely to the community's worship of the Lord. They served in the temple (Ezek. 44:11; cf. Ex. 28:43; Ezek. 45:5; 46:24; Joel 1:13). They were specially appointed to stand before God on behalf of the people—"to represent them in matters related to God, to offer gifts and sacrifices for sins" (Heb. 5:1 NIV). Their role in the sacrificial ministry was crucial, for theirs was the job of slaughtering and burning the animals of sacrifice on the altar. Through their ministry—the performance of this sacrificial ritual—the Israelites could "draw near" to God.

This priestly ministry is a second aspect of Israelite worship that we may call "foundational." Only after Aaron and his sons presented sin offerings and burnt offerings to the Lord, both for themselves and for the people, did the people approach God and stand before Him in worship (Lev. 9:5). No one who was ceremonially unclean or not a descendant of Aaron was permitted to "come near" in this way (Lev. 22:3; Num. 16:40). Only through the atoning sacrifice, performed exclusively by the priesthood, might sinful Israel draw near to God.

Turning, then, to the New Testament church, we are faced with a question. If priests are such an integral aspect of the worship that God finds acceptable, why does the New Testament speak of qualifications for elders and deacons, but not priests? We might be tempted to assume that, according to the New Testament, the office of priest is not necessary for the church to stand before God in worship. But in truth, the role of an mediating priest is as crucial to New Testament worship as it ever was under the old covenant.

For the Christian, the role of priest is fulfilled by Jesus Christ, who is "a merciful and faithful high priest in the service of God" (Heb. 2:17 ESV). He is not only the sacrificial victim, but He is also the priest, representing His people before His Father, living always "to make intercession for them" (Heb. 7:25). It is Christ who has brought believers before God, enabling their worship. "After all," Terry Wardle writes, "Jesus has provided our only access to the Father. Without Him, worship is unacceptable and worshipers undeserving."[30]

It is through Jesus Christ that believers draw near to the Father. By virtue of His atoning sacrifice, Christians may now "draw near with confidence to the throne of grace" (Heb. 4:16). Through His blood, "we have confidence to enter the Most Holy Place . . . [and we may] draw near to God with a sincere heart in full assurance of faith, having our hearts sprinkled to cleanse us from a guilty conscience and having our bodies washed with pure water" (Heb. 10:19, 22 NIV). Through Jesus' high priestly ministry, believers have *immediate access to the Father.*

Jesus is able to fulfill the priesthood in this way because His priestly ministry is superior to that of the priests under the old covenant. Under Mosaic law, priests ministered in a divinely designed, yet human-constructed, tabernacle—a mere "copy and shadow of what is in heaven" (Heb. 8:5 NIV). Christ, on the other hand, ministers at "the true tabernacle set up by the Lord, not by man" (Heb. 8:2 NIV). As the "true tabernacle" is superior to the "copy and shadow," so Christ, the true High Priest, is superior to all earthly priests of the old covenant.

In Christ, the priestly ministry expands beyond its Old Testament framework. Under Jesus Christ's priesthood, believers themselves have become "a kingdom, priests" to serve "His God and Father" (Rev. 1:6;

cf. 5:10; 20:6). In Christ, all worshipers may enter the holy place—all in Christ may draw near to God (Heb. 10:19–22; 12:23).

Jesus is central to Christian worship because He is *both* the sacrificial victim as well as the ministering priest. Should either of these be lacking, worship would be impossible.

Sacred Spaces: Where to Draw Near to God

Realtors often describe the three most important factors in home sales as follows: location, location, and location! Often, *where* something is located is as significant as *what* it actually is.

This principle applies in worship as well. According to God's instruction, priestly service was to take place exclusively at the tabernacle, and then, later, at the temple. The cultic obligations of Israel were to be fulfilled at a specific, divinely ordained location.

Over one hundred biblical texts present the worshiper as "approaching" God, or appearing "before God."[31] To worship, then, is to *come before the Lord*; it occurs in the *presence of God*.

But what does it mean to enter into the *presence* of an *omnipresent* God? Theologically, we affirm that God "is present at every point of space with his whole being."[32] But we also observe the notion of the *presence of God* bears a unique, cultic sense distinguishing it from the notion of God's ontological existence in all places. David affirms God's omnipresence when he rhetorically asks, "Where can I flee from Your presence?" (Ps. 139:7), yet he nonetheless cries out, "Do not cast me away from Your presence and do not take Your Holy Spirit from me" (Ps. 51:11). He suggests that the *presence* of God is directly related to fellowship with God's Spirit. It is this communion with the divine that Cain is denied when, having failed to offer acceptable worship, he was driven "from the presence of the Lord" to live "in the land of Nod, east of Eden" (Gen. 4:16). The land of Cain's exile is not to be understood as a place where God was ontologically absent; rather, Cain, rejected by God, is denied communion with the Lord that comes through an encounter with the divine Spirit.

Prior to the exodus, worshipers encountered God in various locations.[33] However, when God established His covenant with Israel, He also established a specific location at which they would come into His presence. From that point forward, Israel's worship was to take place only where the divine presence would be manifested—namely, at the tabernacle, the "dwelling place" of God on earth. Cultic ritual was forbidden at all other locations. (Deut. 12:5–6, 13–14).[34]

The tabernacle was, literally, the "tent of meeting."[35] Consisting of an outer court, an inner court, and the "holy of holies," wherein dwelt the *shᵉkhînah* glory of God, it was the place where Israel met with God. There, God promised, "I will dwell among the Israelites and be their God" (Ex. 29:45 NIV). And there, at the tabernacle, Israel was to worship the Lord.[36]

But the tabernacle was a temporary, portable dwelling place of the Lord; as such, it was appropriate for the nomadic wanderings of Israel. When the nation became established, however, God's presence took up permanent residence in the temple. The *shᵉkhînah* glory that previously indwelt the tent of meeting now filled the temple, "enthroned above the cherubim" of the ark of the covenant (2 Sam. 6:2; cf. 2 Kings 19:15; Ps. 80:1). God announced, "I have consecrated this temple . . . by putting my Name there forever. My eyes and my heart will always be there" (1 Kings 9:3 NIV). The notion of God's putting His *name* there expressed His sole ownership of the temple, and the anthropomorphic statement about God's "eyes" and "heart" being forever there is an affirmation that the temple was to be God's earthly dwelling place.[37] God's glory was localized for Israel in the temple, and only there were they to worship Him.

But where does the Christian encounter this glory? Where should the Christian worship? When my colleagues and students at Moody Bible Institute gather for worship, surely no one assumes that Torrey-

Gray Auditorium is the exclusive dwelling place of God! When Christians around the world assemble worldwide to worship each week, certainly God is not encountered in but one local church! Where, then does the Christian encounter God's presence?

In the New Testament, we find all Old Testament concepts of sacred spaces localized in the person of Jesus Christ. Jesus Himself indicated that He was to replace the temple in God's program. Even while recognizing the centrality of the temple to Hebrew worship, He proclaimed Himself to be "greater than the temple" (Matt. 12:6). Christ is the place where believers encounter the glory of God. In His conversation with the woman of Sychar, Jesus states that a "sacred space" such as Gerazim or Jerusalem or any other physical location was no longer mandated for true worship (John 4:20–24).

The Hebrew concept of sacred spaces—the tabernacle and the temple—has been fulfilled in Jesus Christ. The *sh^{e}khînah* glory that previously filled these locations has now been enfleshed in the Son of God. The tabernacle stood at the center of Israel, representing God's presence among the people. However, these earthly sites were but a type of the "true tabernacle . . . [that] is in heaven" (Heb. 8:2, 5 NIV). Christians encounter God's presence exclusively in Jesus. Thus, to come into the "presence of God" to worship is to worship at the heavenly tabernacle —to worship *in Christ Jesus*!

John presents this concept quite clearly. In the prologue to his gospel, he teaches that the Word, who both "was with God" and "was God" in the beginning, has now "made his dwelling (*eskēnōsen*; lit. "pitched his tent" or "tabernacled") among us. We have seen his glory, the glory of the One and Only, who came from the Father, full of grace and truth" (John 1:14 NIV). The prophets had foretold that, in the end time, God would "make his dwelling" in the midst of His people forever.[38] John now announces that this prophecy is being fulfilled in Jesus Christ. Christians encounter the glory of God, but not in an earthly tabernacle or temple. Today, when we encounter the glory of God, we see it in the face of Christ.

For the Christian, then, all true worship occurs in Jesus. In his vision of the heavenly kingdom, John writes, "I saw no temple in it, for the Lord God the Almighty and the Lamb are its temple" (Rev. 21:22). God has "tabernacled" in the person of Christ. His glory is localized not in a tent, nor in a temple, nor at any other physical site. He is encountered exclusively in His Son. Consequently, true worship occurs nowhere else. Jesus Christ is, indeed, the heart of worship.

PROCLAIMING JESUS IN CHRISTIAN WORSHIP

Returning, then, to the theme of this book, we note that Christian worship is the proclamation of the redemptive activity in the life, death, and resurrection of Jesus Christ.

The Israelites had been chosen to enjoy a special relationship with God. From among all nations, they alone were given the privilege of coming before God and receiving His Word. The upshot of this relationship, though, was that they were to be the means by which God would fulfill His promise to Abraham to bless all nations of the world (Gen. 12:1–3). Israel was to be a priestly kingdom, dedicated to the worshipful service of the Lord, proclaiming God's will and character to the world.

This proclamatory aspect of the Jews' relationship to God has become fulfilled in Jesus Christ. Only through Him can one offer the "sacrifice of praise" that is "the fruit of lips that confess his name" (Heb. 13:15 NIV). Now this notion of offering a "sacrifice of praise" *could* refer to the church's celebration of Jesus as Savior and Lord in either personal or corporate acts of worship, but in the context of Hebrews 13, such is not the case.[39] The writer's focus here is not on offering the "sacrifice of praise" within the confines of the community of faith. Rather, his concern is to exhort believers to acknowledge Christ *in the world.* In the midst of opposition and suffering, believers are encouraged to proclaim the good news of Jesus Christ and to render His praises *outside the camp.*[40]

Christians must recognize this evangelistic emphasis in New Testament worship. The aim of preaching the gospel is to bring people to acknowledge the lordship of Jesus Christ—to bow before Him in submission, reverence, and commitment. This "bending over" or "bowing" (*proskynein*) before the Lord is the essential response of those who turn to Jesus Christ in repentance and faith. Paul recognizes this connection when he employs several common terms and concepts associated with worship to his ministry among the Gentiles. In Romans 1:9, for example, his gospel preaching is a *service to God.* He views himself as a "minister" (*leitourgeon*) of Christ Jesus. His proclamation of the gospel is a "priestly duty" (Rom. 15:16 NIV). As Jewish priests were commissioned to serve God through performing sacrifices, Paul is charged to minister by preaching the gospel to the Gentiles. The goal of this preaching is that the Gentiles might offer themselves to God as "a living and holy sacrifice, acceptable to God" (Rom. 12:1). The proclamation of the gospel, then, is essentially a call to worship.

WORSHIP: ENGAGING GOD THROUGH JESUS CHRIST

Theologian John Frame speaks of the garden of Eden as a kind of temple. In Eden, Adam and Eve enjoyed life in God's presence. They regularly encountered Him and heard His Word. But, he notes, they failed to render the worship they owed to their Creator. They disobeyed. Consequently, God justly cursed them and cast them out of their Edenic temple. But God did not abandon Adam and Eve. He did want them to be conscious of sin, and to this end, they were cursed. But He also wanted them to know what He was going to do to free them from their guilt. God wants His people to praise Him, not only for His mighty works of creation, but also for the redemption He provides.

Believers today still hear God's Word in worship, and this Word does focus on His provision for our forgiveness. As a result, everything we do in worship is in response to the forgiveness we have found in the cross of Christ.[41] This is why it is not enough to say that Christian worship must be "God-centered." Specifically, Christian worship must be "Christ-centered." "In all our worship, the good news that Jesus has died for our sins and risen gloriously from the dead should be central."[42]

It is the proclamation of the gospel of Jesus Christ, then, that makes Christian worship distinct from that of the Israelites. Even though the New Testament does not prescribe details about precise methods, certainly the heart of Christian worship rests in recognizing the Christ event—the event that represents a fulfillment of the Old Testament system. Any definition of worship that lacks this Christocentric element is insufficient.

The early church recognized the need to distinguish Christian worship from that of the Jews. In the New Testament, we have seen that their understanding of worship struck at the very heart of the Jewish system. In Christ, the Jewish sacrificial system was fulfilled, the role of the priest was realized, and the purpose of the temple was accomplished. Clearly the church could no longer maintain the Old Testament rituals, for their Lord had fulfilled these! "It was becoming evident," Robert Webber writes, "that Jewish and Christian worship did not mix."[43]

The implications of this truth must shape how church leaders view their role as worship leaders. "One may sing and hear of the mighty power of the Father God," Terry Wardle states. "But if the worship service fails to focus on Christ, it is inadequate and incomplete."[44] He goes on to exhort church leaders to place Jesus at the heart of their worship ministries: "Worship services must be designed to intentionally highlight the person and work of Jesus Christ."[45]

This recognition of the Christocentricity of worship is in accord with Paul's view of his own ministry. He makes the Christ event the central focus of his teaching when he writes to the Corinthians, "For what I received I passed on to you as of *first importance:* that Christ died for our sins according to the Scriptures, that he was buried, that he was raised on the third day . . . and that he appeared to Peter, and then to the Twelve. After that, he appeared to more than five hundred of the brothers at the same time, most of whom are still living" (1 Cor. 15:3–6 NIV). Worship *is* a celebration of God; it is an *engagement* with God. But Christian worship is an "engagement with God *through faith in Jesus Christ* and what he has done for us."[46]

We enter God's presence in singing, prayer, the reading of Scripture, the proclamation of the gospel, the Eucharist—in many ways. But always and only, we enter God's presence through Jesus Christ.

Richard M. Weber is assistant professor of theology at the Moody Bible Institute. He has earned the Ph.D. degree from Marquette University, Milwaukee, Wisconsin, and academic degrees from Trinity Evangelical Divinity School and Trinity International University, both in Deerfield, Illinois, and from Millikin University in Decatur, Illinois.

NOTES

1. Matt Redman, "The Heart of Worship," Kingsway's Thankyou Music/Admin. in North America by EMI Christian Music Publishing, 1999.

2. Ronald Allen and Gordon Borror, *Worship: Rediscovering the Missing Jewel* (Portland, Ore.: Multnomah, 1982), 16–18.

3. C. F. D. Moule, *Worship in the New Testament* (Richmond, Va.: John Knox, 1964), 9.

4. Robert G. Rayburn, *O Come, Let Us Worship* (Grand Rapids: Baker, 1980), 78.

5. Ibid., 84.

6. Robert E. Webber, *Worship Old and New* (Grand Rapids: Zondervan, 1994), 33.

7. Allen and Borror, *Worship*, 48–49.

8. John R. W. Stott, *The Cross of Christ* (Downers Grove, Ill.: InterVarsity, 1986), 273.

9. Terry Wardle, *Exalt Him*, rev. ed. (Camp Hill, Penna.: Christian Publications, 1992), 64.

10. Barry Wayne Leisch, *The New Worship* (Grand Rapids: Baker, 2001); Tom Kraeuter, *Developing an Effective Worship Ministry* (Lynnwood, Wash.: Emerald, 1999).

11. Russell P. Shedd, "Worship in the New Testament Church," *The Church in the Bible and the World*, ed. D. A. Carson (Grand Rapids: Baker, 1987), 122–23.

12. Evelyn Underhill writes in her book *Worship* (Guildford, Surrey, Great Britain: Eagle, 1991), 47, "Whatever its ritual expression may be, [worship] always has a theological basis." She adds, "Christian worship is yet always conditioned by Christian belief; and especially belief about the Nature and Action of God, as summed up in the great dogmas of the Trinity and the Incarnation." Furthermore, she writes, "That which is primary for the Christian in this cultus, at least as he moves towards fullness of worship, is the self-giving of the Absolute God—'the love which the Father has us-ward'—flowing out unceasingly to His creation, to evoke from that creation an answering movement of love. . . . For the creative Charity of God, as experienced by man, is a redemptive force. It comes into human life in Christ, His Spirit, His Church, His sacraments, and His saints, not to inform but to transform . . ." (47, 51).

13. Matthew appears to be particularly fond of the use of *prosekynein* to speak of the worship of Jesus Christ. See, for example, Matt. 2:2, 8, 11; 8:2; 9:18; 14:33.

14. See Exod. 3:12, 18; 5:3, 8, 17; 4:23; 5:1; 8:1; Deut. 6:12–13.

15. See Webber, *Worship Old and New*, 30. See also David Peterson, *Engaging with God: A Biblical Theology of Worship* (Grand Rapids: Eerdmans, 1992), 64.

16. See also "spiritual service" (ASV); "reasonable service" (KJV).

17. Were we not limited by length and scope in this study, we might include the Hebrew term *yāre* and Greek terms based on the seb- stem in our discussion. These terms speak of the "fear of the Lord"—i.e., a sober reverence and awe of God. For the purposes of this discussion, however, there is sufficient overlap in the significance of these terms and those of the *hištaḥ*ʷâ/*proskynein* group that a separate discussion will not be included. For further discussion of this particular word group, see Peterson, *Engaging with God*, 70-74.

18. Peterson, *Engaging with God*, 26.

19. Webber, *Worship Old and New*, 22.

20. Rayburn, *O Come*, 52.

21. Anselm of Canterbury, "Why God Became Man," in *The Major Works*, ed. and introduction by Brian Davies and G. R. Evans (New York: Oxford Univ. Press, 1998), 270 (I.v.)

22. Webber, *Worship Old and New*, 41. Rayburn also acknowledges that what we know of the methodology of New Testament worship is "quite limited." Rayburn, *O Come*, 77.

23. Herman Ridderbos, *Paul: An Outline of His Theology*, trans. John Richard De Witt (Grand Rapids: Eerdmans, 1994), 481.

24. Webber, *Worship Old and New*, 34.

25. Sacrifices were also used to seal agreements between people. For example, the agreement between Jacob and his uncle Laban is ratified by means of a sacrifice in Genesis

31:43–55. Soon after this, we read of the confirmation of the covenant God made with Jacob, also sealed by a sacrifice (Gen. 35:6–12).

26. See Lev. 7:11–34.

27. See Lev. 4:1–6:7; 6:24–7:10.

28. Peterson, *Engaging with God*, 61.

29. See Shedd, Worship in the New Testament Church," 121.

30. Wardle, *Exalt Him*, 65.

31. E.g., Psalm 68:3, "Let the righteous be glad; let them exult before God . . ."; Psalm 95:6, "Come, let us worship and bow down, let us kneel before the Lord our Maker"; Micah 6:6, "With what shall I come to the Lord and bow myself before the God on high?" See Bruce Leafblad, *Music, Worship, and the Ministry of the Church* (Portland, Ore.: Western Conservative Baptist Seminary, 1978), 44.

32. Wayne Grudem, *Systematic Theology* (Grand Rapids: Zondervan, 1994), 173.

33. See, for example, Genesis 28, where Jacob encounters God in a vision of a heavenly staircase with angels ascending and descending. This location—christened "Bethel" ("House of God") by the Patriarch—became a recognized place of worship. It must be noted, of course, that the Pentateuch recognizes *heaven* to be the dwelling place of God. For example, when God plans the destruction of Sodom and Gomorrah, He declares that he will *"go down"* to the cities (Gen. 18:21). When the angel of the Lord announces God's plans for Ishmael, he speaks to Hagar "from heaven" (Gen. 21:17). And Abraham plainly describes the Lord as "the God of heaven" (Gen. 24:7) (cf. Gen. 11:5; 22:11; 28:12). Thus, we should not assume that the Old Testament people of God thought of God being somehow confined in places such as Bethel or Mount Horeb. Still, they were aware that God had chosen to sanctify such places by manifesting His presence in clear and significant ways at these sites.

34. The seriousness with which the Israelites took this instruction is illustrated in Joshua 22. The Reubenites, Gadites, and the half-tribe of Manasseh crossed the Jordan to their land in Geliloth, and there they set up an altar, distinct from the tabernacle of the Lord. Shocked, the rest of the Israelites gathered at Shiloh to prepare to go to war with their brothers! Their establishment of this altar was seen as rebellion against God Himself! Only when they were assured that the altar was not intended for burnt offerings, sin offerings, or peace offerings was war averted.

35. Also, "tent of appointment," "tent of rendezvous." Gordon J. Wenham, *The Book of Leviticus* (Grand Rapids: Eerdmans, 1979), 17.

36. Peterson, *Engaging with God*, 33.

37. See Peterson, *Engaging with God*, 44.

38. See Joel 3:17; Zech. 2:10; cf. Ezek. 43:7.

39. This statement is not intended to denigrate personal or corporate worship in the slightest. Within the Christian community, we are instructed to speak "to one another in psalms and hymns and spiritual songs" (Eph. 5:19). We are to "sing psalms, hymns and spiritual songs with gratitude in your hearts to God," while teaching and admonishing each other in the setting of corporate worship (Col. 3:1 6 NIV). But

the context of Hebrews 13 excludes this notion of corporate worship in favor of the church's proclamation of Christ in the world.

40. In the verses preceding Hebrews 13:15, the writer notes that the sin offering was burned *outside the camp*. Likewise, Christ also "suffered outside the city gate to make the people holy through his own blood" (v. 12 NIV). In verse 13, then, he encourages his readers to go "outside the camp, bearing the disgrace he bore." By the time we arrive at Hebrews 13:15 and the exhortation to offer the "sacrifice of praise," the context has clearly established that the writer is *not* confining these praises to the intramural gatherings of believers. See Peterson, *Engaging with God*, 74–75.

41. John M. Frame, *Worship in Spirit and Truth* (Phillipsburg, N.J.: Presbyterian and Reformed, 1996), 6.

42. Ibid.

43. Webber, *Worship Old and New*, 45.

44. Wardle, 64.

45. Ibid.; 65. cf. Rayburn, *O Come,* 79.

46. Peterson, *Engaging with God*, 52; emphasis added

Chapter 13

PROCLAIMING JESUS IN AN ECUMENICAL CULTURE

Unease over "An Evangelical Celebration"

by Mike McDuffee

In today's globalization, characterized by cultural pluralism and fragmentation, "the fundamental level on which the political struggle is waged" as one analyst puts it, "is that of the legitimacy of concepts of ideologies."[1]

What pertains to ideologies in pursuit of temporal rule is also valid for claims to eternal truth. Local or longstanding legitimacy over stories of how the world works under the hand of God and our place in it may no longer be taken for granted. Listeners have to be won by those who tell these stories. Yet present circumstances subject us to two errors.

The first error is to succumb to "weak thought," that is, "the weakening of the idea of truth, and ultimately of reality."[2] The remarks that follow do not address this latest resurgence in ancient skepticism in its traditional forms: of either denying that anything can be known or calling for suspending of judgment over any conflict about what could be known.[3]

A False Premise for Unity

This chapter does examine the second kind of error to avoid—that of relying upon a false surety against wounds to Christian unity. The Roman Catholic Church claims its office of the papacy exclusively guarantees Christian unity. This is the most significant example of the second kind of error we can make in the present setting of postmodernism: making universal truth relative by subjecting it to an authority whose capacity is less than universal. This error puts all true Christians and the universal Christian unity they together bear under the authority of one particular spiritual leader.

As evangelical Christians, we should evaluate the present ecumenical endeavors of the Roman Catholic Church. We best understand these activities as an extension of papal evangelization. As a consequence of this understanding, we should reassess our doctrinal statements about the gospel to ensure they accurately and effectively communicate the good news of Jesus Christ according to the Scriptures, without confusion or ambiguity. What follows is devoted to that goal.

Sociologist of religion Peter L. Berger has long developed the idea of a "religious market"[4] in his assessing the effects of pluralism upon religion. As he has recently said, by this he means, "religious institutions must *compete* for the allegiance of their putative clientele." In a pluralistic social environment, ecumenism is one way by which religious institutions "negotiate with each other to regulate the competition," he argues.[5] In line with this observation, ecumenical circles today condemn proselytism as evangelizing people who have been baptized as Christians. The older ecumenism, housed in the World Council of Churches (WCC), and the new ecumenism, championed by the Roman Catholic Church, agree on this point.[6] Their consensus stakes out the context in which all confessing Christians communicate theological statements to one another. Those who present the good news without being familiar with this ecumenical environment may not realize how others will hear the gospel message. To best anticipate what meaning they carry to others, we should read our evangelical statements of faith in light of this new ecumenical reality.

Effects of the Pope's "New Evangelicalism"

The single most important event of the past generation of church history has been the Roman Catholic Church's decision to pursue a policy of ecumenism inaugurated by the Second Vatican Council (1962–1965). The essence of this ecumenism is the "new evangelization" envisioned by Pope Paul VI and especially advanced by Pope John Paul II. Since Joseph Cardinal Ratzinger—now Pope Benedict XVI—played such an important role in developing the theological thinking girding this ecumenical undertaking, it would be prudent to expect Pope Benedict to continue it.[7]

The gravitational pull of this enormous new "evangelical" Catholicism affects all speech about evangelism outside of it. Theologian Avery Cardinal Dulles tells us that, with Vatican II, the "Catholic Church became in a true sense evangelical."[8] Cardinal Dulles distinguishes a "truly Catholic form of evangelical theology" from "Protestant evangelicalism" on the basis that "it will not be predicated on the doctrine of salvation by faith alone." Catholic evangelicalism, he informs us, embeds the saving of souls in a holistic mandate for the reordering of the secular age in line with the teachings of the Roman Catholic Church:

> It will seek to renew the entire life of believers, of the Church, and of society itself through the leaven of the gospel. Hence it will not separate word from sacraments, or faith from works, or personal morality from social action. It will strive to regenerate the entire community of believers in light of the gospel and to transform the larger secular society in the image of the kingdom of God.[9]

The Papal Quest for Unity

From a Roman Catholic vantage point, all ecumenical endeavors represent inner missions work, the effort to restore full, visible unity among all baptized Christians under the authority of the papacy. It is important, therefore, that evangelical Christians understand the ecclesial character of this Roman Catholic office. According to the First Dogmatic Constitution of the Church of Christ, pronounced at the First Vatican Council (1869–1870), the pope alone holds "a primacy of jurisdiction over the whole Church of God."[10] He is the "true vicar of Christ, head of the whole Church and father and teacher of all Christian people."[11] The pope "governs the whole Church" and "is the supreme judge of the faithful" whose sentence "is not subject to revision by anyone."[12]

The papal office serves the well-being of the whole body of Christ. God gave the "gift of truth and never-failing faith" to the office of the papacy "for the salvation of all." The pope keeps "the whole flock of Christ" safe from "the poisonous food of error" that it can "be nourished with the sustenance of heavenly doctrine." The pope's proper care of the gift of truth and unfailing faith guards against "the tendency to schism" assuring that "the whole Church is preserved in unity, and, resting on its [papal] foundation, can stand firm against the gates of hell."[13]

Pope Benedict XVI believes it is the office of the papacy as articulated by both Vatican I and II that alone provides the "personal expression" to "the unity of the universal Church." As Cardinal Ratzinger, he said, "This will remain the magisterial responsibility for the unity of the Church, her faith, and her morals that was defined by Vatican I and II." He acknowledged that "forms of exercise can change," and "they will certainly change"; however, this will occur only "when hitherto separated communities enter into unity with the Pope."[14]

Pope Paul VI taught that evangelization was the "essential function" of the Roman Catholic Church.[15] The aim of Roman Catholic evangelization is to bring about "a new human race" of "men renewed by baptism and by a life lived in accordance with the gospel."[16] Evangelization encompasses and directs the ecumenical efforts of the Roman Catholic Church:

> The Catholic Church is . . . assiduous in her solicitude for those Christians who are not in full communion with her: she seeks to establish with them that unity which Christ desired and it is her aim to achieve this unity in truth. She appreciates that she would be failing gravely in her duty if she did not bear witness to them of the fullness of revelation of which she is the depositary.[17]

Meanwhile, the 1993 Directory for the Application of Principles and Norms on Ecumenism, released by the Pontifical Council for Promoting Christian Unity, seeks "to motivate, enlighten and guide" ecumenical activities, offering non-Catholics "help [to] evaluate Catholic ecumenical initiatives and to better understand Catholic responses to such activities initiated outside the Roman Catholic Church." For Roman Catholics, the directory is intended to "guarantee that ecumenical activity throughout the Catholic Church is in accordance with the unity of faith and with the discipline that binds Catholics together."[18]

The directory makes clear that the starting point for all ecumenical engagement is baptism, which is the true foundation for Christian unity. By incorporating a person "into Christ and into his Church," baptism "constitutes the sacramental bond of unity existing among all who through it are reborn."[19] "In seeking "the restoration of unity among Christians," the Roman Catholic Church believes "baptismal communion . . . tends towards full ecclesial communion." The Roman Catholic Church's high premium placed upon baptism reaches to the very heights of its eschatological vision of consummation: "To live our Baptism is to be caught up in Christ's mission of making all things one."[20]

Catholics are required to confess that "the entirety of revealed truth, of sacraments, and of ministry"[21] subsist only in the Catholic Church and thus, too, that "the fullness of the unity of the Church of Christ"[22] subsists only in it because these things of God belong to the Roman Catholic Church:

> According to Catholic faith, the Catholic Church has been endowed with the whole of revealed truth and all the means of salvation as a gift which cannot be lost. Nevertheless, among the elements and gifts which belong to the Catholic Church (e.g.; the written Word of God, the life of grace, faith, hope and charity etc.) many can exist outside its visible limits.[23]

In the first papal encyclical teaching about ecumenism, Pope John Paul II declared that the obligation to pursue unity "in fulfillment of God's plan falls to those who through Baptism become members of the Body of Christ."[24] In accordance with this divine plan the pope exercises the "office of unity."[25] Only the papacy manifests the divinely ordained "principle and foundation of unity"[26] The "necessary condition for unity" is restoration of communion of "all particular Churches with the Church of Rome."[27] This is not an option to be entertained but a divine requirement to be obeyed. "The Catholic Church, both in her *praxis* and in her solemn documents, holds that the communion of the particular Churches with the Church of Rome. . . is—in God's plan—an essential requisite of full and visible communion."[28]

The pope lays down as axiomatic the principle that the "imperative of charity is an imperative which admits no exception."[29] Division is to be condemned because it "impedes the very work of Christ"; unity is the "way and instrument of evangelization."[30] The effectiveness of evangelization is measured by how the particular churches will respond to the pope's ministry of bringing unity to Christianity. However, ecumenism is not only an "internal question" among the various baptized Christian communities. "It is a matter of the love which God has in Jesus Christ for all humanity . . ."[31]

Opposition to the papal office of unity and the pope's overtures in behalf of unity would be a most grave matter, because such resistance means to "stand in the way" of God's love. Such action would be sinful, "an offense against him and against his plan to gather all people in Christ."[32] With unity completed, the office of the papacy would continue, "so that under the sole Head, who is Jesus Christ, [the Church] may be visibly present in the world as the communion of all his disciples."[33]

In his capacity as prelate of the Congregation for the Doctrine of the Faith, now Pope Benedict XVI commented in 1996 (as Cardinal Ratzinger) on the ecumenical role of the papacy. The Roman pontiff, according to Ratzinger, is "the perpetual and visible principle and foundation of unity both of the Bishops and of the multitude of the faithful" and, therefore, has a "specific ministerial grace for serving that unity of faith and communion which is necessary for the Church to fulfill her saving mission." [34] How the papacy performs its ministry in bringing about unity is something that "cannot be determined by evaluating the various functions the papacy has completed in the past."[35] In the pursuit of unity, Ratzinger closed his remarks by telling all who call upon the Lord that they "are reminded to trust in the Holy Spirit, to trust in Christ, by trusting in Peter."[36]

Once we understand the nature of the new evangelization that includes ecumenical engagement, which the papal office oversees and seeks to achieve, we can better understand the leverage the Roman Catholic church brings to bear upon the ecumenical movement. A worthwhile place to start this work is a study of the World Council of Churches' Faith and Order paper titled *Baptism, Eucharist and Ministry* (BEM).[37] This is "the most extensively studied text in the modern ecumenical movement, and has elicited responses from almost two hundred Orthodox, Anglican, and Protestant Churches, and the Catholic Church."[38] It is one of only a few documents of ecumenical dialogue that have been received by the papal office for "official response and action."[39] Historian and theologian Thomas E. FitzGerald acknowledges that the "text has been seen as unprecedented in the contemporary ecumenical movement" at expressing "significant theological convergence" on themes of baptism, Eucharist and ministry.[40] A major reason why this convergence is significant is because it includes the Roman Catholic Church as a full member of the Faith and Order Commission.

Ecumenism's Baptismal Unity

A Crucial Definition

Crucial for correctly interpreting the ecumenical field at work today affecting all preaching of the gospel is this statement of the BEM: "The need to recover baptismal unity is at the heart of the ecumenical task as it is central for the realization of genuine partnership within the Christian communities."[41] BEM closely connects a person's receiving of the Holy Spirit with water baptism administered by the church:

> In God's work of salvation, the paschal mystery of Christ's death and resurrection is inseparably linked with the Pentecostal gift of the Holy Spirit. Similarly, participation in Christ's death and resurrection is inseparably linked with the receiving of the Spirit. Baptism in its full meaning signifies and effects both.[42]

Ecumenical Consequences

Ecumenical consequences follow from this definition. First, baptism is the mandate demanding that churches should manifest together full visible unity:

> Through baptism, Christians are brought into union with Christ, with each other and with the Church of every time and place. Our common baptism, which unites us to Christ in faith, is thus a basic bond of unity . . . When baptismal unity is realized in one, holy, catholic, apostolic Church, a genuine Christian witness can be made to the healing and

reconciling love of God. Therefore, our one baptism into Christ constitutes a call to the churches to overcome their divisions and visibly manifest their fellowship.[43]

Second, BEM declares baptism to be "an unrepeatable act." "Any practice that might be interpreted as 're-baptism' must be avoided." The commentary attached to this statement goes on to say,

> As the churches come to fuller mutual understanding and acceptance of one another and enter into closer relationships in witness and service, they will want to refrain from any practice which might call into question the sacramental integrity of other churches or which might diminish the unrepeatability of the sacrament of baptism.[44]

Third, BEM endorses the movement toward mutual recognition of baptism among churches, stating whenever possible that it should be expressed explicitly by the churches. "Mutual recognition of baptism is acknowledged as an important sign and means of expressing the baptismal unity given in Christ. Wherever possible, mutual recognition should be expressed explicitly by the churches."[45]

As an outworking of this thinking, baptismal unity has become the basis for common witness among confessing Christians. Baptism has become the belt buckle of unity that joins in common witness the two ends of the older WCC ecumenism and the ecumenism of papal evangelization. For example, the 1997 WCC report titled, "Becoming a Christian: The Ecumenical Implications of Our Common Baptism," states, "In our baptism we are joined to Christ and his body, the Church."[46] The report further declares, "Our pathway is set and our journey to life eternal is begun, a journey which begins with our death and burial in the baptismal water." (For a historical perspective on the efficacy of baptism in salvation and the dispute it engenders in the church, see Gregg Quiggle's discussion in chapter 5, under the section "Making the Ordinances Effective and Valid.")

In the report, the WCC and the Roman Catholic Church agree that within "the context of the modern ecumenical movement" proselytism "has taken on a negative connotation when applied to activities of Christians to win adherents from other Christian communities."[47] Proselytism "stands in opposition to all ecumenical effort."[48] Insofar as concerns evangelism of men and women already baptized, the group identifies efforts at "the re-evangelization of baptized but non-practicing members of other churches"[49] as a source of tension that could lead to proselytism. All should avoid such evangelistic practices, "even if proceeding with good intentions" because "their approach ignores the Christian reality of other churches or their particular approaches to pastoral practice."[50]

ECT'S FALSE PARITY

Many of us who in good conscience ground our obedience to the faith in Scripture do not believe that baptism brings to pass the benefits of salvation attributed to it by the WCC or the Roman Catholic Church. To stand firm in our faith, we should be prepared at the very minimum to be stigmatized by their representatives. With God's favor, this will not stop us from preaching the gospel to all listeners, regardless of their given religious affiliation received by church-administered baptism.

An Unfortunate Flaw

Our position is also pressed in upon by the ongoing project known as "Evangelicals and Catholics Together," (ECT), an initiative that believes it necessary for confessing evangelical Christians and Roman Catholics to "work with one another, and not against one another, in the great task of evangelization, and to support one another in facing up to the ominous moral and cultural threats of our time."[51] The unfortunate flaw in the Evangelicals and Catholics Together initiative is that it contributes to respecting the various means of gaining Christian identity and growing in Christian virtue advocated by the Faith and Order Commission of the WCC and the Joint Working Group of the WCC with the Roman Catholic Church.

Respecting such various means of identity and growth too easily collapses into a de facto excuse for censoring the preaching of the gospel by trimming its content to promote unity among WCC church members and the Roman Catholic Church. If the ECT perspective becomes established evangelicalism, then all of our past heritage will be read in its light. It will become ecumenically incorrect to preach the gospel and call all men, women, children, and families to live in obedience to the Scriptures by planting and joining Bible-based churches.

For example, in their recently published work *Is the Reformation Over?* Mark A. Noll and Carolyn Nystrom lay down groundwork for ending the evangelical practice of sharing the gospel with Roman Catholics. They propose a multiple language model of Christianity[52], suggesting evangelical Protestantism is but one irreducible tradition God has given to the life of the church. The authors believe evangelical Protestantism and Roman Catholicism are two distinct types of Christianity, which remain "incommensurable." They believe these two kinds of Christianity cannot be compared with Scripture alone operating as the common standard for them both. They tell us the two kinds of Christianity exist owing "more to do with historical circumstances than with sinful error; mistakes, or the exercise of power." They explain their approach to Christian truth "represents a historical or missiological rather than a strictly doctrinal approach to the questions of what Christianity is in its essence and how one strand of Christianity might evaluate another strand of Christianity with insights as well as judgment."[53]

The upshot of setting aside a biblically based doctrinal assessment of the two kinds of Christianity is to award equal status to a Roman

Catholic who has been "baptized into salvation,"[54] with that of an evangelical Christian who upon hearing the gospel believes in the Lord Jesus for salvation. Because they receive salvation via the sacraments, the authors are convinced "it is only marginally useful for evangelicals to quote Bible verses at Roman Catholics." Since "authoritative interpretations of Scripture are deeply ingrained" in the Roman Catholic, he or she would "deny the force of the texts as used by evangelicals." If evangelical Christians will downplay doctrinal differences and decline from sharing the Scriptures with Roman Catholics, then we will fall in step with the growing number of "Christ-followers of one sort" who "are coming to recognize the sanctity, holiness, and telltale manifestations of the Holy Spirit among serious Christ-followers of others sorts."[55]

Noll and Nystrom rightly remind us to temper our criticism of other traditions by exercising Christian love. They also serve us well by encouraging us to give thanks always and for everything, especially for the way God allowed us to repent and believe in the gospel. However, the speculation that "differences in language will continue in heaven" is less helpful in building us up in the faith. The irony of such a tolerant hunch is that it resigns one to concede, "Perhaps a variety of emphases on how much Scripture, tradition, and the church prepared the way for uninterrupted fellowship with God will also continue through eternity."[56]

Rather than entertain such daydreams, we should seek to apply the principle of *sola scriptura* with excellence, and as Carl F. H. Henry once said, make it our goal ever "more precisely to state the redemptive formula."[57] This is especially the case in an ecumenical age strongly influenced by Roman Catholic teaching about salvation through faith in baptism.

Evangelizing without Winning Souls

In the 1998 ECT statement "The Gift of Salvation," the signatories agreed, "We must share the fullness of God's saving truth with all, including members of our several communities." The basis for this commitment to "evangelizing everyone" is cast, however, in the light of disciple building and not the winning of souls (Prov. 11:30). "Evangelicals must speak the Gospel to Catholics and Catholics to Evangelicals, always speaking the truth in love, so that 'working hard to *maintain* the unity of the Spirit in the bond of peace . . . the body of Christ may be built up.'"[58] Similarly, in defense of freedom of conscience, the first ECT statement of 1994 reads:

> There are, then, differences between us that cannot be resolved here. But on this we are resolved: All authentic witness must be aimed at conversion to God in Christ by the power of the Spirit. Those converted—whether understood as having received the new birth for the first time or as having experienced the reawakening of the new birth originally bestowed in the sacrament of baptism—must be given full freedom and respect as they discern and decide the community in which they will live their new life in Christ. In such discernment and decision we dare not interfere with the exercise of that responsibility.[59]

"We dare not interfere"? Woe to anyone who through coercion or manipulation fails to treat another with the dignity and respect she or he deserves by having been created in the image of God, for He is impartial to all and His offspring are held to be precious in His sight. Filled with His love, we should never shrink back from declaring anything that is profitable about repentance toward God and faith in our Lord Jesus Christ or from declaring the whole counsel of God (Acts 20:21, 27). All believers are called to continue to speak all the words of this Life (Acts 5:20).

It is a poor exchange to sanction interchangeability of ways of conversion for upholding freedom of conscience or to safeguard against proselytism. Such good intentions do not justify forsaking the one way by which a person may be saved. The apostle Paul made it clear that he was not sent by the Lord to baptize, but to preach the gospel. "For the word of the cross is foolishness to those who are perishing, but to us who are being saved it is the power of God" (1 Cor. 1:18). Conceding parity of the sacerdotal, sacramental system of salvation offered by the Roman Catholic Church with salvation through hearing the gospel and trusting in Jesus for forgiveness of sin and for guidance in understanding the Scriptures only sows harmful confusion.

The first ECT statement concedes parity not only about how new life begins in a person, but also about how a sinner saved grows in this new life. Therein it is agreed, "there are different ways of being Christian" and thus "different forms that authentic discipleship can take." Such "distinctive patterns of discipleship . . . are amply evident within the communion of the Catholic Church as well as within the many worlds of Evangelical Protestantism." Three points are agreed to in this mutual recognition:

1. Evangelicals and Catholics should affirm that opportunity and means for growth in Christian discipleship are available in our several communities.
2. The decision of the committed Christian with respect to his communal allegiance and participation must be assiduously respected.
3. It is neither theologically legitimate nor a prudent use of resources for one Christian community to proselytize among active adherents of another Christian community.[60]

We can be thankful that evangelicals of the Reformation period or the generations of evangelical Christians that followed refused to accept such principles. Otherwise, there would not be any evangelical Christians today to make these mistaken concessions. Evangelical Christians put at risk any future ministry and legacy the Lord might grant our community of faith if we embrace these principles today. Setting this point aside, it is obvious that the craftsmen of the ECT initiative have designed their doctrinal vessel well, fit to chart a course which best assures its conforming to the cooperative ecumenical efforts of the Faith and Order Commission of the World Council of Churches and its Joint Working Group with the Roman Catholic Church.

The sorry effect of this course of action is that now it is not enough to simply distinguish our evangelical understanding of the gospel according to the Scriptures from what the Roman Catholic Church teaches about salvation. It is now further necessary for us to deny the false parity ECT represents. Beyond this, we must make sure our confessions about the gospel clearly deny that baptism administered by any church brings the benefits of salvation, which the Roman Catholic Church insists it provides to all members of the Christian church.

"Justification" by Faith Through Baptism

The Roman Catholic Church teaches that we are justified by grace through faith alone in Christ. However, it also teaches that we receive this faith through the sacrament of baptism administered by the church. Thus, "all who have been justified by faith in baptism are incorporated into Christ" and "have a right to be called Christians."[61] Since the Roman Catholic Church teaches within it alone subsists the true and complete Christian faith, it confers "*the sacramental bond of unity* existing among all who through it are reborn."[62] It is important in this discussion to avoid haranguing entanglements over whether or not babies should be baptized. As significant as this issue might be, it is secondary to the point at hand. Regardless of what evangelical Christians confess and believe about baptism, it is essential for all of us to realize together that from a Roman Catholic point of view, the baptism any of us administer is efficacious solely "from the very fullness of grace and truth entrusted to the Catholic Church."[63] Indeed, the "many elements of sanctification and of truth" that are "found outside" the "visible confines" of the Roman Catholic Church as "gifts [that] belong to the

Church of Christ . . . are forces impelling towards Catholic unity."[64] Or, as then prelate of the Congregation for the Doctrine of Faith Joseph Cardinal Ratzinger expressed this Roman Catholic teaching, "There exists only one 'subsistence' of the true Church, while outside her visible structure there only exist *elementa Ecclesiae*, which— being elements of that same Church—tend and lead toward the Catholic Church."[65]

REEXAMINING "AN EVANGELICAL CELEBRATION"

Maintaining biblical integrity to hold up under the demands of this ecumenical pressure requires us to revise our 1999 evangelical statement of consensus about the gospel titled, "The Gospel of Jesus Christ: An Evangelical Celebration" (hereafter EC).[66] As members of its drafting committee, J. I. Packer and Thomas C. Oden applaud the fact that EC has been "endorsed by several hundred leaders from all evangelical traditions," and that it lays out "more fully and precisely the imputed righteousness of Christ as the ground for our pardon and acceptance than any representative evangelical statement had yet done.[67] Since this confessional statement "commands the widest range of evangelical leaders' signatures," Packer and Oden with well-deserved confidence declare it a "key consensual statement expressing broadly accepted evangelical convictions throughout the English-speaking world."[68] Other evangelical leaders have said that the widespread support for this doctrinal declaration could only be historically matched by *The Fundamentals: A Testimony for the Truth*, written and distributed in the period 1910–1915.[69]

Since EC is "the first [evangelical statement] to focus primarily on the gospel itself,"[70] it should bear witness to its truths cognizant of the parameters affecting the ecumenical surroundings in which it is communicated. "Much confusion," proponents of EC correctly point out, "can ensue when the gospel is not faithfully proclaimed or when it is not communicated with clarity."[71] All of us should take to heart their advice that "leadership of churches and parachurch ministries might wish to reflect on their own statements of faith in light of 'The Gospel of Jesus Christ: An Evangelical Celebration.'"[72]Before doing so, it is also advisable that leaders should first learn to read EC in its present ecumenical context. Doing so, they may realize its disappointing deficiency at dealing with this new reality.

The glaring omission of EC is its total failure to address the relationship between justification, faith, and baptism. This is unconscionable in an ecumenical age that affirms baptism as the basis for Christian identity and attributes Christian unity to it. There is no legitimate justification for overlooking this obvious factor, which carries enormous effect on relations among confessing Christian across all denominational lines.

This omission is compounded by an inappropriate paraphrasing of our Lord's Great Commission to the church as recorded in the gospel according to Matthew. The EC Drafting Committee placed the order of our Lord's command in the wrong sequence stating that "the Great Commission of Jesus Christ still stands: proclaim the Gospel everywhere, he said, teaching, baptizing, and making disciples."[73] This is unacceptable for a statement expressing the doctrinal consensus among evangelical Christians, who take the Great Commission to be "the church's marching orders from Christ its Head,"[74] and who are impassioned over the ministries of evangelism, church-planting, and cross-cultural missions. Our Lord should be accurately quoted within the most widely endorsed statement among evangelical Christians that specifically focuses on the gospel.

At issue, however, is more than just mere misplacing of the sequence of our Lord's command. By putting teaching first and making disciples last, EC has been enclosed by the ecumenical brackets set out by the WCC, the Roman Catholic Church, and the supporters of ECT, making its content compatible with their statements noted above. Reading EC in the context of the present state of ecumenical activities, which include extensive Roman Catholic involvement, discloses how EC conforms to the teaching that baptism is the beginning of Christian identity.

The brethren . . . those who believed . . . the whole church . . . those belonging to the Way . . . men or women . . . the disciples (Acts 1:15, 4:32; 5:11; 9:2, 26)—all were first called Christians at Antioch during the early formative period of Paul's missionary ministry (Acts 11:26). Evangelicals should retain the right order of our Lord's Great Commission. It rightfully places initial emphasis on the preaching of the Word to make Christians, who then are baptized and instructed in obedience to the teachings of Christ. God has set out preaching to be the way by which Christians are made. "For since, in the wisdom of God, the world did not know God through wisdom, it pleased God through the folly of what we preach to save those who believe" (1 Cor. 1:21 ESV). Hearing the gospel of Christ preached is the one way God saves lost sinners, for "faith comes from hearing, and hearing by the word of Christ" (Rom. 10:17).

The drafting committee rightly denied "that the power of the gospel rests in the eloquence of the preacher, the technique of the evangelist, or the persuasion of rational argument"[75]—all of which are excesses prone to evangelical communicators of the gospel. With equal adamancy, it should be denied that we gain the benefits of the gospel by justification through faith in baptism. Failing to make this denial sets EC in orbit around the larger movements of ecumenism, in which the Roman Catholic Church has assumed a significant role. Because of this failure by silence, all of the careful articulation of imputed righteousness is for naught.

Heard within range of the ecumenical reality in which it is read, EC changes into an example of a solid expression of the biblical doctrine of justification that nonetheless serves a doctrinal position contrary to its content. This is the case because it fails to alleviate all misunderstanding over its tacit complicity with the Roman Catholic teaching of justification by faith in baptism. EC improperly speaks of the gospel because it expresses it outside the proper period of the present, possessed as it is with a deep and sincere hunger for unity among all confessing Christians. We improperly satisfy this wholesome hunger, however, by feeding one another a distorted gospel.

INFORMING A RESPONSE TO EC

Joseph M. Stowell warned his fellow evangelical brothers and sisters in Christ that the "well-intentioned desire . . . to bridge differences through dialogue with representatives of other Christian traditions can also have unexpected negative consequences."[76] He went on to say:

> We need to discern carefully the theology that lies behind the words of any dialogue. The same words used in one theological context can have other connotations in another theological framework. Once again it must be reiterated, authentic unity can only be built upon truth.[77]

Failing to hear our own confession of faith within earshot of papal evangelization with its ecumenical element isolates the theological framework in which we communicate evangelical teaching. An "unexpected negative consequence" of this is that we fail to hear how our statements correspond to views held in a broader ecumenical framework than some of us can embrace in good conscience. We must consider this as we seek to delineate clearly the gospel according to the Scriptures. Evangelical confessions of faith such as EC should always clarify "that the sacraments of the Roman church with their claims that they are necessary for the forgiveness of sins tragically and fatally compromise the principle of grace in human salvation."[78] One example is Moody Bible Institute's position. The footnotes in the undergraduate school catalog elaborate the school's 1928 doctrinal statement on spiritual salvation:

An individual receives the benefit of Christ's substitutionary death by faith as the result of responding to the message of the gospel. Salvation is the free gift of God's grace through faith alone, therefore not dependent upon church membership, intermediaries, sacraments, or works of righteousness to attain or sustain it.[79]

All evangelical Christians who celebrate the gospel of Jesus Christ should clearly affirm that "without faith it is impossible to please [God]" (Heb. 11:6), and that "faith comes from hearing, and hearing by the word of Christ" (Rom. 10:17). We should always hold fast to our confession that a sinner is justified by faith alone in Christ alone to the glory of God alone, according to the Scriptures. The ecumenical environment in which we construct our biblically based theological framework compels us to additionally deny that any are justified by faith in baptism administered by the Roman Catholic Church or any other ecclesiastical element outside of it.

I trust our evangelical leaders will work together to revise as necessary the doctrinal documents guiding our ministries and serving to undergird our fellowship in the present ecumenical environment. May we persevere in prayers for one another that we might boldly proclaim the mystery of the gospel as God gives us opportunity to do so.

Father, make it the testimony of our evangelical conscience that we behaved in the world with simplicity and godly sincerity, not by earthly wisdom but by Your grace, and supremely so toward one another. (cf. 2 Cor. 1:12)

Mike McDuffee is professor of theology at the Moody Bible Institute. He earned a Ph.D. degree from Brandeis University, Waltham, Massachusetts, and holds academic degrees from the University of New Hampshire and Wheaton Graduate School, Wheaton, Illinois. He has served as director of worship at three churches in the Midwest.

NOTES

1. Fredric Jameson, "Postmodernism and the Market," in *Mapping Ideology*, ed. Slovoj Zizek (London: Verso, 1991), 282.

2. Gianni Vattimo, *After Christianity*, trans. Luca D'Isanto (New York: Columbia Univ. Press, 2002), 77.

3. This apt description paraphrases Richard H. Popkin, *The History of Scepticism from Erasmus to Spinoza* (Berkeley: Univ. of California Press, 1979). Stephen R. C. Hicks argues Germanic idealist thinkers created a unique division between reality and reason, which lay down the seed bed for postmodern culture in his study *Explaining Postmodernism, Skepticism and Socialism from Rousseau to Foucault* (Tempe, Ariz.: Scholargy Publishing, 2004).

4. Peter L. Berger, "A Market Model for the Analysis of Ecumenicity," *Social Research* 30 (1963): 77–93.

5. Peter L. Berger, "Pluralism, Protestantization and the Voluntary Principle," a discussion draft for conference on "The New Religious Pluralism and Democracy," April 21–22, 2005, sponsored by Georgetown University's Initiative on Religion, Politics, and Peace. Read from http://irpp.georgetown.edu/conference.htm, available now at http://berkleycenter.georgetown.edu/8986.html/. To be published in *Democracy and the New Religious Pluralism*, ed. Thomas Banchoff (New York: Oxford Univ. Press, 2007), 24–41.

6. Thomas C. Oden has been a leading advocate of the new ecumenism and a bridge-builder of it into evangelical thought. Oden is convinced that the Faith and Order Commission of the WCC is moving away from the modern model of ecumenism to this new ancient and authentic one directed by the Holy Spirit. See "The Emergent Ecumenism, A Response to Robert P. George" by Thomas C. Oden in the *Touchstone Archives*, July/August 2003, vol. 16, issue 6; read from http://touchstonemag.com/archives/article.php?id=16-06-054-f/.

7. See for example, Joseph Cardinal Ratzinger, "The New Evangelization," December 10, 2000, read from http://www.christlife.org/evangelization/articles/C_nevangelratzinger.html.

8. Avery Dulles, "Evangelizing Theology," *First Things* 61 (March 1996): 27–32, read from http://www.firstthings.com/ftissues/ft9603/articles/dulles.html. See too, "John Paul II and the New Evangelization: What Does It Mean?" *John Paul and the New Evangelization*, ed. Ralph Martin and Peter Williams (San Francisco: Ignatius Press, 1995).

9. Ibid.

10. *First Dogmatic Constitution on the Church of Christ*, pronounced July 18, 1870, quoted from *Decrees of the Ecumenical Councils*, ed. Norman Tanner, read from http://www.ewtn.com/library/COUNCILS/V1.HTM/ 4.

11. Ibid., chap. 3.

12. Ibid.

13. Ibid., chap. 4.

14. Ibid.

15. Pope Paul VI, *Evangelii Nuntiandi* (Evangelization Today), ed. Austin Flannery, trans. Dom Matthew Dillon, (Northport, N. Y.: Costellos, 1977), 8.

16. Ibid., 10.

17. Ibid., 27.

18. "Directory for the Application of Principles and Norms on Ecumenism," published by *Pontificuium Consilium ad Christianorum Unitatem Fovendem* (PCPCU), available on official Vatican site, read from http://www.vatican.va/roman_curia/pontifical _councils/chrstuni/general-docs/rc_pc_chrstuni_doc_19930325_directory_en.html, para. 6.

19. Ibid., para. 92.

20. Ibid., para. 22.

21. Ibid., 17.

22. Ibid., 18.

23. Ibid., 104, b.

24. Pope John Paul II, *Ut Unum Sint*, "That They May Be One," promulgated on May 25, 1995, chap. 1, art. 6, read from http://www.vatican.va/edocs/ENG0221/_INDEX. HTM/. For an ecumenical appraisal of this encyclical, see *Church Unity & the Papal Office*, ed. Carl E. Braaten and Robert W. Jenson (Grand Rapids: Eerdmans, 2001).

25. Ibid., chap. 3, art. 95.

26. Ibid., chap. 3, art. 88.

27. Ibid., chap. 3, art. 97.

28. Ibid.

29. Ibid., chap. 3, art. 99.

30. Ibid., chap. 3, art. 98.

31. Ibid., chap. 3, art. 99.

32. Ibid.

33. Ibid., chap. 3, art. 97.

34. Joseph Cardinal Ratzinger, "The Primacy of the Successor of Peter in the Mystery of the Church," in *L'Osservatore Romano-primato inglese*," n. 4 in *L'Osservatore Romano-primato inglese*, read from http://www.ewtn.com/library/CURIA/CDFPRIMA.HTM/.

35. Ibid., n. 12.

36. Ibid., n. 15.

37. "Baptism, Eucharist and Ministry," Faith and Order Paper 111, (1982), Faith and Order Commission of the World Council, read from http://www.wcc-coe.org/wcc/what/faith.

38. Jeffrey Gros, F.S.C., Eamon McManus, Ann Riggs, *Introduction to Ecumenism* (New York: Paulist Press, 1998), 127. The Princeton Proposal for Christian Unity, entitled "In One Body through the Cross" and sponsored by the Center for Catholic and Evangelical Theology, also acknowledges this document as "the most widely studied doctrinal statement of the modern [ecumenical] movement," adding that "Roman Catholic theologians were appointed to the Faith and Order Commission, and played an important part in the elaboration of [this] 'convergence document'" see *In One Body through the Cross,* ed. Carl E. Braaten and Robert W. Jenson (Grand Rapids: Eerdmans, 2003), 23. The Roman Catholic Church has been a member of the Faith and Order Commission of the World Council of Churches since 1968 (*Introduction to Ecumenism,* p. 28).

39. Gros, McManus, Riggs, *Introduction to Ecumenism,* 127. The others with whom the Catholic Church has agreed to pursue formal institutional action are the Eastern and Oriental Orthodox patriarchs, and the Anglican and Lutheran churches— all ecclesiastical bodies with episcopate governance teaching infant baptism.

40. Thomas E. FitzGerald, *The Ecumenical Movement, an Introductory History* (Westport, Conn.: Praeger, 2004), 200.

41. "Baptism, Eucharist and Ministry," Faith and Order Paper 111, Commentary (B6), read from http://www.wcc-coe.org/wcc/what/faith.

42. Ibid., B14.

43. Ibid., B6.

44. Ibid., B13.

45. Ibid., B16.

46. "Becoming a Christian: The Ecumenical Implications of Our Common Baptism," *Faith and Order Consultation* of the World Council of Churches Faith and Order, January 17–24, 1997. Read from http://www.wcc-coe.org/wcc/what/faith/faverg. html/.

47. "The Challenge of Proselytism and the Calling to Common Witness," World Council of Churches, para. 18, read from http://www.wcc-coe.org/wcc/what/ecumenical/ jwgpr-e.html.

48. Ibid., para. 18–19.

49. Ibid., 23.

50. Ibid., 18.

51. *Your Word Is Truth,* ed. Charles Colson and Richard John Neuhaus (Grand Rapids: Eerdmans, 2002), viii. To date, the project has released five statements: "Evangelicals & Catholics Together: The Christian Mission in the Third Millennium," *First Things,* 43 (May 1994): 15–22; "The Gift of Salvation," *First Things,* 79 (January 1998): 20–23; "Your Word Is Truth," *First Things* 125 (August/September 2002) 38–42; "The Communion of Saints," *First Things,* 131 (March 2003): 26–33; and "The Call to Holiness," *First Things* 151 (March 2005): 23–26.

52. Mark A. Noll and Carolyn Nystrom, *Is the Reformation Over?* (Grand Rapids: Baker, 2005), 244–47. The authors concede the analogy needs qualifying since the "varieties of Christian tradition" change over time and are open to ongoing outside influence.

Still they insist, "If reasoning about the major Christian traditions as languages does reflect reality, it explains a good deal about Catholic-evangelical relations" (245). My comments are relevant to the extent evangelical leadership takes the authors' view as a credible analogy truly reflecting the reality of Christianity.

53. Ibid., 241.

54. Ibid., 246.

55. Ibid., 247.

56. Ibid.

57. Carl F. H. Henry, *The Uneasy Conscience of Modern Fundamentalism* (Grand Rapids: Eerdmans, 1947), 86.

58. "The Gift of Salvation," *First Things* 79 (January 1998): 22. Emphasis added.

59. "Evangelicals & Catholics Together: The Christian Mission in the Third Millennium," *First Things* 43 (May 1994): 22.

60. Ibid., 21.

61. *Vatican Council II, The Conciliar and Post Conciliar Documents*, ed. Austin Flannery, para. 3, "Decree on Ecumenism," 455.

62. *Catechism of the Catholic Church*, para. 1271, quoting with emphasis para. 22, Decree on Ecumenism.

63. Decree on Ecumenism, Vatican II, *Unitatis Redintegratio*, 21 November 1964 in *Vatican II, The Conciliar and Post Conciliar Documents*, ed. Austin Flannery (Northport, N.Y.: Costello, 1975), 455, para. 3.

64. *Lumen Gentium, First Dogmatic Constitution*, 357, para. 8.

65. Footnote #56 of *Declaration "Dominus Iesus" on the Unicity and Salvific Universality of Jesus Christ and the Church*, read from http://www.va/roman_curia/congregations/cfaith.

66. All reference to "The Gospel of Jesus Christ, An Evangelical Celebration, 1999" from appendix B of J. I. Packer and Thomas C. Oden, *One Faith* (Downers Grove, Ill.: InterVarsity, 2004), 185–95.

67. Packer and Oden, *One Faith*, 169.

68. Ibid., 32.

69. Akers, Armstrong, and Woodbridge, *This We Believe*, 18.

70. Packer and Oden, *One Faith*, 32.

71. Akers, Armstrong, and Woodbridge, *This We Believe*, 20.

72. Ibid., 27.

73. Packer and Oden, *One Faith*, 187; compare with Matthew 28:18–20.

74. Ibid., 168.

75. Ibid., 191.

76. Joseph M. Stowell, "The Evangelical Family: Its Blessing and Boundaries," ed. Akers, Armstrong, and Woodbridge, *This We Believe*, 292.

77. Ibid., 293.

78. S. Lewis Johnson Jr., "Mary, the Saints, and Sacerdotalism," *Roman Catholicism: Evangelical Protestants Analyze What Divides and Unites Us*, ed. John Armstrong (Chicago: Moody, 1994), 135.

79. "Doctrinal Statement," footnote 3, *2004–2006 Undergraduate Catalog* of Moody Bible Institute, 19.

IN TRIBUTE

by Duane Litfin

The year was 1966, and Sherri and I were attending a reception for incoming students at Dallas Theological Seminary, sponsored by some compassionate faculty members. Most of us freshmen were newly arrived strangers to Texas, feeling as out of place in the Dallas heat as a yankee in King Arthur's Court. But the young, fresh-faced couple standing there seemed friendly enough, so we struck up a conversation.

I don't recall what all we talked about on that occasion, but I know we learned that Joe and Martie Stowell were newlyweds who, like us, had graduated from college just a few months before. Joe was raised in a pastor's home, and I remember discovering that he wanted to follow in his father's footsteps. He wanted to become a preacher of God's Word. It was the beginning of the ties that have bound us as the best of friends for the past four decades.

All this, of course, was before Joe Stowell became *Joe Stowell*. Today Joe is an unwilling celebrity. We can't go anywhere with Joe and Martie that people don't recognize him. They come up to him on the street or approach him in restaurants. We have heard complete strangers greet Joe with words of gratitude for his pulpit, radio or written ministry.

Back in 1966, of course, Joe Stowell was just a tall, boyish-looking first-year student at Dallas Seminary. Yet many in Joe's seminary circle of friends soon recognized Joe's promise. With his heart for Christ and his love for God's Word, combined with his exuberant personality and growing communication skills, it was plain to us all that Joe's ministry future was bright.

Looking back, many of our fondest recollections of those Dallas years turn out to be Stowell memories. During our second year as impoverished students, the Stowells and the Litfins lived on two sides of a ramshackle duplex a few miles from the seminary. To help pay our seminary bills, Joe and I took part-time work in the ladies shoes department of the local Sears store. (Our wives both worked full time.) Among school, work, and home, that meant our lives that year became fully entwined. Those close times formed the basis for a David and Jonathan friendship that has lasted a lifetime.

Upon finishing seminary, Joe moved into his first pastorate, a church plant in Springfield, Ohio, while I headed for a Ph.D. program. In the ensuing decades Joe went on to pastor two other churches, and I became a professor. How odd it seemed, then, when in our forties the Lord moved Joe to the Moody presidency and me to a pastorate. Here was I, the academic, now serving in a church, and there was Joe, the pastor, now serving in an educational setting. Neither of us would have predicted such an outcome, but in a very different way this too made for an entwining of our lives.

Throughout these decades, even though we were usually living in different parts of the country, Joe and I and Martie and Sherri stayed in touch. And periodically, as often as our busyness would permit, the two couples would get together. But each time, the conversation begun so long ago would pick up where it left off, almost as if we hadn't been apart.

When eventually we joined Joe and Martie in Chicago and I took on my own presidential duties at Wheaton, the conversation Joe and I had begun decades earlier entered a new phase. It seems we had more than ever to talk about. In another sense, however, our conversation did not change at all. It gained some new dimensions, but as it turned out, it was just a deeper version of the same conversation we had been pursuing for years, with a common theme to which we have always returned: the proclamation of God's Word, centered, as it must always be, on the person and work of our Lord Jesus Christ. This core theme has been the reference point for our friendship, and for the ministry of Joe Stowell.

That's why this book is such a fitting tribute to Joe's work. Its chapters focus on preaching God's truth from the whole Bible, both to the church and to the world. The chapters emphasize the importance in preaching of theological substance, cultural awareness, and practical application. Such preaching thus combines solid content and clear relevance, a deeper understanding of God's Word that shows itself in fuller commitment to serious discipleship. It is preaching that demonstrates a concern for the life of the church and a mission-driven passion for the lost. But most of all, at the center of such preaching stands the monolithic person and work of Jesus Christ.

Whatever the subject, if we are preaching the Scriptures we are always, in the end, talking about Him. He is our touchstone in every instance, the point of reference by which all the rest is to be understood and evaluated.

A book focused on such priorities is an ideal tribute to Joe Stowell precisely because these are the features that have characterized his ministry. As an expository preacher, and as a teacher of expository preaching, I am sometimes asked who I think best models today the kind of preaching we're after. I always say that one of the best models I know is the work of my friend Joe Stowell. Joe is one of the few preachers whose ministry brings together in such a genial package the various themes of this book.

Above all, Joe is committed to the lordship of Christ. For this reason he is also a serious student of the Scriptures, from cover to cover. He cares deeply about the text, the backgrounds against which it was written, and its message for us today. Further, Joe is an astute observer of our own times, and of the audiences to whom he must apply this biblical message. He is also a gifted wordsmith, someone who knows how to use language effectively to drive home his point. As a result, Joe's has always been a message of both substance and relevance, well packaged and delivered with a style that is uniquely his own, a style shaped by his marvelously affable personality.

To the great benefit of his ministry, Joe is energized by people and genuinely enjoys their company. He understands and empathizes with them. He intuitively grasps their deepest needs, and he understands how wooing them to Jesus can meet these needs.

What make's Joe's preaching so distinctive, then, is the way he manages to pull all of this together so agreeably. I have never heard Joe descend into scolding. That's not his style. Instead, his own good nature shows itself constantly in his preaching. He so often takes recourse to humor in his messages—usually self-deprecating stories told at his own expense—because that is what comes natural to him; that is who Joe is. Phillips Brooks once observed that effective preaching is "truth through personality." If that is so, it explains why Joe's proclamation has been so effective over the years. It is preaching filtered through one of the most amiable of personalities

In the end, of course, Joe will be the first to protest these observations. His protest, with John the Baptist, will be: "No, Christ must increase, I must decrease." It's not about me, Joe will rightly object. It's about Him.

But, of course, such a protest will only reinforce my point. As the title of this collection of essays suggests, Joe's ministry is and always has been about exalting Jesus. It has been a ministry marked by strong, Christ-centered content, applied with clear Christ-centered relevance, effectively communicated through an engaging, Christ-centered personality. This is exactly the kind of ministry God can and does delight to use.

DUANE LITFIN
President, Wheaton College